# Music in the Education of Children

# Third Edition

## WADSWORTH MUSIC SERIES

*Advanced Music Reading,* by William Thomson
*Basic Concepts in Music,* by Gary M. Martin
*Basic Piano for Adults,* by Helene Robinson
*Basic Resources for Learning Music,* by Alice Snyder Knuth and William E. Knuth
*Basic Violin for Adults,* by Albert Lazan
*English Folk Song: Some Conclusions, Fourth Edition,* by Cecil J. Sharp
    (edited by Maud Karpeles)
*Exploring Music with Children,* by Robert E. Nye and Vernice T. Nye
*First Experiences in Music,* by Lyman C. Hurd, III, and Edith J. Savage
*Five Centuries of Keyboard Music,* by John Gillespie
*Foundations in Music Theory, Second Edition, with Programed Exercises,*
    by Leon Dallin
*Harmony and Melody, Volume I: The Diatonic Style,* and *A Workbook for Harmony
    and Melody, Volume I,* by Elie Siegmeister
*Harmony and Melody, Volume II: Modulation; Chromatic and Modern Styles,* and
    *A Workbook for Harmony and Melody, Volume II,* by Elie Siegmeister
*Help Yourselves to Music, Second Edition,* by Beatrice Perham Krone and Kurt R. Miller
*Intermediate Piano for Adults, Parts I and II,* by Helene Robinson
*Introduction to Ear Training,* by William E. Thomson and Richard P. DeLone
*Introduction to Music Reading: Concepts and Applications,* by William Thomson
*An Introduction to Musical Understanding and Musicianship,* by Ethel G. Adams
*Keyboard Harmony: A Comprehensive Approach to Musicianship, Volume I,*
    by Isabel Lehmer
*Keyboard Skills: Sight Reading, Transposition, Harmonization, Improvisation,*
    by Winifred Knox Chastek
*Music Essentials,* by Robert Pace
*Music Fundamentals,* by Howard A. Murphy with John F. Park
*Music in the Education of Children, Third Edition,* by Bessie R. Swanson
*Music Reading through Singing,* by Charles W. Walton and Harry Robert Wilson
*The Musical Experience,* by John Gillespie
*The Musical Experience, Record Album*
*Planning for Junior High School General Music,* by William O. Hughes
*Rhythm in Music and Dance for Children,* by Sally Monsour, Marilyn Chambers Cohen,
    and Patricia Eckert Lindell
*Scored for the Understanding of Music,* by Charles R. Hoffer
*Singing with Children,* by Robert and Vernice Nye, Neva Aubin, and George Kyme
*Talking about Symphonies,* by Antony Hopkins
*Teaching Music in the Secondary Schools,* by Charles R. Hoffer
*Toward World Understanding with Song,* by Vernice T. Nye, Robert E. Nye, and
    H. Virginia Nye
*Toward World Understanding with Song, Record Album*
*The Understanding of Music,* by Charles R. Hoffer
*The Understanding of Music, Record Album*

# Music in the Education of Children

## Third Edition

**BESSIE R. SWANSON**
University of Washington

**WADSWORTH PUBLISHING COMPANY, INC.**
Belmont, California

To My Mother, Primary Teacher and Musician

# Preface

This book is addressed to everyone who is concerned that music be given its proper place in the education of children. It is designed to serve as a textbook for teachers in training and as a practical guide and source of musical information for the teacher in the classroom. School administrators, musicians, and parents will find much of interest here.

Three main aspects of music education must be integrated into a comprehensive study of the curriculum in this field: (1) musical activities appropriate for children, (2) the development of concepts in music, and (3) the use of a wide variety of music literature. However, each area needs to be considered in detail if the student is to arrive at a full understanding of the curriculum. I have met the problem of organization in this book by focusing in Chapter Two on the musical concepts that might be developed by children, and then by devoting individual chapters to each of the musical activities. Throughout the chapters on musical activities, continual reference is made to skills and concepts that grow out of musical experiences and to the broad repertoire of music that is appropriate for elementary school children. Over two hundred musical examples have been included in this textbook; more than seventy are complete compositions that can be found in the basic school music books. In addition, Appendix B lists musical materials, selected school music books, and recordings that should be used continually throughout the study of the activities chapters.

Because the use of bodily movement is central to the young child's understanding of rhythm, this basic element of music is considered first among the musical activities. Immediately following are chapters devoted to the use of rhythm instruments, melody instruments, and harmony instruments, all of which provide concrete and rewarding experiences in music both for children and for teachers in training. Singing and listening to music are given separate consideration, but creative work is highlighted throughout the activities chapters.

Singing has an important relationship to other musical activities, and it is referred to throughout the earlier chapters. However, discussions of the development of voices, the repertoire for singing, and the learning of songs are delayed until Chapters Six and Seven so that understandings and competencies gained in the consideration of the other activities can be brought to bear on these important topics. The college instructor can assign the study of Chapters Six and Seven before the study of the other activities if he prefers to deal with singing first.

The many aspects of music listening are discussed in Chapter Eight. Chapter Nine draws the study to a close with a consideration of "Music and Other Areas of the Curriculum," suggestions for evaluation in music, and practical examples in planning the music lesson at all grade levels.

Three items contained in the section *Activities for College Classes* at the end of each chapter will be particularly valuable to college instructors and teachers in training: (1) "Questions for Review" cover the most important points in each chapter and may be useful in discussion and in the construction of examinations; (2) "Written Assignments" are designed to lead to the development of personally selected music-teaching material that may be used by the student in his early teaching experience; and (3) "Classroom Projects" promote participation in music within the teacher-training class. For many students, a practical application of the music-teaching techniques is necessary for complete understanding. A wide variety of activities and assignments is suggested so that the college instructor can select those that are most appropriate for the individuals in his classes.

Appendix A, *Reference Material for Music Theory and Notation,* along with *Glossary,* will help the student increase his understanding of music notation and terminology. Appendix B, *Guide to Materials,* includes an up-to-date listing of companies supplying useful materials, many of which are cited throughout the text.

This book has grown out of my experience as a special music teacher and supervisor in the public schools, as an instructor in music and teacher-training classes at the University of Washington, Seattle, and at other colleges and universities, and as a student and performing musician, first at the University of the Pacific and then at Stanford University, where I was awarded the Doctor of Musical Arts degree. I am indebted to the many children, classroom teachers, musicians, school administrators, university teachers and colleagues with whom I have been associated.

I would like to express special appreciation to Howard Barnett, University of Victoria, British Columbia, Robert L. Borg, University of Minnesota, Betty Knable, Drake University, Dorothy Kozak, University of Nebraska, and Virginia Simonson Watson, Bowling Green State University, as well as many others actively engaged in teaching courses in elementary music education, for extremely helpful evaluation and criticism of the Second Edition of this book and suggestions for the present edition; to the administration of the Renton, Washington, public schools, to Margaret Rose Anderson, Consultant in Music Education, and to Virginia Houser and Mary Lee Martin, Special Music Teachers, who provided the music-teaching situations in which the photographs for this book were taken. I would also like to thank the publishers of the basic music series and others who were generous in granting permission for the use of their copyrighted material.

*Bessie R. Swanson*

# Contents

**1**

## CHILDREN AND MUSIC—FOUNDATIONS OF THE STUDY    4

**2**

## MUSICAL CONCEPTS    24

# 3

## BODILY MOVEMENT IN THE STUDY OF MUSIC    62

# 4

## RHYTHM INSTRUMENTS IN THE STUDY OF MOVEMENT    98

# 5

## THE USE OF MELODY AND HARMONY INSTRUMENTS    130

# 6

## SONGS AND SINGING VOICES    174

# 7

## MANAGEMENT OF THE SINGING SITUATION    214

# 8

## EXPERIENCES IN LISTENING TO MUSIC    268

# 9

## IMPLEMENTATION OF THE MUSIC EDUCATION PROGRAM    298

# Music in the Education of Children

# Third Edition

# 1

# Children and Music–
# Foundations of the Study

People of all times have recognized the importance of music in education. In ancient Greece Plato wrote, "Musical training is a more potent instrument than any other, because rhythm and harmony find their way into the inward places of the soul, on which they mightily fasten imparting grace . . ."[1] In the New England of 1838 the townspeople acknowledged music as a part of the authorized curriculum in the public school because through music "you set in motion a mighty power which silently, but surely, in the end, will humanize, refine and elevate the whole community."[2]

Whenever parents think of the good things in life that they would like their children to experience in school, they include music and art. Many people are not quite sure what these subjects can do for children, but they intuitively feel the need for the added dimension that these studies give to life. Teachers likewise acknowledge music and art as integral parts of the school curriculum.

The arts are not "practical" subjects in the ordinary sense. There is a difference between feeling their importance in the curriculum and spelling out their real value. Music is especially elusive. It means different things to different people. The *personal* quality of musical experience is one of its highest values, but this quality in itself presents a problem for the teacher who must define objectives and establish a plan for teaching music.

Those who would consider the place of music in the education of children must give some thought to the following questions. First, what is the value of music to the individual? Second, what are the characteristics of children at the various ages for which education in music is to be planned? Third, what kind of experiences and learnings should be provided for children in the elementary school? Finally, who can actively promote the proper role of music in the curriculum and in the lives of the children?

## THE VALUE OF MUSIC

For many people music is almost exclusively entertainment; for others it is a practical aid in worship, in promoting patriotism, or in otherwise helping the individual establish his identity and social relationships. Although music's intellectual and aesthetic values are stressed in the Western world, people of other cultures have utilized its other values. Alain Danielou[3] reports that in India there is deep conviction that some forms of music have definite value as a means of spiritual realization.

There is, of course, widespread use of music as ritual, but in Africa, in India, and within certain religious and psychedelic groups elsewhere, repetitive rhythms and melodic patterns are used to produce an ecstatic condition in the individual.

The values of music may be grouped under three headings, all of them somewhat interrelated: (1) personal enrichment, (2) identification, and (3) a means of expression.

## Personal Enrichment

Music has the functions described above, but at the same time it has become an art form that arouses feelings even when it is unrelated to another immediate experience. Thus, through music, one is able to extend and enrich his life beyond what is practical for him to experience directly.

We can turn to musicians and philosophers to gain insights into the value of music as a personal enrichment. The American composer Aaron Copland believes that there is a basic, primitive relationship between the sentient human being and music. "On that level, whatever the music may be, we experience basic reactions such as tension and release, density and transparency, a smooth or angry surface, the music's swellings and subsidings, its pushing forward or hanging back, its length, its speed, its thunders and whisperings—and a thousand other psychologically based reflections of our physical life of movement and gesture, and our inner, subconscious mental life. That is fundamentally the way we all hear music . . ."[4]

Persons who may never have gone beyond this primitive response to music have found in it lifelong therapy and enrichment. In the school curriculum, where the rigors of academic discipline are often highly prized, music is a subject that can keep the pupil in healthy contact with the important world of feeling.

Daniel A. Prescott and his Committee on the Relations of Emotions to the Educative Process[5] say: "The conscious use of aesthetic experience to maintain morale may be not only a means of social control and integration but also a mark of personal maturity. The use of aesthetic expression as a means of release, escape, or catharsis from unbearable tensions may be a mature means of avoiding less desirable emotional reactions."

In his introduction to aesthetics, Irwin Edman reasons that "every canvas or musical composition that can awaken us more exquisitely and accurately to the infinite and various surface of our experience does that much to sharpen life and render it thereby more alive. If part of the aim of an ordered civilization is to prolong life, certainly part of its ambition is to variegate life and fill its moments with the quality of living."[6] Teachers and parents might well ask this question: is not the enrichment of life through the arts one of the more important objectives of the educational process?

Susanne Langer[7] looks upon music as a symbolic form of feeling. She says "music has all the earmarks of a true symbolism, except one: the existence of an *assigned connotation*." That is, it can mean different things to different people. Langer continues: ". . . what music can actually reflect is only the morphology [the features or shape] of feeling . . ." For instance, some music seems to bear a sad and a happy interpretation equally well; that is because some sad and some happy conditions may have a similar morphology.

Thus music serves man in that it can symbolically express the wide range of feelings involved in the life process. If music is to function most effectively as an enrichment throughout life the individual must have ever broader and deeper experiences with it. Character deepens as one journeys through life, and this depth perspective gives scope and meaning to his outlook on life. The more refined aesthetic experience in music that will enrich adult life beyond that valuable to the child is dependent upon the individual's ability to hear and respond to more of what is expressed in music.

Copland says that the higher forms of music imply a listener whose musical taste has been cultivated, and that "refinement in musical taste begins with the ability to distinguish subtle nuances of feeling . . . The talented listener recognizes not merely the joyous quality of the piece, but also the specific shade of joyousness . . ."[4] The fact that all that music has to offer is not available in the same degree to the experienced and the inexperienced listener or performer is potent justification for education in music. A worldwide heritage of music awaits those who are capable of using it for personal enrichment and pleasure.

## Identification

Music helps people know who they are, for they find in it a means of identifying themselves as individuals and as members of various groups. To be sure, such identification often is a matter of conditioning from childhood when one learns to associate certain patriotic music with the idea of nationality and citizenship. Other music is associated with an individual's church and comes to represent religious ties and beliefs. Everyone has certain songs of sentiment which remind him of romantic moments and important persons in his life; these too are part of his identity.

Many young people identify with a particular kind of music that sets them apart from the older generations of people: the strong percussive beat and hypnotic repetition of music produced by teen-age stage bands and singing groups is "their" music. Other young people find a point of identification and an individual to emulate in the folk singer with guitar accompaniment who comments on social problems. Baroque music with its rhythmic drive and clear blocks of contrasting sound appeals to many young contemporary intellectuals as music that is unaffected and worthy of their attention and commitment.

## A Means of Expression

The arts provide vital forms of self-expression and recreation that people need, but from which they may be cut off because they lack experience and skills. Mechanization of work can free people for more leisure activities, but these, too, can become mechanized. Television has converted young and old alike into passive spectators. Because they have not developed resources within themselves, many people find their chief diversion in what is done *for* them.

Prescott[5] tells us that "Experimentation with various media of expression, carried on in centers of adult education and recreation in various parts of the country, has revealed the hunger which large numbers of people feel for some mode of expressing their feelings. Children, as well as adults, share the same yearning . . ." Later he says, "The large place that the arts have had in all significant cultures makes it apparent that mankind seeks the satisfaction of deep needs through the production and experience of aesthetic materials . . ."

In the visual arts significant advances have been made in helping children express their creative impulses. In appraising music in the school we find that its creative function has been readily acknowledged but often bypassed in actual practice. Where are musical activities comparable to the free creative activities in art? In what directions can early experiences be guided so that adequate expression of mature aesthetic feelings will follow? In all music-making—singing, playing, and improvising—we find opportunities.

In the past, music educators placed much emphasis upon "appreciation." Pupils were taught "the fundamentals" so that they might eventually know the language of music and thereby be privileged to engage in the art. Undue emphasis on mastery of skills isolated the individual from an immediate realization of personal value. In many cases music as an avenue of personal fulfillment was abandoned.

In more recent years, as a reaction to the formalistic approach, music has been brought into the everyday lives of children and brightened with the slogan "Music is fun." Certainly music should be a source of great pleasure and satisfaction for people of all ages; in the early years music-making should be of a type requiring little skill so that children can participate in simple, satisfying ways. However, in presenting music as an immediate source of enjoyment, many teachers find themselves unable to develop a long-range program that assures growth in skills and insights. Pleasure and satisfaction in the use of music in a creative capacity throughout life is dependent upon the development of musical skills and concepts to a functional level. If the simple approach remains the *only* level of contact, boys and girls are deprived of the opportunity to grow into a more mature relationship with music. Music is enjoyable, but its greater values can never be realized if it is experienced solely on the childhood "fun" level.

The development of skill in singing, playing, or writing music demands purposeful involvement in these activities. The "Growth Characteristics of Children" set forth on the following pages describe needs and activities that are natural to children of various ages. Using these as a basis, the teacher must foster interesting, creative musical projects that demand the development of certain skills and insights for their completion. Chapter Two of this book outlines musical concepts that might be developed at various ages, and the activities chapters that follow describe many ways in which children can be involved with music. Music as a means of personal expression can be a reality for children, but they must begin the practice of it as such from their earliest experiences with it and continue throughout their school years.

7

# GROWTH CHARACTERISTICS OF CHILDREN WITH IMPLICATIONS FOR MUSICAL ACTIVITIES AND LEARNING

Certain physical, emotional and intellectual traits of children at different ages have determined the musical materials and teaching techniques used at various levels of music education. The following paragraphs outline distinguishing characteristics of four levels of child development that have implications for music, and give a preview of considerations for the teacher that will be enlarged upon throughout this book. The chief resources for this information have been the research of Arnold Gesell[8] and his associates, and the practical experience of the author of this book. One must consider the growth characteristics outlined here as patterns of behavior that tend to be evident in children of certain ages rather than as norms to which every child will conform.

Since teachers of kindergarten children are often consulted and sometimes involved in planning activities for nursery schools, this outline begins with consideration of the traits of four- as well as five-year-olds. In addition, the upper limit of the study includes twelve-year-olds because there has been increased interest in the "middle school," which incorporates the seventh grade.

## Preschool and Kindergarten— The Four- and Five-Year-Olds

Although four- and five-year-olds tend to be individualistic in their activities they enjoy being in a group. Some group activities in music are possible with children of this age, but the teacher should provide many opportunities for independent music-making by individuals and smaller groups. Musical instruments should be available in various parts of the room so that children can provide accompaniments for their rhythmic activities, withdraw to a quiet corner to pick out a melody on an easy-to-play instrument, or play a favorite selection on a record player. Guidance is provided by the different instruments and records that are made available from time to time. Children develop concepts of pitch and timbre through exploration and concrete experiences with instruments. At this age they can play chords and tone clusters on the piano. When they have learned to play a tune on the piano or bells they are likely to play it over and over. This kind of activity should be permitted.

The four-year-old is a great talker and he likes to dramatize. He can embellish his songs, make up new verses and dramatize them. In his play a few key words extended by nonsense syllables will be made into a chant to accompany rhythmic activities of various sorts. Vocal play and flexible use of the voice in chanting and crooning should be encouraged. Children of four and five like stories and songs with repetitive action and repetitive phrases. Stories about animals, trains, planes, and fire engines are popular. In general, children of this age appreciate the here and now; they have little capacity for insight into activities of other times and places. The repertoire of songs should be selected to reflect these interests.

Both four- and five-year-olds enjoy gross motor activity, but they also have developed some skill and gracefulness in hand movements. Finger plays and action songs are appropriate for these children. Running, walking, bending, stretching, and turning can be utilized freely, but some children have not yet learned to skip and gallop. When accompaniments are provided for such activities they should be adapted to the child's tempo and style of movement.

## Primary Grades—The Years from Six to Eight

During the primary years the child's world expands tremendously. At the age of six he still lives in the here and now, penetrating the future by looking forward to holidays and special events. At the age of seven interests have broadened to include the community in which he lives, and by the age of eight many children are interested in maps and globes, people of earlier cultures such as the Pilgrims and Indians as well as children of other areas of the world. Social studies and language arts programs reflect these interest areas, and school music books usually provide appropriate songs for such expanding interests.

When songs are pleasing to the children and give opportunities for chime-in endings and tone calls, primary children readily join in imitative vocal activities leading to the improvement of voices that is so necessary before group singing is completely satisfactory.

During these years children imitate sounds well and generally have a good capacity for vocabulary building. Some easy folk songs can be presented in the original foreign language (Spanish, French, German, etc.) to further expand the child's facility with word sounds and to broaden his cultural horizons as his maturity permits it.

Interest in dramatization is sustained throughout these years, but the topics which have appeal for boys and for girls begin to be differentiated. Seven-year-old boys prefer cowboy and Indian roles, and dramatization of machines and vehicles, while girls usually relate to dolls, domestic situations, and delicate creatures. Both groups are interested in animals and will readily dramatize a wide variety of these subjects. Songs and recorded compositions that can be incorporated into dramatizations are important in the music program of the primary years.

Since the eight-year-old is only at the beginning of sustained and coordinated group work, the primary teacher must provide opportunities for continued musical activities by individuals and pairs of children. First graders like to work in twosomes or small groups; they have a need for touching and handling materials and for developing skills in fine motor tasks. The playing of instruments and use of projects that provide for the manipulation of musical notation in the process of discovering how to use it are important during these years.

## Middle Childhood—The Nine- and Ten-Year-Olds

The nine-year-old has developed some skill in motor performance; he will do the same thing over and over in order to practice his skill. Since he enjoys repetition, this is a good time to begin instrumental musical studies if he is interested. Both nine- and ten-year-olds like to sing, and many ten-year-olds have developed sufficient control of their singing voices to make this a particularly satisfying activity. For this reason special school choirs usually give preference to fifth graders.

The interest span of ten-year-olds is short and the teacher will find that singing is a favorite activity for a change of pace in the classroom. However, since boys of this age are pressed by family and society to develop "manly" characteristics it is important to avoid singing "sissy" songs that conflict with social expectations. "Those Dissonant Boys"[9] is a realistic discussion of this topic.

At about the age of ten creative talent in music, as well as in other areas, may begin to become evident if the child has had opportunities to develop the necessary tool skills to work in the medium. Since the nine-year-old likes copy work and has considerable capacity to work independently, this is an ideal age to encourage music writing, which when coupled with simple skill in the use of keyboard instruments can permit early independent musical composition. Learning at this age is still initiated through concrete experiences wherein children discover effects and relationships of musical media and their sounds; hence the continued and expanded use of rhythm and melody instruments is important.

Many children during these years are avid readers; the school library should have many children's books on composers and musical subjects that will provide background for a variety of musical pursuits, both for private reading and for simple class reports.

## Later Childhood—The Eleven- and Twelve-Year-Olds

Enjoyment of singing continues throughout the sixth grade, and is especially rewarding when previous training has eliminated singing problems in the group. Sixth graders can learn to sing harmony which remains a favorite activity of twelve-year-olds. Group work such as that undertaken in choirs satisfies the need of these children for physical activity and to be associated with a group.

Occasionally sixth grade boys enter the first stage of puberty and its attendant voice changes. A year later several more will arrive at this point in their progress toward maturity, so it is important that a teacher who works with these boys understand the changing voice and its changing range.

Among twelve-year-olds there is considerable boy-girl interest and cooperative activity, but there generally is no manifestation of sentiment in the relationship. The teacher can use music that has artistic expression and value, but he should avoid song texts that express love interest. Both eleven- and twelve-year-olds prefer choir seating of boys and girls separately even though there is overlapping of voice types between the groups.

At both ages children listen avidly to recorded music, but among twelve-year-olds who lack basic musical interest this activity is supplanted by other pursuits. Eleven-year-olds only begin to be interested in jazz and popular music; this interest increases among twelve-year-olds. The eleven-year-old especially enjoys gross motor activities; folk dancing becomes a favored form of study and recreation. Work with dances of various national groups considered in social studies is a very profitable enterprise for sixth graders.

## THE MANY FACETS OF EDUCATION IN MUSIC

An individual makes use of music in two ways: he listens to it or he produces it. It is generally acknowledged that music offers more to those who participate actively than to those who merely listen. There are many ways to make music, and individuals may find one form of participation more natural than another. Thus, a teacher planning the music program must include many activities to interest children of varied talents and backgrounds.

The curriculum in music for the elementary grades includes both the development of musical skills and the building of concepts about music. Through meaningful experiences, the child becomes aware of the elements of music and of the principles of its composition, and develops an understanding of some of music's expressive qualities.

### Moving to Music

In a discussion of "The Musical Impulse" the American composer Roger Sessions says that on a primitive, direct, and simple level the basic ingredient of music is not so much sound as movement.[10] This statement points up the importance of bodily movement as a related activity in the musical experiences of children.

Children express themselves directly and effectively through movement. When using bodily movement as a response to music, children do more than merely run, skip, and gallop with the music; they use these natural movements to express the more elusive qualities of feeling that the music conveys. Impersonation and dramatization serve a similar purpose and may be used with songs as well as with instrumental music. Through movement children learn to listen to music and to follow its flow through time, both imaginatively and physically. The concepts of space and time that children develop through their varied activities involving bodily movement help them when they listen to music and follow its flow through time. Music listening is more than an auditory response, it has kinesthetic implications as well.

### Singing and Playing Instruments

In the elementary grades the music program often is organized around singing because this is the mode of musical expression closest to the individual, and to it the other activities may easily be related. The child may sing his own tunes or he may choose a folk melody or a composed song to serve as a vehicle for his expression. Singing is literally "the music of the people." Through it children can readily express their feelings and share the feelings of others.

All sorts of simple instruments have been adapted for use by children. They have an important place in the music program for improvising, for accompanying singing, and for the practical study of music. Children often develop dynamic, rhythmic chanting patterns, using the voice and combinations of rhythm instruments. Original melodies grow out of opportunities to play simple melody instruments, and the desire to play a known melody can lead to an understanding of music notation. Children with talent and interest can be encouraged to study the piano and standard orchestral instruments. If the elementary school music program functions effectively, such specialized studies are a natural outgrowth of earlier experiences in playing classroom instruments.

In this book studies of the use of simple instruments follow consideration of bodily movement. All of these activities then are related to singing which is such a basic part of musical studies at the elementary level.

## Creativity in Music

In a broad sense, creativity is a part of all the other musical activities. When children, through bodily movement, through color and design on paper, or through verbalization, express what they hear, they are responding creatively; when they produce desired musical effects with instruments, or when they sing a particular song in a special way, they create a mood.

Adults too often impose their standards on children. They demand that the child develop skills before he has a chance to discover that he can express something from within himself through his own simple type of music. Elementary teachers must first be concerned with promoting situations in which children may explore and use music in their own natural ways. Children can be induced to experiment with voices and instruments to satisfy their instincts to manipulate and to make sounds. More important, they can find ways to express their joy or sadness, their feelings of aggression or loneliness. Watch a group of children producing rhythmic sounds with a drum or with their feet. Observe a first grader picking out a melody on the small xylophone. Listen to a child singing at his work and you will hear the creative music of children.

More specifically, the creative act in music means the composing of melodies. Elementary children do this, sometimes as a group project but often as an individual pursuit. Here, with a little guidance, the gifted child can find an avenue of fulfillment. There are diverse types of creative temperament, and no textbook will explain how they are best aroused and implemented. In Mozart were combined a superb natural talent for music and a facility for expressing it. When he sat down to write his compositions they were often completely worked out in his mind. On the other hand, Beethoven struggled mightily, even with many of his simpler creations, but he often took paths leading to new directions in music. All creative people range between the temperamental extremes of these two types. The teacher may sense such diversity within a class of children, and somehow must bring out the best in both by different approaches. He will find the writings of E. Paul Torrance[11] helpful for many areas of creative work with children.

### Listening to Music

Listening, too, is a creative activity. Roger Sessions states it this way: "The really 'understanding' listener takes the music into his consciousness and remakes it actually or in his imagination, for his own uses."[10]

Listening is basic to all of music-making. As a child sings and plays instruments, he listens. As he interprets music through bodily movement, he listens. All of these activities aid the child in the important project of learning to listen, which is the chief musical activity of the majority of adults. Hence, although listening experiences are discussed in the last sections of this book, they are, in a sense, first in importance in any consideration of music.

### Developing Musical Concepts

A basic condition for learning is interest and inner motivation on the part of the pupil. To satisfy this condition, the teacher must shape the learning program around the physical, emotional, social, and intellectual needs of the child. Many clues to general needs and interests of children of different ages are given in the previous section on "Growth Characteristics."

An activities approach to musical learning allows the pupil to be involved at the direct sensory level. As a result of this involvement, the child develops concepts about instruments, tone production, and the qualities of music itself. Simple intuitions and elementary concepts generated in the arena of practical experience are then combined, related to previous experiences, and formed into generalizations that can be applied to other situations. Chapter Two lists many simple statements about the qualities of music—its *rhythm, melody, texture* and *harmony, tone color, dynamics, form,* and *style.* These ideas are generalizations in that each may apply to many different musical examples.

The fact that the concepts listed in Chapter Two have been expressed in words means that they have been taken to another level in the hierarchy of learning—to the area of verbalization. Ways of talking about these musical ideas can be meaningful only if they are related to previous concrete experience with music.

As a teacher organizes the activities and materials that lead to interaction and learning on the part of the pupil, he must continually evaluate learning that has taken place earlier. To do this the teacher must interpret behavior displayed by the pupil. Here again the musical activities are important, because the child's singing, playing, and moving to music can reveal his musical learning. While musical learning can also be revealed through what is said, the teacher must remember that verbalization itself is an interpretation of what is felt or known about music. Among children who may be equal in their development of musical concepts, some will be less apt in verbalizing, so the teacher must beware of making inaccurate evaluations on the basis of skill in verbalizing alone.

Under the headings shown in Chapter Two are listed many small ideas that support broader, more comprehensive concepts. Learning develops in more than one direction. A broad, general concept may emerge which, as a result of additional experience, thinking, and verbalizing, may be refined and seen in its more complete and complex form. On the other hand, the emergence of a small, discrete idea may be the first of many concepts that later will be organized into a larger concept. The interaction of present concepts and new perceptions arising from continued experience in musical activities can lead both to a refining and a broadening of concepts in music. If he is successfully to foster children's understanding of music, the teacher must give careful thought to the organization of concepts so that he is aware of both large and small ideas. Then he must proceed to arrange interesting musical experiences out of which these concepts can be generated.

## Learning Music Notation

The medium of musical expression is organized sound and silence. Notation is a visual representation of the sound of music but it is not the art itself. Only after a person has had such extensive experience with music that seeing the notation actually promotes an inner *hearing* of the music can "notes" and "music" be considered analogous.

The child's introduction to music is through its sound; then gradually its notation may be used to define and support what the ear perceives. This is the normal development of any musical concept:

1. It is experienced by the ear; e.g., one may hear and sing the "amen" at the end of a hymn.
2. It is identified to the ear; one recognizes the "amen" as a common chord progression that often functions in this capacity.
3. Its notation is related to it; one sees the "amen" chords in notation, he learns how they are formed, their relationship to each other, etc.

The discussion of the music program in this book is designed to follow this developmental pattern. While people need to be able to talk and exchange ideas about music through oral language, they also find value in the use of music's unique symbols to provide a visual representation of music itself. Although in some cultures music remains an aural tradition, those who would participate fully in music-making need to develop skill in the use of music notation.

Throughout this book the teacher is shown ways of planning and guiding the musical activities of children. In connection with all the activities, material is suggested and techniques are outlined that will foster the development of musical concepts and growth in musical skills. As far as possible, the author has suggested age levels at which the various skills and concepts can be developed. Since no grading of this type can be considered valid for every group of children because musical aptitudes and experiences vary widely, the teacher never is relieved of the responsibility for making final judgments on such matters himself.

## WHO IS RESPONSIBLE FOR THE
## MUSICAL DEVELOPMENT OF CHILDREN?

Research today tells us that learning begins in the cradle. As a child grows, his active response to his environment shapes the development of his senses and of his speech as well as his physical dexterity and his formulation of concepts. Parents as well as teachers bear unique responsibilities for providing environment and stimulation that will lead to the optimum growth of the child musically as well as in all other ways.

Education in the elementary school is developed on the basis of a close relationship between a teacher and his pupils. In current practice many elementary schools are organized around the "self-contained" classroom, in which one teacher is responsible for all aspects of the education of the children assigned to him for the year. Many teachers are quite skillful in teaching reading, arithmetic, the social studies, and other such subjects; but when all teachers are expected moreover to provide for the children significant experiences in art, music, and other specialized fields, many feel less than qualified in one or more areas.

Fortunately many school districts provide resource teachers to assist the general teacher in subjects requiring special skills. In some instances a music teacher may be assigned responsibility for most of the music teaching in a school. Decisions relative to teaching personnel usually are in the province of the principal and other school administrators.

### The Contribution of Parents

Research has shown that the home environment can have a significant influence on the musical response of first grade children. John Shelton[12] reported that the following factors show a close relation to musical response at this age:

(1) frequent opportunities for the child to hear singing in the home,
(2) frequent opportunities to sing with other members of the family,
(3) frequent opportunities to hear records played in the home, and
(4) ability of the mother and father to sing and to learn new songs.

In addition to these factors, an environment providing a wide variety of tone-producing media that the child is free to manipulate in experiments with sound and rhythm will make a substantial contribution to his development of elementary concepts in these areas even before he enters kindergarten.

### The Need for the Classroom Teacher

It is true that not all elementary teachers have sufficient skill to meet, unaided, the needs of *all* children in *all* fields of education, although the possibilities for success are greater at the primary level than at higher levels.

But the music program is no exception to the rule that the educating process should be built around the individual needs and abilities of the children, which are best known by the classroom teacher.

Music educators responsible for the program believe that (1) the active interest of the classroom teacher is essential to the promotion of an adequate program of music in the elementary school, and (2) music in the classroom should not be isolated in one period during the day as it is when the special teacher carries on the program alone. Music is an integral part of life and it should function in this capacity in the classroom.

The teacher needs music in his life as much as children need it. By participating in the arts, he achieves self-esteem and personal satisfaction. Almost in self-defense, however, because he fears that music is only for the talented, a person who has little experience with it may claim complete inability and lack of interest. Yet a few successful experiences with music can grip such a person with enthusiasm. Any teacher can find that there is something in music for him and some way in which he can share music with the children in his classroom.

How is it possible to provide a program in music to which the classroom teacher contributes his intimate understanding of the children as well as his own personal interest and presence, and yet make real understanding and skill in music also available? Music educators have found that a good program in music can be achieved through the active participation of two people: the classroom teacher and the music specialist (helping teacher, supervisor, or consultant).

### The Various Roles of a Music Teacher

Most school districts employ music teachers to provide some specialized training for children in the elementary grades. In addition to a teacher who can give instruction on orchestral instruments a music specialist for classroom music may be employed. The classroom music specialist may serve in various capacities: Under one plan the music specialist is a resource person, a technical advisor, and an assistant to the general teacher and his pupils. How much time the specialist spends in any one classroom depends on the skill and musical background of the individual teacher and the generosity of the school administration in providing enough specialists to fill the need. Under optimum conditions, he works in the classroom with the teacher and pupils as often as necessary to provide an effective learning program in music. In some cases the specialist may keep a regular, once or twice weekly appointment with a teacher and his class. Under this plan, the daily music program for the class utilizes whatever skill and understanding the classroom teacher is able to bring to it. Over a period of time the skill of the teacher in guiding musical activities and learning may be strengthened, and the specialist may find that part of his assistance can be gradually withdrawn. Other teachers are so capable musically that a monthly conference, to which the specialist brings requested resource material and suggests new techniques, is enough help.

Under another plan the music specialist may work five days a week with a class, and at the same time assist the classroom teacher in the development of social studies correlations and the integration of music into the children's daily experiences.

With either plan music teaching must be a cooperative project. Regardless of who does the major portion of the music teaching, the classroom teacher's interest in music and his skill as a teacher are indispensable to a vital music program in his classroom. Whether he has sufficient musical background and skills to provide *all* the leadership his pupils require, or whether he must call for assistance in specified areas, the responsibility for music in the classroom remains his. He must prepare himself in whatever ways he can to meet this challenge.

## Planning for Effective Teaching

The music program recommended in this book is both generalized and idealized; it is designed to suggest approaches to be used by those who have little skill and experience, and yet to present a challenge to those who are already well trained in music. The teacher must tailor a music program that he will be able to carry out. His plans, however, must have a certain breadth and scope. Although the teacher may be quite limited as he begins teaching, he will grow in his ability to deal with music in the classroom, and he will find others to assist him in achieving his goals.

Teachers sometimes work from year to year without any organized plan for music, and without making notations of the materials that were most useful in their past years of experience. If music teaching is taken seriously, it must be based on sound planning and continuity. The following suggestions for the organization of a music teaching handbook or a comparable card file can contribute toward these ends.

The development of the individual's music teaching tool should take place as each aspect of the program is studied in this textbook; one section can be devoted to each major activity in music. It is important that the student compile this teaching tool in such a manner that it will be valuable to him, with his particular talents. He should list a limited amount of selected materials for use during the early days of teaching, but he should also make provision for the later addition of material in all sections. The codes established in this textbook for the basic elementary music series books (Appendix B–I) and the basic record series (Appendix B–II) will be useful in the student's music teaching handbook or card file.

If the student is sure that he will teach kindergarten or a specific grade, he will want to select materials with this grade in mind. However, many young teachers find it more realistic to plan for two or more grades, or to compile a general teaching tool to be adapted later to any situation. The decision should be made by the prospective teacher with the advice of his college instructor.

If it seems advisable to develop this teaching tool as a loose-leaf notebook the student should obtain a three-hole binder for 8½″ x 11″ paper with dividers to set off seven sections. If a card file is preferred, 4″ x 6″ cards can be used with two levels of dividers. The teaching tool might be organized as follows with sample materials shown under each heading and ample space left for additions throughout the individual's teaching career.

1. Philosophy and General Resources
2. Bodily Movement
3. Rhythm Instruments
4. Melody and Harmony Instruments
5. Singing Repertoire
6. Listening
7. Creative Activities

This arrangement conforms in general to the organization of material within this textbook wherein numerous suggestions for items that might be included in the teaching tool are made in "Activities for College Classes" found at the end of each chapter. The college instructor can indicate which assignments would be most appropriate for different classes or for individuals with particular objectives in teaching.

This teaching tool should be the result of extensive research in these areas:

1. Musical activities for children and teaching techniques to carry them out.
2. Concepts of music and procedures that assist children in developing appropriate concepts at various ages.
3. Musical materials such as basic school music books, supplementary music, recorded music, and others.

The broad divisions of the collection will outline the musical activities; teaching notes related to each song or other composition should suggest musical concepts that might be developed through the use of the materials as well as the teaching techniques that might be particularly appropriate.

Not every classroom teacher is capable of single-handedly providing the rich program of musical experience his pupils should have. Nor is it usually possible for a music teacher to provide an optimum program unless he works with the classroom teacher. If the two bring to the task valid objectives, well-conceived plans, and a willingness to work together the children undoubtedly will find music a life-enriching enterprise during the school years and thereafter.

## ACTIVITIES FOR COLLEGE CLASSES

A. Questions for Review
1. Discuss the three points established as "the value of music" in this chapter. There are other more limited values. Can you suggest some? Do those you suggest fall under any of the three broad headings established in this chapter?
2. Discuss the growth characteristics of children. Of what value is such an analysis if it does not establish definite norms to which children conform?
3. Describe the six facets of education in music established in this chapter. In what order of importance would you rank them? Can you defend your position?
4. The parent, the classroom teacher, the music teacher, the principal— who is responsible for the musical development of children? Discuss this question.
B. Written Assignment
A successful program in music education is dependent upon a viable philosophy on the part of the teacher. This is something that is developed over a considerable period of time as the teacher himself is involved in musical activities and experiences. Throughout the course of his studies in music education the student should work out a one- or two-page statement of his philosophy and general objectives for music in the school curriculum. Several of the references cited in the following *Chapter Notes* and *Other References* will be helpful.

## CHAPTER NOTES

1. Plato, *The Republic.*
2. Edward Bailey Birge, *History of Public School Music in the United States* (Boston: Oliver Ditson Co., Inc., 1928), p. 47.
3. Alain Danielou, "Values in Music," in *Artistic Values in Traditional Music,* Proceedings of a Conference held in Berlin from the 14th to the 16th July 1965. International Institute for Comparative Music Studies and Documentation. Peter Crossley-Holland, editor.
4. Aaron Copland, *Music and Imagination* (Cambridge, Mass.: Harvard University Press, 1953), p. 14. Reprinted by permission.
5. Daniel A. Prescott, *Emotion and the Educative Process* (Washington, D.C.: American Council on Education, 1966), pp. 93, 102, 284. Reprinted by permission.
6. Irwin Edman, *Arts and the Man* (New York: W. W. Norton & Company, Inc., 1928, 1939), p. 46. Copyright, 1928, 1939, by W. W. Norton & Company, Inc., New York, New York. By permission of the publisher.
7. Susanne Langer, *Philosophy in a New Key,* Third Edition (Cambridge, Mass.: Harvard University Press, 1960), pp. 238–240.

Arnold Gesell, Frances Ilg, and Louise Bates, *Youth: The Years from Ten to Study of Human Growth* (New York: Harper & Row, Publishers, 1949).

————, *The Child from Five to Ten* (New York: Harper & Row, Publishers, 1946).

Arnold Gesell, Frances Ilg, and Louise Bates, *Youth: The Years from Ten to Sixteen* (New York: Harper & Row, Publishers, 1956).

9. Charles H. Slaughter, "Those Dissonant Boys," *Music Educators Journal,* February–March 1966.

10. Roger Sessions, *The Musical Experience* (Princeton, N.J.: Princeton University Press, 1950), pp. 19, 97.

11. E. Paul Torrance, *The Role of Evaluation in Creative Teaching* (Minneapolis: University of Minnesota, 1964, Cooperative Research Project No. 725, Bureau of Educational Research).

————, *Guiding Creative Talent* (Englewood Cliffs, N.J.: Prentice-Hall, Inc., 1962).

12. John Shelton, *The Influence of Home Musical Environment upon Musical Response of First-Grade Children* (Ed. D. Dissertation, George Peabody College for Teachers, 1965), Microfilm Order No. 66–4419.

## Other References

Jones, Archie N., editor, *Music Education in Action* (Boston: Allyn and Bacon, Inc., 1960). Chapter 1, "Philosophical Concepts."

Mursell, James L., *Music and the Classroom Teacher* (Morristown, N.J.: Silver Burdett Company, 1951). Chapter 1, "Why Music for Your Children?"

————, *Music Education Principles and Programs* (Morristown, N.J.: Silver Burdett Company, 1956). Chapter 2.

Music Educators National Conference, *Source Book III, Perspectives in Music Education* (Washington, D.C., 1966). "Philosophy and Practice," pp. 171–206.

Myers, Louise Kifer, *Teaching Children Music in the Elementary School,* Third Edition (Englewood Cliffs, N.J.: Prentice-Hall, Inc., 1961). Chapter 1, "Music in Today's Schools," and Chapter 8, "The Classroom Teacher."

Sheehy, Emma Dickson, *There's Music in Children,* Revised and Enlarged Edition (New York: Holt, Rinehart & Winston, Inc., 1952). Chapter 7, "Music and the Classroom Teacher."

CHAPTER
ONE

**20**

# 2

# Musical Concepts

The curriculum in music for children in the elementary school is planned for (1) broad experience with many kinds of music, (2) the development of skills in musical activities, and (3) the development of understanding about music itself. Chapters in this book are devoted to discussions of musical activities, repertoire, and the development of musical skills. A teacher also needs to know how children grow in their understanding of the elements of music and principles of its construction. In this chapter the author groups concepts in music under the following headings to show those that children can acquire as a result of musical experiences up through the sixth grade:

1. Rhythm
2. Melody
3. Texture and Harmony
4. Tone Color in Voices and Instruments
5. Dynamics
6. Form in Music
7. Style in Music

All of the concepts are stated in terms of generalizations of what is heard (the aural). Marginal notations show the grade level at which an idea might first be encountered. All of the statements listed may be considered at the level indicated, but they also must be reconsidered in the grades above, for children develop deeper musical understanding and better skills as they progress through the elementary grades. Mursell[1] states it this way:

What our understanding of growth and development clearly seems to imply is a *cyclical* sequence or order of topics. . . . Items that need to be presented do not occur once for all at some predetermined time. They appear again and again, always in new settings, always with added meanings.

In observing the grading of the ideas outlined in this chapter the teacher should keep in mind that what may be encountered in a musical setting and on a level appropriate for second graders must be dealt with again by older pupils for broader as well as more precise application in different musical contexts. Some of the musical qualities listed may seem so simple and obvious that one might wonder why they have been included. This author has found that an inexperienced teacher may block his own effectiveness as a teacher because he does not understand that what is obvious to him may not even be noticed by his pupils. The teacher is urged to give attention to the way adult statements of the concepts are cut down to child-size portions.

Music is an art. It often does not conform to descriptions that people establish in their efforts to organize and learn about it. Every musical composition is unique; once some reasonable generalizations are established one can observe in what ways a particular composition adheres to or deviates from the usual in such characteristics as rhythm, melody, and form. Experience with a repertoire of music that is broad and varied, within a program of interesting and creative activities, will give children opportunities to develop all the necessary concepts.

In order to deal effectively with the varied musical repertoire that will be used and to meet the needs of children in various learning situations, the teacher must analyze songs and other music to find out what qualities are noticeable in each. The following resources will be helpful:

1. The compositions the instructor of a college class uses to provide experience with music and to show how such analysis is done. At the end of this chapter two songs are analyzed in some detail; other musical examples throughout this book can be studied in the same way.
2. Teachers' manuals for the graded music series which analyze the song material and point out important characteristics in each composition.
3. Notes for teachers that analyze recorded instrumental music in the educational record libraries for elementary schools (see RCA Victor ADVENTURES IN MUSIC and the BOWMAR ORCHESTRAL LIBRARY).
4. A specialized publication, "The Study of Music in the Elementary School—A Conceptual Approach,"[2] which gives a detailed analysis of concepts and provides good musical examples for each.
5. Other specialized publications in music education, containing numerous compositions from the common elementary school repertoire, showing how the music can be analyzed and studied within the framework of the musical activities. Examples for every grade will be found in Bergethon and Boardman,[3] Knuth and Knuth,[4] and Schubert and Wood.[5]

A teacher who may need to improve his own understanding of music is referred to Aaron Copland's very readable book, What to Listen for in Music,[6] and Leonard Ratner's Music—The Listener's Art.[7]

---

## RHYTHM

All music has rhythm, for music, just as man and all of nature, moves through time with rhythmic ordering of movement. Rhythm, a basic element of music, is infinitely variable.

In this chapter concepts of rhythm that might be grasped by children in the elementary grades are outlined under four headings. The listing is broad, but it is not necessarily complete. The musical experiences which the children have may give them opportunities to develop additional ideas about rhythm that are fully as valid. The activities of bodily movement and use of rhythm instruments, described in Chapters Three and Four, are essential to the development of these concepts, and in building rhythmic skill.

When children see notation on the printed page, they can begin to learn the accepted terms and the meanings of notation for rhythm. Learning notation should be merely a matter of attaching symbols to something already familiar. Visual examples should be used where possible to support aural experience when dealing with rhythm.

A child's first ideas about rhythm come as a general awareness of its pace and character: that it can move fast or slow, and that it can be characterized as graceful, majestic, heavy, nimble, etc.

The smallest rhythmic unit is the motive, a grouping of one or more unaccented tones in relation to an accented one. In elementary education the use of the term "rhythm pattern" is preferred because it sometimes may be a larger unit than the musician's concept of "motive." In children's musical studies, music is analyzed in terms of its meaningful parts; there should be no attempt to dissect it at the technical level of a music theorist. In further musical studies, rhythm patterns can be seen as groups in larger, interrelated units that comprise the musical phrase.

After learning the general characteristics of rhythm and the way it falls into patterns, children will be ready to study the different organizations of beats that underlie rhythm in music. The teacher must be sure that he and his pupils do not equate "rhythm" with "beat." Peter Yates has said, "Beat is a condition not of rhythm but of performance accuracy, a point from which and a point to which rhythmic relationships can be directed, a coordinating device for group performance and, in many musical traditions, for dance."[8] Children can learn that a rhythm pattern is directly related to the meter of the music and that different rhythm patterns have different relationships with the underlying beat.

## Pace and Character of Movement

1. Music can move fast or slowly. (Later, pace in music is called *tempo*.)
2. Some fast music may be light; other fast music may be heavy and vigorous.
3. Slow music may be calm and quiet, or it may be ponderous and heavy.
4. Some music has a steady, even movement like running or walking, but other music may have a steady, uneven short-long movement, like galloping or jumping.
5. One piece of music can be played or sung at faster or slower speeds, arousing different feelings at each different speed.
6. Usually the rhythm of a piece of music moves at the same speed throughout, but sometimes it slows down gradually near the end or at some place in the middle. (Later this effect is identified as a *retard*.)
7. Sometimes the rhythm of a part of a composition is speeded up gradually, often to make up for a previous slowing down. (Later this effect is called *accelerando*.)
8. Sometimes only the melody is accelerated or slowed, while the accompaniment keeps a steady pace. (Later this effect is called *rubato*.)
9. Different speeds and qualities of movement in

*first grade upward*

music are designated by certain English and Italian terms:

*grave*—slow, solemn  
*largo*—very slow and broad  
*lento*—slow  
*adagio*—leisurely  
*andante*—moderate and flowing  
*cantabile*—in a singing manner  
*dolce*—sweetly  
*grazioso*—gracefully  
*moderato*—moderate  

*allegretto*—moderately fast  
*animato*—animated  
*allegro*—quick, lively  
*vivace*—brisk, fast  
*presto*—very fast  
*leggiero*—light, graceful  
*maestoso*—majestic  
*molto*—very much  
*poco*—a little  

*fifth grade upward*

10. A moderate tempo is about the speed of a heart beat (72 pulses per minute). Sometimes the composer specifies the tempo as a certain number of beats per minute.

*sixth grade upward*

## Rhythmic Motive or Pattern

1. Rhythm in music consists of groups of rhythm patterns; the tones in some rhythm patterns are regular and even, but in other patterns some tones are short and some are long.
2. A rhythm pattern may consist of tones that are long and slow-moving; a piece with such rhythm patterns can be restful and quiet, reverent and solemn.
3. A rhythm pattern may consist of tones that are short and fast-moving; a piece with such rhythm patterns can be brilliant and exciting, lively and dancing.

*second grade upward*

4. A rhythm pattern usually can be played by itself as a satisfactory repeated figure; sometimes the syllables and words in a song help determine the length of a rhythm pattern.
5. One tone in a rhythm pattern usually seems heavier than other tones; the heavier tone often is the second or third, but sometimes it is the first or last tone in the pattern.
6. A rhythm pattern that has regular and even tones is less exciting than one in which the tones are irregular in length and occurrence.
7. A rhythm pattern may be repeated once or several

*third grade upward*

**MUSICAL CONCEPTS**

times in one composition; it is usually alternated with other patterns.

8. Two short rhythm patterns may be grouped together to form a longer pattern; sometimes only part of the pattern is repeated.

*fourth grade upward*

9. Rhythm patterns within a phrase may be even in number, symmetrical, and balanced; sometimes an unbalanced, asymmetrical effect is desired so the rhythm patterns are designed to help achieve this effect.

10. A rhythm pattern can be varied (developed) in a number of ways: it may be lengthened (extended), shortened (fragmented), played twice as fast, or played half as fast.

*fifth grade upward*

## Beat, Meter, and Accent

1. The beat is regular and continuous throughout most pieces of music. Particularly in marches and dances the beat is felt strongly as a framework for the rhythm patterns in the music.

2. Lullabies and other gentle pieces have an underlying beat but in these it is less obvious.

*first grade upward*

3. The beat must be set at a suitable speed (tempo) for each piece; it can vary considerably from one composition to another. (Older pupils can see that ease in beating time is one reason for such different meters as $\frac{2}{4}$, $\frac{2}{2}$, $\mathcal{C}\!\!\!|$, and $\frac{2}{8}$.)

4. When beats are grouped in sets of two the music is said to be in *duple meter*. The steady beat for a march or a dancing song in duple meter is sounded *one-two, one-two*. (Older pupils can discover that $\frac{2}{4}$, $\frac{2}{8}$, fast $\frac{2}{2}$, $\mathcal{C}\!\!\!|$, and fast $\frac{6}{8}$ represent duple meter.)

5. When beats are grouped in sets of three the music is said to be in *triple meter*. A waltz or a minuet is sounded *one-two-three, one-two-three*. (Older pupils can discover that $\frac{3}{4}$, $\frac{3}{8}$, fast $\frac{3}{2}$, and fast $\frac{9}{8}$ represent triple meter.)

6. In any meter the first beat is slightly stronger than the other beats in the set; it is called the *accent*. Measure bars mark off accents and metric units.

*second grade upward*

7. In *quadruple meter* the beats are grouped in sets of four with an accent on the first beat and a lesser accent on the third beat. (Older pupils can discover that quadruple meter is represented by $\frac{4}{4}$, $\mathbf{C}$, $\frac{4}{8}$, fast $\frac{4}{2}$, and fast $\frac{12}{8}$.)

*third grade upward*

CHAPTER
TWO

28

8. A slow duple meter that has a swing is counted in six beats: *one-two-three, four-five-six.* In this meter there is an accent on the first beat and a lesser accent on the fourth beat. (Slow *compound duple meter* is shown by $\frac{6}{8}$ and $\frac{6}{4}$. *Compound triple meter* is shown by $\frac{9}{8}$).

*fourth grade upward*

9. In some folk and contemporary music unusual meters containing sets of five or seven beats are encountered. In such meters as $\frac{5}{4}$ and $\frac{7}{4}$ the beat is steady, but the occurrence of the accent on an odd-numbered beat gives an asymmetric rhythmic effect.

*sixth grade upward*

10. When the beat continues at a steady pace throughout a composition while the meter changes so that the accent is shifted, an exciting, asymmetrical rhythm is achieved. This effect is found in some folk dances and contemporary music.

## Rhythm Patterns Related to Meter

1. A rhythm pattern can have a smooth movement when its tones flow evenly, twice as fast as the beat. (Later various patterns of even quarter, eighth, and sixteenth notes in $\frac{2}{4}$, $\frac{3}{4}$, and $\frac{4}{4}$ meter can be shown to have this characteristic.)

2. A rhythm pattern can give a feeling of roundness and flow when the tones of the pattern divide the beat into three parts. Many nursery rhymes have rhythm patterns of this kind. (Later various eighth, quarter, and dotted-quarter note patterns in $\frac{6}{8}$, $\frac{9}{8}$, or $\frac{12}{8}$ can be shown to give this effect.)

*second grade upward*

3. A rhythm pattern may have tones that move exactly with the beat; in other patterns, some tones may move half as fast as the beat, and they can be combined with faster and even slower tones. Various combinations of quarter, half, dotted half, and whole notes are used in such patterns.

*third grade upward*

4. A rhythm pattern may not take up all of the beats in a meter; sometimes the pattern is repeated, another is sounded, or there is a period of silence called a *rest.*

5. Occasionally a rhythm pattern begins with its most important tone on the first beat of the meter, but in many other rhythm patterns one, two, or three quick light tones precede the most important tone. Such short tones leading to the accent are said to be

**MUSICAL CONCEPTS**

**29**

on the *upbeat*. Rhythm patterns with upbeats may cut across measure bars.

6. Many rhythm patterns have tones that divide the beat unevenly. A common pattern is that in which the beat is divided into four parts with the long tone getting three parts of the beat, and the short tone one part. Various combinations of dotted quarter and eighth notes or dotted eighth and sixteenth notes represent such patterns.

7. When a rhythm pattern is arranged so that its important tone does not coincide with the strong beat in the meter, the pattern is said to be *syncopated*. Many syncopated Latin-American rhythm patterns have a short tone on the beat, followed by a longer tone on the unaccented part of the beat, or a rest on the beat with tones sounded after the beat.

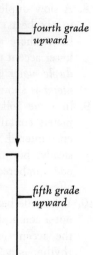

*fourth grade upward*

*fifth grade upward*

## MELODY

All understandings about melody must emerge from direct experience with it, by singing, moving, playing instruments such as glockenspiels, resonator bells, and the piano, and by manipulating notation during these music-making activities. Attempts to have children memorize statements about the characteristics of melody rather than to discover qualities and relationships in the music itself is a travesty of the learning process. Labels or words describing an effect can help direct attention after the effect itself has been noticed, but they are important only when one wishes to talk about music.

Because notation for pitch is important, it is included in this chapter. The teacher must know how the visual symbols can be related to the aural experience of melody when the children are ready for a visual representation.

On the following pages are listed the qualities of melody that are revealed in the experiences children have with it. The activities through which children discover these characteristics of melody will be found in Chapter Five, "The Use of Melody and Harmony Instruments" and in Chapter Seven, "Management of the Singing Situation."

Children in the early primary grades can notice the rise and fall of the melody line and observe its natural division into phrases. Second grade children can begin to sense the influence of a scale system upon a melody; they will notice that a melody that stops on a certain tone (the tonic) has more feeling of repose than a melody that stops on another tone.

A motive is a short, self-contained, expressive fragment of melody. The melodic motive is called a tonal pattern in primary level music education, for the same general reasons that the rhythmic motive is called a rhythm pattern in the early grades; the use of the term "motive" can be initiated at about the fifth grade level. In the intermediate grades children begin to be aware of the interrelationships of melodic motives in a phrase. At about the fourth grade level the teacher can begin to refer to the difference in pitch between two tones as an interval.

## Melody as a Complete Unit

1. A melody may rise, it may fall, or it may stay generally on one level.
2. In rising or falling, a melody can move by scale steps (*conjunct*), or it can move by larger steps (*disjunct*).
3. The tones of a melody may seem to flow in one long continuous line, or they may be shaped into small groups (*motives*).

*first grade upward*

4. Certain tones in every melody are restful, but other tones seem restless and tend to lead toward a restful tone. The home tone (*the tonic*) is the most restful tone.
5. A melody may have two or more *phrases*, the first being set off by a *half cadence*, and the second coming to a more definite ending (*authentic cadence*).

*second grade upward*

6. The mood a melody arouses is determined to some extent by the way it moves. A slow-moving melody that remains near one level, using *repeated tones* and *neighboring tones*, can seem calm and restful. Lullabies have this characteristic.
7. Some melodies sound unusual because they use only five different tones. (Older pupils can learn that these melodies are written in the *pentatonic* scale.)
8. Some melodies have a slightly different, darker sound than others; they are said to be in the *minor mode*, whereas many brighter sounding melodies are in the *major mode*. (Pupils can change a major scale to minor by lowering the third and the sixth degrees.)

*third grade upward*

9. Scalewise movement in a melody can suggest strength if it rises steadily, relaxation if it falls. A melody that moves up or down by large steps may suggest boldness.
10. A melody may have a high point of interest called a *climax*. This may be early in the melody but more often it comes near the end. Often the climax coincides with the highest tone of the melody but sometimes it does not.

*fourth grade upward*

**MUSICAL CONCEPTS**

**31**

11. A melody may have both very high tones and very low tones; such a melody is said to have a wide *range*.

12. A melody that moves through the tones of a chord is said to move *chordwise*. Much folk music is organized around chord tones.

13. A melody often has a framework of chord tones that is filled in by other tones.

14. In many songs each syllable in each word is given one tone, but in some music one syllable is given several tones. (Later these two types of melody may be identified as *syllabic* and *melismatic*.)

*fifth grade upward*

15. Sometimes many words are sung or recited on just a few tones. This is characteristic of *recitative* used in opera or oratorio for the narrative parts of the text.

## Melodic Motives (Tonal Patterns)

1. Some tonal patterns are longer than others; some are as short as two tones, others may be six or seven tones in length.

*first grade upward*

2. A tonal pattern consisting of tones moving one step at a time up or down the scale is called a *scalewise* pattern.

3. A tonal pattern may consist of a few tones that are far apart—that is, going from low to high or high to low in wide leaps.

4. A tonal pattern consisting of the tones of a chord is called a *chordwise* pattern.

*second grade upward*

5. A longer tonal pattern may contain both scalewise and chordwise movement among the tones.

6. Some tones within a pattern may be *repeated tones*; others may be *neighboring tones*.

7. Rhythm is part of the tonal pattern; if the tones remain the same but the rhythm changes, the pattern is different.

8. In a motive (tonal pattern), one tone is usually more important than the others; this important tone may be in the middle of the pattern, at the beginning, or at the end.

9. Within a melody, a motive can be repeated exactly, or it can be changed slightly the second or third time it is used.

*fourth grade upward*

10. When a motive is repeated on a higher or lower level, the repetition is said to be *in sequence*.

11. Sometimes two adjacent motives are quite differ-ent from each other; they are said to *contrast*.
12. A motive can be changed (*developed*) in a number of ways: it may be lengthened (*extended*), or shortened (*fragmented*), changed in rhythm, turned upside down (*inverted*), and so on.

*fifth grade upward*

## Melodic Intervals

1. The distance from low *do* (1) to high *do* (8) is a very wide leap. (Older pupils can count the beginning and the ending scale steps and all the steps between to find that there are eight tones in this interval, called an *octave*.)
2. The distance from *do* (1) up to *re* (2), and the distance from *re* (2) up to *mi* (3) is one step. (Later it is identified as a *major second*.)
3. The distance from *do* (1) up to *mi* (3) is an easy skip; it is the first part of the tonic chord and is used for tuning up to sing. (Later it is identified as a *major third*.)

*second grade upward*

4. The distance from *mi* (3) up to *fa* (4) is a half step, and the distance from *ti* (7) up to *do* (8) is a half step; this is a very small interval. (Later it is identified as a *minor second*, which is one half step smaller than a major second.)
5. The distance from *mi* (3) up to *so* (5) is a small skip, as is the distance from *la* (6) up to *do* (8). Brahms' "Cradle Song" has this skip as its first ascending interval. (Later it is identified as a *minor third*, which is a half step smaller than a major third.)

*third grade upward*

6. The distance from *do* (1) up to *so* (5) is a firm leap; this interval is heard when the open strings of the violin are tuned. (Later it is identified as a *perfect fifth*.)
7. The distance from *so* (5) up to *do* (8) is a leap, as is the distance from *do* (1) up to *fa* (4). This interval is the first ascending interval in "Taps." (Later it is identified as a *perfect fourth*.)
8. The distance from *do* (1) up to *la* (6) is a comfortable, wide leap, as is the distance from *so* (5) up to *mi* (3). This interval is heard in the first two tones of "My Bonnie." (Later it is identified as a *major sixth*.)

*fourth grade upward*

MUSICAL
CONCEPTS

**33**

## The Organization of Tones within Scales

1. Every melody is based on an organization of tones called a scale. The scale most often used for melodies in our music is the *major scale:* seven different tones, in a prescribed pattern of whole steps and half steps, having names corresponding to the first seven letters of the alphabet. (See diagram in Appendix A.)

2. The pentatonic scale, used as the basis for some folk songs, has only five tones. The most common form of this scale can be made by playing the black keys on the piano, or by omitting the fourth and the seventh steps of any major scale.

*third grade upward*

3. The chromatic scale has twelve different tones, each a half step apart. In the ascending chromatic scale, a tone with a sharp (♯) is one half step higher than the same named tone with no sharp. In the descending chromatic scale, a tone with a flat (♭) is one half step lower than the same named tone with no flat.

4. A major scale can be built on any tone of the chromatic scale. When a major scale is made, certain tones of the chromatic scale are not used. The sound of the major scale is achieved only when whole steps occur between all tones of the scale except 3–4 and 7–8, where half steps occur.

5. The *natural minor* scale is heard when the syllables for any major scale are sung beginning and ending on *la*. Since the half steps fall between different steps, the minor does not sound the same as the major scale.

*fourth grade upward*

6. A minor scale has more harmonic strength when the seventh step of the scale is raised (then called the *leading tone*). Raising this tone creates another form of the minor scale, the *harmonic minor*.

7. The harmonic minor scale can be made in another way: by beginning on the first tone of the major scale and flatting each third and each sixth scale step.

*sixth grade upward*

## Notation for Pitch

1. The pitch of musical tone, referred to as high or low, is shown as high or low on a music *staff*. Each step of a scale is represented by the consecutive lines and spaces of the staff. (See diagram in Appendix A.)

*third grade upward*

2. The first seven letters of the alphabet are used to name the lines and spaces of the staff, just as they are used to name the piano keys and resonator bars. These are repeated at higher and lower levels.
3. When a tone is so high or low that it cannot be shown on the staff, *leger lines* are added above or below the staff to show the pitch. Music for bass voices or instruments is written on another staff.
4. A clef sign at the beginning of the staff shows what tones are represented by the lines and spaces of a staff. The *treble clef* (G clef) is used for high voices and instruments; the *bass clef* (F clef) is used for low voices and instruments.
5. The lines and spaces of both staffs conform to the whole- and half-step arrangement of the C major scale; that is, half steps occur between E–F and B–C; all other consecutive lines and spaces represent whole steps.
6. When notes other than those in the scale of C major are to be written, half-step changes of pitch can be shown by a sharp or a flat placed on a line or space before the note.
7. When a melody is written in a scale other than C major, the necessary sharps or flats are placed at the left of the staff (as the *key signature*) rather than before every note that needs to have a sharp or a flat. The music is then said to be in the key of the tonic note of that scale.

*fourth grade upward*

## TEXTURE AND HARMONY

Texture is a quality of music resulting from the interrelationship and action of two or more instrumental or vocal parts sounding together. There are two basic types of musical texture:
1. Homophonic—that in which one principal melody is present and other tones support and enrich this melody.
2. Polyphonic—that achieved when two or more distinct and separate musical lines are sounded simultaneously.

Harmony is the relationship of the tones of music, either within a single melodic line or from the point of view of the melody and its accompaniment. The tones within a melody can be organized around a chord or a series of chords. In the development of musical understanding, experimentation with chords and their relationships to each other and to a melodic line should grow out of musical activities involving tuned instruments.

Since so many teaching aids are available today, boys and girls can arrive at an elementary understanding of musical texture and harmony by the end of

MUSICAL CONCEPTS

**35**

the sixth grade. Particularly useful are the many kinds of recorded music and the special classroom instruments, such as resonator bells and the Autoharp. Concepts of harmony can be developed when children learn to play the Autoharp and sing with it; as early as the second or third grade, children can hear the difference between the tonic and the dominant chords. Later they can sing rounds that represent a different texture in music. Listening to music offers opportunities for encountering more varied use of musical harmony and texture.

Within the generalizations given on the following pages, all of the items in the first two groups could be understood by children without reference to music notation. It is important that these effects first be pointed out as they are heard. Later, children should see the notation for the particular effect.

It is only in the fifth and sixth grades that children build chords and use their understanding of melody as the basis for an introduction to some of the specifics of the system of harmony. The desire to play chord accompaniments on resonator bells and on the piano can lead to an understanding of all the items listed under "Seeing and Building Chords."

Procedures outlined in Chapter Five, "The Use of Melody and Harmony Instruments," and in Chapter Seven, "Management of the Singing Situation," will provide the teacher with sufficient ideas for pupil activities that can lead to the development of skills related to the concepts outlined in this section.

Although some items are explained, the following outline is not a study of harmony. It is merely a listing of the musical properties that children can find meaningful. These concepts should grow out of musical experiences; they do not need to be studied in depth in these grades. Appendix A–IV shows definitions and notation of chords and scales for the college student who needs this assistance.

## Variety in Texture

1. When a chord accompaniment supports one main melody the effect is called *harmony*. (In advanced study, this is called *homophonic texture*.) — *first grade upward*

2. When a melody is harmonized, the harmony may have different qualities of texture: slow-moving chords that are held while the melody moves through several tones; chords that are played on almost every tone of the melody; chords that are broken and played in arpeggios or in repeated accompaniment figures.

3. Two or more melodies of equal importance sounding at the same time create *counterpoint*. The *round* and the *canon* are simple types of counterpoint. (In more advanced study, this is called *polyphonic texture*.) — *third grade upward*

4. An accompaniment that consists of a rhythmic-melodic pattern repeated over and over is called an *ostinato*.

5. Sometimes two or more voices within a composition move for a short or a long time in *parallel motion*. The intervals between the voices usually are thirds or sixths, which are *consonant intervals*. This kind of harmony is found in two-part songs for children's voices and between the upper parts of "barbershop quartet" arrangements.

6. Sometimes two parts within a composition move in opposite directions, or in *contrary motion*; a *descant* is often set in contrary motion to the melody.

*fourth grade upward*

## Chords and Their Relationships

1. A chord is a group of tones sounded together. The *tonic chord* (I) is the "home" chord and gives the feeling of restfulness and arrival. Musical compositions often begin with tonic-chord harmony and usually end on it.

2. The *dominant chord* (V) is an active, restless chord; its tones tend to lead to tones in other chords, usually the tonic.

*second grade upward*

3. The *subdominant chord* (IV) is called the "amen" chord because its smooth, pleasant sound is heard as the first chord in the "amen" at the end of a hymn.

*third grade upward*

4. The tonic chord (I), the dominant chord (V), and the subdominant chord (IV) are the three chords most often used in simple harmonies of hymns and folk music. All of these are bright-sounding *major chords* when a major scale is used.

5. When a melody is harmonized, chords that fit with its important tones must be used. Some tones that are short or that do not occur on accented beats in the melody can be treated as *passing tones* or *neighboring tones*, which are not harmonized.

6. When a minor scale is used the tonic chord (I) and the subdominant chord (IV) are *minor chords;* such chords have a sweet, pleasant sound that is darker in quality than that of major chords.

7. When the harmony moves from the dominant chord to the tonic chord at the end of a piece, it creates a feeling of arrival and finality (later identified as a *full cadence*).

8. When the harmony moves from subdominant (IV) to tonic (I), the result is a less strong,

*fourth grade upward*

MUSICAL
CONCEPTS

37

"amen" cadence (later identified as a *plagal cadence*).

9. Sometimes a phrase or larger section of a composition ends on tones of the dominant chord; this is a temporary kind of ending (later identified as a *half cadence*).     *fifth grade upward*

10. In a major key the *supertonic chord* (II) is a minor chord, and it sometimes is used to provide a quality of sound that contrasts with the major chords.

11. Some chords in modern music produce tense, clashing sounds that are called *dissonant*. The composer uses dissonance to produce an effect or create feeling through his music; it is not necessarily unpleasant.

12. Composers of modern music sometimes use chords from two different keys at the same time (*polytonality*). Such combinations of tones create variety and interesting musical effects, although they may seem dissonant and jarring to listeners accustomed to traditional harmonies.     *sixth grade upward*

### Seeing and Building Chords

1. The simplest chord, a *triad*, consists of three tones built up in thirds from any step of a scale. The tone on which a chord is built is called its *root*.

2. Chords are labeled in three ways: with a Roman numeral, indicating the scale step on which the chord is built; with a capital letter (as seen on the Autoharp) showing the letter name of the note on which the chord is built; or by a name indicating its harmonic function, such as *tonic* (I) or *dominant* (V).     *fourth grade upward*

3. The dominant seventh chord ($V_7$) has four tones and is used instead of the dominant (V) when a richer, more dynamic quality is desired. (This is the form of the chord available on the Autoharp.) The dominant seventh is a major chord with an added third on top, which is an interval of a seventh from the root of the chord; this is a dissonant chord that forces the harmony to move.     *fifth grade upward*

4. Some chords having the same letter name and formation are found in different keys. The function and harmonic effect of a chord depend upon its relationship to the *tonal center* of the key in which

**CHAPTER TWO**

38

it is used, just as each tone of the scale has its own relationship to the key tone (tonal center). | *sixth grade upward*

5. A chord can have some tones doubled, or it can be inverted and still retain its general characteristics and function.

## TONE COLOR IN VOICES AND INSTRUMENTS

Tone color (timbre) in music can be explored and studied in the elementary school in a number of ways. When tone is the center of a study of instruments and voices, the children should have an opportunity to play instruments and to hear them in performance, either live or recorded. The first experiences and observations come in the kindergarten and primary grades, where children hear differences in singing voices and where they explore the tone quality of various classroom instruments. By the time they have completed the sixth grade, children should be acquainted with the tone quality of most instruments and voices; they should have some understanding of the importance of tone color as an element of music.

This section deals only with the essential characteristics of tone quality of the different voices and instruments. To get an idea of the scope and importance of this subject to a composer, the teacher is advised to read Copland, *What to Listen for in Music,*[6] Chapter 7. Procedures for studies of orchestral instruments are outlined in Chapter Eight of this textbook.

### Vocal Tone

1. Some voices are higher than others; the voice of a child or a woman is usually much higher than the voice of a man.

2. A voice can be made to sound soft and gentle, or loud and brilliant, or exciting, depending upon the feeling that is to be conveyed in the song. (This list of adjectives identifying vocal expression should be expanded in successive grades.) | *first grade upward*

3. Voices of different people have different qualities of sound; some voices have a smooth, velvety sound, others may sound rough or nasal, or dark and veiled. (Other adjectives can be used to describe vocal tone quality as children hear a greater variety of voices in successive grades.) | *second grade upward*

4. When people sing together under the direction of a leader, they may be singing in a *chorus* or a *choir*. Groups that sing sacred music are called choirs. (Later, as children hear different singing groups, they can learn what voice parts make up a | *third grade upward*

MUSICAL CONCEPTS

children's choir and an adult chorus or choir. An a cappella choir is unaccompanied.)

5. Girls, some women, and boys with unchanged voices are classified as *sopranos*. Such voices are high, light, and bright in quality.

6. Women with lower, darker, or heavier singing voices are classified as *altos*. Some children who sing lower tones better than upper tones take the lower (alto) part in two-part music.

*fourth grade upward*

7. The highest and brightest man's voice is the *tenor*; a man's voice that sounds four or five tones lower and is deeper and more somber in quality is called a *bass*.

8. When people sing together in small groups, with each voice on a different part, they may sing in a duet, a trio, a quartet, a quintet, or a sextet. (Pupils may become acquainted with "barbershop" quartets and famous ensembles from opera or oratorio.)

*fifth grade upward*

9. Among highly trained singers, voices are classified according to musical expression and the dramatic roles played. The voice of the *coloratura soprano* is brilliant and agile with a very high range; the *lyric soprano* voice is sweeter and lighter in quality. The *dramatic soprano* has a heavier voice.

10. The quality of voices among men singers is likewise varied. There are *lyric, heroic,* and *robust* tenor voices; each voice reflects to some extent the qualities associated with the name. The *baritone* is the full, middle-range male voice, and the *basso profundo* is the deep, powerful male voice often playing the solemn role of a king or priest in opera.

*sixth grade upward*

**CHAPTER TWO**

## The Strings

1. On some instruments a musical tone is made when a tightly stretched string is plucked with the finger, set in vibration by a bow drawn across it, or struck by a small felt hammer. (In successive grades, children can become further acquainted with the plucked or strummed instruments, such as *guitar, ukulele, banjo, Autoharp, psaltery, zither,* and *harp*; they should learn to differentiate between the tones of the bowed stringed instruments and the keyboard instruments.)

2. Strings that are long and thick produce heavy, low

**40**

tones of long duration; strings that are short and very thin produce high, bright tones of shorter duration. (In successive grades, the concept of *pitch* is related to high- and low-sounding strings on different instruments; children learn how strings are stopped by the fingers at higher or lower positions on plucked or bowed instruments to make higher or lower tones.)

3. All stringed instruments have a sounding board or a resonating body that vibrates when the string is sounded, reinforcing the tone so it is loud enough to be heard. (Children touch different instruments to feel the vibrations created; later they learn how the player controls the *volume* of the tone by various playing techniques.)

4. On many stringed instruments the *duration* of the tone depends upon the length of time the string continues to vibrate after it has been struck or plucked; the violin and other bowed instruments can produce a singing tone because the player can use the bow to draw a smooth, continuous tone. (In successive grades, children can hear how the bow is used on instruments of the violin family to create very short, dry tones called *staccato;* long, connected tones called *legato;* or light, lifted tones called *spiccato.*)

5. The piano has the widest *range* of tones from low to high; it has a different string (usually double or triple) for each pitch. The strings of the harp are similar to the strings of the piano, but the harp is played by plucking the strings with the fingers rather than by striking them with a hammer, as on the piano. (Later, children can learn to recognize such musical effects as *glissandos, arpeggios,* and running *scale passages* on both instruments, and uses of the pedals of the piano.)

6. Among the bowed stringed instruments, the *violin* is the highest in pitch and tonally the most versatile; its tones can be soft and lyric, soulful, or dramatic and exciting. The *viola,* which is a little larger, has a darker, more sonorous tone. The *cello,* not so agile or brilliant in tone as the violin, can sound dramatic, robust, or tender and soulful. The *double bass* has the lowest and most powerful tones of this group of instruments.

7. The harpsichord looks like a grand piano, but its tone is produced by a mechanical plucking of the strings with leather plectrums. The tone, although

*first grade upward*

*fourth grade upward*

**MUSICAL CONCEPTS**

**41**

limited in dynamic range, is crisp and sparkling; the harpsichord is considered the ideal keyboard instrument for much music by Bach, Handel, and other composers of the baroque period.

8. The bowed strings make up half of the symphony orchestra, providing the basic tone quality for that group. There are some orchestras with nothing but strings.

9. The string quartet is an ideal small group because the tones of the instruments blend to form a well-balanced musical ensemble. The quartet consists of first violin, second violin, viola, and cello. Their parts are comparable to soprano, alto, tenor, and bass in vocal groups.

*fifth grade upward*

## The Woodwinds

1. On some instruments a musical tone is made when a person blows across a hole in a short pipe, as across a bottle. The *flute* and its half-sized relative, the *piccolo,* are played this way. The higher tones of the flute can be very bright and penetrating; the lower tones may sound hollow and dark. (In successive grades, children can learn more about playing the flute and about its tone quality; they can compare it with the *recorder,* an end-blown flute with a soft, more intimate tone quality.)

2. In all woodwinds, the player raises or lowers the tone by opening or closing holes down the length of the instrument. Since the mechanism that closes the holes lies conveniently under the fingers of the player, he can play very rapidly, leaping from low to high tones easily. (Later, children can learn the different musical effects of legato and staccato played on these instruments.)

*second grade upward*

3. Some wind instruments have a *single-reed* mouthpiece at the end of the instrument. The *clarinet* is the most important of this group; its tone is rich and full, but quite bright on the high notes. (Later, children can learn to know the different qualities of the clarinet in its three registers; they can become acquainted with the rich, low tones of the *bass clarinet* and the mellow but sometimes reedy tone of the *saxophone.*)

*third grade upward*

4. Other wind instruments have a *double reed* (flattened "soda-straw" type) mouthpiece. Of this group the *oboe* is well known. It is about the size of a

CHAPTER
TWO

42

clarinet, but it has a relatively unchanging tone that is somewhat nasal and sometimes pastoral or oriental in quality.

5. The *bassoon* is a larger double-reed instrument; it has a wide dynamic range and such tonal versatility, from grandiose to plaintive or humorous, that it is sometimes called the clown of the orchestra. (In successive grades, children can become acquainted with the plaintive, reedy tone of the *English horn* and the heavy, somber tones of the *contrabassoon*.)

*fourth grade upward*

6. The woodwind instruments are important "color" instruments in the symphony orchestra because their tones contrast well with the string tone. They can also carry the melody line or provide modest fill-in parts for the whole ensemble. Concert or marching bands, which seldom use strings, depend upon the many woodwind instruments to set the basic tone quality.

*fifth grade upward*

## The Brasses

1. The most brilliant, commanding tone of any instrument comes from the *trumpet*. This instrument evolved from the *bugle* which, being limited to only five tones, is used for signaling, e.g., reveille and taps. Because it has three valves, the trumpet can sound any tone and carry a melody beautifully. (At a later time, children learn that the *cornet* is similar to the trumpet, but slightly shorter and less brilliant.)

2. One of the largest instruments of the orchestra is the *tuba*. It is an armful of wound brass tubing with a flaring bell. Because its tone is so heavy and slow moving, the tuba is used primarily to support the bass rather than to carry melody. (Later, children can learn that the *sousaphone* is a tuba wound so it can be carried on the player's shoulders in a marching band.)

*second grade upward*

3. A characteristic common to brass instruments is the cup-shaped mouthpiece. The lips of the player produce the tonal vibrations; the tubing and bell amplify the tones; the size and shape of both mouthpiece and instrument determine tone quality.

4. The *trombone* is the baritone-bass of the brass family. It has a sliding cylindrical tube that is used to form different pitches. The tone quality of the trombone is rich and powerful, but more solemn

*fourth grade upward*

MUSICAL
CONCEPTS

**43**

and dignified than the trumpet; it can sound brilliant when played loudly.

5. The *French horn* is descended from the natural hunting horn; it is circularly wound, has a large flaring bell and, with its three circular valves, can sound all tones of the scale. Its tone, lower than that of the trumpet, is noble and full, sometimes majestic and brassy. It can be muted for an effect of distance or solitude.

6. The trumpet, the tuba, the trombone, and the French horn add body and brilliance to the orchestral sound. These and other brass instruments are used in greater numbers in the band, where they often provide massive effects.

*fifth grade upward*

## The Percussion

1. Some drums emit a deep, resonant tone of long duration; other drums have a tone that is short and penetrating, with a dry quality. (In higher grades, children can become acquainted with the tone quality of untuned drums such as *tom-toms, bongo* and *conga drums,* and the *snare* and *bass drums* of the symphony orchestra. They learn that the size of the drum, the type of material in the drumhead, and the method of beating all are factors contributing to the different tone qualities.)

2. Some single-toned percussion instruments produce short, dry sounds, and others produce ringing sounds of longer duration. (Later, children learn to recognize subtle differences in the tones of instruments such as the *claves, castanets, woodblock, maracas, triangle, sleighbells, cymbals,* and *gong.* They observe how different qualities of sound can be produced through different uses of the instruments.)

3. Some percussion instruments are tuned, and melodies can be played on them. *Glockenspiels, bells,* and *resonator bars* have a bright, bell-like tone. The tone of the *xylophone* is dry; it can be either brittle or muffled, depending upon the type of mallets used. (Later, children learn that pitch in these instruments is related to the length of the tone bar or size of the bell.)

4. There are two kinds of drums in a symphony orchestra: tuned drums and those of indefinite pitch. Both the *snare drum* and the *bass drum* are of indefinite pitch. The *kettledrums (tympani)* are

*first grade upward*

tuned drums with the shape of large copper kettles. A symphony orchestra usually has two or three tuned to different pitches; the tone is deep, resonant, and important to majestic or triumphant expression by the orchestra.

5. Many single-toned percussion instruments, such as *castanets, triangle, cymbals,* and *gong,* are used in the symphony orchestra for special effects. The xylophone and glockenspiel are used occasionally.    *fifth grade upward*

6. Among the tuned instruments with bell-like tones is the *celesta,* which is essentially a glockenspiel attached to a keyboard (it looks like a small piano). Its tone is very delicate, with little carrying power. The *orchestra chimes,* tuned metal tubes, are struck with a wooden hammer to produce a tone of great resonance and duration.

## DYNAMICS

Among the refining, expressive factors of music are the various dynamic qualities which the composer indicates or which a musician incorporates because he knows the performance tradition of music in a particular style. Music of the romantic period is known for the plentiful use of *crescendo* and *decrescendo,* contrasts between loud and soft, as well as various dynamic accents. In contrast, in the music of the great composers of the classic period such expressive factors are used with restraint, supporting but never detracting from the total effect of the musical elements themselves.

Young children can learn to hear loudness and softness in music and to sense how these factors affect the mood and expression of the music. The development of these concepts can come through several activities in music: singing songs which have dynamic contrasts, moving to music which demands changes in the quality of movement because of obvious changes in dynamics, playing rhythm instruments with musical compositions featuring changes from loud to soft, or listening to music in which the mood or story is expressed in part by changes in dynamics.

The following are suggested concepts about dynamics in music which children might develop as a result of their musical experiences in the elementary school.

**MUSICAL CONCEPTS**

### Relative Strength of Sound

1. Some music should be played or sung loudly in order to create an appropriate mood for the piece. Marches and heavy work songs might be quite loud.

**45**

2. Some music should be played or sung softly in order to create an appropriate mood for the piece. Lullabies and other gentle pieces usually should be sung softly.
3. In a musical composition some phrases or sections may be sung or played louder than others in order to convey contrasting ideas or moods.
4. There are various degrees of loudness and softness in music. The performer must select the level of loudness or softness that is most appropriate to the mood and ideas in the music. (In the intermediate grades signs for various gradations of loudness and softness can be learned. See Appendix A–II).
5. When many instruments or voices play or sing together they may sound louder than a single instrument or voice. However, either an individual or a group can vary the loudness or softness of their playing or singing in order to produce the desired mood in the music.

*first grade upward*

## Types of Dynamic Changes

1. Music may become suddenly louder or suddenly softer within a composition because the players simultaneously play or sing louder or softer to obtain a desired effect.

*first grade upward*

2. Music may become suddenly louder or suddenly softer within a composition because singers or players are added or dropped out of a performing group. (In the intermediate grades children may learn that the "terrace" dynamics of some music in the baroque style is created by the alternate playing of large and small groups.)
3. Music may become gradually louder or gradually softer within a composition. This effect is called *crescendo* (louder) or *diminuendo* (softer); it is achieved by careful control on the part of each player or singer so that the gradual change is achieved.

*third grade upward*

**CHAPTER TWO**

## Interrelationship of Dynamics with Other Musical Elements

1. Music that goes faster may become louder unless the performers take care to maintain the same dynamic level.

2. A melody that goes higher sometimes sounds louder because of a difference in the tone quality of certain voices and instruments in a higher register.

3. The texture of the music may influence the effect which the dynamics of a composition produce. That is, a single line played loudly by many instruments will produce an effect very different from that heard when many instruments play several different parts at the same dynamic level.

*fourth grade upward*

4. The composer and the performer achieve expressive effects that help convey the mood and meaning of the music by using dynamic changes interrelated with other factors in music (melody, rhythm, harmony, texture, and timbre).

*fifth grade upward*

---

## FORM IN MUSIC

Form has been characterized as the intellectual aspect of music because the mind must remember and compare the use of rhythmic, melodic, and harmonic elements heard at one point with their development and continued use throughout the composition. While the comprehension of form in large works like symphonies requires skill and experience in music listening, many aspects of form and design in music are well within the understanding of children.

The aspects of form in music within the grasp of elementary school pupils are listed on the following pages. This study begins early, as children expand their singing repertoire. At that time they use and observe melodic motives and phrases that are basic units in musical design; they learn how phrases are put together and how a melodic motive can be developed and varied in small ways. Concepts about fundamental aspects of form are outlined in the section that follows. It is only after children understand some of the techniques a composer can use to create variations on one theme that they are ready to undertake a study of the larger forms in music.

The entire activities program in music offers opportunities for observation and use of principles of musical form (see especially Chapters Three, Four, Seven, and Eight). The teacher should study this listing of concepts and then consider how they can be developed in activities that incorporate the improvisation and writing of music as well as a desirable repertoire of songs and recorded instrumental music.

**MUSICAL CONCEPTS**

### The Phrase as a Unit of Musical Form

1. Music is built up of phrases and sections that, together, make up a whole composition.

2. A song or other short piece of music usually consists of several well-defined phrases, some alike and some different.

*first grade upward*

**47**

3. Often there is an even number of phrases in a composition, but sometimes the number is uneven.

4. Within one composition, the phrases usually are the same length, but sometimes a phrase is longer or shorter than others.

5. A phrase can be repeated exactly (AA); it can be repeated, but with some changes (AA'); or it can be followed by another that is in contrast to it (AB).

*second grade upward*

6. Sometimes two phrases sound like a question and an answer within a longer musical unit. (Later these are identified as *antecedent* and *consequent phrases* within a musical *period*.)

7. Some phrases give the impression of a long flowing line; others readily divide into short melodic motives.

*third grade upward*

8. A phrase may consist of one important motive that is repeated and expanded, or it may consist of two or more different motives.

*fourth grade upward*

## Sectional Forms in Music

1. Some songs and short instrumental pieces seem symmetrical and balanced, because a second section completes or answers the first section; some marches, dances, and songs having a stanza followed by a refrain have this form. (Later this may be called *two-part* or *binary form* and shown as AB in analysis.)

*third grade upward*

2. A musical composition may have a satisfying first section that is followed by a contrasting second section. When the first section is repeated at the end, the whole piece seems well balanced and complete. Some cradle songs, waltzes, minuets, preludes, and other short pieces are written in this form. (Later this may be called *three-part* or *ternary form* and shown as ABA in analysis.)

3. Sometimes a first section is alternated with two or more other sections. Since the first section comes around after each different section is played, this form is called a *rondo*. The rondo usually is lively and cheerful in nature. (Later the rondo form may be diagrammed as ABACADA, or some other form of the basic pattern with A recurring.)

*fourth grade upward*

4. A composer can use any arrangement of sections that is suitable to his musical material. Some compositions that are clearly divisible into sections do not

fit any of the prescribed plans. (Later these can be called *free sectional* form and analyzed as ABB, ABCA, and so on.)

5. Sometimes a composer selects a short song or dance (or composes an original one) and writes a series of *variations* on it. Each section is the same length as the original melody, but each is treated in a different way:

   (a) the theme may be ornamented; passing tones, turns, and other decorations can be added to the melody or the accompaniment;

   (b) the theme may have a change in its basic rhythm, melody, or mode;

   (c) the accompaniment may be altered by a change in rhythm, harmony, tone color, or dynamics.

   *fifth grade upward*

6. Two large sectional forms in music are the *sonata* and the *symphony*. The sonata is written for one or two instruments; the symphony is written for full orchestra. These large forms consist of three or four related but separate *movements*. A single movement might be a three-part form, a rondo, a theme with variations, or a *sonata-allegro form*. In the sonata-allegro form, usually the first movement in a symphony, the composer contrasts and develops his themes in some generally prescribed ways. (More specific consideration of these large developmental forms is undertaken by students at the secondary level.)

   *sixth grade upward*

## Nonsectional Forms in Music

1. Sometimes a melody in one voice (vocal or instrumental part) is followed by successive voices that enter separately, imitating the first voice throughout. The different voices, singing in *counterpoint* to one another, overlap any phrase endings so that the whole seems to be one continuous composition. (This can be identified as a *canon*, of which one form is the *round*.)

   *fourth grade upward*

2. A short composition may sound unified and unbroken if the composer has used a single pattern of rhythmic movement and textural treatment throughout. (Bach composed some well-known preludes on continuous broken-chord patterns.)

3. One or two musical motives can be so skillfully handled by the composer that they grow into one small unified composition, with no repetitions or

**MUSICAL CONCEPTS**

**49**

contrasting sections. (Debussy composed some piano preludes in this way.)

4. When a composer uses a story or other descriptive idea as the basis for a composition, he may choose not to follow a prescribed design in his music. He may compose the piece in a single movement so that he has greater freedom to develop musical continuity and feeling that express the programmatic ideas. (*Tone poems* often are written in such a *free form.*)

*fifth grade upward*

5. In another kind of continuous, imitative counterpoint, a composer may present a *theme* in a single voice (A) which is imitated in turn by two or three other voices; however, when one voice (A) turns the main theme over to another (B) it then carries a *countertheme* until the main theme moves on to the third voice (C); then the first voice (A) has a free part (nonimitative) until the main theme again returns to it (A). (These can be identified as important characteristics of a *fugue.*)

*sixth grade upward*

## Suites and Dramatic Forms

1. Many composers have written music based on episodes and stories to be portrayed in ballet. When the music offers listening pleasure without the dancing, the composer may arrange its strongest parts into a *ballet suite* of contrasting movements for concert orchestra.

2. Any collection of related musical compositions might be a suite. The *classic dance suite,* a popular musical form at the time of Bach, consists of a group of contrasting dances such as the sarabande, the minuet, and the gigue. In more recent times, composers have written *descriptive suites* that might be called musical pictures of one subject.

3. Almost every motion picture film is accompanied by background music that contributes to the ideas and feelings conveyed by the film. A composer may arrange an *orchestral suite* from the film music. In earlier times, *incidental music* written for plays was arranged into a suite for separate concert performances.

*fourth grade upward*

4. When drama, stage sets, costumes, singing, orchestral music, and dancing are all combined, the impressive stage production is called *opera*. Opera includes music for solo voices and ensembles, chorus, and orchestra to create dramatic effects while por-

traying a story. The main musical themes of an opera often are introduced in the *overture,* which the orchestra plays before the curtain rises.

5. When a large dramatic work is based on a contemplative or religious subject, it may be performed as a concert without costumes, stage sets, or drama. In such music, called an *oratorio,* solo voices and ensembles, chorus and orchestra, and sometimes a narrator are used.

*fifth grade upward*

## STYLE IN MUSIC

Style is the result of particular ways of using the various elements of music and procedures of composition. Each period in history has brought developments of compositional techniques. The composer's use of rhythm, melody, tone color, and harmony has been influenced to some extent by the social and artistic attitudes of his day. The term "style" can be used in different contexts; for general purposes in elementary music education, we consider the broad style periods that have produced music with certain notable characteristics.

Several basic music series for elementary schools include study units about famous composers. While there is need for some historical and biographical information of the type provided in these books, children also must be helped to build a musical frame of reference for the varied styles of music they hear. The chief concern of elementary music education is to establish an idea of the sound characteristic of each period. This process begins in the primary grades when children hear music by composers of different styles. Gradually, as they grow to recognize characteristic uses of rhythm, melody, harmony, tone color, and form, children in the fifth and sixth grades find that they can begin to identify the music of different composers.

The earlier style periods are easily defined, but as one moves into the twentieth century he encounters a variety of trends in musical composition. Some music of the twentieth century represents the machine age and its impersonal outlook on life. Composers explore all kinds of sound including that which is electronically produced; they are not "fenced in" by traditional concepts of tone, rhythm, melody, and harmony. Other contemporary composers show their interest in the native music of people everywhere by incorporating the melodies, rhythms, and harmonies of folk music in their compositions. Diverse though the musical composition of contemporary composers may be, general characteristics unique to this age can be identified. An outline of unique aspects in the structure of contemporary music with related musical examples can be found in *Experiments in Musical Creativity.*[9]

**MUSICAL CONCEPTS**

### The Baroque Style

1. Baroque music has a strong, steady rhythm and a firm bass line. The treble voice is somewhat florid, using distinctive figurations and embellishments of the melody.

**51**

2. A baroque composition features a single theme that is extended, elaborated, and intensively explored. The variation form and the fugue lend themselves to such treatment.
3. Instrumental music of the baroque period features alternation of solo passages with ensemble passages.
4. Baroque composers like to give a vivid representation of words, ideas, and feelings in the music itself.

*Composers:* Bach, Corelli, Couperin, Handel, Lully, Scarlatti, Vivaldi. (See Appendix B–II for listings of recordings by these composers; see basic music series references and teaching suggestions.)

### The Viennese Classic Style

1. Melodies of the classic composers have some qualities of folk songs and dances of that day; they have a simple expressiveness and clear-cut beauty of line.
2. Regular metric groupings provide the rhythmic basis for classic music. The effect of clear, well-balanced phrases, periods, and larger sections is characteristic of the style.
3. Music of the classic period makes ingenious use of motives and themes that are set in contrast to one another, elaborated and developed throughout an entire section of the work.
4. The predominant texture of classic music is homophonic—that is, one melodic line stands out. However, melodic material is shared by instruments of the ensemble; there is skillful use of counterpoint that is subsidiary to the leading voice.

*Composers:* Beethoven (early works), Gluck, Grétry, Haydn, Mozart. (See Appendix B–II for listings of recordings by these composers; see basic music series references and teaching suggestions.)

### The Romantic Style

1. The large orchestral piece of one grand, unbroken movement is characteristic of the romantic style; picturesque episodes within the composition suggest different aspects of an idea or event.
2. Instrumental tone color is used to convey feeling and effect in this music; massive, rich, low-pitched sound may provide heroic effects, and unusual combinations of high and low may be used for brilliant contrasts and flashes of color.
3. Chromatic tones, indefinite cadences, and some irregularity of rhythmic flow contribute to a mood or pictorial image. Chords are used for their color effects and emotional qualities; certain complex, dissonant chords create rich enchanting sound as well as strong movement in music.
4. Groups of short pieces in different moods, written for solo voice or instrument, especially the piano, are characteristic of the romantic style.

*Composers*: Berlioz, Bizet, Borodin, Brahms, Chopin, Dvořák, Franck, Grieg, Hanson, Mahler, Mendelssohn, Moussorgsky, Rimsky-Korsakov, Saint-Saëns, Schubert, Schumann, Sibelius, Tchaikovsky, Wagner, Wolf, Verdi. (See Appendix B–II for listings of recordings by these composers; see basic music series references and teaching suggestions.) Note: Several of the French and Russian composers writing within this period reflect nationalistic musical traits as well as some of the qualities of the romantic style.

## The Impressionist Style

1. Melodies in this style tend to be vague; they consist of short motives rather than long singing lines.
2. Rhythms of the impressionist style often have a vague pulse, and are obscured by syncopation. Subtle use is made of dynamic changes.
3. Chords are used for their color value and sonority rather than for the dynamic quality of movement. When sectional forms are used, the outlines are blurred.
4. Tone color in impressionist music is rich but subdued, pastel, and misty. The harp is frequently heard; many instruments are muted; piano solos use much pedal to sustain and mix chord colors and tonal outlines.

*Composers*: Debussy, Delibes, Delius, Falla, Griffes, Ravel, Respighi. (See Appendix B–II for listings of recordings by these composers; see basic music series references and teaching suggestions.)

## Contemporary Music

1. Rhythm is energetic and driving in music of the twentieth century. Often it seems erratic. Sometimes there is no regular duple or triple grouping of beats; accents seem shifted or misplaced.
2. Tone sometimes is generated by media that in an earlier age would be considered nonmusical sources, including electronically produced sound.
3. Melodies in contemporary music tend to be jagged and fragmentary. Sometimes folk tunes and motives are used, but seldom in long, flowing lines.
4. Contemporary harmony can be dissonant and clashing. Much use is made of counterpoint, and it, too, may produce dissonance. Opposing musical lines may be written in different scales; different sections of the orchestra may play chords simultaneously in different keys.
5. Contemporary music often shows sectional forms. Phrases can be heard in a question-and-answer relationship. Sections may end with an abrupt shift to a different harmony or texture rather than with a cadence.

MUSICAL
CONCEPTS

*Composers*: Bartók, Britten, Cage, Cowell, Copland, Ginastera, Guarnieri, Harris, Honegger, Ives, Kabalevsky, Khachaturian, Kodály, McBride, Menotti, Milhaud, Prokofiev, Schoenberg, Shostakovich, Stravinsky, Thom-

**53**

son, Varèse, Vaughan Williams, Villa-Lobos, Walton. (See Appendix B–II for listings of recordings by these composers; see basic music series references and teaching suggestions.)

## APPLICATION IN THE ANALYSIS OF MUSICAL COMPOSITIONS

In every song or other musical composition of merit one finds a unique utilization of the elements of music. Among simple folk songs there is a variety of melodic, rhythmic, and structural characteristics. The following analyses are designed to show the teacher how he might look at a piece of music before he decides which characteristics to bring to the attention of his class.

### THE GREEN DRESS

*South African Song*
*Josef Marais*

*Gaily*

"The Green Dress" is a pleasant, conversational-type song with a rather repetitive melody and a single simple idea in the text. It is from the South African collection of the folk singer Josef Marais.

*Rhythm.* The song has an easy walking rhythm in duple meter, $\textstyle\unicode{x2669}\ \ \unicode{x2669}\ |\ \unicode{x2669}\ \ \unicode{x2669}$, that is appropriate to the idea conveyed in the words.
one - two,  one - two
Since the text begins on an unaccented part of a word, an upbeat leads into the first phrase. An upbeat also leads into the second long phrase and into

two short phrases in the refrain. This characteristic adds to the lilt and on-going quality that is so important in this music. Two rhythm patterns are used in various ways: ♫♫ and ♩ ♩ ♩ 𝄾 . Sometimes these patterns are unified and sometimes they begin on different parts of the measure so the accent is shifted. Notice that in the early part of the song the four eighth notes are followed by three quarter notes: ♫♫ | ♩ ♩ ♩ , while in the latter part of the song the eighth notes are framed by quarter notes in a somewhat different motive: ♩ | ♫♫♩ . Thus rhythmic interest is maintained in this very simple song.

*Melody.*   The melody is predominantly scalewise, but has some movement between adjacent tones of a chord. In the first phrase it has repeated motives within a rising sequence that provides a little tension and interest in the melody. In general however, the melody is quite repetitive with two slight climaxes in the measure prior to each cadence:

There is prominent use of the rising fourth (5,–1) as the opening interval of the first two phrases.

*Harmony.*   The harmony of the song is quite ordinary in that it is organized around the tonic and dominant seventh chords in the major mode (G). However, a slightly unsettled, ongoing quality results from the fact that the entire refrain, up to the last tone, is built on the dominant seventh chord. The first cadence in the refrain goes to the third of the tonic chord, giving an incomplete ending in contrast to the final cadence on the tonic. Both of these qualities can be noticed by children if these musical characteristics are pointed out.

*Form.*   Each phrase in this song is four measures long, but each may be subdivided because it is composed of smaller, related rhythmic-melodic motives. The second phrase begins like the first phrase, but is set as question and answer (antecedent and consequent phrases) in contrast to the first phrase which has a rising sequence. Although the refrain contains material related to the stanza it begins with a new repeated motive; thus the total form is two-part (binary), which is shown as AB, but since it has two similar phrases in each section it can be diagrammed a a′ b b.

Of all the interesting characteristics seen in this simple folk song, children in the primary grades would be expected to notice only the most obvious, which could be highlighted by their musical participation with it. Since the teacher never can be sure just what direction creative musical participation will take, he should alert himself to possibilities for helping children discover whatever musical characteristics are most naturally brought out by their activities with a particular composition.

# THE SHEEPSHEARING

*Legato*                              *English Folk Song*

From *100 English Folk Songs* edited by C. Sharp, © 1916 the Oliver Ditson Co. Used by permission.

While "The Sheepshearing" is a folk song it has some musical characteristics quite unusual to folk songs in general. The text is narrative, but of equal importance with the ideas in the text is the independent flow of the melody.

*Melody.* Some phrases in this song move chiefly along chord lines and others follow the scale. There is a complete upward scale line in one long phrase; at the end of that phrase is a stepwise, sequential descending pattern. A three-note descending sequence, which is a melisma on the word "told," alternately outlines notes of the tonic and dominant seventh chords with a passing tone between each chord tone. A long flowing vocalization on one word rarely is seen in folk songs of the Western world.

This melody is quite varied in interest, with the climax occurring at the top of the long rising scale line. Following the climax the song circles quietly down to its cadence. The rising fourth (5 –1) used at the beginning of the first phrase and the last phrase gives the song additional lilt and movement.

*Rhythm.* "The Sheepshearing" is in a smooth-flowing triple rhythm. Upbeats at the beginning of every phrase push the rhythm along. Two principal rhythm patterns are used. One is even; the other has a dotted rhythm: ♫ | ♩ ♩ ♩ | ♩ and ♩. ♪♩ . This simplicity of rhythmic material provides a sense of unity in the song.

*Form.* The opening phrase in this song is eight measures long; it is unified by the use of three similar two-measure motives ending in a cadence. The second phrase opens with two similar two-measure motives, but moves on into a rising scale line followed by descending sequences so that an extended phrase of ten measures is achieved. This long phrase ends on the dominant chord, making a half cadence. The last phrase of four measures is similar to the last four measures of the first phrase; both end in a full cadence. While the phrases are uneven in length, the essential structure of this folk song is ABA.

Partial analyses of several musical compositions are shown in other chapters of this book. Art songs such as Brahms' "Cradle Song" (page 234), "Papageno's Magic Bell Song" by Mozart (page 203), "Whither?" by Schubert (page 196), and "The Shadow March" by Rowley (page 205) are shown with the composers' accompaniments and therefore offer greater opportunities for study of the music. "March Past of the Kitchen Utensils" (see page 121) is analyzed with respect to its form and instrumentation. Listening to discover how a composer achieves certain musical effects is an activity appropriate in all grades, but at different depths of study.

The "Minuetto" from *L'Arlesienne Suite No. 1* by Bizet was composed in the middle of the nineteenth century and so it has some of the interesting orchestration and melodic characteristics of that period. The music has such clear lines and well-defined form that it is not difficult to determine how the composition is constructed.

The Teacher's Guide to ADVENTURES IN MUSIC Grade 4, Volume 2, shows considerable background material and detailed analysis of this composition. Here we will be concerned only with the outstanding qualities of the music that can be discovered by children involved in creative movement and rhythm orchestration of this music.

The first thing to be noticed is the short crisp quality of the melody in the first section as contrasted with the smooth legato lines of the second section. The predominant tone color is that of string and woodwind instruments playing first in a short detached style, then in a flowing legato style.

*Rhythm.* This composition is written in a rather lively $\frac{3}{4}$ meter with upbeats prominent in the first section. The rhythm is very regular with an opening rhythm pattern of ♩ | ♩. ♪ ♩ ♩ | ♩ soon modified to ♩. ♪ ♩ ♩ | ♩ ♩ with a written accent on the first beat of the second measure. This rhythm alternates with a related pattern on the subdivided beats ♫ | ♫ ♫ ♫ | ♫ ♫ ♩ and often is joined by bass instruments playing an *um pah pah* accompaniment: ♩ ♩ ♩ | ♩ ♩ ♩ | . The second section has a consistently running eighth-note pattern in the higher instruments set against the slower moving rhythm of the lower melody ♩ ♩ | ♩ ♩ | .

This music is of a pleasant colorful dance character, but it has no specific descriptive connotations. It should be enjoyed and studied for its interesting interplay of rhythm, melody, and tone color.

**MUSICAL CONCEPTS**

**57**

*Form.* There are three distinct large sections in this music, ABA. Section A is divided into two parts, each of which is repeated as follows:

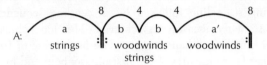

Section B is likewise well balanced but somewhat longer with the main theme in a lower voice:

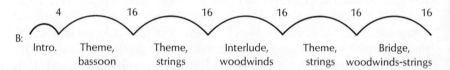

The final section is a replaying of Section A without the repeats and with an eight-measure coda. The form of this music (three-part or ternary) follows the classic models with predictable balanced phrases, a contrasting middle section that is readily noticed, and a short graceful ending.

*Melody and tone color.* In this music the contrast between the two sections is so evident that it seems best to listen to the details of the form before studying the melodies. Section A has two melodies that are quite closely related in character. The alternation of the strings and woodwinds is as important as the change in melodic detail. The strings predominate in the first eight measures (repeated), then woodwinds alternate with strings in a high-low pattern, followed by an eight-measure phrase for woodwinds, all of which is heard twice.

The melody of Section B is very singable and can readily be followed, first as it is heard played by the bassoon and then by the strings:

*Harmony and Texture.* The music is chiefly in the major mode (E♭) but it moves briefly to the related minor (c) in the second part of Section A and to a closely related major key (A♭) in Section B. Although these changes of key may not be readily noticed by the untrained listener they add a subtle quality of freshness and variety to the different sections of the music.

The texture of Section A is homophonic; that is, all of the parts move as a single unit with one predominant melody. In Section B two related but independent melody lines are heard: the slower moving melody with accompaniment in lower instruments and the embellishing counter-melody above.

*Dynamics.* There is interesting use of dynamic contrasts throughout this composition. Sometimes loud sections are contrasted sharply with soft sections and at other times the music tapers off from loud to soft as at the end of the final section. The alternation of instrumental tone color is closely related to the dynamics in this music.

The development of the ability to hear interesting details that contribute to the total effect of a musical composition requires much experience in purposeful listening; it cannot be achieved with any single composition. It is important that a teacher develop his own ability to recognize the significant characteristics in different compositions so that he can facilitate children's musical discoveries.

---

## ACTIVITIES FOR COLLEGE CLASSES

A. Questions for Review

1. What are the seven broad areas under which musical concepts are organized in this chapter?
2. Outline the large ideas to which smaller concepts are related in any one of these seven broad areas.

B. Written Assignments

1. Select a song from any basic series music book at the grade level of your choice and analyze it in terms of the musical concepts children at that age might develop through study of the song.
2. Select a short recorded instrumental composition and analyze it in terms of the musical concepts children at a given grade level might develop through study of that composition.

---

## CHAPTER NOTES

1. James L. Mursell, "Growth Processes in Music Education," in Nelson B. Henry, editor, *Basic Concepts in Music Education* (Chicago: University of Chicago Press, 1958), p. 157.
2. Charles L. Gary, editor, *The Study of Music in the Elementary School—A Conceptual Approach* (Washington, D.C.: Music Educators National Conference, 1967).
3. Bjornar Bergethon and Eunice Boardman, *Musical Growth in the Elementary School* (New York: Holt, Rinehart and Winston, Inc., 1963).
4. Alice Snyder Knuth and William E. Knuth, *Basic Resources for Learning Music* (Belmont, Calif.: Wadsworth Publishing Company, Inc., 1966).
5. Inez Schubert and Lucille Wood, *The Craft of Music Teaching* (Morristown, N.J.: Silver Burdett Co., 1964).
6. Aaron Copland, *What to Listen for in Music,* Revised Edition (New York: McGraw-Hill Book Company, 1957).
7. Leonard Ratner, *Music—The Listener's Art,* Second Edition (New York: McGraw-Hill Book Company, 1967).
8. Peter Yates, *Twentieth Century Music* (New York: Pantheon Books, a division of Random House, Inc., 1967), p. 248.
9. Contemporary Music Project, *Experiments in Musical Creativity* (CMP₃) Washington, D.C.: Music Educators National Conference, 1966), pp. 31–42.

# 3

# Bodily Movement
# in the Study of Music

Rhythm, one of the four elements of music, is basic to man's existence; the individual experiences rhythm in his breathing, in the beating of his heart, in the act of walking, and in his observation of the alternation of night and day. The building of tension followed by relaxation is basic to all of these. In walking the muscle contracts to raise the foot and relaxes momentarily as the foot contacts the ground; in breathing the lungs alternately expand and contract. Primitive man elaborated on these rhythmically based experiences in his dances and in his use of drums and rattles. Both Roger Sessions[1] and Aaron Copland,[2] contemporary American composers, have pointed out this elemental relationship between man and his music.

Children are rhythmic psychophysiological organisms gradually becoming aware of rhythm in their lives, perceiving and developing concepts about movement, time, and the interrelationship of the two that are fundamental aspects of music. The teacher has only to begin with the child's natural activities in movement, to reinforce and expand these experiences in such a way that the child responds more precisely, perceives more clearly and understands more fully this sense of movement through time that is conveyed in music.

Expressive movement, as an activity in music, is related to the programs in physical education and creative dramatics; skills in movement and freedom for expression are necessary in all. The objectives in the use of music differ among these areas. In physical education, the objectives of expressive movement are physical development, health, and poise; music assists by helping to make the movement rhythmic. In creative dramatics, movement expresses what the individual himself feels; music is selected or composed to support ideas already present. In both of these areas music is an assistant.

The objectives for movement in the music program are to identify music as an expression of gesture and feeling, to learn to listen to music, and to explore it with natural movements and imagination. Whether the immediate activity is creative movement, folk dancing, or a study of rhythmic patterns and phrases, this objective for the music program remains the same. However, work in the other fields is valuable and contributes toward a richer musical experience, for the more flexibility and physical control one has, the greater are his possibilities for expressing what he feels in the music. The imaginative approach to movement that is developed in creative dramatics gives the individual the necessary feeling of freedom to express confidently what he hears in the music.

The development of rhythmic movement as an activity leading to musical development may be initiated at any age. If it is not undertaken in the kindergarten or first grade and developed continuously throughout the grades, teachers of older children will find it necessary to take special steps to establish attitudes and skills that will permit bodily movement to be used fruitfully in conjunction with the music activities.

## APPROACHES TO RHYTHMIC AND CREATIVE MOVEMENT

The teacher must approach rhythmic movement at the point of understanding for the child, develop in him the physical ability and freedom to move in expressive ways, and then relate this movement to music. The early steps can be taken in several classroom or playground situations.

### Child-Created Movement

During "sharing time," when children tell of their experiences, the teacher may say in response to a child's narration, "Yes, Jeanie, show us how you walked to the store. Did you feel happy? Were you in a hurry?" And perhaps Jeanie will be able to reconstruct her mood and movement so that the whole class may know how she felt. This is creative dramatics; it is not related to music at this point, yet it is the type of experience on which the interpretation of music is based. The teacher may guide the rhythmic experience a step further by suggesting that other children "go with Jeanie to the store just as she went." The experience becomes an impersonation when the other children follow the pattern set by Jeanie.

Stephen may one day give his physical interpretation of the way the bear moved in a story. The teacher may support his movement by playing a deep-sounding drum or sandblocks in the rhythm Stephen establishes. If the teacher is able, he may improvise a piano accompaniment for Stephen's "bear"; other children may join in or take turns being the bear. In these early stages of rhythmic training, a rhythm instrument or the piano provides the best accompaniment for movement because the teacher can adjust the tempo to that of the child so that he will have the optimum freedom in movement.

Tired children, happy children, "bears," and "elephants" will walk in their distinct ways. "Ponies" will trot and gallop in the pasture; children will run and skip to school and they will begin to listen for rhythms and sounds that suggest particular ways of moving. To assist in the gradual development of movement responses to music, the teacher must:

1. work from the child's fundamental movements, such as walking and running,
2. help the child find freedom of movement within limits of the classroom,
3. show him in what respect his movement is rhythmic,
4. relate his movement to rhythmic sound,
5. provide opportunities for him to move with other children in their rhythm,
6. help him learn to move in any of the fundamental rhythmic patterns at will,
7. help him to arrive at the point of being able to adjust his movement to music in a predetermined tempo.

The individual children, the group, the situations that arise, and the teacher's own way of working, all help to determine how the steps are accomplished.

Activities in physical education develop coordination and skill in movement, and a program in creative dramatics encourages freedom of expression. The teacher will find Chapters Five and Six of *Creative Rhythmic Movement for Children*[3] by Andrews particularly helpful in establishing freedom in movement. The film "Learning through Movement"[4] shows the development of flexibility and variety in different kinds of movement.

Children need space in order to feel free to respond in movement. Skipping, galloping, and twirling require more space than walking and marching, and when the space is limited fewer children are able to respond simultaneously. Those who do not participate in the full body motion may use movements of the arms and the trunk as they sit in their chairs. This permits them to respond in a limited way and orients them to the rhythm so that they will be more successful when it is their turn to move with the full pattern. For each lesson the teacher should select some music for large free movements and other music for more limited movements such as swaying, stepping, or rocking so that the entire class may respond occasionally as a group.

A fruitful program in rhythmic movement in the classroom often requires readjustment of furniture so that there are two or three wide aisles or space at the front of the room. The classroom has the advantage of being available at any hour and many teachers feel that a finer response to music is obtained in the friendly atmosphere of the home room.

A multipurpose room or a gymnasium has more space for movement. However, in a very large room, there may be so much space that movement seems to have no limitations. When free creative movement is the goal, this is ideal; but when the objective is the interpretation of music, the intimacy of the project may be lost and the teacher's directions and the music may be difficult to hear.

Children should experiment with movement, going in different directions to develop freedom and originality. Even in marching, children should not always follow in a line, but should learn to "go different ways" for more freedom of ideas and movement. Some children are very creative and imaginative; a few prefer to follow the lead of other children. To get the timid child started, the teacher may suggest, "Tommy, go with Joe," or "Sue, follow Mary." Children who feel insecure in this activity generally will be happier moving in a group than individually.

One or two children may be very well coordinated, imaginative, bursting with ideas, and eager to "perform." If the child is sincere and creative rather than craving attention for its own sake, the teacher sometimes may use this child to initiate ideas, but he must be careful not to promote a "star." Such a child can discourage other children from participating.

### Early Interpretive Movement

In progressing from child-created movement to the interpretation of music, children are asked to adjust their movements to what they hear, rather than having the accompaniment pick up their rhythm. It will be a gradual transition in which the teacher must patiently accommodate a wide variety of individual aptitudes for movement. The interpretation of songs with dramatic interest provides an avenue for this development.

In many songs, both the text and the rhythm of the music suggest the activity. In some of these, rhythmic movement may be combined with pantomime. For "The Elephant" (Bir J–74)* children may clasp both hands, bend from the waist, and let the continuous arc of the back, head, and arms suggest the head and trunk of the elephant.

## THE ELEPHANT

*Rhythmically*                                             *French Folk Song*

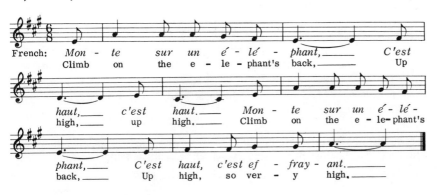

French: Mon - te sur un é - lé - phant, C'est
Climb on the e - le - phant's back, Up

haut, c'est haut. Mon - te sur un é - lé -
high, up high. Climb on the e - le- phant's

phant, C'est haut, c'est ef - fray - ant.
back, Up high, so ver - y high.

From *Teacher's Guide for Beginning French*, © 1955, 1959, Modern Language Association of America. Used by permission.

Since the elephant is a heavy fellow, all movements are ponderous and slow. Experience of this kind helps children understand that music can suggest size and weight as well as movement. The class may need to sing the song several times, readjusting the tempo of music and physical movement until both synchronize in a swaying rhythm that is just right for the elephant the children have in mind. Different groups of three or four children may move as "elephants" while the other children sing.

As they learn to sing the song and enter into the physical interpretation, the teacher should lead the children to observe the outstanding musical characteristics of the song. Notice and count its swinging rhythm that moves

in two's,  and feel the upbeat that leads to the heavy
           1   2   1   2

downbeat ♪ | ♩. ♩ ♪ | ♩. ♩ .
         "up   high,   up   high."

Pantomiming the rhythmic movements of a heavy piece of machinery such as the wrecking machine in "Old House" (MMYO II–24) will please the boys. "What kinds of movements does a wrecking machine make?" "How heavy is it? Show us." "How fast does it move?" "Yes, we have several good ideas now. Let's sing our song again, thinking about the movement, and see if we can get the music going at a good speed for these wrecking machines to operate."

* See Appendix B, Section I, for key to code of song books.

BODILY
MOVEMENT IN
THE STUDY
OF MUSIC

**65**

## OLD HOUSE

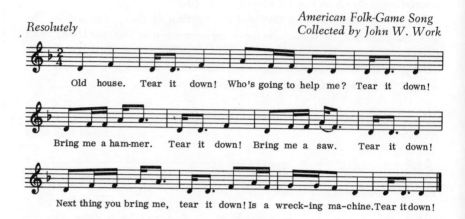

From *Book Two* of MAKING MUSIC YOUR OWN Series, Silver Burdett Company. Used by permission of John W. Work.

Thus, through leading questions and encouragement, the teacher helps the children develop rhythmic movement that reflects both the text of the song and the musical setting. The rhythm of this song swings in two's

♩ ♩ | ♩ ♩ , but it has an uneven rhythm pattern: ♫ ♩.
1  2   1  2                                              "Tear it down."

This is a good rhythm pattern to chant and clap so that this uneven quality is noticed.

Ideally the teacher is a guide, helping the pupils develop, evaluate, and refine their responses rather than imposing his own ideas. Rhythmic activity related to songs can provide an early means for promoting expressive movement in the classroom. In the words of the song are the ideas upon which to build an impersonation. In the music, if the music and text are well mated, are the rhythmic characteristics for the movement. Some songs, in which the text describes an animal or other character, may have a musical rhythm that is not appropriate for movement. Teacher and children should evaluate the rhythmic possibilities of their songs, using movement only when it is convincing.

CHAPTER
THREE

### Percussion Instruments Used in Accompaniments

Any percussion instruments may be used to provide accompaniments for the rhythmic movement of children. The teacher who cannot play the piano in the traditional manner can use it as a percussion instrument to provide rhythmic accompaniment. He can select two or three notes from one chord, in different octaves for each hand, and play the chord alternately high and low in a running, walking, or galloping rhythm. By sounding three or four of the black keys simultaneously he can create what are called "tone clusters." These can be played alternately at two different levels in any desired rhythm and with variety in dynamics. Some simple approaches to improvisation at the piano are given by Glenn Mack (MMYO K–168–177).

For marching, pupils may add a drum on the steady beat or on the accent. Special effects may be produced by sounding cymbals, gong, or triangle on climaxes or on selected accents. The rhythm sticks or two halves of a coconut shell struck together may suggest running:

The same pattern played more slowly may suggest walking. Young children may accompany galloping and skipping by playing a steady beat:

But the teacher and older children may make a more exciting accompaniment by playing the characteristic recurring pattern on coconut shells or a drum, alternately sounded in the middle and tapped on the rim:

The rhythm patterns for skipping and galloping are interchangeable. However, the $\frac{6}{8}$ pattern gives a feeling of flow and roundness to skipping. Galloping is a more sharply defined movement, for which the following $\frac{2}{4}$ pattern is more suitable:

Some instruments, like drums, tambourines, or maracas, can be played by children who are dancing. This is shown in two films that are highly recommended: "Building Children's Personalities with Creative Dancing,"[5] and "Music for Children."[6] In the first, children play rhythm instruments, chiefly maracas, as they dance to recorded music. In the second, one pupil plays claves or a drum while she dances, accompanied by other children playing an ensemble of tuned percussion instruments.

The Orff method of teaching music to children is referred to several times both in this chapter and in Chapters Four and Five of this book. Basic to that approach is the idea that "music and movement ought to be taught simultaneously, supplementing one another and intimately connected."[7] The musical training that Carl Orff developed began with the idea that pupils should improvise on instruments to provide accompaniments for their own dances and rhythmic exercises. For this they used percussion instruments of many kinds, including primitive types. Orff also developed tuned percussion instruments, adjustable xylophones, glockenspiels, and other instruments that children could play easily. These and some techniques for their use are discussed in Chapter Five.

Many teachers of young children believe that children should use bodily

BODILY
MOVEMENT IN
THE STUDY
OF MUSIC

**67**

movement both for self-expression and as an interpretation of music. With these approaches accompaniments utilizing various types of percussion instruments, played by children and teacher, are extremely useful and often are more appropriate than piano accompaniments because they are rhythmically flexible and provide fine shadings of dynamics and tone color.

## The Fundamental Movements and Musical Interpretation

Children should be led to notice how their fundamental ways of moving, running, and walking are expressive of different purposes and moods, depending upon the tempo, weight, and energy used. The teacher can provide music that supports the different kinds of movement and children can begin to transfer their understanding of expressive movement to an understanding of music. They learn that music has tempo in that it moves fast or slow, that melody can flow smoothly or dynamically or in a halting manner, that a musical phrase has shape that is governed by its movement, that rhythm can be regular and in a continuous pattern, or that it can alternate in long and short tones to suggest other kinds of movement.

Since running and walking are the movements in which most young children have the greatest facility these should be used first. Gradually skipping and galloping rhythms can be added. Part I, pages 8–15, of *Rhythm in Music and Dance for Children*[8] offers some good suggestions for helping children discover and experiment with their own movement potential.

One composition may suggest several movements. Children should be encouraged to try out these possibilities in order to judge which seems the most appropriate. "Gigue" from *Suite Number 3* by Corelli (MMYO K–44) is suitable for skipping, galloping, walking, bending, swaying, or "rowing boats."

CHAPTER
THREE

## GIGUE

*Leggiero*                                               *Arcangelo Corelli*

From *The Kindergarten Book* of OUR SINGING WORLD Series, Enlarged Edition. Used by permission of Ginn and Company, owner of the copyright.

There is nothing boisterous or heavy about this composition. Whatever movements are adopted should be carried out in a gay dancing spirit with a sense of freedom and flow. Movement in response to music must be conceived in terms of its melodic flow and textural qualities as well as its rhythm, and therefore the ideas expressed will go beyond thinking merely that "this is music for skipping" or "this music sounds like running."

The teacher should plan for variety in the music used during one lesson. When the children hear obvious differences in rhythm, tempo, and dynamics, they understand the necessity of moving in different ways. Every kindergarten and first grade book provides music for the fundamental movements such as walking, running, marching, skipping, and galloping. The following compositions are suggested for different types of movement:

**BODILY MOVEMENT IN THE STUDY OF MUSIC**

*For walking:*

"Andante," Beethoven (GwM I–158)
"Gavotte and Variation," Pachelbel (ExM I–24)
"Morning Stroll," Gretchaninoff (MoM K–39)

*For running:*

"Country Dance," Beethoven (MoM K–130)

"Russian Folksong," Beethoven (Joy–51)
"Theme in D," Tchaikovsky (ABC I–120)

*For marching:*

"March," Prokofiev (Joy–46)
"Soldier's March," Schumann (GwM I–149)
"When Johnny Comes Marching Home," Lambert (MMYO K–37)

69

*For swaying:*

"Bagatelle," Beethoven (ExM I–26)
"Little Lullaby," Opus 124, No. 6, Schumann (TiM I–185)
"Skater's Waltz," Waldteufel (MMYO K–96)
"Waltz," Opus 39, No. 2, Brahms (GwM I–156)

*For skipping or galloping:*

"Gigue" from *Suite No. 3*, Corelli (MMYO K–44)
"Sicilienne," Schumann (MoM K–29, Joy–52)
"The Wild Horseman," Schumann (Joy–84)

The folk tunes and other selections in *Music for Active Children*[9] are suitable for young children. The music is arranged in classified rhythmic groupings for easy location of appropriate compositions for the fundamental movements. In his own piano repertoire a teacher may find portions of compositions that move at a steady pace suitable for rhythmic activities.

In their most informal setting, singing games are played by small groups of children on the playground, clapping, walking, skipping, or using other suitable movements. Younger children often learn the games from older children. Traditional singing games afford good opportunities for children to develop skill in fundamental movements. "Santy Maloney," an old singing game, provides children with a fine accompaniment for either skipping or marching.

## SANTY MALONEY

*Lively*                                                    *Old Singing Game*

Can you dance, San–ty Ma – lon – ey? Can you dance, San–ty Ma – lon – ey?

Can you dance, San–ty Ma – lon – ey, As we go round a – bout?

Transposed from G.

**CHAPTER THREE**

Most kindergarten and first grade song books contain a variety of singing games. "Ring Around a Rosy" is an example (see page 138). Other traditional titles are:

"Did You Ever See a Lassie?"
"The Farmer in the Dell"
"The Muffin Man"

"London Bridge"
"Looby Loo"
"Mulberry Bush"

## Using Recorded Music

After the children have learned to follow rhythm played on percussion instruments or the piano, the teacher can begin to use recorded music. This should be carefully selected, and in the earlier experiences of primary children it is important that this music be:

1. In a tempo to which children are able to adjust their movements easily. Music suitable for the free rhythmic activities of young children is somewhat faster than that appropriate for adults.
2. Steady in rhythm without breaks or retards to interrupt the basic movement.
3. Musically good in all respects: rhythmic, rich in tone color, and conveying mood and feeling as well as rhythm. Quality is important because a musical experience is only as valuable as the music used. In the early stages of rhythmic movement, the music must be simple; but there is a difference between simple, uncomplicated music and music that is poor in quality and unappealing.

City and county music consultants as well as teachers of music education in the colleges usually have samples of the available records. The teacher may keep in touch with new releases through these persons or he may obtain one of the annual catalogs published for school use (see Appendix B for names and addresses of record companies and for the code used in this book to identify record albums).

The six albums in *Rhythmic Activities* (RCA Victor RECORD LIBRARY FOR ELEMENTARY SCHOOLS) have been useful for rhythmic activities. Although these recordings have been available for many years they still have value and can be found in many schools. More recent publications, the RCA ADVENTURES IN MUSIC Series and the BOWMAR ORCHESTRAL LIBRARY, are especially valuable because they contain the music of composers representative of several periods of musical style. (See Appendix B–II for a complete listing of the musical contents of these two record series.)

Some instrumental recordings include narration or singing, and others feature the piano or small instrumental ensembles. The Greystone Record Corporation has "A Visit to My Little Friend," "My Playful Scarf," and others under the *Children's Record Guild* label. Among their *Young People's Records* are "When the Sun Shines," "A Rainy Day," and others. *Rhythm Time* and others by Bowmar, and *Rhythms of Childhood* by Ella Jenkins (Folkways) are some good recordings created especially for rhythmic response in early childhood.

In addition to these special educational recordings, the teacher is advised to look for suitable compositions in his own record collection or in that available at his school. Excerpts from many compositions, especially suites of classic dance forms, incidental music from opera and ballet, as well as primitive and folk dances, are usable.

Gertrude Knight included several of these types in her work with children, as exemplified in the film "Building Children's Personalities with Creative Dancing."[5] Encouragement, a sense of freedom for movement, discovery and yet supporting guidance are evident in her work. Children begin with skipping, galloping, and bouncing, and then move into more varied spontaneous dance involving the whole body. When this teacher wants the children to feel the rhythm within themselves, she suggests, "Find the ball way down inside of you and make it bounce" . . . "Bounce inside so the bounce comes

**BODILY MOVEMENT IN THE STUDY OF MUSIC**

**71**

outside," etc. Musicians know that a feel for rhythm is not limited to the fingers or toes, but is deep inside the body. As early as possible, children should find this deep feeling for rhythm.

The use of descriptive, "feeling" words helps children loosen up and move expressively with all parts of the body. Mrs. Knight says, "My fingers are the end of me." . . . "How far can you grow out of your fingers?" . . . "How tall can you get?" . . . "Grow from inside like a tree." . . . "Put your fingers in the sky and pull it right down."

The music used in this film ranges from the baroque and classic compositions:

*Brandenburg Concerto No. 1*  Rondo *Alla Turca,* Mozart  
(Menuetto and Trios), Bach

to primitive dances with direct rhythmic and sensuous appeal:

Hopi "Butterfly Dance"  *Suite Primeval* by Skilton: Cheyenne  
Sicilian "Tarantelle"  Indian "War Dance" and Rogue River  
Indian "Deer Dance"

Other recorded music such as that by the following French composers can be useful in the early stages of expressive movement:

"Carillon" from *L'Arlesienne Suite No.*  "Golliwog's Cakewalk" from *The Chil-*  
1, Bizet  *dren's Corner Suite,* Debussy (BOL  
"Farandole" from *L'Arlesienne Suite*  #63)  
No. 2, Bizet (A in M VI–1)  "Dance of the Automatons" from *Cop-*  
*pélia Ballet Suite,* Delibes

This music has rhythmic strength and general continuity. It is colorful and expressive, and it appeals to the imagination.

The march is a historically important musical form. Its rhythmic appeal makes it a natural musical study for intermediate grades. If the boys and girls have not had previous experience in moving to music, the march might open the way to expressive movement in the interpretation of music. Marching may first be done in the multipurpose room or gymnasium where the pupils can work out interesting two- or four-abreast formations. A rousing Sousa

**CHAPTER**  march such as "Stars and Stripes Forever" (BOL #54 or A in M IV–2) leads  
**THREE**  children to participate eagerly because they can identify with a marching band or a regiment of soldiers. Such marching, however, is only a beginning, a means to an end and not the musical objective.

When marching has produced an enthusiasm for participation and the pupils have developed an appreciation of moving in rhythm with the music, the teacher should begin to look for variety in marches. Good sources are the BOWMAR ORCHESTRAL LIBRARY Album #54, *Marches,* as well as other albums throughout the Bowmar series and the ADVENTURES IN MUSIC series. To begin, pupils and teacher may discuss the different uses for marches: military or school-band marches, wedding and other ceremonial marches may be suggested. "How do these differ and why?" Excerpts from two marches

**72**  might be played and discussed. "March" from *Aida* by Verdi (BOL #61)

may be compared with "March of the Little Lead Soldiers" by Pierné (BOL #54). The former is triumphant and military, the latter is a crisp, rather rapid "short-legged" march.

Teaching notes in the albums provide themes to play and sing, and give historical backgrounds for each composition. These are helpful in preliminary discussions. After hearing the compositions, part of the class may march in a manner appropriate to the music. Encourage the children to experiment with body carriage and steps of different lengths in their attempts to portray the spirit of the march. This is the beginning of *expressive* movement. Costumes and props may aid in establishing the mood.

In addition to the rhythmic experience, it is important that pupils determine what use of musical elements produces the characteristic sounds in each march. Listen to and sing the melodies. How do they differ? How do the tempo and rhythm differ between these marches? Does the instrumentation contribute to the general character of the music in a significant way?

Other marches may be used in the same manner with these objectives for the study: (1) rhythmic movement, (2) expressive movement, (3) continuing growth in understanding of the elements of music, and (4) familiarity with a basic repertoire of musical compositions.

The following marches make interesting studies in rhythm, form, and instrumentation:

"March" from *The Love for Three Oranges,* Prokofiev
"Marche Militaire," Schubert
"March of the Pilgrims" from *Harold in Italy,* Berlioz
"Polonaise Militaire," Chopin

"Pomp and Circumstance," Elgar
"Procession of the Sardar" from *Caucasian Sketches,* Ippolitov-Ivanov
"Wedding March" from *Lohengrin,* Wagner

---

## STUDYING DETAIL IN MUSICAL COMPOSITION

Primary children may successfully move in response to the metric beat, general rhythmic swing, and mood in music. The musical purposes for this early experience are to give the children a meaningful reason for listening to music, to direct their imaginations to it as an expressive medium, and to give them experience with its rhythmic elements. There is no better way to sense the ongoing flow of music than to move through time and space with it. It is impossible to overemphasize the importance of this kind of musical awareness. However, bodily movement also can be used with both songs and recorded music to analyze and to develop a more precise understanding of details in melody, rhythm, and musical form.

BODILY MOVEMENT IN THE STUDY OF MUSIC

### Folk Dances as Patterned Movement

Although singing games are the first group dances used in the classroom, very soon the children will enjoy simple folk dances that have words to tell what to do. The words may be incidental, and singing is not expected to be the only accompaniment, as it may be in the singing game. It is not until the children are able to enjoy a rhythmic, patterned movement that they use the folk dance rather than the singing game. A few such as "Bow Belinda" are used in the first grade, but more extensive participation in folk dances begins in the latter second and third grades.

## BOW BELINDA

*American Singing Game*

Bow, bow, bow Be-lin-da; Bow, bow, bow Be-lin-da;

Bow, bow, bow Be-lin-da; You're the one my dar-ling.

There are two essential parts to a folk dance. The foot pattern is the response to the basic recurring rhythm of the music. Primary children need not learn such definite steps as the schottische, polka, two-step, and waltz. The easiest foot patterns are skipping, marching, a bouncy walk, or a step-slide to the side. For many dances more than one type of foot pattern is suitable; the selection of a particular one is determined by the tempo of the music and the children's skill in dancing.

Phrasing and sectional form in the music determine the floor pattern, the directional movement that the dancers take. The words may tell them in what direction to move. American square dancers follow the directions of a "caller"; in other dances the participants learn the sequence of movement and follow the phrasing and sectional changes in the music. The most beautiful folk dancing is that in which the dancers keep precise rhythm and execute the various directional patterns in perfect coordination with the changing phrases and sections of the music.

**CHAPTER THREE**

Folk dancing contributes to the social and physical development of the child. The musical values are not so easy to realize. If the activity is to be a part of the music program, the teacher should keep these musical objectives well in mind:

1. To give the pupils another opportunity to respond rhythmically to music and to study its rhythmic components.
2. To help them hear and respond to phrasing and form in music through an enjoyable physical activity.

As they dance, the children must learn to listen, to feel the rhythm, and finally to experience the synchronization of movement with music. The activity must be a joyous one, and at the same time the teacher must call attention to rhythm, phrase structure, and musical form. To point up the rhythm, he may have some children sing and clap while others use the basic foot pattern in a simple line or circle formation. A few rhythm instruments may be played to underline the metric beat.

In most folk dances the foot pattern remains the same throughout, but the floor pattern follows the phrase changes in the music. To help the children notice the phrase construction, the teacher may omit the regular floor pattern and ask the children to use the foot pattern as they move in a line formation and then go in the opposite direction on each new phrase. "Paw-Paw Patch" may be danced with one of several foot patterns, and the short phrases may be worked into varied floor patterns.

When using "Paw-Paw Patch" in this way, make a single circle formation with hands joined. Using a bouncy walk, move toward the center of the

## PAW-PAW PATCH

From *The American Singer, Book III.* By permission of American Book Company.

circle on the first phrase and move backward out of the circle on the second phrase. On the third phrase drop hands and let each child turn in place, looking for "Nellie." During the last phrase the dancers can move counter-clockwise, pointing "way down yonder." Repeat and pantomime different movements during the third phrase of successive stanzas.

The following dances are suitable for third grade pupils using the techniques described; these will be found as songs in the basic music series or in instrumental recorded versions.

"Old Brass Wagon" (TiM III–13)    "Rig-a-Jig-Jig" (GwM II–23)
"Paw-Paw Patch" (DMT III–8)    "Shoo Fly" (Bir III–2)
"Pop Goes the Weasel" (ABC III–10)    "Skip to My Lou" (ExM II–10)

In the intermediate grades American dances such as the following are used:

"Brown-Eyed Mary" (ABC V–3)    "Four in a Boat" (GwM IV–41)
"Buffalo Gals" (Bir VI–98)    "Goin' to Boston" (TiM V–85)
"Down the Ohio" (MMYO V–8)    "Sourwood Mountain" (MoM IV–152)

A wide variety of dances from different countries can be used in the intermediate grades. It is not necessary to work out all the intricacies and variations the native dancers put into their art, although pupils should, if possible, learn to appreciate and understand those dances. The general procedures in developing dancing are these:

1. Promote a feeling for the basic rhythm of the song and learn to move with the characteristic foot pattern of the dance. Some of the pupils should play rhythm instruments and sing while others do the pattern individually or in a line around the room.
2. Determine how the appropriate foot pattern is related to the metric beat and accent of the music.
3. When partners are needed, learn to do the foot pattern with another person in the manner suggested.
4. Develop floor patterns that follow the phrase structure of the music. Using a circle or a line formation, some basic floor patterns are these: reverse direction on alternating long phrases; move into and back out from the center of the circle on shorter phrases; turn around a partner on shorter phrases, and so forth.

Songs and dances used in a program correlated with social studies include the polka, which is a couple dance of Bohemian origin in lively $\frac{2}{4}$ meter. The schottische is similar to, but slower than, the polka and is often used with songs in $\frac{4}{4}$ meter. Adaptations of both can be used in the intermediate grades. The foot pattern for the schottische is smooth and even:

step - step - step - hop

The polka is a combination of slide, step, and hop; its pattern varies, depending on the beat on which the music begins. Children can learn to do these patterns for the polka:

$$\frac{2}{4} \quad \flat \quad \flat \quad \flat \quad \flat$$

step - slide - step - turn
L    R(up)  L    L
or
step - slide - step - hop

"Holla Hi! Holla Ho!" (TiM VI–148, DMT VI–94, ExM IV–47) is a good song with which to practice any of these patterns.

## HOLLA HI! HOLLA HO!

*Lively*

*German Folk Song*
*English by Peter Kunkel*

Who comes up the mead-ow way? Hol-la hi! Hol-la ho!

Sure-ly 'tis my sweet-heart gay? Hol-la hi-a-ho!

She goes by the__ o-pen door, Hol-la hi! Hol-la ho!

Must not love me__ an-y more. Hol-la hi-a-ho!

From *Work and Sing,* Copyright 1948, Cooperative Recreation Service, Inc., Delaware, Ohio. Used by permission.

When this song is danced as a schottische or polka, a step is taken on each quarter-note value; in other songs the step may be taken on each half-note value. Boys and girls in these grades should study out such problems and be aware of the relationship between dance steps and metric beat. The following are dancing melodies of this type:

"Ach Ja!" (ABC V–134)           "Sweet the Evening Air" (Bir V–14)
"Stodola Pumpa" (GwM V–98)      "Weggis Song," (MMYO IV–171)

Many songs are in waltz rhythm. Because it is important that the pupils be free to respond to the rhythm of the music rather than to learn complicated steps, it is recommended that the simplified "waltz-walk" be used first. A large step is followed by two smaller steps as the dancers progress around in a single circle. As soon as they are able the children may try leading first with the left and then with the right shoulder so that a swaying effect is achieved. "Du, Du Liegst Mir im Herzen" and the following are suitable for waltzing:

"Little White Dove" (DMT IV–69)     "The Charro" (Bir IV–82)
"Sweet Rosie O'Grady" (GwM IV–56)   "The Skaters" (MoM IV–26)

**BODILY MOVEMENT IN THE STUDY OF MUSIC**

**77**

## DU, DU LIEGST MIR IM HERZEN
### (You, You Live in My Heart)

*Waltz tempo*　　　　　　　　　　　　　　　　　　*German Folk Song*

German: *Du,　du　liegst mir im　Her - zen,　Du,　du*
　　　　You,　you　live　in　my　heart,___　You,　you

*liegst mir im　Sinn,　　Du,　du　machst mir viel' Schmer - zen,*
live　in　my　mind,　　You,　you　make me feel　sad,___

*Weisst nicht, wie　gut ich dir　bin;___*　{　　　*Ja,　ja,*
Do　you not　know I love　you;___　}

*ja,　ja*　{ *Weisst nicht, wie　gut ich dir　bin!___*
　　　　　{ Do　you not　know I love　you.___

From THIS IS MUSIC, *Book VI*, by William Sur, Robert E. Nye, William R. Fisher, and Mary R. Tolbert. Copyright © 1962 and 1967 by Allyn and Bacon, Inc. Used by permission.

Waltzes and tangos of the Latin-American tradition are varied and colorful. Boys and girls should hear the music and move rhythmically in appropriate patterns. The tango is associated with Argentina and has African origins, as have the habanera of Cuba and the samba of Brazil. The basic step of the tango embraces two measures of $\frac{2}{4}$ meter:

**CHAPTER THREE**

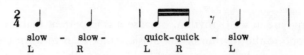

slow - slow-　　　quick-quick - slow
L　　R　　　　L　　R　　　L

"In Bahía" lends itself to this foot pattern as do the following:

"La Conga" (ABC V–96)　　　　　　　"Sambalele" (DMT VI–61)
"San Sereni" (MMYO V–184)　　　　　"The Count of Cabra" (GwM IV–82)

78

## "IN BAHÍA"

Spirited

Brazilian Folk Song
Words Adapted

From *Book Six*, EXPLORING MUSIC Series, © 1966, Holt, Rinehart and Winston, Inc. Reprinted by permission of the publisher, Holt, Rinehart and Winston, Inc.

Many good recorded folk dances are available. Examples for all levels are found in these collections:

RCA VICTOR series: *The World of Folk Dances*, (LPM–1619 to 1615) or single records such as "Kinderpolka," "Klappdans," "Shoemaker's Dance," "Dance of Greeting"

BOWMAR RECORDS: *Singing Games and Folk Dances*, Albums 1–6.

Folk dancing is musically valuable when the dancers can listen to and follow the music rather than simply count the steps. Many teachers make the mistake of selecting a dance in which the foot pattern is too intricate or the floor pattern too varied for an inexperienced group. To promote the desired *musical* objectives, the traditional dance may be simplified or a new, easier one created.

**BODILY MOVEMENT IN THE STUDY OF MUSIC**

### Portraying Melodic Movement

The melodic line is an important element to which the children may direct their attention. As the melody rises and falls, circles, or moves on one plane, the children move their arms and bodies in these ways. The basic rhythm in "Hobby Horse" from *Album for the Young* by Tchaikovsky (BOL #68) is a light running pattern, but the melody moves in long flowing lines, sometimes circling and at other times climbing steadily. While the feet of the children move in the running pattern, their arms and bodies can reflect this melodic flow. Sometimes rapid rises and falls in a melody line suggest turns and whirls. "Little Windmills" by Couperin (BOL #64) seems to do this within a lively running pattern.

The melodic movement of "Gigue" from *Suite for Strings* by Corelli (BOL #63) can be studied in considerable detail by children in the intermediate grades. This music, in $\frac{12}{8}$ meter, has an easy skipping rhythm throughout and falls in two sections with a break between and an extended retard at the end. The form is AABA with seventeen measures in each A section and nine measures in the B section. The second of three long phrases in A has distinct rising and falling melodic sequences that would be very easy to depict with flowing arm movement and changes in body elevation. Individuals should have plenty of space to experiment with the type of movement that best represents this music.

### Unison Expressive Movement

Some songs have a type of melodic movement that pupils can portray as a group. Movement in this setting is free and creative; the musical elements may be of more importance than the text itself. "Down the Stream" may be dramatized with simple movements.

### DOWN THE STREAM

*Smoothly*

*Miwok Indian Song*
*Derrick Norman Lehmer Collection*

In such a song children may express the ideas of the text as well as the musical elements of the song. In this there are two ideas: (1) "Down the stream all the leaves go." Smooth-flowing movements of the body accompanied by rippling hand motions may be used here. (2) "Who can say, who can know where the leaves go?" This may suggest uplifted, outreaching arms as though asking the question. In addition, there is a gradual rising line in the melody at the beginning and a falling line leading to the ending. This might suggest body elevation from a low crouch at the beginning to an upright position on the climax of the third phrase and back to a position of rest at the end.

Other songs that might be interpreted in a similar fashion are these:

"Above the Plain" (MMYO V–131)  "Long John" (Bir V–90)
"Aloha Oe" (TiM V–158)  "Roll On, Columbia" (GwM IV–114)
"For the Beauty of the Earth" (ABC  "The Sunrise Call" (ExM V–140)
IV–60)

Songs that are suitable for unison expressive movement have characteristics distinct from dialogue songs (discussed in the next section) and those for dancing. They have a sincerity of thought that evokes dramatic movement. The phrases are often majestic and flowing in contrast to the more sharply patterned rhythm of a dance. As a result, the movements are broad and sweeping, using hands and arms as well as body pose and elevation to suggest meaning.

Some instrumental compositions have long flowing lines which intermediate grade children might work out as a dynamic group expression of the music's mood and movement. "Ase's Death" from *Peer Gynt Suite No. 1* by Grieg (BOL #59) is dynamic and expressive within a flowing melody line. It is a lament beginning with a repeated three-tone rising theme in the first part. The music rises in pitch and intensity to a climax and then sinks gradually away on a repeated three-tone descending phrase in the second part. Changes in body elevation and intensity of movement within the slow rhythm of this music could make a dramatic portrayal of the lament.

### Following Breaks and Retards

Breaks, holds, and retards in music capture the attention and make a composition interesting. When these additional techniques are encountered, several hearings are necessary before the children know the music well enough to follow it accurately. A familiar composition, such as "The Wild Horseman" by Schumann, may be played on the piano with a break at the end of the first phrase to show the children how unpredictable the galloping horses might be.

## THE WILD HORSEMAN

*Allegro con brio*                                                                                       *Robert Schumann*

Or, instead of galloping full speed throughout the composition, the children can learn the effective use of a retard if the teacher will play one at the end of this piece.

A composition such as "Waltz" by Brahms can be used to illustrate the hold. At a break all movement stops, but at the hold there is a continuity that may be shown by the slow rising of the arms or turn of the body.

## WALTZ

*Dolce*

*Opus 39, No. 2*
*Johannes Brahms*

Some recorded pieces can also be used to help children notice such musical details. "Petite Ballerina" from *Ballet Suite No. 1* by Shostakovich (A in M II–1) has a slight retard and a hold before the last entrance of the theme. Brahms' *Hungarian Dance* No. 5 (BOL #55) has numerous examples of the hold, retard, and accelerando that older children would be challenged to include in their interpretation of the music.

## Interpreting Contrasting Sections

To give variety and dramatic interest to longer compositions, the composer uses contrasting sections. He achieves balance as well as variety by repeating the original section after the contrasting one. To interpret the music, the pupils must listen as they move and change their movements with the music. Contrasts are present in all music from the simple dance suite to the symphony. When children learn to understand and listen for sectional changes in conjunction with their work in expressive movement, they develop their potential powers as music listeners and performers as well.

Preliminary experience in following changing rhythms may be had with rhythm instruments or the piano. The teacher might play eight measures for walking, then, without a break, change to a running or skipping rhythm. Any of the piano compositions suggested for fundamental movements may be used if they are in the same key and sound good played consecutively. Hood and Schultz, in *Learning Music through Rhythm*,[10] give a detailed study and several piano compositions suitable for preliminary work in changing rhythms.

Contrasting sections are a challenge as the children try to interpret music in terms of imaginative characters and situations. "March" from *Ballet Suite* by Lully (A in M III–2) is a clear example of three-part sectional form in music. In the first and last sections the rhythm is bold and martial, suggesting a colorful but dignified processional. In the middle section the rhythm moves in an even, rapid pattern, broken regularly by longer notes; the melody moves in winding scale patterns. This section might be interpreted as a dance, following the short patterns with rapid steps combined with bending and lifting the arms on longer notes. See *Teacher's Guide* to ADVENTURES IN MUSIC, *Grade 3, Volume 2,* for an interesting, detailed analysis of this composition. "Norwegian Dance" in A by Grieg (BOL #63) has sharply contrasting sections in three part form (ABA) that might be interpreted by alternate groups of girls and boys.

"Romanze" from *Eine kleine Nachtmusik* by Mozart has five broad sections, which may be labeled ABACA. The main theme (A) is a graceful flowing melody in two parts. It is followed first by a more playful melody (B) with little turning patterns, and then by a more animated section (C) with repeated tones in the accompaniment and a kind of question-and-answer melody played alternately by high and low sounding instruments. The A section could be interpreted with graceful stepping movements, B by fast and slow steps interchangeably following the rhythm of the melody, and C by tiny running steps with the question-and-answer effect taken by two alternate individuals or small groups. The five sections, with the main theme returning after each new theme, comprise a rondo form.

When working with the smaller unit of musical form, the phrase, children can express contrast through bodily movement by (1) changing the direction

**83**

of movement at the end of a phrase, as suggested with folk dances, (2) moving the arms in broad arcs, or (3) raising and lowering the body and arms to indicate the rise and fall of a phrase. Phrases may be represented on the chalkboard as broad arcs. If phrases are the same length, the arcs should be the same length.

Physical response to rhythmic, structural, and descriptive elements in music is an important and interesting activity for all classes. It is often a part of singing and listening and should be used more extensively as a basic experience in the music program.

## CHARACTERIZATIONS AND DRAMA

When does a child's interpretation of music through fundamental movements become drama? It is impossible to distinguish between the two. One moment he may be creeping on tiptoe as himself; the next moment his imagination may have added dramatic locale and characters. There is no reason to be concerned about the presence or absence of the dramatic situation, but the child who throws himself into a characterization may lose some of his self-consciousness and move with more freedom.

The imagination cannot be forced, but the teacher can encourage its use for the sake of the freedom and vitality it brings to rhythmic movement. Just a suggestion of a costume, ears for a rabbit, a simple mask for a bear, helps a child achieve a sense of realism. Scarves help to create the flowing line that is needed in the interpretation of some compositions. A scarf should be about 2½ times the height of the child so that he can hold it extended between both outstretched arms or let it flow freely behind him to give a feeling of elongation and grace to his movement.

### Short Sketches for Interpretation

It is important that over a period of time boys and girls have experience interpreting short sketches from various musical styles. Some music may be equally appropriate for boys and for girls. However, in the early stages of interpretive movement, when the subject is of greater importance to the children than the movement itself, the boys may prefer to characterize animals and bolder subjects while girls may be fascinated with fairies or butterflies. The teacher must be sensitive in his selection so that in every lesson there is something of appeal to each group.

Many composers have tried to bring characters to life through music. Among the animal sketches available for piano are these:

"Elephants Walking," Hansi Alt (Joy 180)

"The Bear," Rebikoff (MMYO K–163)

"Papillons," Opus 2, No. 12, Schumann (Bir II–T194)

"The Wild Horseman," Schumann (Joy 84)

Like the painter, the composer may use a combination of techniques to create a small composition depicting one character. When such compositions are interpreted through bodily movement, quite varied techniques must be used. "The Little White Donkey" by Ibert (A in M II–1) is a favorite of children. "Fairies and Giants" by Elgar (A in M III–1), "Dance of the Mosquito" by Liadov, and "Flight of the Bumble Bee" by Rimsky-Korsakov (BOL #52) are delightful musical characterizations. Of special appeal to boys is the heavier movement of Bartók's "Bear Dance" (A in M III–2), or "Bydlo" from *Pictures at an Exhibition* (A in M II–1) by Moussorgsky.

A teacher may wish to relate the music to a poem or a story that will influence the movement of the children. The various series of records listed in Appendix B have teaching suggestions that include poems, stories, and pictures that might be used with the compositions. A teacher may have other material that is appropriate to certain pieces of music. Too many stories and pictures, however, can deprive a child of the opportunity to make his own interpretation of the music. A balance must be achieved between guidance and freedom, if the children are to learn to respond directly to music itself.

Sometimes the teacher may tell the children the title of a composition before they listen or attempt to move to the music. Most often, it is best to let the music itself suggest the movement because the title may limit the imagination, and the idea it suggests may not be as appropriate as the interpretation of the children.

In the use of bodily movement as a means of response to music, a continuous awareness of the music is fully as important as the physical response, and certainly the emotional response must be an integral part of the total activity. The different parts of the music program cannot be isolated, for whatever happens in the listening activities, to be discussed in Chapter Eight, is surely akin to this.

## Longer Dramatic Projects

Generally, short, separate musical sketches provide the greatest experience with different musical rhythms and characterizations. On occasion, several of these sketches, developed individually, may be combined in a story sequence. Or, after the children have had considerable experience, a larger piece of music may be interpreted. *The Nutcracker Suite* by Tchaikovsky (BOL #58), a group of eight short compositions based on a fairy tale, is a considerable challenge. The story and the music are delightful, the sections are short and varied and lend themselves to expressive movement. For the story and musical themes see *The Music Box Book;*[11] THIS IS MUSIC, *Book Three*, pages 34 to 42; or EXPLORING MUSIC, *Book Two*, pages 80 and 81.

*Peter and the Wolf* by Prokofiev has the narration of the story integrated with the music and offers children interesting opportunities for character portrayal. The music makes the listener feel that Peter is an active, happy, outgoing boy with lots of friends. Grandfather is a gruff, stern old man, who walks stiffly and heavily. The cat, of course, is an agile, stealthy creature. Whether or not the complete story is dramatized, it is a fine experience for the children to portray some of these characters through movement. Such activity will help them direct their attention to details in the music which suggest the character even more than does the narrator. For musical themes and pictures of instruments see THIS IS MUSIC, *Book Three*, pages 62 to 64.

*The Comedians* by Kabalevsky is taken from incidental music that the composer originally wrote for the children's play *Inventor and Comedian*. This suite has ten short sections, all evocative of characterizations and dramatic action in expressive movement:

"Prologue," which is lively and jocular, has some suggestion of stiff mechanical movement.
"Gallop" is vigorous and rapid, suggestive of rodeo activities or other good-natured, vigorous sporting play.
"March" suggests tiptoeing and stealth with some grotesque qualities.
"Waltz" has graceful running or soaring lines. It suggests birds, butterflies, and bees.
"Pantomime" certainly should be music for bears. Several big, gruff bears!
"Intermezzo" is lively, witty, and dancing.
"Little Lyric Scene" is a short restful interlude, perhaps a night scene.
"Gavotte" is an early morning dance of sunbeams and fairies in a meadow.
"Scherzo" may suggest a chase.
"Epilogue" brings back some of the vigorous activity and jocular character of the first two sections.

Any of these sections can be used separately (see BOL #53, #55, A in M I–1, and A in M III–1), but the suite as a whole is well balanced and may be tied together in a story sequence if the pupils are imaginative enough to create one.

In order to interpret such varied music a child must use a combination of rhythmic movements, following important melody lines and retards as well as sectional changes. In doing so he may become so immersed in his impersonation that he is unaware of the movements he uses. This is not a problem, for of prime importance is the fact that he is developing a sensitivity to music, to its rhythm, tone color, and mood.

Children should be encouraged to "live" the character they portray; facial expression, body weight, and posture as well as rhythm should be representative. To do this the class must have a seriousness of purpose. Part of this work should be teacher-directed so that the children expand their understanding of what may be heard in music and the varied ways of expressing these ideas through movement. Balancing this directed work there should be ample opportunity for the pupils to listen carefully and develop their own interpretations.

## Ballads and Dialogue Songs

Important values can be derived from the dramatization of songs, and success in simple dramatization prepares children for more significant expressive movement with other music. Actual rhythmic movement may be of less importance than the sincere portrayal of an idea. A dramatization involves two or more characters in related action. Here the possibilities are limited only by the imagination of the pupils and the time available for working out the details. "The Old Gray Cat" (MMYO K–17) is an excellent song for creative dramatic play by young children.

## THE OLD GRAY CAT

*Dramatically*                                                      *Alabama Folk Song*

1. The old gray cat is sleep - ing, sleep - ing, sleep - ing, The
2. The lit - tle mice are creep - ing, creep - ing, creep - ing, The

old gray cat is sleep - ing in the house.
lit - tle mice are creep - ing through the house.

3. The little mice are nibbling in the house.
4. The little mice are sleeping in the house.
5. The old gray cat comes creeping through the house.
6. The little mice all scamper through the house.

Used by permission of Dr. Byron Arnold from whose collection of Alabama folk songs it is taken.

Some of the children are mice who creep and nibble around the house, always slightly fearful and watching as the old gray cat sleeps; but watch how they scamper when the cat wakes up!

The musical interpretation of this song should be adjusted to fit the ideas in the text. The children can learn something about change in tempo and dynamics if the first stanza is sung moderately softly and very smoothly so that the cat will continue to sleep. The second stanza will be quiet, but with a little more movement, and so forth, until the final stanza which must move rapidly and with excitement as the mice scamper away from the cat. The teacher should discuss these changes with the children so their musical awareness will be sharpened. The following songs lend themselves to dramatization, and they can be found in several of the basic song series:

"Count of Cabara" (GwM IV–82)      "Johnny Sands" (TiM V–81)
"Deaf Woman's Courtship" (MoM      "Soldier, Soldier" (Bir IV–153)
IV–116)

**BODILY
MOVEMENT IN
THE STUDY
OF MUSIC**

**87**

## "OH NO, JOHN!"

*Moderately fast*

*English Folk Song*
*Collected by Cecil J. Sharp*

1. On yon-der hill there stands a— maid-en, Who she is I do not know; I'll go and ask her hand in— mar-riage, She must an-swer yes or no.

*Refrain*
Oh, no, John! No, John! No,— John! No!

2. My father was a Spanish captain,
   Went to sea a month ago;
   First he kissed me, then he left me,
   Bid me always answer no.

3. Oh, madam, in your face is beauty,
   On your lips red roses grow;
   Will you take me for your husband?
   Madam, answer yes or no.

4. Oh, madam, I will give you jewels;
   I will make you rich and free;
   I will give you silken dresses;
   Madam, will you marry me?

5. Oh, madam, since you are so cruel,
   And that you do scorn me so,
   If I may not be your husband,
   Madam, will you let me go?

6. Oh, hark! I hear the church bells ringing;
   Will you come and be my wife?
   Or, dear madam, have you settled
   To live single all your life?

Used by permission of Novello and Company, Ltd.

In this old English ballad a boy and a girl may act out the story told in the solo parts. The entire class or a smaller group might pantomime appropriate movements to underscore the progress of ideas in the song and join in on the refrain after each stanza. For young actors the greatest problem is filling in suitable movement when there are no directions in the song text. Considerable experimentation and some guidance is necessary before they can find movement patterns that are satisfying to them.

## LEARNING TO CONDUCT SONGS

Within the framework of traditional gestures available to him, the conductor of a symphony orchestra conveys to the orchestra all the feeling of musical rhythm, melody, dynamics, and other expressive factors that make possible the interpretation of any musical work. Conducting is a highly developed use of movement and gesture which untrained individuals can only approximate in simple ways. However, from the fourth grade upward pupils can begin to apply gesture and arm movement to the interpretation of music by learning to conduct their own songs. Rhythmic arm movements of a general nature should be an early kind of participation. When rhythmic response is well established, pupils can learn the conductor's patterns for the common meters of $\frac{2}{4}$, $\frac{3}{4}$, $\frac{4}{4}$, and $\frac{6}{8}$. The conductor's pattern can be of great help to a singer in analyzing and singing the rhythm of a song. When the pupils can keep the proper metric beat, they will automatically hold long notes and provide time for rests.

In conducting, the child should hold his hand palm down with a supple rather than a rigid or flabby feeling. His elbow should be slightly away from his body. Only when directing very large groups should he raise his arm high. It takes practice to develop an expressive conductor's beat, and with intermediate children the initial objective is to establish the rhythmic movements in the proper direction. The patterns shown are for the right-handed person; when the left hand is used, the opposite left-and-right directions are taken. When the children are learning the hand movements, they should practice conducting well-known songs that begin on the first beat of the measure. Songs meeting these requirements are shown below in conjunction with each basic conducting pattern.

In conducting $\frac{2}{4}$ meter, the movement is essentially down and up with a slight movement to the right preceding the upward stroke. Every conductor must give a preparatory beat to let the singers know when to start; this takes the form of a slight upward movement preceding the downward stroke when the singing begins.

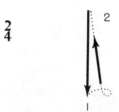

"Merrily We Roll Along":

For $\frac{3}{4}$ meter the conductor's pattern is in effect a triangle moving to the right. The $\frac{4}{4}$ pattern moves first to the left across the body and then to the right.

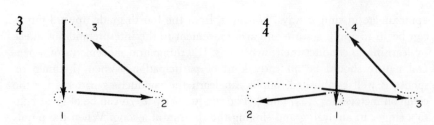

Other than the preparatory beat, which comes only at the beginning of the composition, the dotted lines indicate the slight rebound of the hand between beats which gives the conductor's pattern the necessary fluid rhythmic movement.

"America":

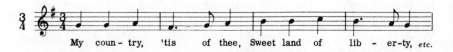

"Lovely Evening":

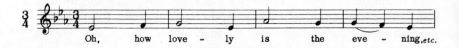

"All through the Night":

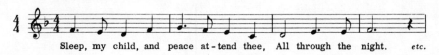

A two-beat pattern is usually used with $\frac{6}{8}$ meter, so that there is a subdivision of three on each beat, in contrast to the "1-and-2-and" two-part subdivision in $\frac{2}{4}$ meter. If a song is sung in slow $\frac{6}{8}$ meter each beat is indicated.

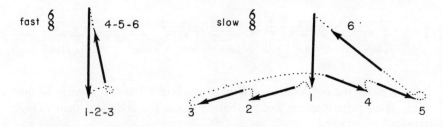

"Row, Row, Row Your Boat":

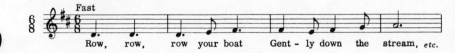

"Sleep and Rest":

In learning to direct songs the child should first establish an automatic rhythmic movement of the hand in the pattern for each meter. Although a conductor does not outline the beat pattern with both hands, in the early stages both hands should be used so that (1) left-handed pupils will not be confused in direction, and (2) the teacher may face the group and not confuse the students by his reverse movement. The $\frac{3}{4}$ pattern when done with both hands is:

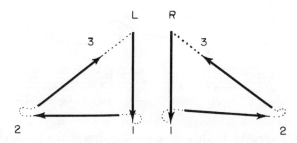

Many songs begin on other than the first beat of the measure. In such cases the preparatory beat will be that preceding the beat on which the song begins. "The Star-Spangled Banner," in $\frac{3}{4}$ meter, begins on the third beat; therefore the preparatory beat will take the form of a short movement in the direction of the second beat in $\frac{3}{4}$ meter:

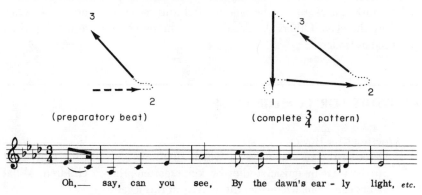

(preparatory beat)   (complete $\frac{3}{4}$ pattern)

Oh,— say, can you see, By the dawn's ear-ly light, etc.

Other well-known songs beginning on upbeats are:

"America, the Beautiful" in $\frac{4}{4}$ meter (see page 200)

"Oh No, John!" in $\frac{4}{4}$ meter (see page 88)

Brahms' "Cradle Song" in $\frac{3}{4}$ meter (see page 234)

"Down in the Valley" in $\frac{9}{8}$ meter (see page 165)

Inexperienced song leaders sometimes count out the entire measure when a song begins on a fragment of a measure. Songs such as "Oh! Susanna" pose special problems because they begin on the *last half* of the second beat. In this song the leader can establish the tempo by saying as he conducts:

"Believe Me, If All Those Endearing Young Charms" is in $\frac{6}{8}$ meter but has two beats to the measure. The conductor can conduct the whole measure in duple pattern and say:

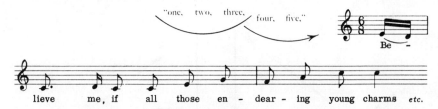

In the early stages the teacher must be selective in the songs children are asked to conduct. However, after skill is developed, more advanced problems may be met successfully in well-known songs.

All intermediate children should be taught the accepted conductor's patterns. Those who develop the necessary skill should be encouraged to serve as song leaders. Fifth and sixth grade groups may elect a song leader for a one- or two-week period. Often children who are especially interested and have richer musical backgrounds become natural musical leaders and are so recognized by the class. Others should also have the opportunity to develop their potential as leaders.

## ACTIVITIES FOR COLLEGE CLASSES

A. Questions for Review
1. Describe the several ways in which rhythmic and creative movement can be used in music studies by kindergarten-primary children. What values can be realized from the activity at this level?
2. Describe the ways in which rhythmic and creative movement can be used in music studies by intermediate grade children. What values can be realized from the activity at this level?
3. What details in musical composition can be studied and portrayed through bodily movement?
4. At what grade level and how should song conducting be introduced? What are the values of this activity?

B. Written Assignments
   1. From one or two graded music series used in the school district in which you expect to teach select representative songs to show the different ways bodily movement may be used in the music program at the grade level of your choice. Develop brief teaching notes for each song, suggesting the type of movement to be used and the musical concepts to be developed. Cite the source and page of each song. Exclude titles cited in this text.
   2. If you plan to work in the kindergarten or primary grades select or create an easy piano accompaniment that you can play for walking, running, and skipping activities of children. Write out one short composition of each type so you will have it available when you begin teaching.
   3. Find short recorded compositions that would be suitable for fundamental movements by children at the grade level of your choice. State how much of each recording would be used and what type of movement would be appropriate. Exclude titles cited in this text.
   4. Find recorded compositions that would be suitable for creative interpretive movement of different kinds by children at the grade level of your choice. Describe the type of movement that might be appropriate, and point out the more obvious concepts in rhythm, melody and form that the children might develop through experience with the music selected.
C. Classroom Projects
   1. As others move, accompany at least two contrasting fundamental rhythmic movements in one of the following ways:
      a. improvisation on the piano as worked out in written assignment No. 2 above.
      b. suitable piano compositions
      c. a rhythm instrument
   2. Make a simple costume that creates a sense of realism for a particular character. With a piano or recorded accompaniment, create movement that effectively characterizes the subject.
   3. In small groups, work out movement that is expressive of selected numbers from the suite "The Comedians."
   4. In a small group, select and create an appropriate dance and arrange a suitable accompaniment for a song in one of the following groupings:
      a. schottische or polka
      b. American reel or circle dance
      c. Latin-American waltz or tango

## CHAPTER NOTES

1. Roger Sessions, *The Musical Experience of Composer, Performer, Listener* (Princeton, N.J.: Princeton University Press, 1950), pp. 11–16.
2. Aaron Copland, *Music and Imagination* (Cambridge, Mass.: Harvard University Press, 1961), pp. 13–14.

3. Gladys Andrews, *Creative Rhythmic Movement for Children* (Englewood Cliffs, N.J.: Prentice-Hall, Inc., 1954).
4. "Learning through Movement," S. L. Film Productions, Los Angeles.
5. "Building Children's Personalities with Creative Dancing," University of California, Extension Division, Film No. 5844.
6. "Music for Children," Contemporary Films, New York.
7. Carl Orff, translated by Arnold Walter, "The Schulwerk—Its Origin and Aims," *Music Educators Journal,* April–May 1963. Also *The Canadian Music Educator,* October–November 1962.
8. Sally Monsour, Marilyn Chambers Cohen, and Patricia Eckert Lindell, *Rhythm in Music and Dance for Children* (Belmont, Calif.: Wadsworth Publishing Company, Inc., 1966).
9. Elsie Braun, *Music for Active Children* (New York: Stephen Daye Press, Inc., 1957).
10. Marguerite V. Hood and E. J. Schultz, *Learning Music through Rhythm* (Boston: Ginn and Company, 1949), Chapter 3.
11. Syd Skolsky, *The Music Box Book* (New York: E. P. Dutton and Co., Inc., 1946).

## Other References

Cole, Natalie Robinson, *The Arts in the Classroom* (New York: John Day Co., Inc., 1940). Chapter 4, "Free Rhythmic Dancing."

Driver, Ann, *Music and Movement* (London: Oxford University Press, 1947).

Driver, Ethel, *A Pathway to Dalcroze Eurhythmics* (New York: Thomas Nelson & Sons, 1951).

Gray, Vera, and Rachel Percival, *Music, Movement and Mime for Children* (London: Oxford University Press, 1962).

Humphreys, Louise, and Jerrold Ross, *Interpreting Music through Movement* (Englewood Cliffs, N.J.: Prentice-Hall, Inc., 1964).

Mursell, James L., *Music and the Classroom Teacher* (Morristown, N.J.: Silver Burdett Company, 1951). Chapter 4, "Expressive Bodily Movement."

Perham, Beatrice, *Music in the New School* (Park Ridge, Ill.: Neil A. Kjos Music Co., 1941). Chapter 6, "Music and Rhythms."

Saffran, Rosanna B., *First Book of Creative Rhythms* (New York: Holt, Rinehart and Winston, Inc., 1963).

Sheehy, Emma Dickson, *Children Discover Music and Dance* (New York: Holt, Rinehart & Winston, Inc., 1959). Chapter 7, "Dance," and Chapter 8, "Guiding Movement and Accompaniment."

See Appendix B for *Guide to Materials* (including basic series music books and records).

**4**

# Rhythm Instruments
# in the Study of Music

From the earliest times man has used instruments in his music-making. In almost all ethnic groups, chanting, singing, and dancing have been accompanied by them. Children are fascinated by sounds of all sorts; their natural tendencies to touch and to manipulate make the use of simple instruments a vital part of any program of music in the schools. Singing and sound-making with instruments go together. Only after the teacher understands the place of simple instruments in the music program is he in a position to teach songs and promote the varied program recommended in this text.

Simple percussion instruments (those that are struck to produce the tone) long have been standard equipment in the kindergarten and primary grades. These instruments, when properly used, have undeniable value throughout the elementary music program. Although all instruments may play rhythm, those ordinarily classed as "rhythm instruments" sound only one pitch and so are incapable of playing a melody line. In the percussion section of the symphony orchestra a number of these are standard equipment: tambourine, triangle, castanets, drums of various kinds, cymbals, gong, claves, and others. Small copies of these have been adapted for young children, and a number of folk instruments such as bongo and conga drums, maracas, and guiro are added to the collection used by older children in arrangements of Latin-American songs and dances. Multitoned percussion instruments (xylophone, glockenspiel, piano, and others) are included among melody instruments in Chapter Five.

## RECOMMENDED INSTRUMENTS

Any musical instrument planned for active use in a classroom must be durable enough to last for a long time, and parts of it that wear out should be replaceable. A drum, to be more than a decorator's item, must have a head that is sturdy enough to be struck repeatedly with a padded mallet. After two or three years of active use, it may be necessary to replace the drumhead, but at a small part of the original cost.

The quality of sound in the instruments is also important. If there is anything that will put such an instrumental program in the "toy" classification, it is the use of instruments with poor and indistinctive sound. Many teachers, for lack of funds, have provided home-made substitutes for instruments. This can be a practical solution to a problem if the substitute has fine tone quality. In fact, almost any group of children can benefit from a project in which they explore quality of sound in metal and wood objects in an attempt to find substitutes for instruments not otherwise available to their classroom.

## A Basic Group of Rhythm Instruments

When a teacher plans to obtain rhythm instruments for his classroom he should know that (1) if a complete set of instruments is not available immediately, he may gather a basic group first and then accumulate the remainder over a period of time; (2) some homemade instruments are more durable and have better tone than those which are bought.

Instruments basic to primary musical activities are described in the following paragraphs. After that, additional desirable instruments are listed. Finally, the more authentic folk type is suggested as the distinguishing feature of rhythm instruments used in the intermediate grades.

*Drums.* Every classroom should have at least one drum and, where possible, two or more of contrasting size. A tunable, 14-inch modern dance drum is a light-weight, versatile instrument that can be used to produce interesting variety in tonal and rhythmic effects. Primitive drums with skin heads are available in many sizes from the small hand drum to the large ceremonial drum that rests on the floor. These are durable and have a splendid tone but they are quite expensive and therefore may not be available to the average classroom.

A less expensive drum with a reasonably good sound may be constructed with these materials:

1. *A wooden barrel, keg, or pail, 10 or 11 inches in diameter.* This should be quite sturdy, open at one end and with a smooth rim or edge over which the drumhead material is stretched. If the barrel is old and dry, soak it for several hours so that the tacks may be driven in more easily. The larger barrel results in a drum with a deeper tone.
2. *Hide or gum rubber for the drumhead.* Scraped rawhide, chamois, or old bass drumheads can be used if they are soaked in water until they are pliable enough to be stretched over the drum. Commercial, pure gum, sheet rubber, $\frac{1}{16}$-inch thick, also can be used as a drumhead. Buy a square slightly larger than the diameter of the barrel; by the time it is stretched it will have ample edge for tacking.
3. *Upholstery tacks with large heads.* Drive these in about an inch from the edge of the rubber or hide. Put three tacks in rather close together, and then pull the drumhead across the opening and drive in three more tacks. Work on alternate sides around the drum. Putting in a group of tacks will prevent tearing of the material.

The life of the drum will be longer if the hand or a *padded* drumstick is used to strike it.

*Rhythm sticks.* In the symphony orchestra or in a Latin-American orchestra the claves are a pair of resonant wooden sticks, which are struck together. Rhythm sticks are their counterpart among the primary rhythm instruments. The most resonant tone is made when the sticks are held loosely in the hands as they are tapped together. These may be purchased, but the homemade version is simple to make, much less expensive, and just as satisfactory.

Buy ⅝-inch doweling in a lumber or hardware store. Cut it into 12-inch lengths and stain any desirable color. For a lighter, contrasting sound, use inexpensive chop sticks or ¼-inch doweling. Each classroom can use three or four pairs of both sizes.

*Triangle.* The 5-inch triangle with striker is adequate. For quality in sound the commercially-made triangle is best, but a large nail struck with another nail will produce a similar tone. The triangle or nail must be suspended by a short piece of twine so that the tone will ring freely. Two or three triangles are necessary for bell and other tinkling effects.

*Sandblocks.* Two or three pairs of sandblocks are useful. Those available commercially are generally too small and not durable. Long-lasting sandblocks with an excellent sound may be made with

1. Two half-sheets of fine emery cloth (9″ × 5½″).
2. Two pieces of plywood (3″ × 9″).
3. A 4-inch piece of ¾-inch scrap lumber for a handle.

The construction is simple. Attach the handle with short nails driven through from the plywood side. Draw the emery cloth smoothly around the plywood base and thumbtack on the top side. Do not glue it down because it makes a better sound when merely drawn tightly around the wood base.

*Coconut shells.* Nothing makes a better sound for galloping and trotting horses than hollow halves of coconut shells tapped together. Two pairs are recommended. To prepare them, drain the milk from a coconut, cut it evenly in half, and scrape out the meat. When the shells are dry, they may be scraped and polished.

*Sleigh bells.* It is best to buy medium-size bells that are attached to a handle. Three or four of two different sizes are enough.

With the above group of instruments the teacher will have variety and will be able to promote very worthwhile instrumental activities. It is desirable, of course, to have a greater selection of instruments. As the budget allows, some of the following may be added:

*Tambourine.* Homemade varieties are rarely adequate in quality of sound. It is worth the money to buy a good quality instrument. Two or three 7-inch tambourines are sufficient.

*Tone blocks.* Two sizes of these are very useful for clock sounds. The tone block is tapped with a small wooden mallet. The commercial variety is recommended.

*Cymbals.* One pair of small 7-inch cymbals is enough. Many commercially made small cymbals leave something to be desired as far as tone quality is concerned, so it is worthwhile to get the best quality available.

*Gong.* This is a more expensive item, but one that is important because it can be used to enhance climaxes and dramatic effects. It should be suspended, struck with a padded mallet and allowed to vibrate freely.

*Maracas.* One or two pairs of the commercial variety of resonant wood maracas is recommended. It is worthwhile to buy a better quality instrument, for the handles of the cheaply made kind come off. Teachers have made good-sounding maracas out of dried gourds that have been cut open, cleaned and shellacked inside, and resealed with a small amount of fine rattling material inside (rice, shot, etc.). If the gourds have been buffed on the outside they may be painted and lacquered in colorful Mexican designs.

*Guiro (gourd rasp).* One of these will serve special purposes from time to time. It is played by rhythmically stroking a light stick over the notched area. This is quite easily made by filing notches in the side of a large dried gourd and shellacking the instrument.

*Handcastas.* These are the childhood counterpart of castanets. They are less expensive and easier to play.

*Finger cymbals.* Two pairs will provide special effects as needed.

*Bells.* Any small bells are useful.

## Folk Instruments at the Intermediate Level

Although authentic rhythm instruments from different countries are useful in the primary classroom, they play a more important role at the intermediate level. Prestige is given this work when such instruments are used. Instead of rhythm sticks, substitute claves, the authentic Cuban instrument. It is necessary to buy these instruments in order to get the desired tone quality. Tambourines should be larger than those used in the primary grades. Maracas, castanets, guiros or other types of rasps are especially valuable with Latin-American songs.

Triangles, cymbals, or gong may be used occasionally for specialized effects and, when possible, should be of the standard orchestral size. If such instruments are not available, pupils may explore the potential of different metal objects that, when suspended and struck, make sounds of an acceptable quality.

Drums may be of varied types, but the bongo and conga drums are of particular interest to children this age. Because Latin-American and West Indian songs are included in the basic music books, there is a reason for having authentic native instruments. Bongo drums are a pair of small drums, one higher in pitch than the other, bound together so that one player can sound them with both hands as he holds them between his knees. Very intricate rhythms can be played on the bongos. A conga drum is much lower in pitch because it is longer. It may stand on the floor, tilted at an angle so that the sound is free; or it may be held between the legs as the player sits on the floor and plays it with both hands.

A homemade version of bongo drums can be made out of two short lengths of cardboard tubing taken from the inside of a linoleum roll or out of two small butter kegs, bolted together, the open tops of which have been covered with goatskin. Some firms sell the complete materials for bongo drums, and these are assembled by the purchaser. Homemade substitutes for conga drums can be made of fiber waste pipe which has been cut in lengths up to 26 inches. The application of goatskin drumheads and tuning procedures are described in detail in *Make Your Own Musical Instruments* by Mandell and Wood.[1]

As pupils become acquainted with people of other cultures they become interested in the typical instruments, such as drums and rattles of the American Indian, Chinese woodblocks and gong, and Hawaiian uli-uli and drums. Often authentic instruments of these types are available in the community and can be obtained for display or limited use. The construction of such instruments makes an excellent arts and crafts project for intermediate grades. *Drums, Tomtoms, Rattles,*[2] which describes the construction of primitive instruments for modern use, is one of the best sources of information for such a project.

## THE EXPLORATION OF SOUND AND
## THE ENRICHMENT OF SONGS

Important objectives of the instrumental program are to develop sensitivity to different tone colors and qualities in instrumental sound, and to establish basic concepts in regard to pitch, dynamics, and duration of tone. Therefore, children must have opportunities to experiment with the instruments. Children's natural interest in sound should be cultivated to the end that they discover differences:

1. The drum has a booming sound and the triangle has a tinkling, bell-like sound.
2. The drum has a low tone and the triangle has a high tone.
3. Some drums have lower tones than others.
4. The tones of triangles, cymbals, and drums resound for a longer period of time than does the tone of the rhythm sticks.
5. Instruments may be played in more than one way with varied effects.

This is only a sampling of many musical discoveries to be made. In this work some teacher-guided group experimentation is possible, but much individual, free exploration should be arranged.

In many classrooms, activity centers are established, and music has its center where instruments are kept. Since sound-making and listening are the basis for exploration, there are limitations on acceptable times for the activity. Some small groups may use the instruments before school, after school, or during recesses and activity periods. During good weather, the more durable instruments may be taken to a specified location out of doors.

In the kindergarten the teacher can guide free exploration by limiting the number of available instruments. Drums are often the first instruments placed in the instrument center. As an introduction, the teacher may arrange a demonstration-discussion in which the pupils show and tell what they know about the instruments. He may suggest ideas that would lead the children to explore the instruments further. Later, when some interesting discovery is made (a new combination of instruments or a new and effective way of playing an instrument), the teacher may wish to bring it to the attention of the entire class. In *Children Discover Music and Dance*,[3] pages 85 to 95, Emma Sheehy gives interesting examples and suggestions for this use of the instruments.

## A Classification of Sounds

Although in the beginning a classification of the effects produced is not important to children, two or three years of work with the instruments should lead them to a summarization of the representative sounds:

1. Short, dry sounds can be produced by:

| | |
|---|---|
| *rhythm sticks* | *skinhead drum* |
| *tone blocks* | *coconut shells* |
| *sandblocks*—short, quick stroke | *tambourine*—tapped |
| *guiro*—quick stroke | *castanets* |

2. Sustained, dry sounds are produced by:

| | |
|---|---|
| *maracas*—shaken | *guiro*—stroked slowly |
| *sandblocks*—rubbed slowly together | |

3. Sustained tones with greater resonance are produced by:

*larger drum* with skin head          *tambourine*—shaken
*drum* with rubber head

4. Tinkling sounds, higher in pitch, are produced by:

*triangle*—tapped                     *finger cymbals*
*cymbal*—tapped lightly with hard stick

5. Ringing sounds of longer duration are produced by:

*triangle*—struck repeatedly and rapidly at one corner (for a louder tone, the striker can be rung repeatedly around the entire inside of the triangle)
*bells*—allowed to vibrate freely

*cymbals*—crashed together or struck with a padded mallet and allowed to vibrate freely
*sleigh bells*—shaken for the desired duration
*gong*

## Techniques in Enriching Songs

Group exploration of sound and rhythm can be an outgrowth of selecting suitable instruments for use with songs and rhythmic activities. In the kindergarten and first grade, instruments as well as hands and feet are used to create sound effects as they are needed with particular songs. Several pairs of chop sticks tapped rapidly and lightly or many fingernails clicking on desk tops or on paper provide excellent rain-on-the-roof effects. Sandblocks make train sounds. Pupils should be guided to experiment, to listen, and to decide what instrument produces the sound desired in a particular song. "Who's That Tapping at the Window?" suggests the use of two instruments, one that produces a light "tapping" sound and another that has a heavier "knocking" sound.

### WHO'S THAT TAPPING AT THE WINDOW?

*Moderately fast*                                                    *Virginia*

Who's that tap-ping at the win-dow? Who's that
knock-ing at the door? Mam - my tap-ping at the
win - dow, Pap - py knock-ing at the door.

Reprinted by permission of the publishers from Dorothy Scarborough, *On the Trail of Negro Folk-Songs* (Cambridge, Mass.: Harvard University Press, 1925, 1953).

**103**

These instruments may be sounded in a steady rhythm throughout the song or played only at the end of each phrase. The children may wish to try it both ways. Some of the following songs suggest the use of instruments for sound effects:

"The Angel Band" (MMYO K–92)          "Horsey! Horsey!" (TiM I–129)
"The Bells" (DMT I–18)                "Jingle at the Window" (GwM II–19)
"By'm By" (Bir II–95)                 "Little White Duck" (ExM I–16)

Drums, rhythm sticks, or sandblocks can be sounded on the metric beat of marching songs like "Yankee Doodle" (see page 106). When the drum sounds the steady 1–2 beat, it follows the rhythm of the marchers' feet. Rhythm sticks might play the metric beat in "Clap Your Hands" (MMYO I–12), or they may be used to furnish the steady clock sound in "Ticktock" (Joy–54).

The rhythm of the melody can also be played. Often, after the children know a song thoroughly, it is the easiest response, for they merely follow the rhythm pattern of the words throughout all or part of the song. In "Chickama Craney Crow" rhythm sticks can be played on the rhythm of the words "Chickama, chickama, craney crow." Later, the rhythm of the words may be played throughout the song.

### CHICKAMA CRANEY CROW

*Whimsically*                                                    *Southern Folk Song*

Chick - a - ma, Chick - a - ma, Crane - y Crow, I went to the well to___ wash my toe; When I came home, one chick-en was gone! Oh, Chick-a-ma, Chick-a-ma Crane - y Crow!

From Berg, Burns, Hooley, Pace, and Wolverton, Music for Young Americans, *Kindergarten Book*. American Book Company. Used by permission.

Such simple enrichment of songs can be quite worthwhile both at the intermediate and at the primary level. Although the techniques are essentially the same, the older pupils are more interested in the effects produced than in the use of the instruments for their own sake. A song such as "Down the Stream" (see page 80) can be enhanced by the sounding of a single drum on the first beat of each measure. To maintain the feeling of dignity and wonder expressed in this song, the drummer should start softly and crescendo to the third phrase of the song. A diminuendo toward the end, letting the drum continue fading away for two measures after the voices conclude, will add to the dramatic effect.

Simple instruments should be used as an enrichment in the singing program at all grade levels. The teacher must be sure, however, that each song has its own intrinsic appeal and is not selected if its sole merit is that it offers an opportunity to introduce the instruments.

## A STUDY OF THE ELEMENTS OF RHYTHM

The use of instruments in the singing program should lead to a study of the basic elements of rhythm. In addition to the metric beat the position of the accent beat within the metric framework is studied by older children. Special rhythm patterns can be discovered and studied in relation to the rhythm of the melody as a whole.

### The Metric Beat and the Melody Rhythm

The essential concept to be developed in this study is that the durational values of tones in the melody line are related to the basic metric framework that underlies the melody. The metric beat is ongoing at a certain tempo and in a particular pattern of pulses, that is, groups of two or groups of three beats (see meter signatures, $\frac{2}{4}$, $\frac{3}{4}$, etc., Appendix A–I).

Sometimes a melody consists of short rhythm patterns that are repeated; in contrast, another melody may be long-lined and more smooth-flowing in character. If children are to understand rhythmic notation, their experiences should be designed to point up the varying relationships of melody rhythm and metric beat.

The rhythm instruments are especially appropriate for this study because they are easy to play, and when instruments with contrasting sounds are used, the different aspects of rhythm are clearly defined.

Experience in playing the metric beat should first be related to bodily movement such as walking or marching, which would be appropriate for "Yankee Doodle."

RHYTHM
INSTRUMENTS
IN THE STUDY
OF MUSIC

**105**

## YANKEE DOODLE

*Briskly*                                           *Traditional*

During kindergarten, first grade, and second grade, children should have much experience playing this "steady beat." As they march and sound the steady beat on rhythm instruments younger children can say

"ta,   ta,   ta,   ta."

to identify the beat. Older children who are beginning to know the meaning of the meter signature can count the beat by saying

"one, two, one, two."

They can learn that the beat is consistent and ongoing; some will need a longer time than others to develop this understanding and the skill to play rhythm sticks, drum, or sandblocks freely and rhythmically. The following songs have two strong beats per measure and are suitable for such early response:

"Ha, Ha, This-A-Way" (MMYO I–63)

"Little Gray Ponies" (GwM I–36)

"Rig-a-Jig-Jig" (ExM II–20)

"Santy Maloney" (Bir II–11)

"This Old Man" (DMT II–9)

"Toodala" (TiM I–46)

Young children should not attempt to play the rhythm of the melody until they know the words of the song well. In general, the lighter, drier sounds produced by chop sticks or rhythm sticks are preferable for this use. The task for the children is to play the syllabic pattern of the words as they sing.

"Chickama Craney Crow" (see page 104) or any songs of the type listed above, but not used for playing the metric beat, are suitable.

In the early experiences with metric beat and melody rhythm the teacher should keep the techniques separate, never asking the children to respond to both elements in one song. After sufficient skill and understanding have been developed, the teacher can help the children play *both* elements of rhythm on the same song with different sounding rhythm instruments. During the second grade most children are able to maintain sufficient concentration to play *at will* either the metric beat or the rhythm of the melody.

From the second or third grade upward pupils will be ready to study the relationship between these elements of rhythm. To demonstrate the relationship between the metric beat and the melody rhythm in "Yankee Doodle" or any other strongly rhythmic song, the teacher might follow this procedure:

1. Have one instrument, perhaps rhythm sticks, play the steady metric beat as the children sing the song.
2. Sing again, this time having chop sticks sound the melody rhythm.
3. A third time establish the metric beat with the rhythm sticks (be sure it is going well), then have the singers and those playing the chop sticks add the melody rhythm.
4. Repeat the process and urge the children to listen to both sounds. If the children playing the chop sticks know the melody rhythm well, perhaps those singing can merely whisper the words so that the two elements of rhythm can be heard more easily.

Songs that have strong rhythms, such as marches and dance tunes, are best for such rhythm study. It would be entirely inappropriate to accompany a lullaby or an art song with rhythm instruments. We must not lose sight of the fact that music is expressive and that it must always be studied in ways that will help the children feel its message.

Rhythmic song-chants are studies in the relationship of metric beat and word rhythm patterns. Primitive chants, such as those of the American Indian, lend themselves to interesting uses of rattles and drums. The primitive use of rhythm instruments is startling and dynamic. If possible, the pupils should hear recordings of such chants and songs. *The Columbia World Library of Folk and Primitive Music*[4] and *Folkways*[5] recordings are excellent sources for ethnic music. The following songs can be quite authentically combined with instruments:

"Breezes are Blowing" (MMYO III–105)
"Corn Grinding Song" (ABC III–35)
"Duck Dance" (DMT III–65)
"Hunting Song" (Bir III–99)
"Magic Feathers" (TiM III–30)
"Navaho Happy Song" (ExM III–34)

The pupils may also explore jingles and short poems to determine how the rhythm of the words is related to the steady beat. "Diddle, Diddle Dumpling" begins on the strong beat and has a few evenly divided beats:

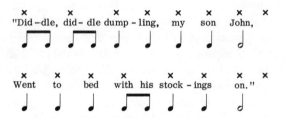

The children can clap the rhythm of the steady beat as they chant the rhyme until they discover that some of the words move right along with the beat and others move twice as fast. Then they should use some system of verbalizing the rhythm. In the first and second grades the system shown here helps children define simple relationships of rhythm and metric beat.

"Did – dle, did – dle dump – ling, my son John,..."

"tah  toh, tah  toh, tah,  tah  tah  tah tah-ah

From the third grade upward, when the children begin to learn the function and meaning of the meter signature, more conventional verbalization of the rhythm should be used:

"Did – dle, did – dle  dump – ling,  my  son  John,..."

One  &  two  &  one, two,  one, two,  one, two..."

This system lends itself to effective verbalization of more intricate rhythms (see Appendix A–I).

Many familiar rhymes fall in compound duple meter [$\frac{6}{8}$] in which there are three parts to each beat. Young children can verbalize such rhymes as follows with "tah" always sounded on the beat [ $\downarrow$.]:

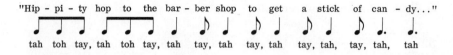

"Hip - pi - ty hop to  the bar - ber shop  to  get  a  stick  of  can - dy..."

tah  toh tay, tah  toh tay,  tah  tay, tah  tay, tah  tay, tah,  tay, tah,  tah

Throughout this book verbalization in the analysis of rhythm is recommended. Children in the intermediate grades should learn to say or think the underlying metric framework for any rhythm they play. In the early primary grades the melody rhythm for any rhythmic song can be played, but only easy rhythms of the type shown above are chanted and studied. From the late third and early fourth grade, depending on the ability of the children, more complex rhythms can be verbalized. Suitable examples at more advanced levels will be shown throughout this chapter.

## Learning Written Notation for Rhythm

After the children respond well to the basic elements of rhythm and understand the relationship between them, the teacher may begin to present rhythmic notation. The following steps, with some variations, are suggested. "The Bridge of Avignon" will serve as an example.

### THE BRIDGE OF AVIGNON

*Gracefully*                                              *French Singing Game*

French: *Sur le pont    d'A -vi - gnon,    L'on-y  dan - se,    L'on-y  dan - se;*
       On the bridge,    A - vi - gnon,    All  are danc - ing,    gai - ly  danc - ing;

       *sur le    pont    d'A - vi - gnon,    L'on-y  dan - se    tout en rond.*
       On the bridge,    A - vi - gnon,    All are  danc - ing    in  a  ring.

1. The class sings the song with a previously developed instrumental accompaniment, rhythm sticks on the metric beat and sandblocks playing the melody rhythm.
2. The child playing the metric beat is asked to continue as the other children chant the beat using the syllable "tah." The teacher makes short vertical lines on the chalkboard to represent the beats:

   |        |        |        |
   tah     tah     tah     tah

3. The children then sing the first two measures of the song as a child plays the sandblocks on the rhythm of the melody and the teacher points to the beat marks on the chalkboard. They discover that sometimes there are two syllables to each beat, so the teacher adds another vertical line and links the two together within the space of one beat:

   ⌐¬ |    ⌐¬ |
   tah toh tah    tah toh tah

4. The children then chant the rhythm using the syllable "tah" on the beat and "toh" on the second part of the beat when necessary. The teacher can add note heads to the rhythm pattern and later put it on a piece of tagboard to be identified by the children at another time.

The teacher should help the children learn to recognize short rhythm patterns for many songs using combinations of quarter and eighth notes early in the second grade. As suggested on page 108 the rhythm of childhood rhymes can be chanted using rhythm syllables somewhat earlier than the notation is used. In the late second grade or in the third grade children who have had consistent rhythmic training of this kind can write out rhythm patterns independently and may combine this skill with melody writing as described in Chapter Five, page 146.

**109**

When the children are secure in their use of rhythm patterns having even divisions of the beat as in $\frac{2}{4}$, $\frac{3}{4}$, or $\frac{4}{4}$ meter, they may begin to see and use simple rhythm patterns with uneven divisions of the beat as in $\frac{6}{8}$ meter.

### RIG-A-JIG-JIG

*Lively*                                                                                                      *Singing Game*

As I was walk - ing down the street, Heigh - o, heigh - o, heigh - o, heigh - o, A pret - ty girl I chanced to meet, Heigh - o, heigh - o,___ heigh - o. Rig - a - jig - jig, and a way we go, A - way we go, a - way we go; Rig - a - jig - jig, and a - way we go, Heigh - o, heigh - o,___ heigh - o.___

From *Singing Together* of Our Singing World Series, Enlarged Edition. Used by permission of Ginn and Company, owner of the copyright.

In a study of the rhythm of "Rig-a-Jig-Jig" the teacher might begin with the refrain. Ask some children to sound the rhythm sticks on the metric beat as shown by the X-marks and ask others to sound the rhythm of the melody using sandblocks. The children can discover that sometimes there are three strokes of the melody for each beat and at other times there are a long stroke and a short stroke for each beat. The system of rhythmic verbalization will be enlarged to allow its application to such rhythm patterns:

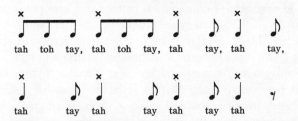

tah toh tay, tah toh tay, tah tay, tah tay,

tah tay tah tay tah tay tah

Other well-known songs in $\frac{6}{8}$ meter that are suitable for such early rhythmic study by second and third graders are these:

"Calico Pie" (ExM II–34)  "Looby Loo" (ABC II–30)
"Follow Me" (GwM II–30)  "The Dairy Maids" (DMT II–45)
"Lazy Mary" (Bir II–27)  "The Darby Ram" (TiM II–126)

At several stages in the program of rhythm study, the children may be encouraged to create original rhythm patterns. Echo clapping, wherein the teacher or a pupil claps a short rhythm pattern and others imitate, can be a useful means of developing rhythmic freedom and skill.

The teacher should (1) establish the speed of the metric beat, (2) clap the pattern, and (3) have the children clap it as an immediate echo, at the same time chanting the rhythm as shown above. Many exercises of this kind are shown in *Music for Children, I—Pentatonic,*[6] pages 53 to 55, "Rhythms for Imitation."

Second and third grade children can learn to clap or use rhythm instruments to play "question-and-answer" rhythm games with the teacher or another child. The leader should set the tempo and help the children feel the beat over which a rhythmic "answer" would be improvised by a child immediately after hearing the rhythmic "question." There should be no break in the rhythm between "question" and "answer" and both should be the same length:

*Music for Children, I—Pentatonic,* page 74, gives examples of rhythm canons that can be undertaken when greater rhythmic skill has been developed. In a canon the second part enters a measure or two after the leader and sounds the rhythm he heard in the first pattern as he listens to the rhythm he will sound in the following pattern. Needless to say this procedure requires that children develop memory for rhythm and the ability to listen for one pattern as they clap another.

RHYTHM
INSTRUMENTS
IN THE STUDY
OF MUSIC

## Playing the Accent

Another kind of rhythmic response that can be used in rhythm ensembles and in another phase of the study of rhythm is the sounding of the accent in the underlying meter of a song. Playing a rhythm instrument on the accented beat is appropriate for "This Old Man," a song in which marching or playing the metric beat intensifies the feeling for the natural rhythm. Playing the accent is a technique that should be developed after the children have learned to respond with ease to the metric beat and the melody rhythm (usually sometime during the second grade).

### THIS OLD MAN

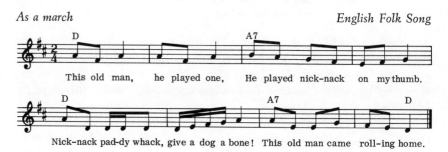

*As a march*                                    *English Folk Song*

This old man, he played one, He played nick-nack on my thumb.

Nick-nack pad-dy whack, give a dog a bone! This old man came roll-ing home.

In developing an understanding of accent, it is well to work from the metric beat. A few of the children can play the metric beat on the rhythm sticks, counting with the beat, "one two one two" (instead of "tah tah tah tah"), while the class sings the song. Following this, the drummer is instructed to play only the "ones." The counting helps him to find the accent; if he has no difficulty, counting aloud soon may be dispensed with. To help children clap or play on the accent have them move the hand or drumstick rhythmically in the opposite direction on the unsounded beat. Thus their total response is rhythmic and following the meter; yet if they count silently they will sound only the proper beat. Other rhythmic songs that are appropriate for the early study of the accent are these:

*Songs in duple meter:*

"Angel Band" (ExM II–6)
"Paw-Paw Patch" (see page 75)
"Rig-a-Jig-Jig" (see page 110)
"Ring around a Rosy" (see page 138)
"Santy Maloney" (see page 70)
"Skip to My Lou" (MoM II–152)

*Songs in triple meter:*

"Circle Around" (GwM II–17)
"Du, Du Liegst Mir im Herzen" (see page 78)
"El Coquí" (TiM II–29)
"En Cadiz" (MMYO II–75)
"I'm Learning to Dance" (Bir II–47)
"My Father" (DMT II–35)

At this stage, the children speak of rhythms that swing in "twos" or "threes." They know this because they have learned to listen and respond to meter rather than because they have been drilled on the meaning of meter signatures. After children have had much experience playing the metric beat and accent combination, the teacher should show them that when the music "swings in twos" the meter signature is $\frac{2}{4}$. The point of observation is only that the upper number in $\frac{2}{4}$, $\frac{3}{4}$, or $\frac{4}{4}$ shows how the music "swings" and how often the accent occurs. The pupils should have much experience with $\frac{6}{8}$ meter, as one that "swings in twos." During this period of study rhythms in this meter can be verbalized

"1 lay lay, 2 lay lay."

In some elementary music texts nonfractional markings for the meter signatures are used:

4    or    3    or    2

These are much more meaningful to young children and convey the same intent as standard meter signatures.

We must stress the point that the earliest experiences in rhythm analysis of any kind should be aural rather than visual. Children first feel, hear, and learn to respond to the separate elements of rhythm; then they listen for a combination of two or three of the elements and learn to play any of them at will. Most third grade pupils readily learn to play the melody rhythm, metric beat, or accent at will if they have had, in the first and second grades, extensive experience using the instruments as song enrichments to play one element at a time. If children in the intermediate grades do not have understanding and skill enabling them to play any of these elements at will the teacher will find many good marching and dancing songs that will lend themselves to such a study.

## Playing Afterbeats

After they have had much experience with such elemental rhythmic responses, intermediate grade boys and girls may begin to clap and play the afterbeats, a common form of rhythmic participation in reels and dance songs. "Sandy Land" is a relatively simple song that may be treated in this manner.

### SANDY LAND

*Lively*        *American Singing Game*

Make my liv-ing in Sand-y Land, Make my liv-ing in Sand-y Land,

Make my liv-ing in Sand-y Land, La-dies, fare you well.

In order to play the afterbeat successfully, the children must hear and feel the downbeat. Often the spectators at a square dance tap a foot on the downbeat and clap on the afterbeat.

The ability to play afterbeats successfully will strengthen the students' preparation to play more complicated syncopated patterns. Children can learn to play afterbeats at a moderate tempo and then increase the speed as demanded by the dance. To maintain continuous rhythmic movement, let the hands move outward on the downbeat. If instruments are used, a deeper-sounding instrument can be played on the accent and one with a short, dry sound on the afterbeats.

In ¾ meter the accent may be played on one instrument and the two after-beats on a different instrument as in "Du, Du Liegst Mir im Herzen" (see page 78).

Play a deep-toned drum on the accent and a higher-toned drum or tone block on the second and third beats of each measure. To sustain the dotted half notes, rap on the first beat and shake the tambourine on the second and third beats. In the early experiences with such a pattern it may be necessary for fourth grade children first to play the continuous metric beat in combination with the accent and then *count* but do not *sound* the "ones" as they learn to play "two-three" as afterbeats.

## Playing Repeated Rhythm Patterns

Playing the melody rhythm of a song sometimes can lead to the discovery of rhythm patterns which may then be played as repeated patterns (ostinati) in a rhythm instrument accompaniment. The stanza of "The Bridge of Avignon" (see page 109) contains two rhythm patterns:

Different students might alternately play the two patterns on different instruments as they occur in the song (sandblocks and chop sticks would be good choices). A drum sounding the accent would give added depth and unity to such an accompaniment. Then either of the patterns could be played repeatedly, as a rhythmic ostinato in the rhythm ensemble accompanying the singing.

Often a single specialized rhythm pattern provides a very suitable accompaniment for a song. Such a pattern is not selected arbitrarily, but is integral to the rhythmic scheme of the song for which it is suggested. For example, in "Rig-a-Jig-Jig" (see page 110) coconut shells can be played throughout the song in the galloping rhythm:

This is a more advanced use of the instruments, for the player sometimes must respond independently of the melody rhythm that is heard in the song. Some third graders may be able to play such a pattern. This kind of rhythmic response can be a frequent activity in the fourth grade and above. If such a rhythm pattern is played as an introduction for two measures before the singing begins, the player will establish a security that will permit him to continue it more successfully throughout the song. The repetitive playing of a single pattern found in the song may serve as an accompaniment for songs such as these:

"Mister Banjo" (ABC III–97):

"Down the River" (DMT IV–48):

"John Robertson" (Bir IV–34):

"The Kicking Mule" (TiM IV–37):

Folk songs from Italy, Spain, and central Europe make interesting uses of rhythm. Latin-American songs are filled with the uneven dotted rhythm patterns of the habanera and the syncopated patterns of the tango:

At first such special rhythm patterns are experienced as they are found in the melody of the song. The words of a song such as "Tinga Layo" support the pattern and make it possible for the students to play it.

# TINGA LAYO

*With an easy swing*

*Calypso Song from the West Indies*

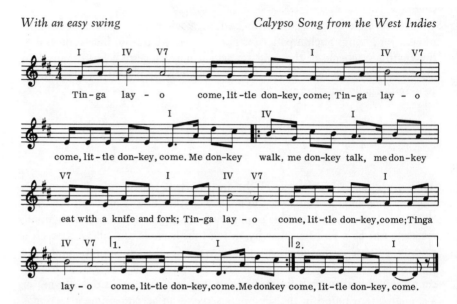

Tin-ga lay-o come, lit-tle don-key, come; Tin-ga lay-o
come, lit-tle don-key, come. Me don-key walk, me don-key talk, me don-key
eat with a knife and fork; Tin-ga lay-o come, lit-tle don-key, come; Tinga
lay-o come, lit-tle don-key, come. Me donkey come, lit-tle don-key, come.

From *Calypso Songs of the West Indies* by Patterson and Belasco. Copyright 1943 by M. Baron Company. Used by permission.

As the children learn this song, they may accompany it with bongo and conga drums, claves, and maracas. At first the claves might be played on the metric beat and the conga drum on the accent. As the melody becomes familiar, bongos and maracas may be used to play the melody rhythm, and a shake of the maracas can be used to sustain the half notes. After this is successfully carried out, the teacher should help the children discover and isolate the typical rhythm patterns. These may be placed on a chart or chalkboard for observation. The particular characteristics of the rhythm patterns are brought out by being played against the metric beat, which is sounded on another instrument:

**CHAPTER FOUR**

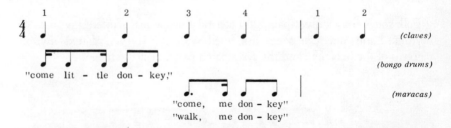

These patterns may then be chanted with rhythm syllables and played continuously over and over, one on the bongo drums and the other on the maracas as the song is sung. A conga drum may be added on the accents or played continuously in the pattern shown below. Such an accompaniment could be worked out by fifth or sixth graders.

**116**

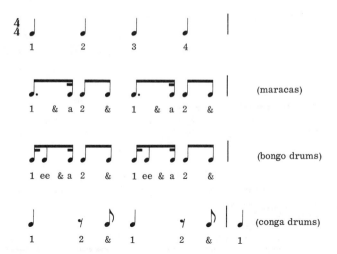

(maracas)

(bongo drums)

(conga drums)

Most intermediate pupils need many simple experiences before they are ready to play continuous complex patterns. Playing one pattern at a time will suffice in the early stages. Rhythm instruments can provide introductions and codas as well as accompaniments. Combinations of the accent, metric beat, afterbeats, or specialized rhythmic patterns from the melody may be used. Specific suggestions for introductions and codas are made in many of the basic music books.

At the fifth and sixth grade level pupils should be given a practical method for reading more complicated rhythm notation. In order to help children organize their concepts of rhythm the teacher can make charts such as the following in which the beat is divided into as many as four parts with a different syllable for each part.

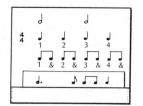  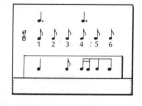

When an analysis of a particular rhythm pattern is desired, the notes (properly spaced) can be written on a strip of chart paper and inserted in a pocket below the charted metric beats and their subdivisions. After establishing the beat and chanting the rhythm (1 & 2 &, etc.), the pupils can easily determine the rhythm of the pattern. When such a procedure for rhythmic analysis is used consistently in the intermediate grades, sixth grade children will have some dependable means of working out rhythm patterns without the teacher's help.

There is need for three forms of rhythm verbalization for ⁶⁄₈ meter, which is used in many nursery rhymes and children's songs.

1. In the primary grades a verbalization related to that used for simple duple meter is recommended:

2. When fast ⁶⁄₈ is encountered and the meter is clearly duple the "one-two" can be counted by older students in a manner related to that used for simple duple meter:

3. In slow ⁶⁄₈ where some of the eighth notes are divided intermediate grade pupils find it useful to know how to count this meter in six beats with the secondary accent on the fourth beat:

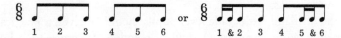

Although the system of rhythm analysis and counting recommended in this book has been in use for many years, other systems can be used. A discussion of the problem will be found in "How to Think Rhythm" by Otto Miessner.[7] The 1-&-2-& system recommended in this book makes possible the analysis of rhythm at a level that meets the general needs of most adults if the teacher is consistently accurate in his subdivision of the beat. Some teachers use common words such as

as reminders of common rhythm patterns. Such a system breaks down when people give different stress to different syllables in the words, and it does not show the relationship of one rhythm pattern to another as does the ♪♪ ♪♪ system.

After pupils have had considerable experience, they may wish to create their own interesting rhythm combinations using two, three, or four different instruments. Early experiences should be with simple ²⁄₄ or ³⁄₄ meter. Later more advanced combinations may be created:

1. Establish the metric beat with the claves

$\begin{smallmatrix}4\\4\end{smallmatrix}$

2. Add a habanera rhythm with the maracas

1   2 & 3   4   1   2 &

3. Furnish an accent with the congo drum

4. Top it all with a lively bongo pattern

1 & 2 & 3 & a 4 &   1 & 2 &

The film "Percussion, the Pulse of Music"[8] is excellent to show in the intermediate grades as an introduction to improvisatory use of rhythm instruments.

## THE STUDY OF MUSICAL FORM AND INSTRUMENTATION

In working out instrumental accompaniments for their songs, children learn to listen and to analyze in order to reflect the particular qualities of the music in their playing. It is but a short step from the more advanced work in enriching songs to the creation of rhythm orchestrations for recorded music. Children can learn to listen for contrasting sections in the recorded instrumentation that suggest changes in the rhythm orchestration. An understanding of the tone qualities of the rhythm instruments, skill in playing them, and skill in responding to the elements of rhythm are necessary before this more advanced work is undertaken.

### Old and New Concepts of the Rhythm Ensemble

Up to this point the "rhythm band," which in the past has been such an important activity in kindergarten and first grade, has not been discussed. If one considers the musical objectives that are to be achieved through the use of rhythm instruments, and the type of activity needed to achieve those objectives, it can be seen that the kindergarten or first grade is too early for beneficial *mass* use of the instruments. In the traditional rhythm band, promoted at this early age, we see practices that are in direct opposition to the approach to rhythm instruments recommended in the early pages of this chapter.

1. Young children are individualists who have not yet learned to work together. To put a rhythm instrument into the hands of every child is to promote indiscriminate sound-making rather than to develop sensitivity to the tone quality of the various instruments.
2. In a rhythm band the children are required to learn *how* to play the instruments at the same time that they learn *when* to play them in the orchestration.
3. When an orchestration is predetermined by the teacher, as it must be at

this level, the children must learn the various parts by rote. Their response is not prompted by an understanding of the elements of rhythm and musical form.

4. While the project may strengthen the children's automatic response to certain elements of rhythm, bodily movement is a much more effective way to develop such response.

5. Generally, only a few especially talented children are ready at this age to participate in the rhythm band. Their talents are exploited and "stars" are developed while the majority of the children have little opportunity to benefit as they would have in a more educational rhythm instrument program.

There is a place for an organized ensemble of rhythm instruments from about the third grade level upward. Rather than using a predetermined orchestration, children of this age can work out their own arrangements on the basis of their understanding of rhythm and their skill in the use of the instruments. Out of experience in arranging comes an understanding of musical form and instrumentation, along with further experience in discriminating listening.

Early emphasis can be given to the importance of listening for changes in instrumentation by working with a composition such as the first section of "March Past of the Kitchen Utensils" from *The Wasps* by Vaughan Williams (A in M III–1). Throughout this section a deliberate marching accompaniment is carried by the bass instruments. This could be played in the rhythm orchestra by selected drums. The accent at the end of each of the five eight-measure phrases in this section of the composition suggests a bold crash of cymbals. The instrumental contrast is in the melody, which is carried alternately by trumpet and piccolo (a), and by violins and bassoon (b). To reflect this change in instrumentation (a, b, a, b, a) the children should select different rhythm instruments. The brassy quality of the trumpet might be suggested by finger cymbals on the melody rhythm and triangles on the accents of each measure. In contrast, the violin-bassoon sections might suggest the use of drier sounds such as rhythm sticks or tone blocks.

Other compositions that might be used in an initial study of instrumentation and musical form are these:

"Air Gai" from *Iphigenia in Aulis*, Gluck (A in M I–1)
"March" from *Soirées Musicales*, Rossini-Britten (A in M I–1)
"Marche Militaire," Schubert (BOL #54)

"Polka" from *Mlle. Angot Suite*, Lecocq (BOL #53)
"Village Dance," Liadov (BOL #53)

## Working Out an Orchestration

Once the children understand how the rhythm instrument arrangement should change with the form, instrumentation, and character of the music, more advanced work can be undertaken. The orchestration is not pre-planned by the teacher, but he must be so well acquainted with the music that he is able to guide the children as they make observations and determine their orchestration.

As a study in musical form, the entire composition, "March Past of the Kitchen Utensils," might be used. (The *Teacher's Guide*[9] to the ADVENTURES IN MUSIC record series will be a great aid to the teacher in analyzing the music.) The composition has three large sections which can be labeled ABA. Within the first A (as described above) there are five eight-measure phrases, each further divided into two parts. The latter A is similar, but with only three eight-measure phrases. Section B is a sharp contrast in rhythm, mood, and use of instruments. It has five phrases, each only four measures long.

To label the sections in the composition and to remember what instruments are selected to play the different parts, the teacher and pupils should, as a result of their listening, discussion, and experimentation, develop on the chalkboard an outline such as the following.

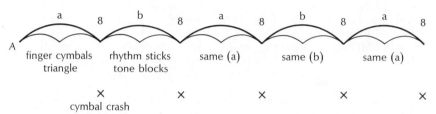

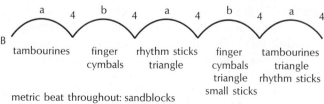

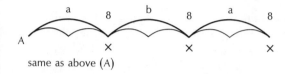

Making one orchestration may take three or more periods of work. During the first session in which the composition is heard, its general form is sketched out, and perhaps a rough idea of the orchestration for the first section is developed. Between lessons, some students who are particularly interested may give some thought to the project. If the music is recorded and a record player with headsets is available, individuals may hear the music several times and be prepared to make recommendations at the next lesson.

The composition chosen for rhythm orchestration must be appealing as a piece of music in itself and yet be suitable for the particular class to work with competently. Its rhythmic characteristics must be appropriate for use with rhythm instruments. The rhythm of some compositions is too intricate, or there are syncopated passages and such rapid fragmentary figures that children are not able to play them. Compositions with interwoven contrapuntal lines do not lend themselves to this use. The addition of rhythm instruments is entirely incompatible with many compositions having slow, smooth-flowing melodic lines.

The following compositions will provide worthwhile musical experiences and may lead to some very interesting rhythm orchestrations:

"Can-Can" from *Mlle. Angot Suite,* Lecocq (BOL #56)
"Dance of the Comedians" from *The Bartered Bride,* Smetana (BOL #56)
"Marche Militaire," Schubert (BOL #54)
"Petite Ballerina" from *Ballet Suite No. 1,* Shostakovich (A in M II–1)
"Tambourin" from *Céphale et Procris,* Grétry (A in M II–1)
"Viennese Musical Clock" from *Háry János,* Kodály (A in M II–1)

A creative project, designed to develop musical taste and discrimination, cannot be imposed on the pupils; it must be guided so that experience in the activity itself is the real teacher. Good judgment on the part of the teacher is essential. At one extreme, too many instruments may be played so loudly and poorly that the result is very unmusical. At the other, the teacher may be so sensitive about tone quality and volume that the children are given no freedom to explore the sound possibilities for themselves. The instruments should never be played so loudly that they obscure the recorded music. A dynamic balance can be found between recording and instruments that permits a sense of freedom in playing.

The instruments suggested at the beginning of this chapter provide a reasonably well-balanced ensemble. Not all of the children need to play instruments at the same time. Emphasis should be on the music and on the appropriate orchestration created rather than on the mass playing of instruments. Pupils should take turns so that everyone will have an opportunity to play the various instruments.

Listening to the music, discussing the form and notating on the chalkboard the possible uses of instruments, trying out each idea to hear the effect, and deciding upon the orchestration to be adopted are the important activities. As in any other creative session, the teacher needs to be skillful in developing the chain of ideas so that many pupils contribute suggestions and participate in the experimentation. The great difference between the program suggested here and that of the old school "rhythm band" is one of musical and creative values. If the music is appropriate and worthwhile, if the approach is exploratory and furthers the understanding of musical concepts, then ensemble playing of rhythm instruments can be a valuable experience.

## Composers' Use of Rhythmic Effects

Some composers have made continuous specialized rhythm patterns a basic ingredient in orchestral compositions. Children can play these rhythm patterns with the recorded music even when the development of a rhythm orchestration is not an objective. "Spanish Dance No. 1" from *La Vida Breve* by Falla (A in M VI–1) has castanets as an outstanding percussion instrument. Sixth grade students may play these rhythm patterns throughout much of the composition:

If castanets are not available or if the playing technique is not sufficiently developed, pupils may play the pattern on claves, with alternating hands on the knees or on dry-sounding drums.

"Bolero" by Ravel has the following rhythm patterns which are easily heard:

The upper pattern can be played on high and low drums. Since the lower pattern moves very rapidly, pupils will be more successful if they use maracas or bongo drums so that both hands may be used alternately.

Throughout the "Habanera" from *Carmen* by Bizet, "Jamaican Rumba" by Benjamin (BOL #56), and "Grand Walkaround" from *Cakewalk Ballet Suite* by Gottschalk-Kay (A in M V–1), the habanera rhythm pattern can be played almost continuously:

"Aragonaise" from *Carmen* can be accompanied by these patterns:

"Ritual Fire Dance" by Falla is brilliant and exciting. Pupils need to direct their attention to basic rhythms in order to play the following patterns with different toned drums. Experimentation for appropriate tone quality and dynamic level is important.

Haydn's *Symphony No. 101* is titled "Clock" because the second movement, Andante, has a clock-like effect produced by the pizzicato rhythm of the lower strings and bassoons. Likewise, *Symphony No. 8* by Beethoven (A in M VI–1 or BOL #71) has in the second movement a metronomic rhythm which may be played on tone blocks or rhythm sticks.

Other compositions may be used but the basic rhythm patterns must be obvious and continuous enough to permit the children to hear and play them with satisfaction. Pupils should not only direct their attention to the basic rhythm, but should hear the melodic flow and improvisation above it. Through this activity the pupils become acquainted with some of the world's most colorful music.

Here is a means of exploring music that will appeal to all, if intelligent guidance goes with it. The instruments provide a convenient way to point up rhythm in the music. However, from the beginning and throughout, they must serve as an enjoyable means of experiencing music. If the technical studies become so pedantic or overemphasized that the expressive factors are beat right out of the music, then the project is in vain.

The use of rhythm instruments quite often is very successfully established in the primary grades. It can only be hoped that more intermediate classes may be given an opportunity to explore these interesting musical activities. The teacher must continually draw rhythm to the attention of the pupils. They should learn to create and to respond to increasingly complex patterns. They must learn the music symbols which represent rhythm. Consistent use of chalkboard, charts, and flannel board is necessary to show the relationship of metric beat, accent, and rhythm patterns. Gradually the approach must be shifted from explanation and the development of concepts about such symbols to the interpretation of them as they are met in new musical material. Only then will the students begin to be independent music makers.

## ACTIVITIES FOR COLLEGE CLASSES

A. Questions for Review
  1. What quality and types of rhythm instruments are recommended for use in the kindergarten and the primary grades? In the intermediate grades?

2. Describe the early informal uses that can be made of rhythm instruments in the study of music.
3. Describe how rhythm instruments are used in a study of the elements of rhythm.
4. Describe how rhythm instruments can be used in a study of musical form and instrumentation.

B. Written Assignments
   1. Find songs to exemplify the several ways in which rhythm instruments may be used at the grade level of your choice. Make brief teaching notes for two songs under each heading cited in questions 2, 3, and 4 above, stating (a) how particular instruments could be used and (b) what concepts in music might be developed through this activity. Cite the source and page number for each song.
   2. Create a rhythm orchestration for one short recorded composition suitable for use at the grade level of your choice. Diagram it and state why you suggest specific instruments for certain effects. What concepts about music might the children in this grade develop as a result of the experience?
   3. Write rhythm notation for (a) the names of four people and (b) two 2-line nursery rhymes.

C. Classroom Projects
   1. Make some basic rhythm instruments outside of class. A drum, rhythm sticks, and sandblocks would be a good beginning. Give careful consideration to the tone quality. Bring the instruments to class so that the instructor and other students may evaluate your results and benefit from your experience.
   2. In a small group, prepare to sing a song and use rhythm instruments as worked out in written assignment No. 1.
   3. Direct the college class in playing the rhythm orchestration worked out under written assignment No. 2, above. Evaluate the results. In what way could you improve the orchestration?

## CHAPTER NOTES

1. Muriel Mandell and Robert E. Wood, *Make Your Own Musical Instruments* (New York: Sterling Publishing Co., Inc., 1957).
2. Bernard S. Mason, *Drums, Tomtoms, Rattles* (New York: A. S. Barnes and Co., Inc., 1938). Out of print, but available in many libraries.
3. Emma Dickson Sheehy, *Children Discover Music and Dance* (New York: Holt, Rinehart & Winston, Inc., 1959), pp. 85–95.
4. *The Columbia World Library of Folk and Primitive Music,* compiled and edited by Alan Lomax (New York: Educational Department, Columbia Records, 799 Seventh Ave., New York, N.Y. 10019).
5. Folkways Records, 121 West 47th St., New York, N.Y. 10036
6. Carl Orff and Gunild Keetman, *Music for Children, I—Pentatonic,* English version adapted by Margaret Murray (Mainz, Germany: B. Schott's Söhne, Edition 4865).

7. Otto Miessner, "How to Think Rhythm," *Music Educators Journal,* June–July 1963.
8. "Percussion, the Pulse of Music," from *Music for Young People* series, National Educational Television, Audio-Visual Center, Indiana University, Bloomington, Ind.
9. *Teacher's Guide to* ADVENTURES IN MUSIC (A New Record Library for Elementary Schools) prepared by Gladys Tipton and Eleanor Tipton, by Radio Corporation of America, 1960.

## Other References

Coleman, Satis, *The Drum Book* (New York: The John Day Co., Inc., 1931).

Morales, Humbert, *Latin American Rhythm Instruments* (New York: H. Adler Publishers Corp., 1954).

Nash, Grace, *Rhythmic Speech Ensembles (Famous Sayings, Lines and Rhymes)* and Teacher's Manual (Scottsdale, Ariz.: G. C. Nash, 1966).

Orff, Carl, and Gunild Keetman, *Music for Children, I—Pentatonic,* English adaptation by Doreen Hall and Arnold Walter (Mainz, Germany: G. Schott's Söhne, 1956; Associated Music Publishers, Inc., N.Y.). See "Studies in Rhythm and Melody," pp. 66–87.

————, *Music for Children* (recording), Angel Records 3582 B.

————, *Music for Children* (film), Contemporary Films, 267 West 25th Street, New York, N.Y. 10001.

See Appendix B–V for listing of companies supplying rhythm instruments.

CHAPTER
FOUR

**126**

# 5

# The Use of Melody and Harmony Instruments

One of the best ways for children to develop understandings about melody and harmony is through playing tuned instruments. These may range from tuned glasses, bells, and small xylophones to the piano and standard orchestral instruments. In early playing experiences it is important that the instruments be of simple construction and demand little skill in playing. Then the freedom to play rhythm on untuned instruments will carry over into the playing of tuned instruments.

Children should do much of their playing in conjunction with the singing program. Instruments can help enrich the singing activities, develop the ability to listen and to discern different pitches and combinations of tones, and promote interest and skill in interpreting simple melodies and tonal patterns from the printed score. In addition, children can be led to create melodies and sound effects through individual as well as group experimentation and study. Children in the intermediate grades can combine melody instruments and singing to produce harmonic effects. The Autoharp also provides an easy approach to harmony.

## THE MELODY INSTRUMENTS

The xylophone and glockenspiel are classed as percussion instruments because they are struck with mallets. They are also called keyboard instruments because the tone bars are arranged in the same order as the piano keyboard. Some of them may be simplified so that only a few tones are used.

Instruments of the xylophone type have wooden tone bars and those of the glockenspiel type are made of metal. The larger sizes are chromatic; that is, they have tone bars representing both black and white keys on the piano, and therefore can be played in any key. Smaller instruments that have only eight or ten tones of the diatonic scale are used in many classrooms.

Very good-sounding school xylophones in both chromatic and diatonic models with adjustable tone bars are available from musical instrument firms in Western Germany.[1,2] Some teachers have successfully made their own xylophones out of hardwood. Detailed instructions for construction are found in special sources such as *Creative Music in the Home*.[3] The distinctive tone quality of the wooden instrument is valuable when ensemble playing is undertaken.

The instruments with metal bars have a bell-like quality. They are most useful in early singing-instrumental work. Sets of diatonic "bells" with fixed tone bars in the key of C have been used in primary classrooms for many years. They consist of eight or ten tone bars sounding an octave above:

West German firms[1,2] produce diatonic glockenspiels of one-and-one-half or two octaves in which the tone bars are removable. When desired, the F and B or other tones may be omitted so that a pentatonic or other limited scale is obtained. Alternate B♭ and F♯ tone bars are supplied with the diatonic instrument so that the keys of F and G major may be used. This expands the playing possibilities of the instrument considerably.

Of all the audio-visual tools available for teaching music notation in the early grades none offers more promise than a staff-lined felt or flannel board with tone bars attached at the left side, directly related to the lines and spaces. Tone bars in this position can be used for playing tonal patterns and phrases from songs as well as for children's independent melody writing.

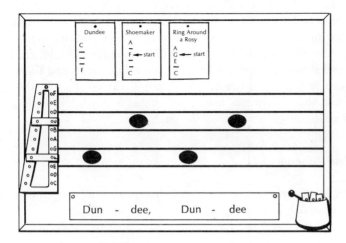

The Glockentürm (bell tower), made by Studio 49,[2] can be used for this purpose, or one of the other adjustable glockenspiels can be bolted to the flannel board. If a rigid flannel board (24″ × 36″) is used it can remain in playing position in a classroom so that children may use it for practice and creative purposes at any time during the day. Throughout this chapter reference will be made to this audio-visual aid for use in the lower grades.

Chromatic glockenspiels, Song Bells or Melody Bells, are used extensively in the intermediate grades. On these instruments the tone bars are arranged in two rows, as on the piano keyboard, and the children can play melodies in any key. In the intermediate grades, when the children have sufficient knowledge and skill to play easily, these are the desirable instruments to use.

Resonator bells are tuned metal bars, each of which is mounted on a separate block of wood. These form the chromatic scale when properly arranged, or they may be rearranged to form any single scale, chord, or selected group of tones. They are more expensive than some other bell types but they are also more versatile. Resonator bells are available in both higher and lower registers. The lower, which corresponds to the singing voice, is generally preferred.

All melody instruments should be correctly tuned because the children must become accustomed to the correct sound relationships of the tones in the scale. Cheap, carelessly tuned toy instruments do not serve the purposes of

**THE USE OF MELODY AND HARMONY INSTRUMENTS**

**131**

music education. Instruments played in combination must be tuned to the same standard of pitch.

Children enjoy playing individual hand-bells, each of which has a handle and may be rung separately. If these are well tuned, they are useful for young children exploring different qualities of tone and pitch relationships. The children may be able to play a few tunes on them, but the instruments having tone bars that are struck with small mallets are easier to play rhythmically, and they have a more direct relationship to the piano keyboard.

Some teachers substitute tuned glasses if other melody instruments are not available. If the glasses ring well and are accurately tuned, their quality is pleasing, quite mellow, and easy to match with the voice. Eight-ounce glasses may be tuned in the key of C; to get the complete scale, smaller glasses should be used for the higher tones. If the glasses are to be played regularly, the water line and correct scale number should be permanently marked on each glass so that the children can keep them in order and fill them correctly. The F and B tuned glasses can have the water line for F♯ and B♭ marked for alternative tuning when needed. Older pupils should share in the scientific experiment that determines how much water is needed in each glass; the more water in the glass, the lower the pitch.

## Song Enrichments

A simple example of the use of bell instruments in early singing experiences is provided in "Hickory, Dickory, Dock."

### HICKORY, DICKORY, DOCK

J. W. Elliott
from Mother Goose

Lively

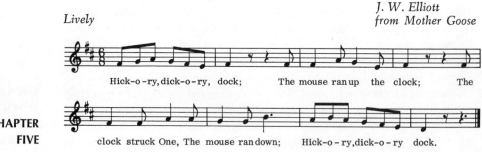

A child may play a glissando up the bells after "the mouse ran up the clock" and a downward glissando at the end of the song. This embellishment will objectify *up* and *down* on the bells. When the instrument is held vertically the children more readily understand the concept of a high pitch as they play toward the top of the bells. Later they should play from low to high in a left-to-right movement as on the piano keyboard.

*Introductions and Codas.* Fragments of melody may be played as introductions or codas (endings) that add interest to the song. These provide experience in playing the instruments and working with specific combinations of tones. As an introduction to "Are You Sleeping?" younger children may sound the key note (F) on the bells a specified number of times to represent the hour that "Brother John" should arise. The same tone may be struck several times as an ending to the song.

### ARE YOU SLEEPING?
### (Frère Jacques)

*Cheerfully*                                                    *French Round*

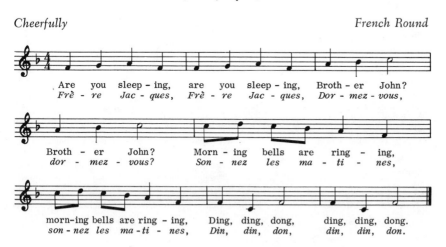

Are you sleep - ing, are you sleep - ing, Broth - er John?
*Frè - re Jac - ques, Frè - re Jac - ques, Dor - mez - vous,*

Broth - er John? Morn - ing bells are ring - ing,
*dor - mez - vous? Son - nez les ma - ti - nes,*

morn-ing bells are ring - ing, Ding, ding, dong, ding, ding, dong.
*son - nez les ma -ti - nes, Din, din, don, din, din, don.*

Older children may create an introduction or a coda by playing the tonic and dominant tones in the pattern found in the last phrase of the song:

The same technique may be used for other songs in which clocks or bells are the topic, such as "Fray Martin" (MMYO K–63) and "The Bells" (DMT I–18).

Imaginative pupils and their teacher can find many things that suggest introductions for songs. Some second and third grade song books suggest introductions, codas, and special effects such as those shown for "White Choral Bells" (DMT II–125), "Goodnight to You All" (GwM II–122), and "Pirate Bold" (TiM II–44). It usually is best to have the introduction end on the note on which the song begins. Unity is provided when the introduction or coda utilizes a melodic idea found in the song itself.

*Tonal Patterns within Songs.* Even in the kindergarten, children should have the experience of playing melodic fragments in songs they know. "Clean Up!" (Bir K–19) has a rhythmic two-tone motive that a child can play with two fingers on the piano, on two resonator bells, or on two bars of the adjustable glockenspiel as others sing. Likewise, in the Scottish folk song "Dundee, Dundee" the interval of a fifth occurs four times and may be played when the children sing that portion of the song (see brackets):

**133**

## DUNDEE, DUNDEE

*Jauntily*                                                                    *Scottish Folk Song*

From Berg, Burns, Hooley, Pace, and Wolverton, MUSIC FOR YOUNG AMERICANS, *Book Two*. American Book Company. Used by permission.

The children should use different levels of the hand to show the low and high pitch level as they sing, and if the tone bars are mounted vertically they can readily see the relationship between low and high on the instrument.

When the adjustable glockenspiel is used and just the necessary tone bars are placed on it, first grade children can play more extensive patterns that they have previously sung, such as the following from "Bye'm Bye" (GwM I–41, ExM II–56).

They do not see the staff notation, but a card attached to the flannel board can show them what tones to use and where to start in playing the pattern:

BYE'M BYE

*Freely*                                        *Texas Folk Song*

Occasionally an entire song is based on a scale line as in "Gretel, Pastetel" (DMT II–50), "Old King Cole" (TiM I–137), or "The Diesel Train" (GwM II–76). As the group sings the song, one child may play this scale in time with the singing. Sometimes a complete phrase within a song moves scalewise and can easily be remembered and played. In "Dundee, Dundee" the four-measure phrase preceding the refrain moves stepwise up and down four tones of the scale. If an adjustable instrument with B♭ is available, five tone bars can be placed on the instrument and this phrase can be played in conjunction with the tone call marked with brackets.

Early song enrichments of this kind should be confined to the scale and to simple patterns that are easily remembered and played rhythmically by the children after they know the song. In the first paragraph of this chapter it was stated that the freedom to play rhythm on untuned instruments carries over into the playing of tuned instruments. It should be pointed out that in order to play a melody accurately and rhythmically a child needs some awareness of the syllabic rhythm of the words upon which the melody is based. When a child plays "Dun-dee, Dun-dee" he plays two different tones on one word; when he plays the word "gos-sip-y" (in the same song) he plays three syllables on one tone. If he has had experience playing the melody

**THE USE OF
MELODY AND
HARMONY
INSTRUMENTS**

**135**

rhythm with chop sticks as outlined in Chapter Four this will be something he understands. Aural awareness is sharpened as children learn to listen for these details.

When the larger chromatic bells or the piano is used, the teacher must mark the tone bars or keys to be played for a particular pattern, or he can make a keyboard diagram to show the position of the tones. The pattern for "Dundee, Dundee" would be shown:

The following considerations are important in regard to group singing with these tuned instruments:
1. The singers should take their pitch from the instruments with which they are going to sing.
2. Very rarely are the bells so tuned that they may be used in combination with a recorded song.
3. Bells are easily covered by the voices. When the entire class participates the children must sing lightly and listen carefully so that they stay in tune.
4. The rhythm of the singers should not be broken by halting performance on the instrument. The teacher can assure rhythmic playing by careful selection of the tone calls and phrases to be played and by the use of adjustable tone bars, resonator bells, or an appropriately marked keyboard.

### Playing Melodies

Children as well as adults enjoy playing familiar melodies. If the teacher is able to remove some of the technical obstacles, children can pursue this activity with continuous satisfaction. It is best to begin with songs having a limited number of notes. There are a few appealing songs with just three tones; other songs use only four or five tones. If resonator bells or other adjustable instruments are available, just the tones in the song may be arranged in the proper order. When the children know the song they can play rhythmically by ear without having to search for the necessary tones.

## THE SHOEMAKER

*Simply*                                                    *Puerto Rican Song*

From Berg, Burns, Hooley, Pace, and Wolverton, MUSIC FOR YOUNG AMERICANS,
*Book Three.* American Book Company. Used by permission.

"The Shoemaker" has just three tones. The teacher, using a 3″ × 5″ card,
can make a chart to show the children the position of the tone bars on the
vertical adjustable glockenspiel (left) or on the resonator bells placed in a
horizontal position (right).

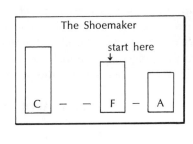

The following songs are among those that can be played easily by first and
second grade children using adjustable tone bars:

*Three-tone songs*

"Hop, Old Squirrel" (TiM I–60)
"Hot Cross Buns" (Bir I–147)
"It's Raining" (ExM I–22)
"Jeremiah, Blow the Fire" (GwM I–35)

*Four-tone songs*

"Berceuse Française" (TiM I–150)
"Bought Me a Cat" (AFlk–104)
"Mary Had a Little Lamb" (MoM K–106)
"Ring around a Rosy" (see page 138)

**THE USE OF
MELODY AND
HARMONY
INSTRUMENTS**

When an adjustable instrument is not available, children must learn the
position of the necessary keys of tone bars in relation to the total keyboard.
This is a keyboard diagram for "The Shoemaker" as found in MUSIC FOR
YOUNG AMERICANS, *Book Three:*

so    do mi
5     1  3

**137**

The use of keyboard instruments in combination with such a diagram is an important step in developing an understanding of tonal relationships as represented on the keyboard. First the child notices the black key combinations in alternating patterns of two and three; then he learns to find a white key "to the left of two black keys" or "to the right between three black keys," etc. Later these positions are related to notes on the staff, and letter identification is established.

The teacher should think in terms of acquainting children with the arrangement of the keys and their relationship to the musical staff rather than of "teaching piano" per se. A functional use of piano and bells, exploring, improvising, and playing known melodies by ear, are valuable activities. A number of the basic music books suggest interesting uses of the keyboard.

*Pentatonic Songs.* Many melodies are based on scales other than the major scale (seven tones) that we hear so often. The pentatonic or five-tone scale is very easy to play. The most common form of the pentatonic is that which corresponds to a major scale with the fourth and seventh scale steps omitted (see Appendix A–IV). Although we often think of it as an oriental scale, it is the basis of many children's chants as well. Music educators in Germany have made extensive use of adjustable keyboard instruments, and have done much work with the pentatonic scale. Simple children's chants that are first sung and then played on five-toned glockenspiels or xylophones provide the early song material for this work. "Ring around a Rosy" is an example of a four-tone chant within the pentatonic scale.

### RING AROUND A ROSY

Steadily                                                    *Children's Singing Game*

Ring a-round a ros - y, A poc-ket full of po - sies,
Ash - es, Ash - es, All fall down!

This song may be played on the black keys of the piano beginning with D♭, or on adjustable bell instruments in which the tones are arranged as shown.

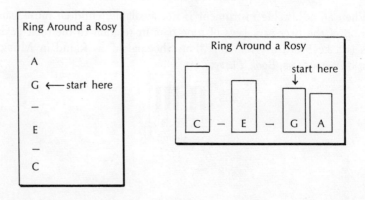

| Ring Around a Rosy |
|---|
| A |
| G ←—start here |
| — |
| E |
| — |
| C |

Ring Around a Rosy

start here
↓

C – E – G A

The following are well-known pentatonic songs that can be used in this way:

"Band of Angels" (TiM I–36)
"Everybody Loves Baby" (MMYO K–95)
"Goodbye, Ol' Paint" (GwM III–16)
"Hoosen Johnny" (MMYO II–84)

"Mary Had a Baby" (Bir I–95)
"Old MacDonald Had a Farm" (TiM III–80)
"The Hole in the Bucket" (MMYO IV–181)

The advantage of using this scale, in addition to the fact that it has a limited number of tones in a particular pattern, is that as children mature they can easily be taught to improvise counterparts for pentatonic songs they know. This technique will be shown later in this chapter.

*Early Uses of Staff Notation.* When children in the second grade can play several three- and four-tone songs on the melody instrument, the teacher can use the flannel board with adjustable tone bars to help them understand staff notation for pitch. The words of a tonal pattern or a phrase from a song that the children know are written on a strip of chart paper and pinned to the bottom of the flannel board (see diagram of "Dundee, Dundee," page 131). Flannel notes are placed on the proper line or space above each syllable of the words and the children are shown how the note represents the tone bar struck and also how it is related to the word below it.

Placing notes on a music staff is similar to using a graph: both the vertical (pitch level) and the horizontal (flow through time) need to be considered. Teachers should take into account both the intellectual and the visual difficulties in this activity and give the children many simple patterns in these early experiences with notation. Two- and three-tone patterns should be used first.

It is desirable that all children become aurally aware of tonal patterns, and the early music training should be designed to promote this development. However, a few individuals may have limited talent in pitch recognition and tonal memory; the *exclusive* use of the aural approach can result in continual insecurity and frustration for these children. Consequently it is important in the second grade to begin to use visual representation for the tonal patterns and phrases that are sung and played. Notation can be used in three ways:

1. Placing notes on the staff to represent tonal patterns and melodies that have already been played and sung (reinforcing an aural experience with a visual representation of pitch).
2. Placing notes on the staff to represent a newly created melody (a music writing activity).
3. Placing notes on the staff and learning a tonal pattern or melody from the notes (a music reading activity).

If the staff-lined flannel board is three feet long, a short phrase as well as tonal patterns can be shown and played on the related tone bars. Songs in which one phrase occurs several times are useful in this work. The first phrase of "Old MacDonald Had a Farm" occurs three times in one stanza. A number of the children might learn to play it on the adjustable tone bars after singing it in connection with the use of hand levels. Other children might for the first time feel secure in playing the melody when they can rely on the notation to guide them.

THE USE OF MELODY AND HARMONY INSTRUMENTS

**139**

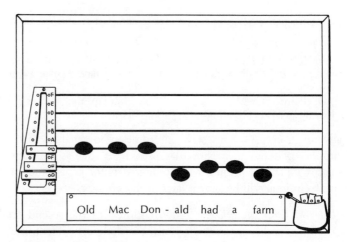

Old Mac Don - ald had a farm

Although in the early study of notation for musical pitch it is not necessary to include rhythm notation (quarter notes, half notes, stems, bar lines, etc.), it is important that phrases and tonal patterns be sung and played rhythmically. The early study of rhythmic notation was described in Chapter Four; representation of melody and pitch can be brought together in staff notation after a great deal of aural experience has been provided and some understanding of the notation of each has been developed separately.

First steps in melody writing, described on page 146, should be developed concurrently with the first and third points on the above outline of activities for learning music notation. When the flannel board with staff-related tone bars is used, second grade children readily learn to make staff notation for the simple tunes they create.

When the children are ready to read musical notation for pitch for the first time the teacher can use a short phrase from a song they have not yet learned. Put the correct notes over the words and the necessary tone bars on the flannel board. "Hush, Little Baby" (see page 192) will serve as an example.

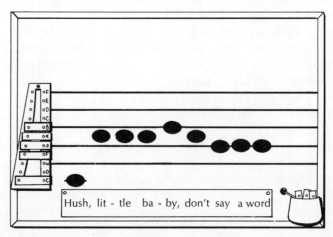

Hush, lit - tle  ba - by, don't say  a word

1. Help the class chant and clap the phrase aloud in the proper rhythm (not too fast).

2. Sound the first note on the tone bar and ask the class to whisper the words and show with hand levels how the tune goes; point to the notes as they do this.
3. Ask one child to play the tune as the others listen and prepare to sing back what he plays if it is correct.
4. Make any necessary corrections in the rhythm and have the class sing the phrase again, using hand levels.
5. Leave the tone bars and notation on the flannel board so that others can practice during their free time.

For other music reading experiences the teacher might put a new melody on the flannel board and ask the children to practice it individually in their free time. During the music lesson some individuals can play it for the class. After the children have had further experience with notation, the teacher might ask a child to transfer a tonal pattern or phrase from a song in his music book to the flannel board; individuals might study and practice it in their free time and the class can then hear, play, and discuss it during the music lesson.

If, in addition to the flannel board with staff-related tone bars, the teacher has resonator bells in the classroom, he can now place them in the music corner for the children's use. In the late second or in the third grade he will find some of the children transferring their music playing skills to these horizontal tone bars. The children do this by referring to the letter names that are printed on both sets of tone bars. When this occurs children are learning an important aspect of music theory as a result of their own musical motivation.

A fundamental idea resulting from research by Jean Piaget on the development of children's thinking is that sensorimotor skills and the intellect are not separated, that the development of concepts in children is continuous with simpler forms of psychological functioning.[4] If this is the case, teachers would be well advised to help children develop concepts of musical pitch, tonal relationships, and flow of melody through the use of tuned instruments and audio-visual aids such as the flannel board which permit children to deal with these elements in a concrete, manipulative way.

*Using Number Notation.* The relationship between tones within a scale is shown by scale numbers or sol-fa syllables. The latter will be discussed in Chapter Seven, but the use of scale numbers has its proper place in connection with the playing of instruments described in this chapter.

Through the use of the adjustable tone bars related to a staff we have seen how children can be led to play melodies directly from musical notation. In this work children readily learn the names of the lines and spaces and learn to use letter names to designate pitch because the tone bars are marked with these letter names. Also important is our musical system of tonality wherein one tone becomes the key center of a group of seven tones. This group may be a major scale or a minor scale (see Appendix A-IV), depending upon the location of whole and half steps within the scale. The use of number notation, in which the key note is designated as "number one" of the scale, can help boys and girls think in terms of scale organization and begin to learn the sound of intervals and chords within a major or a minor scale.

If the flannel board with the staff-related tone bars is not available, a primary teacher will need to make considerable use of number notation as he helps his pupils gain the basic skills in playing melody instruments. Several music series provide material and directions for this work. The diatonic key of C bells, tuned glasses, the adjustable tone bars or resonator bells can be used. The earliest songs played should have an easy rhythm and a predominance of scale movement in the melody:

"Evensong" (GwM II–113)                "Riding in a Sleigh" (TiM I–131)
"Go Tell Aunt Rhodie" (ExM II–105)     "Row Your Boat" (ABC III–44)
"My Little Ducklings" (DMT I–35)       "Twinkle, Twinkle, Little Star" (TiM
                                        II–35)

The following example shows the scale numbers in relation to a song in the key of D:

### GRETEL, PASTETEL

*Cheerily*                                                    *German Folksong*

From DISCOVERING MUSIC TOGETHER, *Book Two,* by Charles Leonhard, Beatrice Perham Krone, Irving Wolfe, and Margaret Fullerton. © 1967 by Follett Publishing Company, Chicago, Illinois.

When the children are provided with number notation for a familiar song, they play partly by ear as well as from the numbers. With the aid of the following notation children can play this song on an adjustable instrument, including tuned glasses, set up in the key of D, or on a fixed diatonic scale in the key of C.

| 1 | | 1 | 1 | | 5 | 5 | 5 | | 6 | 6 | 6 | | 5 - | |
|---|---|---|---|---|---|---|---|---|---|---|---|---|---|---|
| Gret- | | el, | Pas | | tet- | el, | oh | | where | is | your | | goose? | |
| 5 | | 4 | 4 | 4 | | 3 | 3 | 3 | | 2 | 2 | 2 | | 1 - | |
| She | | sits | on | her | | nest, | and | I | | can't | get | her | | loose. | |

If the teacher is using the diatonic key of C bells, number notation can be used with only a few songs. However, when resonator bells, glockenspiel, or tuned glasses with alternate F♯ and B♭ tones are available, scales in the key of G or the key of F can be built, and then number notation can be used successfully for many songs. The pupils will need to know what tone bars are necessary to each key and where the number-one note is located. Charts can be made to serve this purpose:

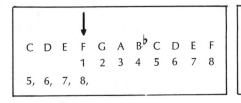
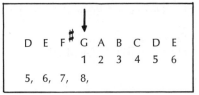

When a song goes below the tonic, a small mark at the base of the number indicates the lower octave.

As they play and replay their favorite songs, the children will memorize the number notation and the intervals in the melody. They should then be encouraged to play the melodies on the piano at school or at home. All that needs to be done for songs in the key of C is to show the children that C, the number-one note, is the white key just to the left of the two black keys in the middle of the piano keyboard.

Keyboard mock-ups showing the letter names of the keys are generally provided inside the back cover of the basic music series from the third grade upward. Such an aid is very useful to children who are motivated to play familiar tunes on the piano.

Third grade children who have had a year or more of experience playing songs on the diatonic tone bars may begin to play the same melodies on the chromatic bells. When a familiar song such as "Baa, Baa, Black Sheep" is played in the key of F the pupil will discover that, in order to play the melody correctly, he must use B♭ for the number-four note.

$\frac{4}{4}$  1   1   5   5   | ⑥ ⑥ ⑥ ⑥ 5  –  | 4   4   3   3   | 2   2   1   –   | etc.

Having this sort of keyboard experience with several songs and learning to hear and sing tonal patterns in their singing activities will prepare third grade children to play simple melodies directly from the staff notation in their books.

**THE USE OF MELODY AND HARMONY INSTRUMENTS**

*Transition to Staff Notation.* In the description of the work with the flannel board and its staff-related tone bars it was shown how natural is the transition to the use of notation to help the pupil play a familiar melody or to learn a new phrase of music. When this audio-visual aid is not available the teacher must make use of scale numbers (or syllables) and keyboard diagrams to effect the transition.

At first tonal patterns and easy phrases are read; later, easy songs are read. Songs in the keys of F and G may be played because the children, as a result of the keyboard experiences described above, will understand the function and necessity for the sharp or flat note. The following are good songs for early reading experiences:

**143**

*In the key of C:*

"Down in the Meadow" (ABC III–45)   "Spring Flowers" (TiM III–70)
"In a Clock Store" (DMT III–34)      "Vesper Hymn" (ExM III–90)
"On St. Paul's Steeple (GwM III–89)  "Walking Song" (GwM III–94)

*In the key of F:*

"For Health and Strength" (ExM III– "I Am a Gay Musician" (TiM III–58)
5)                                   "Why Cats Wash after Eating" (ABC
"Frère Jacques" (MMYO III–5)         III–87)
"Hush My Babe" (GwM III–96)

*In the key of G:*

"Bingo" (DMT III–54)                 "Old Boatsum" (Bir III–11)
"My Burro" (ABC III–116)             "Sur le Pont d'Avignon" (ExM III–
                                     23)

In all of their work with melody instruments the children should have many opportunities to play individually. Learning to play an instrument is a personal thing; a child cannot experiment and learn by doing as the entire class waits and watches. The teacher should provide opportunities for children to practice and improvise on melody instruments privately in the music center.

Number notation may be introduced in the latter part of the first grade or in the second grade. If the flannel board with staff-related tone bars has been used, number notation, representing tones within the scale, can be presented in the third grade; then one or two lessons with a very familiar song will make clear the relationship between the numbers and the scale tones. A few children can follow the teacher's example in relating the number notation to the numbers on the bells. Then they will be ready to practice by themselves during their free time with the bells and the notation set up for them in the music center. If the rubber eraser of a lead pencil is used instead of the wooden mallet, the tone will be so soft that it will not disturb the other children. Periodically the teacher should ask individuals to play for the class the songs they have learned.

CHAPTER
FIVE   **Exploratory and Creative Uses**

In their eagerness to teach "music," teachers should not neglect to let children discover the sound and functional characteristics of tuned instruments. Useful musical insights can be gained by investigations that do not damage the instruments. Children may discover that the instruments made of metal have a more sustained, ringing tone (longer duration) than the xylophones, which are made of wood. They can notice that the longer bars have a lower pitch than the shorter bars on both types of instruments, and that pitches of the strings on the piano, psaltery, Autoharp, and violin are determined by both length and thickness. In tuned glasses the height of the column of water affects the pitch of the tone.

**144**

The piano is a magnificent instrument to investigate, to learn what makes the strings vibrate, how many strings are struck by one hammer, how the high tones sound, how the lowest string rumbles, what the pedals do, etc. Chapter Six, "The Piano," in *Children Discover Music and Dance*[5] gives excellent suggestions of how young children may use the piano in unusual and satisfying ways.

*Early Melodic Improvisation.* In early creative uses of the melody instruments children can work with the two tones, E and G, or the three tones, E, G, A, that provide the basic intervals in their natural chanting songs (see page 177). They can chant and clap short jingles and then play the same rhythm on the selected tone bars, experimenting with different combinations of the available tones.

Chanting choral speech, using rhythm instruments for background and dramatic effects, is valuable preliminary training for improvisation. The recording *Music for Children*,[6] made by children's classes trained in the method developed by Carl Orff and Gunild Keetman, provides excellent examples of this type of rhythmic speech work. Carl Orff has described music that is combined with movement, dance, and speech as "elemental music." He believes that it is "pre-intellectual" and is the appropriate approach to music for children. The article "The Schulwerk—Its Origin and Aims"[7] will provide the student with important orientation for this work.

Some of the principles of the Orff method are utilized with materials that are given in the basic music series THIS IS MUSIC (*Book I*, page 141, *Book II*, page 54) and in GROWING WITH MUSIC (*Book II*, page 86).

In using a short jingle as the basis for rhythmic improvising the children should learn (1) to chant the words and clap the metric beat, (2) to chant the words and tap the syllabic rhythm of the words:

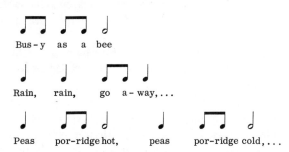

and (3) to tap the syllabic rhythm on the selected tone bars. The freedom to improvise, to hear and to enjoy what one has created, is of great value to the individual. In this work children have an opportunity to combine words and tones in a creative way on a level especially suited to them.

Other easy rhymes to use as a basis for early improvisation are:

Bus-y as a bee

Rain, rain, go a-way,...

Peas por-ridge hot, peas por-ridge cold,...

THE USE OF
MELODY AND
HARMONY
INSTRUMENTS

**145**

As a part of this creative work, the teacher can help children develop skills in the use of the ear, the voice, and tonal memory. When an individual creates a five- or six-tone melody, the class can sing back and show with hand levels the pattern sounded on the melody instrument. When the vertical adjustable tone bars are used, there is a direct relationship between the placement of the tone bars and the hand levels used. This enables other children to replay the melody that has been created.

*First Steps in Melody Writing.*   With the use of the flannel board and the staff-related tone bars, the writing of melodies poses no problems beyond those described in connection with playing tonal patterns and phrases from known and unknown songs (see pages 136–141). When second grade children have had considerable experience improvising on three tones, the teacher can place the words for the chant on a strip of chart paper and pin it to the bottom of the flannel board. One child can create a melody and repeat it as often as necessary while another child places the notes on the proper lines or spaces.

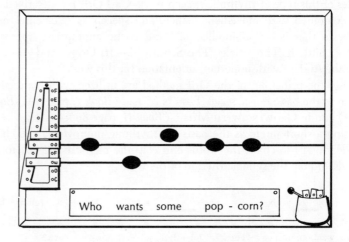

When the flannel board is available for the children to use individually during their free time throughout the day they get a great deal of experience with improvisation and using musical notation. As the children mature in tonal memory, singing skill, and rhythmic response, this work can be expanded in three directions:

1. Use longer chants such as the traditional "Diddle, diddle dumpling, my son John . . . ," the children's own jump-rope chants, "Lollypop, lollypop red and green . . . ," etc. Many examples are given in *Music for Children, I—Pentatonic.*[8]

2. Add a fourth tone (C) and later a fifth tone (D), which completes the pentatonic scale. When more tones are needed add others of the pentatonic scale in a higher octave.

3. Add accompaniments with other instruments: one child may use the pentatonic scale to play a free improvisation (not repeated or necessarily remembered) based on the syllabic rhythm of a longer nursery rhyme. Other children provide an accompaniment by playing selected rhythm

instruments on the metric beat and accent. Later they can use other tuned instruments as accompaniment.

The first stage of independent melody writing should deal only with rhymes in simple duple meter ($\frac{2}{4}$). Several months prior to the first melody writing (found by this author to be most successful in the last half of second grade) children should have had much rhythmic training of the type described in Chapter Four, pages 105–111. Such training will enable them to deal independently with easy rhythms of this kind. After they have succeeded in getting notation for the melody on the flannel board they can copy it onto staff-lined paper and add the necessary notation for the rhythm of the rhyme that was used. Second graders readily see the need for writing notation for the melody lines they create, but it takes longer for them to appreciate the value of notation for rhythm.

This kind of creative melody writing can readily be developed with third graders if they have had the necessary training in rhythm. It is in the third grade that easy drone and ostinato accompaniments for pentatonic melodies can be improvised by the children. Techniques in developing accompaniments for pentatonic songs will be explained in the next section of this chapter and can be studied in depth by referring to the Carl Orff materials previously cited.

The next steps in creative melody writing with the staff-related tone bars are to accustom the children to the placement and sound of other tones in the diatonic scale, and finally to write melodies using a complete scale. In moving toward this objective it is best to continue to use gapped scales so the children will have some visual orientation to help them remember and write the melodies they play. Several weeks of experience with each of the following configurations have been found to be satisfactory:

| B♭ | as in "Hush | D | as in "Bow | C | as in "Bye'm |
| A | Little Baby" (see | — | Belinda" (see | — | Bye" (see |
| G | page 192) | B | page 74) | — | page 135) |
| F | | A | | G | |
| — | | G | | F | |
| — | | F# | | E | |
| C | | — | | D | |
| | | D | | C | |

Following are photographic reproductions of two examples of melody writing out of a collection of 85 which second graders did completely unaided through the use of the flannel board with staff-related tone bars.[9]

Star-light, star bright, First star I've seen to-night;

Wish I may, wish I might Have this wish I wish to-night.

You get a line, and I'll get a pole;

We'll go fish-ing in the craw-dad hole.

*Playing Countermelodies.* As a result of the song-enrichment activities and the development of skill in responding to the elements of rhythm, students from the third grade upward can begin to create and play countermelodies for songs they know. Essentially, these are instrumental parts that go all the way through the song but do not follow the melody itself. Many basic music books show countermelodies, but teachers who understand simple harmony can guide children in creating their own instrumental arrangements.

Rounds are useful for this work because their basic harmony is simple and is repeated in each phrase. The last phrase of "Are You Sleeping?" (see page 133) may be used as a counterpart that is played repeatedly as the song is sung. The following round, "Bells," lends itself to a variety of uses with instruments.

## BELLS

*French Round*
*Words by Vivian Cooper*

*Stately*

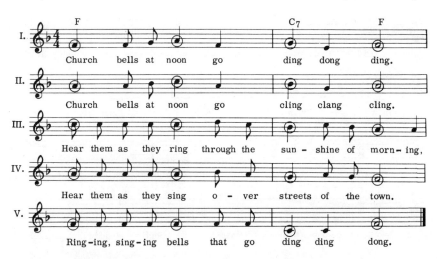

I. Church bells at noon go ding dong ding.

II. Church bells at noon go cling clang cling.

III. Hear them as they ring through the sun - shine of morn- ing,

IV. Hear them as they sing o - ver streets of the town.

V. Ring-ing, sing-ing bells that go ding ding dong.

1. In an early acquaintance with the song one pupil playing the bells can join the singers when the voices arrive at the last phrase.
2. The last phrase may be used as an introduction and continuous counterpart throughout the song.
3. Any one of the two-measure phrases can be played repeatedly as a counterpart while the whole song is sung.
4. If enough melody instruments are available each can be used to play a two-measure pattern repeatedly; build up from one to five parts at two-measure intervals, and then let each instrument drop out in reverse order.
5. Play the encircled first and third beats throughout the song as the "skeleton" of the melody. Notice how all the other notes serve as embellishments to this melodic framework: some function as passing tones (G in first measure); others function as upper neighboring tones (D in fifth measure).

Other rounds may be treated in a similar manner:

"Christmas Greeting" (GwM IV–181)   "Spring Gladness" (see page 250)
"French Cathedrals" (ExM IV–69)     "Why Shouldn't My Goose" (ExM
"Morning Is Come" (Bir IV–62)        IV–97)

Songs based on the pentatonic scale are useful for early experience in the creation of counterparts because almost any combination of the five tones makes an acceptable sound, and improvisation can go on without a knowledge of harmony. In addition to the easy pentatonic songs listed on page 139, "Skye Boat Song" (DMT VI–101) and "Land of the Silver Birch" (ExM III–35) are in this mode.

**THE USE OF MELODY AND HARMONY INSTRUMENTS**

**149**

## LAND OF THE SILVER BIRCH

*Steadily*                                                    *Canadian Folk Song*

Land of the sil-ver birch, home of the bea-ver Where still the
might-y moose wan-ders at will, Blue lake and rock-y shore,
I will re-turn once more. Boom de de boom boom, Boom de de boom boom,
Boom de de boom boom, Boom_____ boom boom._____

From EXPLORING MUSIC, *Book Three,* by Eunice Boardman and Beth Landis. © 1966
by Holt, Rinehart and Winston, Inc. Reprinted by permission of the publisher.

Either of the following patterns might be played repeatedly as a counterpart
for this song.

The Italian term for such persistent, repetitious melodic-rhythmic passages
is *ostinato.* Often the most simple rhythmic basis for an ostinato figure is the
metric beat or a doubling of the metric beat. Note that in the above example
the ostinato consists of patterns taken from the song itself. Other ostinato
patterns may be improvised and played, either above or below the melody,
depending upon the tone quality of the instrument used. The black keys of
the piano or the upper row of the chromatic bells may also be used to
improvise other accompaniment parts if this song is sung one half step higher.

*Playing Drone Accompaniments.* The drone bass or "bourdon" is an
accompanying effect usually associated with bagpipes. It is common in
Scottish folk music and was also used by composers of an early dance, the
musette. For children who have learned to play the accent beat freely, this is
a very easy part to add to songs in the pentatonic mode. "Ring around a Rosy"
(page 138), which uses four tones of a scale built on C, is accompanied by a
drone when the tonic and dominant tones are sounded simultaneously:

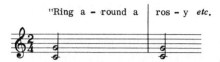

"Ring a - round a | ros - y *etc.*

"Old MacDonald Had a Farm" (page 140) is in the pentatonic scale on G and could have a drone accompaniment using G and D.

It does not require a great deal of equipment to use the techniques outlined here. In addition to an adjustable instrument for playing the melody a teacher should have, first, a low-pitched metal instrument (alto glockenspiel or resonator bells) and, later, a xylophone for the wood tone quality. The following chart shows how seven adjustable tone bars on either instrument can furnish three pentatonic scales for limited accompaniments. The tonic and dominant tones (for use as a drone) are circled in each scale.

|  | C | D | E | F | G | A | B |
|---|---|---|---|---|---|---|---|
| C pentatonic: | Ⓒ | D | E | — | Ⓖ | A | — |
| F pentatonic: | Ⓒ | D | — | Ⓕ | G | A | — |
| G pentatonic: | — | Ⓓ | E | — | Ⓖ | A | B |

Extensive examples of work with the pentatonic are given in *Music for Children, I—Pentatonic*.[8] The system outlined there is based on early rhythmic training, making use of chanting, clapping, patting, and playing rhythm instruments. The development of creative improvisation and the use of contrasting tone qualities in instruments are of paramount importance in the Orff method.

## Recorder-Type Instruments

The recorder or fipple flute is a classic among wind instruments. Made of wood, it has a two-octave range and a pleasing tone. Much music was played on recorders during the Renaissance, and its use in ensemble playing has been revived. Of the several sizes, the soprano recorder is most often used in the elementary music program. Good-sounding recorders for school use now are available.[10]

Instruments similar to the soprano recorder, but molded of plastic and less expensive, have been used for many years in the public schools. The Song Flute and the Tonette are limited in range to a ninth and are quite easy to play.

The teacher who intends to use such instruments in the classroom should learn to play them in order to understand the problems involved and to guide the pupils more effectively. If he can go beyond the plastic instruments and learn to play a recorder, he will be able to enrich the music program further and show the children an avenue for musical exploration which they can enjoy for a lifetime.

The recorder-type instruments, like the keyboard instruments, are useful because they specifically define tonal relationships. When the melody moves along the scale, the fingers move consecutively; when the melody skips a third, two fingers are raised, etc. Keyboard instruments generally are preferred because the child can sing as he plays. However, some benefits can be derived from recorder-type instruments if they are used wisely in conjunction with the singing program.

Recorders, Tonettes, and Song Flutes are often used in the third or fourth grade. Some of the basic music series provide helpful teaching aids for use with these instruments. The following approach will enrich the singing program and will teach children to play the instruments:

1. Teach the children to play selected portions of songs they know and sing well. Their ears then will guide their fingers as they form the pitches on the instruments.

2. It takes considerable finger coordination to cover all of the holes successfully and thus obtain a good-sounding middle C, which is the lowest available tone. This tone is also the hardest to sound in tune. The first melodies played should use only the upper tones of G, A, and B, which can be made with only one hand on the tone holes. As skill is developed, lower tones may be added. (See the progression suggested in *The Elementary Method for the Soprano Recorder*,[11] *Melody Fun*,[12] and THIS IS MUSIC, *Book III*, page 116.) Many basic song books contain melodies or fragments that employ only a few notes; these may be used when the children are learning to sound their instruments.

| | |
|---|---|
| "Grandma Grunts" (GwM IV–14) | "Little Fox" (ExM IV–118) |
| "Haul on the Bowlin'" (Bir IV–115) | "May I?" (GwM III–18) |
| "Jingle Bells" (chorus) (DMT IV–61) | "The Greedy Girl" (ABC IV–21) |

3. When the pupils are able to play some familiar melodies by ear, select simple songs and fragments to be played directly from the notation. Later these songs will become part of the singing as well as the playing repertoire.

4. Combine singing with playing of obbligatos and counterparts found in the song books, and assist the children in working out simple arrangements.

Success in playing an instrument depends on practicing the skills. When a singing-playing program is undertaken, all children in the class should have an opportunity to learn to play simple melodies, but a major portion of the classroom music time should never be given over to drill on technique. Pupils should be so motivated and the work so set up that they will practice and improvise in their free time. An instruction book is helpful in organizing an approach to be used in the classroom and will facilitate individual practice outside of class. Some children will develop greater skill than others and will become the natural leaders in this activity. When the class sings, they will play a melodic accompaniment while others provide harmony on keyboard instruments or the Autoharp. The most interesting, vital classroom music program is achieved when musical activities are intelligently combined.

In combining different instruments, one of the chief problems is that of tuning. Both teacher and pupils must constantly be aware of the fact that *sound* is the important consideration. If instruments that are played together are not tuned to the same standard of pitch, poor musical experiences result. When recorders, Tonettes, or Song Flutes are played in groups by unskilled players, the total intonation may be poor. The problem can be met in part by the use of the same brand of instrument. Further, students must learn to adjust breath pressure to correct the pitch. This skill requires maturity in listening and experience in playing.

Facility in playing a recorder-type instrument can lead directly to the study of the clarinet, flute, or other woodwind instruments, because the basic techniques are similar. However, it is of greater concern to the classroom teacher that, through the use of these instruments, pupils learn to play and sing, to listen, to develop valid musical concepts, to evaluate, and to progress steadily in the ability to enjoy their own music-making as their musical judgment matures.

## The Orchestral Instruments

In many schools children may have instruction on band and orchestral instruments if they wish it. Special instrumental teachers usually carry on this important project, but the classroom teacher is concerned in these ways:

1. He promotes interest and assists in discovering students who have special aptitudes, interests, or needs that would make participation in the program valuable to them.
2. He cooperates in the scheduling of such special classes so that they are carried on with greatest effectiveness and yet do not unduly disturb the working of the classroom.
3. He promotes an outlet for the skills and interests developed in the special instrumental classes.

The attitudes of the classroom teacher have a great influence on the opinions and interests of his students. If the special instrumental program is worth having, it deserves the interest and support of the classroom teacher. He must look upon it as an expanded opportunity for his pupils. Some children have innate musical talent that should be developed; others are superior intellectually, and the challenge of learning to play an instrument may enrich their educational experience. It is not wise, however, to limit this experience to those who are the better scholars, for occasionally a child who has not found satisfaction in his academic studies may succeed in such a music activity.

The special teacher must work during the school day, taking pupils from their classrooms. Instruction is most effective in small classes of homogeneous instruments (strings, brasses, and woodwinds separately). However, since a child's preference in an instrument must be considered, a classroom teacher may have pupils in each group absent from the room at different times.

When the special teacher can teach different groups on different days the classroom teacher can set up a study or activity period so that the absent pupils do not miss some vital subject presentation. Very often, however, a specialist must teach all of the instrumental classes in one school on one day of the week. In such schools the classroom teacher is hard pressed to find enough hours in that day to accomplish his classroom presentations with all students present. However, when the school principal appreciates the value of special music studies, and when the teachers appreciate each other's responsibilities, mutually agreeable solutions can be found.

As students acquire skill in playing their instruments, they should be given opportunities to play in the classroom. The players will not only further acquaint the other children with the standard instruments, but will have an early, sociable use for their skills. Many music books show simple instrumental accompaniments. When accompanying classroom singing, the treble instruments can play descants and obbligatos, and the bass instruments can play drones, root tones, and chanting parts. (Such accompaniments will be discussed under harmony instruments.)

Those children who are studying piano in class or private lessons can contribute to classroom activities. Many of the accompaniments provided in the teachers' editions of the basic song series are easy enough for older children to play. Piano students should be encouraged to improvise chording accompaniments for songs they know. Some of the suggestions given in the next section of this book can be adapted to the piano. Those students who have a piano in the home will thus find more ways to utilize their developing skills. When they can perform small solos, their classmates may serve as a surprisingly attentive audience.

## PLAYING HARMONY PARTS

In the intermediate grades, continued musical experiences prepare pupils for more extensive work with harmony. The playing of simple counterparts along with singing is a type of harmonic experience suitable for children in the third grade and above. The Autoharp is a stringed instrument that sets up chords when a bar is pressed. Before the invention of the Autoharp it was not a simple task to provide classroom experiences in playing harmony parts on instruments; in order to sound a chord, one had to know what tones the chord contained and how to make them sound simultaneously. The experiences in harmony came as children sang or played different parts together or listened to harmony produced by others.

When the children can become acquainted with chords through the use of an automatic chording instrument such as the Autoharp they can move on to a successful use of other instruments, on which they build the chords themselves. These include the keyboard instruments and the fretted instruments like the ukulele and the guitar. Because the Autoharp is the simplest of the automatic chording instruments, a discussion of its use in the intermediate grades will show in what direction a study of harmony might be pursued.

## The Autoharp as an Introduction to Harmony

Twelve-bar and fifteen-bar Autoharps are available; the latter offers more variety in keys and is the instrument referred to in the following discussion. However, the twelve-bar Autoharp is very satisfactory for most elementary school use. At the first few group lessons with the Autoharp, when only one instrument is available, each student should have a diagram the size of the Autoharp's chord mechanism to familiarize him with the marking and relative position of the chords. Techniques may be presented to the class as a whole, but the development of skills is an individual matter. Arrangements must be made so that students may practice during their free time.

*Techniques in Playing the Autoharp.* The primary chords are the tonic (I), the subdominant (IV), and the dominant seventh ($V_7$). On the Autoharp, the bars that define the chords are pressed down one at a time by the left hand. When the pointer finger is placed on the tonic chord of a given key, the middle finger falls on the dominant seventh chord and the ring finger on the subdominant chord of that key.

### KEYS AND CHORDS ON THE FIFTEEN-BAR AUTOHARP

*You have this choice of chords:*

| 6<br>4<br>II (2)<br>Supertonic | 1<br>6<br>IV (4)<br>Subdominant | 4<br>2<br>7<br>$V_7$ (5)<br>Dominant<br>Seventh | 5<br>3<br>I (1)<br>Tonic | You may play<br>in these keys: |
|---|---|---|---|---|
| D minor | F major | $G_7$ | C major | G major |
| A minor | C major | $D_7$ | G major | C major |
| G minor | B♭ major | $C_7$ | F major | F major |
| — | E♭ major | $F_7$ | B♭ major | B♭ major |
| — | G major | $A_7$ | D major | D major |
| — | G minor | $A_7$ | D minor | D minor |
| — | D minor | $E_7$ | A minor | A minor |
| — | — | $D_7$ | G minor | G minor |

IV   $V_7$   I

left hand

When this finger pattern is established, the player may use any of the keys on the Autoharp with equal facility and may transpose from one key to another. The pressure of the finger on the bar must be firm so that all unneeded strings are stopped.

The Autoharp is strummed with a pick held in the right hand. A plastic pick makes a loud, sharp tone, a felt or leather pick a softer tone. The beginner strokes the strings just to the right of the bars. The advanced player may cross the right hand over and stroke nearer the center of the strings, just to the left of the bars, to produce a more resonant tone.

In stroking the strings, the most common method for the beginner is to give equal-length strokes on the first beat of each measure, or on the first and third beats, depending upon the tempo and meter of the song. The experienced player will discover different styles of playing.[13] Some songs suggest a banjo style accompaniment, using a plastic pick to produce alternating low and high chords. Other songs need a smoother, more sustained stroke.

Before two-hand coordination is established, one player may press the bars with his left hand to make the necessary chords while another strokes the strings in the appropriate rhythm. It is important that the students understand the two functions of the Autoharp: to provide the key and harmony and to establish the tempo and meter for the song.

To sing with the Autoharp the group must first find the beginning pitch of the song by some variation of the following method:
1. Determine the key and the scale degree on which the song begins (see Appendix A–IV).
2. Sound on the Autoharp the tonic chord in that key; or, better, play the chord progression $(I–IV–V_7–I)$ to establish the key in the ear.
3. In the tonic chord, recognize and sing the tonic tone, then sing to the scale tone on which the song begins. If the player or singers are unable to sense which of the chord tones is the tonic, that string and the string for the tone on which the song begins may be plucked with finger or plastic pick.

Next, the player must establish the meter and tempo by strumming a two-measure introduction. If the meter is $\frac{3}{4}$ he may make one long and two short strokes, or he may merely strum on the accent beat and count silently on two and three. If the meter is $\frac{4}{4}$ he may make one, two, or four strokes for the measure, depending upon the tempo and character of the song, that is:

| strum | | | | | strum | | strum | |
|---|---|---|---|---|---|---|---|---|
| 1 | 2 | 3 | 4 | *or* | 1 | 2 | 3 | 4 |

| | strum | strum | strum | strum |
|---|---|---|---|---|
| *or* 1 | 2 | 3 | 4 |

## DIAGRAM OF CHORD MECHANISM OF THE AUTOHARP *

*Press the buttons down with the left hand, using the pointer finger on the tonic chord. Strum with the right hand either to the right or to the left of the chord mechanism.*

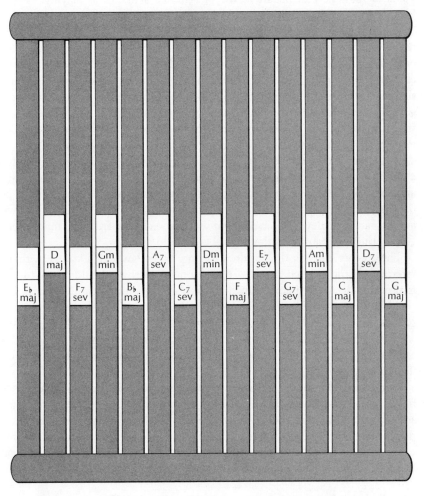

* Autoharp is the registered trademark of Oscar Schmidt-International, Inc.

**THE USE OF
MELODY AND
HARMONY
INSTRUMENTS**

By playing the Autoharp, children can acquire many important musical concepts. Some teachers, however, fail to pass along an understanding of what is being done, and the process is largely a mechanical, rote acquisition of a skill. Other teachers insist that all technical barriers be hurdled before the students take part in any of the pleasurable activities of playing. A fine balance in these matters is the mark of a good teacher.

When the Autoharp is introduced to an entire intermediate grade class, the teacher should select familiar rhythmic songs that can be accompanied with only two chords. The approach should be both by ear ("When must we change the chord in order to have it sound right with the melody we are singing?") and by chord indications in the book. In the past, music educators gave so much attention to helping children *read* music that they neglected to train the ear to *hear* it properly. Learning to chord by ear is as important as learning to follow notation.

If it is familiar to them, "Paw-Paw Patch" (see page 75) is a good song for children to try to chord by ear. The teacher should choose songs that begin and end on the tonic chord. Help the class tune up to begin singing as outlined above; explain to them that this song can be chorded with two chords, but that they will have to find where the change from the tonic chord (G) to the dominant seventh chord (D₇) should occur.

The teacher can ask the children to sing "Paw-Paw Patch" softly without referring to the printed music. At the same time they should listen to the tonic chord accompaniment, which the teacher supplies on the Autoharp. He should refrain from changing the chord at the beginning of the second phrase so that the children have the opportunity to hear the need for the dominant seventh chord; he can then correct the harmony and continue on through the song, letting the reaction of the pupils prompt the change in harmony when it is necessary.

Many songs that need just two chords are provided in the basic song series for the intermediate grades. Pupils are capable of playing these Autoharp accompaniments quite independently after they have learned the fingering pattern and the techniques of strumming and tuning up outlined in this chapter. "Down in the Valley" (see page 165) and the following are good first songs to sing with the Autoharp:

**CHAPTER**
**FIVE**

"Bow Belinda" (see page 74)  "Paw-Paw Patch" (see page 75)
"Came A-Riding" (see page 163)  "Polly-Wolly-Doodle" (DMT IV–14)
"De Glendy Burk" (TiM VI–75)  "Red River Valley" (ExM V–109)
"Go Tell Aunt Rhodie" (see page 216)  "Sandy Land" (see page 113)
"Love Somebody" (ABC V–21)  "Skip to My Lou" (see page 252)
"Michie Banjo" (MMYO V–110)

*Tuning the Autoharp.* Like any stringed instrument, the Autoharp must be tuned periodically. A new Autoharp will need to be tuned at least twice before the strings are set at the required tension for each pitch. Variations in temperature affect the tuning of the instrument; therefore, when not in use the instrument should be stored in its case.

In general, the quickest way to tune the Autoharp is to match the pitch of a well-tuned piano. A key with which to turn the tuning pegs is supplied with each instrument. Care should be taken not to turn the peg too far nor to loosen it from the wooden frame during the tuning process. Turning the tuning key in a clockwise direction will raise the pitch.

Begin with middle C and tune all strings for the C tonic chord (C–E–G) upward and downward from that position. Strike the piano key and then pluck the corresponding string, turning the key to raise the string to the pitch of the piano. If the pitch of the string is raised too much, turn it slightly counterclockwise to lower the tone and then clockwise again to bring it exactly in tune. After the tonic chord throughout the range of the instrument is in tune, begin near the middle of the Autoharp and tune each successive string so that it matches the pitch of the corresponding key on the piano.

An Autoharp may need tuning every two to four weeks, depending upon climatic conditions and the type of use it receives. If an Autoharp is noticeably out of tune it should not be used: if it is to be played in combination with other pitched instruments it should be tuned to the same standard of pitch.

*Learning Chord Names and Characteristics.* During early experiences when accompanying is limited to two chords, pupils should be led to hear the distinctive qualities of the tonic and dominant seventh chords. The tonic chord is built on the key note of a scale and has qualities of arrival and stability; it is commonly called the "home" chord. In contrast, the dominant seventh chord has qualities of restlessness and instability so that movement to the tonic chord is desired.

Later, as children play in different keys and make simple transpositions, they will find it important to know that these chords are named in three different ways: in *any* key the tonic chord is built on the first step of the scale and is often labeled with a Roman numeral I. In a *specific* key it has a letter name. Thus in the key of G, the tonic chord (I) is the G chord. The dominant chord is built on the fifth step of the scale and is labeled V. On the Autoharp the form of the dominant chord is the dominant seventh ($V_7$). This four-tone chord is used because the added tone gives a special color and dynamic quality. The following chart shows the relationships between chords in the three common keys.

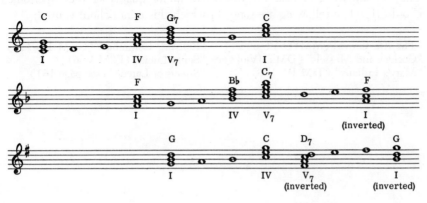

After mastering two-chord songs, children can readily play three-chord songs and begin exploring the sound of the subdominant chord (IV). The chord progression IV–I has the familiar sound of the "Amen" at the end of hymns. Pupils should compare the sound with that of the $V_7$–I progression, which is the most common harmonic ending (cadence) in a song. To follow chord indications in a score, it is essential that the automatic fingering pattern for the Autoharp be well established. With the fingers moving by touch, the pupil is able to keep his eyes on the notation. In some books, chords are marked over every measure whether the chord changes or not. If the teacher will circle in red the chord letters or numbers at places where the chord actually changes, the children will be more successful in following the score.

Since not all keys are represented on the Autoharp, it is often necessary to transpose a song in order to accommodate the instrument. When this is done the chord numbers (I, IV, $V_7$) rather than chord letters (e.g., G, C, $D_7$) should be marked above the song. As an example, a song in the key of A might require transposition one whole step lower to the key of G. If the chord letters for the key of G are placed above a song written in the key of A, there is a serious discrepancy in the notation, but chord numbers can refer to the chord needed in either key. An understanding of chord numbers as well as chord letters enables an individual to generalize his knowledge of harmony to any key.

"In Bahía" (see page 79) is a simple three-chord song. Other three-chord songs that can readily be played on the Autoharp are these:

"Aloha Oe" (ABC VI–95)
"Cindy" (MMYO IV–180)
"Dogie Song" (ExM V–142)
"Fiddle Dee Dee" (GwM II–128)
"Four in a Boat" (GwM IV–41)
"Liza Jane" (see page 183)
"Night Herding Song" (MoM III–136)
"Noah's Ark" (TiM IV–104)
"Oh No, John!" (see page 88)

"Old Folks at Home" (ExM IV–104)
"O Susanna" (DMT IV–12)
"Red River Valley" (DMT V–52)
"Sarasponda" (TiM V–40)
"Silent Night" (ABC V–82)
"Sing Your Way Home" (ExM V–178)
"Sweet Betsy from Pike" (ABC VI–4)
"Tinga Layo" (see page 116)
"Yankee Doodle" (see page 106)

When facility and understanding of the primary chords is achieved, some intermediate children will be able to play songs containing other chords. They should learn to hear the distinctive minor quality of the supertonic chord (II). The following are songs in which this minor chord is used:

"The Ash Grove" (MMYO VI–68)
"Cockles and Mussels" (DMT IV–43)
"Mary's Lullaby" (TiM IV–176)

"Roll on, Columbia" (GwM IV–114)
"Santa Lucia" (ExM V–61)
"Streets of Laredo" (see page 161)

## STREETS OF LAREDO

*Simply*

*American Cowboy Song*

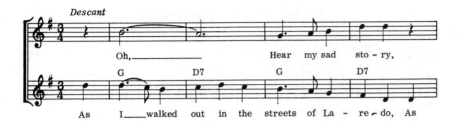

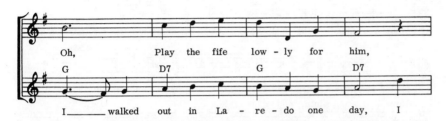

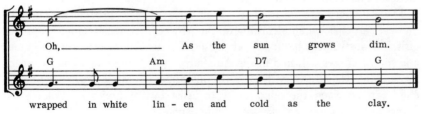

From *Music around the World.* © 1956, Silver Burdett Company.

**THE USE OF MELODY AND HARMONY INSTRUMENTS**

Sometimes a song seems to fluctuate between a major and a minor key. Usually the two are "related" keys—that is, they share the same key signature. Songs with this kind of fluctuating major-minor harmony are these:

"Blue Tail Fly" (MMYO III–90)
"Frog Went Courting" (DMT V–12)

"Johnny Has Gone for a Soldier" (ExM VI–3)
"The Wee Falorie Man" (MMYO IV–131)

**161**

Songs such as "Wayfaring Stranger" (TiM V–86), "Erie Canal" (DMT V–116), and "All the Pretty Little Horses," when chorded for Autoharp, provide opportunities to sing minor songs with this accompaniment.

## ALL THE PRETTY LITTLE HORSES

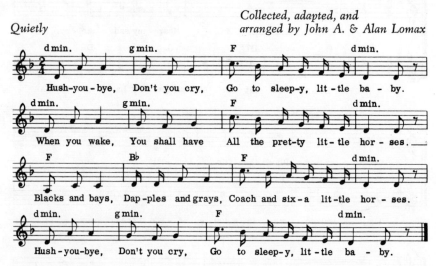

*Quietly*

*Collected, adapted, and arranged by John A. & Alan Lomax*

Transposed from E minor.

Copyright 1934 by John A. and Alan Lomax in the book *American Ballads and Folk Songs*. Copyright assigned 1958 to Ludlow Music, Inc., New York, N.Y. Used by permission.

Experiences in minor keys are limited by the chords available on the Autoharp, but there are sufficient resources to acquaint pupils with the minor mode and its relationship to the major.

The Autoharp can be used in all of these ways to provide avenues for musical participation and learning on the part of intermediate grade boys and girls. The instrument has many other uses. The teacher of the primary grades and special classes will find in the Autoharp a very satisfying accompaniment for singing. Usually he will play the instrument himself, but sometimes a child can be given the opportunity to assist by rhythmically stroking the strings as the teacher provides the chord changes.

Children with handicaps in physical coordination can be motivated to strum rhythmically when they "help" the teacher provide the Autoharp accompaniment for class singing. Children who are deaf or hard-of-hearing like to feel the vibrations the instrument creates in a tabletop on which it is played. In these and in other ways the Autoharp has proved to be a valuable musical tool in elementary classrooms.

## Harmony with Other Instruments

Following their experiences in making harmony with the Autoharp, children can learn to play bass parts and to build chords on other instruments. The resonator bells sound well when the tones are struck simultaneously in block chords. Intermediate pupils can play the same chords on the

**CHAPTER FIVE**

piano, the ukulele, or the xylophone to accompany classroom singing. The value of such activities in building interest is as great as its value in increasing skills and understanding in harmony.

*Playing Root Tones.* Intermediate grade pupils may use the classroom melody instruments or the stringed instruments of the orchestra to provide accompaniment for songs using only two chords. Even a pupil who has not studied the cello can pluck the open strings (C and G) to play the root tones of the tonic and dominant chords in a song such as "Came A-Riding."

### CAME A-RIDING

Moderato

Song from Czechoslovakia
English by Martha Ramsey

THE USE OF
MELODY AND
HARMONY
INSTRUMENTS

From *Joyful Singing,* Cooperative Recreation Service, Inc., Delaware, Ohio. Used by permission.

**163**

An easy approach to part singing is provided when some of the children sing the bass part two octaves above the bass instrument while others sing the melody. The Metallophone,[1,2] which is a glockenspiel-type instrument with long tonal duration sounding in the tenor range, is especially valuable for playing root tones and drone-bass accompaniments.

Stringed instruments of the orchestra are often available in an elementary classroom and it is helpful to know what easy-playing opportunities they afford. These instruments are tuned as follows:

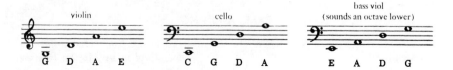

The open strings of these instruments may be used as root tones for tonic and dominant chords in the following keys:

| Key | Chord Roots | | Instrument |
| | (I) | (V₇) | |
|---|---|---|---|
| G | G | D | violin, cello, bass |
| D | D | A | violin, cello, bass |
| C | C | G | cello |
| A | A | E | violin, bass |

Open strings of any of the instruments listed above can be used to play the root tones for "Streets of Laredo" (page 161). The low tones of the bass viol would add depth and resonance to the chord accompaniment of the Auto-harp. Notice that the tonic (G) and the dominant (D) alternate regularly throughout the song, except in the last phrase where A, the root tone of the minor chord, is needed. The tone on these instruments can be produced most easily by plucking the string (pizzicato), but it can also be sustained by bowing the open string.

*Supplying Chord Accompaniments.* When Autoharp chords are given for a two-chord song it is not difficult to use other instruments in accompanying parts. Later, three-chord songs can be treated in a similar manner. "Down in the Valley" (see page 165) is harmonized by the tonic and dominant chords in the key of G. This basic harmony can be used in several ways to create an accompaniment on tuned instruments that fifth and sixth grade children can play:

1. Follow the chord markings and pluck the open G and D strings on any of the stringed instruments, or sound these tones on a bell instrument in a lower octave, on the downbeat of each measure throughout the song.
2. Notice that the fifth of the scale (D) is a tone common to both chords; therefore this tone can be sounded continuously throughout the song. The open D string of the violin could be sustained, or D in the higher range of a bell instrument could be struck at the beginning of each measure.

3. Sound all of the tones for each chord on resonator bells on the first beat of each measure in which the chord is used. Three children can play G, B, and D rhythmically during the first four measures, then four other children can play D, F♯, A, and C on the downbeat until the tonic chord returns in the last measure of the song.

### DOWN IN THE VALLEY

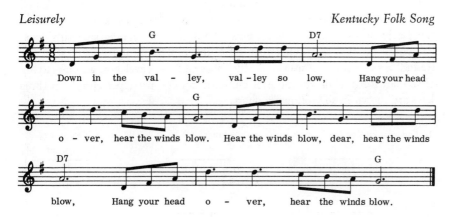

*Leisurely*                                                                  *Kentucky Folk Song*

Down in the val - ley, val - ley so low, Hang your head o - ver, hear the winds blow. Hear the winds blow, dear, hear the winds blow, Hang your head o - ver, hear the winds blow.

Pupils who wish to build chords on resonator bells must know the letter names of the notes within each chord. This is called spelling the chord. The key signature must be taken into account; flats and sharps must be used to alter the names of the chord notes as necessary. Thus the activity of accompanying songs with harmonic chording provides motivation for learning the names of the staff degrees and the key signatures if these have not previously been learned. A chart such as that on page 159 can help fifth and sixth grade pupils see the relationships between the primary chords in the keys of C, F, and G with which they will work most often.

Because the piano and the chromatic bells are fixed-scale instruments, the positions as well as the names of the tones in the chord must be known. On the piano certain arrangements of the tones within the various chords facilitate the change from one chord to another. To play consecutive tonic and dominant seventh chords for "Down in the Valley" the following placement of notes for the left hand would be used by the beginning pianist. Notice that the player needs to move two fingers only one half step in order to change from one chord to another:

**THE USE OF MELODY AND HARMONY INSTRUMENTS**

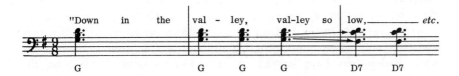

"Down in the val - ley, val-ley so low,_____ etc.

G                              G        G        G              D7        D7

Positions of tones within chords in the keys of C, F, and G are shown in Appendix A-V of this book. In a simplified approach to piano chording the relative position of the chord tones shown there is used for every key. The elementary teacher who has mastered this keyboard technique can share it with his pupils. The publications of Robert Pace[14] are helpful in such a study.

The principle of the fretted instruments (ukulele, banjo, and guitar) is this: when a string is depressed by a finger, it is brought into contact with the fret just ahead of the finger; the vibrating part of the string then is shortened and produces a higher pitch. Fretted instruments are tuned so that the hand can easily produce the primary chords. However, to change smoothly from one chord position to another requires practice. The ukulele, smallest of the fretted instruments, is useful at the intermediate level for accompanying Hawaiian songs. The tuning and tablature for the principal chords in three keys are shown in the following chart:

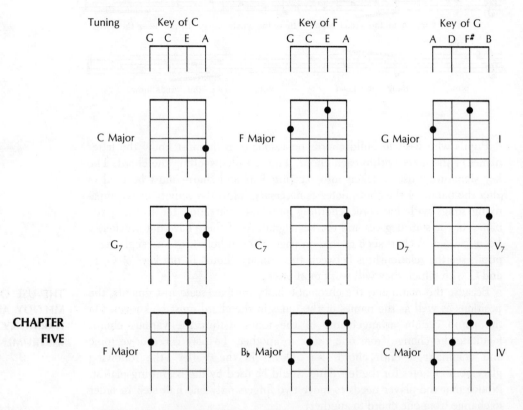

The guitar is an excellent, authentic accompanying instrument for many folk songs, especially of the United States and Latin America. The instrument has a long history dating back to the sixteenth century in Spain and other European countries. A teacher who plays the guitar will find it a very useful accompanying instrument for elementary classroom singing. Some sixth graders who have learned the basic principles of chording on the Autoharp and keyboard instruments may be encouraged to begin learning to play the guitar. Numerous instruction books and three-quarter-size guitars are available. The tuning and tablature for the principal chords in three keys are shown in the following chart:

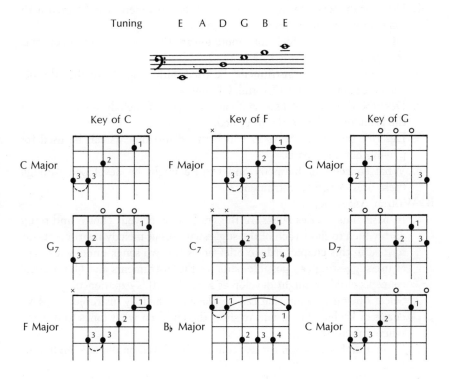

The playing of melody and harmony instruments in the ways described in this chapter leads to the development of basic musical skills and concepts. The understanding and effective use of *rhythm* is necessary to any concerted playing of the melody and harmony instruments. Through the use of these tuned instruments children are made aware of details in *melody* and can learn to use musical notation effectively. The field of elementary *harmony* opens up when children in the intermediate grades begin to use the Autoharp and to combine other instruments for harmonic purposes. *Tone color* and *dynamics* are considered when different kinds of instruments are used and when they are played in ensemble. *Musical form* and *texture* are observed when children create introductions and codas, and play rounds and ostinato patterns.

There is enough of interest in instrumental activities to provide vital musical experiences every day of the school year. However, the other activities in music are important too, and so the teacher must be selective and use instruments in the ways most musically rewarding to his class.

**THE USE OF MELODY AND HARMONY INSTRUMENTS**

## ACTIVITIES FOR COLLEGE CLASSES

A. Questions for Review
   1. Describe the several ways in which melody instruments can be used with songs in the primary grades; in the intermediate grades.
   2. Of the above uses, which contribute toward the development of concepts of melody?
   3. How might melody instruments be used with songs to further the development of concepts of form? Of timbre?
   4. Describe the creative uses that can be made of melody instruments in the primary grades; in the intermediate grades.
   5. Describe the several ways in which tuned instruments can be used for playing harmony parts.
   6. What concepts of harmony and texture might be developed through these uses of tuned instruments?

B. Written Assignments
   1. In basic music series books for the grade level of your choice find songs with which to show each of the suggested uses of melody instruments described in this chapter. Make brief notes for two songs under each type of use suggesting (a) possible parts for the instruments and (b) musical concepts children might develop as a result of this experience.
   2. Select three easy songs that can be played on melody instruments. Make charts or keyboard diagrams to show the children what tones to use and where to start the song.
   3. Write number notation for two songs to be played on diatonic eight-tone bells.
   4. Create an easy countermelody for a song. Copy the original song on staff paper and write your countermelody on the staff below.
   5. Select a nursery rhyme and create a melody using the five tones of any pentatonic scale. Be sure the rhythm of your song conforms to the rhythm of the rhyme.
   6. Select and copy a pentatonic song from one of the basic music series. On the staff below it write an original ostinato for the song.
   7. Select a round and show at least two counterparts that could be played repeatedly on melody instruments throughout the song.
   8. Select a song that can be accompanied by a chording instrument (Autoharp, piano, guitar, or ukulele) and one of the stringed instruments of the orchestra. Write out the part to be played on the stringed instrument.

C. Classroom Projects
   1. Be prepared to sing and to play instruments for one song selected in written assignment No. 1.
   2. Play on selected tone bars one song from written assignment No. 2.
   3. Be prepared to play on the chromatic bells in the key of C either song for which you made number notation under written assignment No. 3. Transpose and play the same song in the key of F or G.

4. Arrange a pentatonic scale on resonator bells. Play a pentatonic song using these tones; then play the same song using the black keys of the piano.
5. Sing and play the melody you created under written assignment No. 5.
6. Select a song that the college class or a small group will sing as you accompany in one of the following ways:
   a. with I, IV, V$_7$ chords on the Autoharp.
   b. with three chords on the piano.
   c. with the ukulele or the banjo.
   d. with the Autoharp or ukulele in combination with the root tones of the appropriate chords played on the bass viol or cello.

## CHAPTER NOTES

1. Instruments made by the Sonor Drum Co., Western Germany, are distributed in the United States by M. Hohner dealers (see Appendix B–V).
2. Studio 49, Percussion Instrument Makers, Western Germany, makers of Orff-Schulwerk Instruments (see listing of Magnamusic-Baton, Inc., in Appendix B–V).
3. Satis N. Coleman, *Creative Music in the Home* (Valparaiso, Ind.: Lewis E. Myers and Co., 1927), pp. 144–157.
4. Michael A. Wallach, "Research on Children's Thinking," in *Child Psychology—The Sixty-second Yearbook of the National Society for the Study of Education* (Chicago: NSSE, distributed by the University of Chicago Press, 1963), Part I, Chapter VI.
5. Emma Dickson Sheehy, *Children Discover Music and Dance* (New York: Holt, Rinehart & Winston, Inc., 1959), Chapter 6.
6. Carl Orff and Gunild Keetman, *Music for Children,* Angel Records 3582 B.
7. Carl Orff, translated by Arnold Walter, "The Schulwerk—Its Origin and Aims," *Music Educators Journal,* April–May 1963. Also *The Canadian Music Educator,* October–November 1962.
8. Carl Orff and Gunild Keetman, *Music for Children, I—Pentatonic,* English adaptation by Doreen Hall and Arnold Walter (Mainz, Germany: B. Schott's Söhne, 1956; Associated Music Publishers, Inc., N.Y.), pp. 66–78.
9. Bessie R. Swanson, *An Analysis and Evaluation of Individual Melody Writing by Seven-Year-Old Children in Public School Classes* (Doctor of Musical Arts Research Study, Music Department, Stanford University, June 1967). See principally Chapters Four and Five and Appendix B.
10. *Hargail Music Press,* 157 West 57th St., New York, N.Y. 10019. Specialists in recorders as well as music for recorders and other instruments.
11. Gerald Burakoff, *The Elementary Method for the Soprano Recorder* (New York: Hargail Music Press, 1967).
12. Forrest L. Buchtel, *Melody Fun* (Park Ridge, Ill.: Neil A. Kjos Music Co., 1938).
13. Meg Peterson, *The Many Ways to Play the Autoharp* (Union, N.J.: Oscar Schmidt-International, Inc., 1966).
14. Robert Pace, *Music Essentials for Classroom Teachers* (Belmont, Calif.: Wadsworth Publishing Company, Inc., 1961).

## Other References

Bishop, Dorothy, *Chords in Action* (New York: Carl Fischer, Inc., 1956).

Fox, Lillian Mohr, *Autoharp Accompaniments to Old Favorite Songs* (Evanston, Ill.: Summy-Birchard Publishing Company, 1947).

Krone, Beatrice, and Max Krone, *Harmony Fun with the Autoharp* (Park Ridge, Ill.: Neil A. Kjos Music Co., 1952).

Nash, Grace C., *Music with Children*, Series I, II, III, Recorder Book. (Scottsdale, Ariz.: G. C. Nash, 1965).

Nye, Robert Evans, and Bjornar Bergethon, *Basic Music, An Activities Approach to Functional Musicianship*, Third Edition (Englewood Cliffs, N.J.: Prentice-Hall, Inc., 1968).

Nye, Robert E., and Vernice T. Nye, *Music in the Elementary School*, Second Edition (Englewood Cliffs, N.J., Prentice-Hall, Inc., 1964), Chapter 5.

Pace, Robert, *Piano for Classroom Music* (Englewood Cliffs, N.J.: Prentice-Hall, Inc., 1956).

Reser, Harry, *The Harry Reser Guitar Method* (New York: Remick Music Corp., 1952).

Sistrunck, Sara Dunn, *Resonator Bells, A Means of Musical Growth* (New York: Mills Music Inc., 1967).

Slind, Lloyd H., *Melody, Rhythm and Harmony for the Elementary Grades* (New York: Mills Music, Inc., 1953).

Trapp Family Singers, *Enjoy Your Recorder* (Sharon, Conn.: Magnamusic Distributors, Inc., 1954).

**CHAPTER
FIVE**

# 6

# Songs and Singing Voices

Singing is an important part of any school music program. Teachers should be concerned not so much that children become great singers, but that they become enthusiastic singers. In singing, young and old alike find both a very personal way to express themselves and another means through which the feelings of others are conveyed to them. A varied repertoire and opportunities for singing, both in the classroom and in other situations, must be provided during all the elementary school years.

In planning a music education program in which singing is a central activity the essential concerns of the teacher are (1) what characteristics he may expect to find in children's voices, (2) how children learn to sing, and (3) what kinds of songs they find easiest and most appealing.

These and related topics will be discussed in this chapter. Here also songs of many kinds are reprinted to be sung and evaluated. A list of the basic school music books and a code to identify the sources of songs used as examples throughout this book are included in Appendix B–I.

## CHILDREN'S VOICES AND THEIR DEVELOPMENT

The idea that singing is for all children is not new. In *Creative Music for Children* (1922) Satis Coleman expressed it very well when she told of her observations of what she considered a "singing school" for baby robins which took place in her garden in the early summer. Relating this to her considerable experience in teaching music to children she said: "I believe that any child who would begin relatively early and sing as much as those robins sang, with a simple and correct pattern ever ready for him to imitate, would be able to sing well and accurately no matter what his lack in musical inheritance might be."[1]

Children learn to speak and sing, as do robins, in imitation of what they hear and in response to an inner urge to express themselves. Beatrice Landeck points out that a mother's modulated speaking to her child easily slips into chanting and singing in relation to the child's daily routine. She suggests ways in which nursery rhymes and other familiar tunes can be adapted to fit the objects and activities of the child's daily experiences.[2]

It is unfortunate that few children have an extensive and early contact with such flexible uses of the voice, and that in the average human situation singing is not necessary for communication, nor is it encouraged. As a result, some kindergarten and first grade children do not sing, or their singing is not recognized as such, when they first come to school. Some of these children will learn to sing merely by associating with those who do and by experiencing a pleasant singing situation. Others, unfortunately, may be classed as "nonsingers" or "monotones" until they encounter a wise teacher and an environment in which they can acquire a concept of singing and comfortably practice the skills necessary for them to master the art themselves.

## Variations in Young Children's Singing

Some people account for the wide variation in children's singing skill by referring to "ability" or "talent," but a great many other factors are involved. A few children sing as easily as they speak, perhaps more easily, because singing is not necessarily tied to words. Nor it is limited to known melodies. Some uninhibited early singing can be considered "vocal play" and occasionally extremes in vocal range are heard. In an example recorded by the Pillsbury Foundation Studies[3] a 4½-year-old-child utilizes a range of over 2½ octaves in free vocalization.

On the other hand, a child with an innately cautious temperament may refrain from singing, not because of any limitation in his vocal mechanism, but because he has not been assured that this is an acceptable use of the voice. Both Reynolds[4] and Shelton[5] found a significant relationship between the home environment and the musical responses of first grade children. Thus, a child's need for expression in sound patterns, his temperament, his confidence, his environment, and his vocal inheritance are factors influencing his singing practices and general musical response.

When singing is considered an extension of speech, one can more readily understand why there is such a wide range of ability among kindergarten and first grade children. It is influenced by the same factors that affect the development of speech. Because singing is very closely associated with the emotions it is also readily affected by psychological problems.

*Tone Quality.* The quality of the child voice is a variable, dependent on such factors as experience, available vocal examples, and physical structure. Not only do children imitate what they hear but they elaborate on it and explore their own sound-making mechanisms; some are more curious and exploratory than others. Since children imitate rather realistically the high whine of a siren or the deep whistle of a steamboat, the teacher should expect that the singing voice might be capable of considerable variation; it is produced by the same mechanism. Within musical limits such variation in vocal tone quality is desirable, for singing should be expressive of many ideas and moods.

We should not *always* expect children in the primary grades to conform to the traditional concept of the child voice—that it is high, light, and flutelike. This quality is ideal for certain songs, and the teacher should promote it through the mood and feeling to be expressed in these songs, rather than because it is the only quality ever heard in the child voice. The folk song "Bye'm Bye" (see page 135) is such a song. It should be sung lightly, in a very dreamy mood. No heavy cowboy voices here, please! Similar, yet different in character, are "Away in a Manger," "Lavender's Blue" (ExM II–60), and "Five Angels" (MMYO I–46), which require a sweet, floating quality characteristic of lullabies.

Some children emulate a more vigorous voice quality, which is suitable for exuberant songs. Their enthusiasm for such songs may be an important factor as they learn to use the singing voice. The sea chantey "Up She Rises" (MMYO I–67), game songs like "Santy Maloney" (Bir II–11), and folk songs such as "Train Is A-Coming" (AFlk–150) are examples of rhythmic songs that should be sung with as much vigor as possible.

## UP SHE RISES

*Vigorously*                                                                 *Sea Chantey*

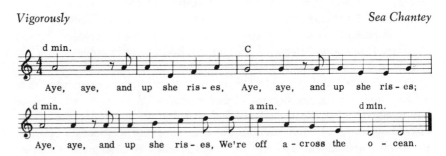

From MAKING MUSIC YOUR OWN, *Book I*, Teacher's Edition, © 1968, General Learning Corporation. Used by permission of Silver Burdett Company.

*Voice Range and Flexibility.* The term "monotone" is an unfortunate one that should never be used, for it implies that the individual sings or speaks on one level with no pitch variation. One need only listen to the speaking or crying voice of a child to hear the natural variation in pitch. Out-of-tune singers may be more accurately described as "conversational singers," who "sing" much as they speak. This condition can be found in children who did not learn to sing in a spontaneous intuitive way at an early age, and who arrive in the kindergarten and first grade without being aware of the possibilities of their vocal mechanisms.

Children who do not learn to sing before they are six may have to attack the problem in a cognitive way and observe that singing is a combination of changes in pitch as well as in word rhythms. In such cases these two dimensions need to be separated so that children can practice singing several syllables on one pitch as in a chant, then two or more pitches on one syllable, as in a call:

Persons differ in sensitivity to pitch. Those who are most sensitive and are not impeded by psychological factors tend to sing without instruction when they have a voice to imitate and when they become aware of the flexibility of the vocal mechanism. Others may need to have their attention directed to pitch levels before they begin to notice the details in melody, just as some need a guide to point out details in visual design in order to appreciate what is there.

Greater use brings wider range and flexibility to the voice, just as exercise and training build skills and coordination in other muscular activities. In general kindergarten and first grade children have a practical vocal range from middle C to D or E above the octave.

Others seem to be limited to four or five tones centering around F or G.

This fact has some bearing on the songs selected for young children. It has been observed that groups of nursery school and kindergarten children engaged in rhythmic play employ chants similar to those heard in cultures uninfluenced by music of Western civilization. A limited middle-of-the-voice range is used, and a tonal center is established on one pitch level. From this point the voice drops a minor third and may then rise to the tone a full step higher than the tonal center.

The pattern is heard in many variations. "Ring around a Rosy" (see page 138) is an example of a children's chanting song heard in many different countries.

Young children who have never sung can most easily be helped if their first songs incorporate the tonal range and intervals that children sing most naturally. One such song is "Who's That Tapping at the Window?" (see page 103). Notice that this song conforms to the required limited range and that it suggests participation with sound-making and simple dramatization that would capture the interest of young children.

Kindergarten and first grade teachers must expect a wide variation in singing skill among children when they first come to school. No one factor is responsible for this wide range. Additional discussions of reasons why children do not sing may be found in *Children Discover Music and Dance*[6] by Sheehy and MUSIC FOR YOUNG AMERICANS, *Book One*, page 177.

*Vocal Development through Tone Calls.* Children who are unable to sing an entire song should be encouraged to repeat short song fragments or tone calls. When a child recognizes his success in singing one or two tones, he will have established a concept about singing in tune that will enable him to repeat the process with longer melodic fragments. Song-related tone calls are

SONGS AND
SINGING VOICES

**177**

especially valuable because they can be used as a natural part of the song-learning process and need no separate motivation.

"Over in the Meadow" is found in several of the basic song series and is a song that children like:

## OVER IN THE MEADOW

*Not too slowly*                    *Traditional American Folk Song*

O - ver in the mea - dow, in the sand, in the sun, Lived an

old Moth - er toad__ and her lit - tle toad - ie one;

"Wink!" said the moth - er, "I wink," said the one; And he

winked and he blinked__ in the sand, in the sun.

Transposed from F.

From Berg, Burns, Hooley, Pace, and Wolverton, MUSIC FOR YOUNG AMERICANS, *Book One,* American Book Company. Used by permission.

One motive in the song is a fine tone call:

"Wink!" said the moth - er,

Its characteristics are these:
1. It has unity and completeness in itself and thus is satisfying to sing.
2. It is a melodic pattern (so–do or 5–1) found in many simple songs.
3. It lies in the most advantageous range of the child voice.
4. It has rhythmic interest but is not difficult to sing.
5. Other activities of the toadies may be discussed to capture personal interest, e.g., "Hop," said the mother, "Dive," "Swim," etc.

When first singing the song for the children, a teacher may make a game of this simple tone call. One small group after another may sing it, imitating the teacher, who sings about other toadie activities suggested by the children. Individual children may sing it, imitating the teacher or another child. When the song is learned, individuals may sing their choice of activities after the group has sung the song together. The objectives of this procedure are that the song fragment will be sung in tune, and that the children will discover how it sounds and how it feels to sing it so.

If it is not advisable to have a particular child sing alone, he will be given an opportunity to participate within a small group singing a tone call. Many children are eager to sing alone, and hearing them often arouses a less competent singer to try also. In such cases the teacher must arrange that the tone call the child attempts is very easy, in the most favorable range for him, and that it has been heard correctly several times before the weak singer has an opportunity to try it. Following such an attempt, approval and encouragement must be forthcoming.

Tone calls from many songs must be used. For some children singing success will come only after several months. The process demands considerable ingenuity and imagination on the part of the teacher. A pleasant "game spirit" must prevail so that the children do not become tense or anxious in any way but can give full attention to the melodic fragments they are singing.

The following are suggested as further examples of tone calls taken from familiar primary songs:

"Rig-a-Jig-Jig" (see page 110):

"Are You Sleeping?" (see page 133):

"See Saw, Margery Daw" (GwM K–133):

Very often the ending phrase makes the most appropriate tone call because it has a sense of unity and completeness in itself. It must, however, be short and have rhythmic interest. It is important that it be sung rhythmically. The discussion and examples in "Tone Plays and Phrase Repetitions," pages 39 to 42 of *American Folk Songs for Children*,[7] are helpful. *The Kindergarten Book* and *Book One* of Music for Young Americans give song fragments in the form of one-tone and two-tone calls.

*Other Remedial Techniques.* Some children are "conversational singers" because they do not have established concepts of what singing a *particular* melody really is. Occasionally the teacher should sing with "la" or "loo" the first phrase or two of a song the children know; a singing game such as "London Bridge" or "Mulberry Bush" may be used. The children may be asked to identify it and in turn, as individuals, in small groups, or as a class, sing it back to see if they can make it identifiable without the words.

At other times a teacher can contrast singing with speaking by saying rhythmically a pattern such as "Heigh-o, heigh-o, heigh-o" from "Rig-a-Jig-Jig." He can ask the children, "Did I *say* it or *sing* it?" They should then say it rhythmically. After that, the teacher can sing the pattern and then ask the children to sing it. Kindergarten children respond well to this procedure.

Other techniques can be used to establish the singing voice in children. Satis Coleman said that "to speak in a singing voice with abandon, without having to conform to a set song, is a great help in freeing the voice." She suggested practicing utter freedom in vocal sounds and holding conversations on one tone, later moving to two tones, using a higher tone on the word to be emphasized.[1]

In the privacy of the music corner, as he picks out his favorite song on the bells, many a child finds the necessary quiet concentration that enables him to match the melody of the bells with his own voice. Thus another beginning for singing is found in a situation removed from the singing group. Such freedom for individual work is important and requires special planning on the part of the teacher.

In the second and third grades good results may come from individual voice instruction. By this time, children have learned to accept special help in several areas of their school studies. The type and extent of the special help to be given in singing depends on the child and the teacher.

From his kindergarten days, Robert had a husky speaking voice and was not able to sing. In spite of customary remedial measures in the first and second grade classrooms, he showed no improvement. During Robert's third grade term the music consultant gave him special private work because he seemed interested in improving his singing voice. First they read character lines from children's stories: e.g., "What did the wolf say when he came to the door of the first little pig's house?" Robert had a good voice for the big wolf; and the consultant encouraged him to make it sound even bigger and deeper. "How did the little pig reply?" This was more of a problem, but, given an example, Robert soon produced a high, frightened-little-pig reply.

Now that he knew how to change his voice, Robert experimented with other dramatic recitations. After a few lessons the music consultant showed him how to sustain any of the pitch levels of his newly flexible speaking voice into a singing tone. Robert understood the process and began to experiment with his voice and to practice sustaining tones at various levels.

Frequent opportunity must be given boys and girls to sing alone, in pairs, or in small groups, for this will build confidence and enable other members of the class to listen objectively to voices of various qualities. Children are aware of differences in voices, but they accept them just as they do differences in the ability to read or to play ball.

## Voices in the Intermediate Grades

Those concerned with the music program of the intermediate grades must provide for the continued development of the singing voices of boys and girls. After the fourth grade, the vocal tone is more brilliant. The *practical* range for *all* voices in general classroom singing is about the same as that for the primary grades, but with good training many children are able to sing several tones higher or lower:

Vitality and energy are essential to good singing and, fortunately, most children have an abundance of both. Good singing is the result of clarity in enunciation and adequate breath support which gives the musical phrase its continuity. When pupils are enthusiastic about singing, breath support is no problem because the muscular framework is strong and flexible. If interest wanes, bodies sag in the chairs and tone quality deteriorates. In the intermediate grades breath support is achieved only indirectly through (1) good posture, promoted as far as possible through interest and enthusiasm, and (2) the message of the song—how it should be sung to achieve an expressive melody or vital rhythm.

One of the most common faults of children's singing is breathiness. A little attention to measured exhalation, taking a deep breath and exhaling evenly and gradually on a soft ss sound, can be helpful if the principle is then applied to a song with long smooth phrases.

Precise enunciation of words is important. Children can be careless or simply untrained in proper habits of enunciation. A flexible use of tongue and lips is necessary for clear speaking as well as for good singing. Singing is intoned speech, and unless the words are understood it does not fulfill its intended function. The teacher's example and his insistence upon clarity of speech in all language usage will aid in the development of good singing.

Singing has the added dimension of predetermined pitch not found in speaking. Throughout the elementary school there must be continued attention to singing tone calls and intervals in tune. The greatest problems occur on rising intervals when untrained voices tend to make the leap too short, basically because the singing lacks vitality, but also because the children have not yet learned precisely how a particular interval should sound. Consistently good training, beginning in the primary grades, could eliminate this problem. Some practices that lead to a better sense of pitch are:

1. Consistently singing a particular song in the same key,
2. Learning songs accurately from good recordings, with the aid of a tuned instrument, or from a teacher with an excellent sense of pitch,
3. Hearing and signing tone calls and intervals of the scale with particular attention to correct pitch.

*Boys' Voices.* Although the range and general quality in the voices of elementary school boys and girls is essentially the same, psychological factors occasionally result in more vocal problems among the boys. Problems may arise because singing voices were not well established in the primary grades. As they grow older, boys are less interested in developing a high singing voice; they would rather believe that their voices are low and "manly." At puberty the boy's larynx grows and the vocal cords lengthen and thicken so that his voice drops in pitch. During the fifth, sixth, and perhaps seventh

**181**

grades, prior to the change in voice, he has his last opportunity to sing in the high register. At this time his soprano voice tends to develop more brilliance than the girl's and, when properly trained, may have a range even higher than that given above. When these two facts are appreciated by the boys, there is usually little difficulty in promoting interest in the development of the unchanged voice.

Occasionally a teacher may find a boy in the fifth or sixth grade whose voice and general physical development indicate his early approach to adolescence. At this time the voice may temporarily be limited to about an octave upward from G or A below the treble staff. Although the unusual quality of the voice may make it sound lower, this is still within the normal range of the mature alto voice. A fifth or sixth grade class also may include boys whose voices are not yet beginning to change but who have not earlier learned to use their high singing voices. At this age they may have no inclination to do so. The teacher's problem then lies in helping them learn to sing in a lower limited range, knowing that within a year or two the normal lengthening of the vocal cords will permit them to extend the range downward. A practical range for these voices is:

Obstacles to the development of both of these types of boys' voices are that the normal singing range for the class does not include all of the low notes, and that almost every sixth grade song goes above this range. Three suggestions are made:

1. The teacher should help the boys identify the effective vocal range they possess and should encourage them to sing with the class whenever the song goes within that range.
2. Occasional songs with a short range should be transposed and sung in the lower octave by these voices and in the higher octave by the normal voices. "Go Tell Aunt Rhodie" (see page 216), when sung in the key of A, has this range:

3. Some melodic sections of songs may be sung by these lower voices while the others sing harmony parts. The stanza of "Liza Jane" is an example. "Down Mobile" (TiM VI–16) can be used in a similar way when sung in the key that gives the lower voices the most advantageous range.

## LIZA JANE

*Lively*          *Old American Song*

Come, my love, and go with me, Li'l Li - za Jane, Come, my love, and go with me, Li'l Li - za Jane, O E - li - za, li'l Li - za Jane, O E - li - za, li'l Li - za Jane!

Transposed from C.

From Beattie, Wolverton, Wilson, and Hinga, THE AMERICAN SINGER, Second Edition, *Book Six*. American Book Company. Used by permission.

There is no easy solution to the problem, for there may be only one or two such voices in a classroom. However, when the range of the voice has been determined, the teacher or music consultant can usually find suitable song material and ways to help the individual achieve some vocal satisfaction.

*Outstanding Voices.* Occasionally an intermediate pupil may possess an unusually beautiful voice that floats free and true without apparent effort. When such a voice is discovered the teacher may be concerned about its proper development. Private lessons and any special training of the voice itself should be delayed until the singer is fifteen or sixteen years old when the vocal cords have completely adjusted to the physical change of puberty. (It should be noted that there is growth in the larynx of the girl during puberty. The vocal cords do not lengthen, but in some individuals a strengthening of the lower tones of the voice gives evidence of the emergence of a true alto voice.) The general musical education of such a child should be promoted so that he will be in a position to use his voice to greatest advantage when it does mature.

Such a gifted child should be encouraged to sing in a natural, free voice and to develop a repertoire of folk and other songs which he enjoys sharing with others. He can participate in the school choir, sing occasional short solos with the group to develop his confidence in solo work, and participate in small ensembles with other good singers. In order to develop his musicianship

**SONGS AND SINGING VOICES**

he should study a musical instrument during his intermediate years. The piano is a most practical instrument for a singer to know, but musicianship can be improved through the study of other instruments.

A musically gifted child should have broad experiences in listening to fine singers of all types and to a variety of instrumental music so that he develops an intuitive sense of good musical expression. All of the classroom activities in music will combine to give this child basic understandings upon which he may later develop more specific music skills in accordance with his needs.

*Remedial Work with Voices in the Intermediate Grades.* If the previous training has been adequate, there should be few voices in the fourth or fifth grades that need special attention. For those that do, the teacher should work with the entire class in such a way that individual voices will improve. Focusing attention on the sound of short phrases and tonal patterns from the song is a valuable technique. However, in these grades it becomes increasingly necessary that those who do not sing in tune be given special private assistance. Work with groups of three or four students can be very successful. Usually twice-weekly lessons (ten minutes in length) over a period of two or three weeks will begin to yield results.

One music consultant gradually worked this type of service into her weekly visits to the various schools. Because the children enjoyed music and liked the consultant, an offer of a "private lesson in singing" became a hoped-for privilege for good as well as poor singers. The classroom teachers usually selected the three or four in greatest need of assistance.

The pupils would bring their song books, and the first question asked would be "What song do you like to sing?" She knew that poor singers are most readily successful on middle-of-the-voice folk-type songs. Songs like "Polly-Wolly-Doodle" or "Go Tell Aunt Rhodie" were chosen in preference to the more difficult "Star-Spangled Banner" or "Old Folks at Home." When the song had been agreed upon all began to sing it together. The result was more spirited than accurate and often came out in as many keys as there were singers. At the end of a phrase or two the consultant would say to the singer who seemed to have the most promising voice, "You were doing very well. Let's hear you sing it."

The pupil then sang alone or with the aid of the consultant in whatever key seemed to fit his voice. Usually he managed to sing the song quite recognizably for one or two phrases. Having found the best singer in the group, she asked others to sing with him. If the group succeeded in sounding a whole phrase accurately together, they were asked to repeat it and listen to the sound; some were asked to listen as others sang together. "Was everyone on the same tune?"

If a small amount of success was recognized, another favorite song might be used in the same way. The chief objective was to work on a phrase or two to get it going together in the most appropriate key for the voices. Encouragement was essential. After the pupils were successful in singing the melody in a lower key, the consultant might move up a whole step to see who could sing it at a higher level.

If one or two of the voices were so inflexible that they did not get on tune at all, the consultant would try another approach: "In the early days of aviation, when an airplane pilot had to fly 'blind' he followed a radio signal. He called it 'getting on the beam.' You have to get your voices 'on the beam' in order to learn to sing. This is the tone of the radio beam; see if you can match it." The consultant often found that C above middle C

was a good "radio beam" tone. Sometimes those who could not match lower tones proved to be good "pilots" at this level. If the singers did not hit the tone immediately, they were asked to slide up to it like a siren. At other times a lower tone was used and, once contact was made with the radio beam tone, this became the first tone of a song;

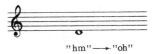

became

The pupils should be given simple things to practice: making siren sounds outdoors, matching radio beam tones with each other and listening carefully to match the pitch pipe tone when the class tunes up to sing a song. If melody instruments are available, the number notation may be written out for the phrases of the songs that the students sing correctly; in their free time they can then practice matching tones as they play the melody on the bells.

The classroom teacher who can give this remedial work himself, or who knows what the consultant is working toward, will know what to expect of less skilled singers during the classroom singing time. He will see that care is taken in the tuning-up process so that all pupils have a chance to match the key tone; he will see that one or two simple songs in an appropriate but limited range are included in the song selections so that the newly developing voices will have a better chance to sing in tune; he will provide these opportunities but he will not call attention to, nor embarrass by too much attention, those who are trying to get their voices in tune.

## OPPORTUNITIES FOR SINGING

SONGS AND SINGING VOICES

In the elementary school the grade-level classroom and playground provide the setting for the basic development of voices and skills in singing. When such skills have been acquired opportunities for broader singing experiences must be provided. Numerous suggestions for singing in both situations are offered on the following pages.

## SINGING IN THE CLASSROOM

Under favorable conditions most children enjoy group singing in the classroom. With younger children it is more an experience of "feeling" than of hearing; in the beginning the teacher should not expect conformity to melody and rhythm by all pupils. Only after ears have been trained to listen

**185**

and when the beauty of a *particular* melodic line is appreciated will fine unison singing begin to emerge.

## The Need for Informal Singing

Considering the individuality of each child, his lack of experience in cooperative activity, and often his lack of singing skill, it is nothing short of amazing that a kindergarten or first grade teacher achieves any sort of unified singing response from the group. Yet, in spite of obstacles, group singing is a tradition in the early years. It is a satisfying experience because it captures the spirit in an unusual way. When conformity to a particular melody and rhythm is achieved, it is chiefly through response to mood and feeling.

These facts develop a case for individual and informal small-group singing as an early experience, for until a child has sung he can hardly be expected to master the more difficult task of singing together with others. Consequently, the classroom teacher must look for varied times and places to foster individual singing during the school day. In the kindergarten many of the informal periods when children work alone or in small groups might be used to promote individual singing. As children build with blocks, play at housekeeping, paint, or color, they should feel free to sing and croon.

In this informal singing, a song need not be complete; phrases, repeated tone calls, make-up songs, and chants are natural and satisfying. The important thing is that the child sings because he feels free to do so, and this continued vocalization leads to greater facility in the use of the voice. The teacher, of course, gives encouragement and a good example when it may be beneficial. As other activities progress, the teacher may sing with a small group, accompanying them on the Autoharp, the ukulele, the guitar, or the piano; children will be encouraged to share new or original songs with the class.

Informal activity periods are less frequent in the first grade, because more time is given to reading, numbers, and writing. To promote informal individual and small-group singing, the teacher can use moments before school, after school, and at recesses, as well as during the classroom activities periods. Often as he stands talking with a few children, he will notice and encourage singing. For this purpose the children's original chanting songs or short folk songs are appropriate; some of the following may be sung anytime, anywhere, with complete informality: "The Old Gray Goose" (TiM III–10), "All Night, All Day" (ExM II–48), "Mary Wore a Red Dress" (Bir K–17), and "Gretel, Pastetel" (see page 142). Observe how readily other verses concerning the everyday interests of children may be added to this song: "Nancy, dear Nancy, oh where is your coat?"

For the child who has no natural inclination to sing, larger group activities may stimulate an interest or an unconscious first participation. Singing games, action songs, and finger plays are appealing to most children and encourage participation. Some children respond to ideas and picture images, and therefore storytelling and descriptive songs are important. Pupils may sit in a semicircle around the teacher as he talks and sings; they in turn join in.

The teacher must bear in mind that individual and small-group participation, as well as singing by the entire class, must be provided to meet the needs of every child.

Singing is an important classroom activity that should be continued throughout the intermediate grades. The teacher can establish the use of singing during opening exercises and at other appropriate times throughout the school day. Two or three music lessons during the week can have singing as a central interest, with related activities such as playing instruments, discussing and interpreting notation, etc. Chapter Seven gives special consideration to classroom management and techniques for teaching songs at all grade levels.

## Scheduling and Seating

Many teachers include music both at a definite time and at varied points throughout the day as needed for enrichment and for a change of pace. In the kindergarten and the first grade a scheduled music time may last only ten minutes on some days, more on others. The length of time depends on the type of activity engaged in and the frequency of informal uses of music at other times. Twenty minutes of the school day should be given to music in the primary grades and twenty-five minutes in the intermediate grades. When music has its assigned time in the daily schedule, the teacher is less likely to omit it when pressed by other demands of the curriculum. When unscheduled, the musical experiences become random and less unified. A short period set aside can draw these experiences together, help define them and relate them to one another.

The kindergarten schedule is flexible, and there is no problem in finding a time for music. The grade teacher, however, is pressed to find time for all the subjects in the curriculum, and musical activities are worked into the schedule in various ways. Some teachers use music time as a morning activity break, following reading or number work. Others prefer it as a relief in the middle of the afternoon or as a pleasant activity at the end of the day. However, music itself is important, not only as a refreshing break in the day, but as an activity worthy of the best that children and teacher can bring to it. As often as possible, music should be scheduled for a time when the children are rested and responsive.

To create an informal atmosphere for singing, many teachers have younger children sit in a semicircle on chairs or on a rug much as they do during storytelling time. The intimacy achieved by this arrangement is good, but singing is dependent upon a proper use of the lungs and diaphragm and the posture assumed by children seated on a rug does not permit this. As a daily practice it is preferable that chairs be used. The teacher should sit where he can easily communicate with every child in the group. In such an arrangement, the child with a poor voice should be seated next to a stronger singer so that he will consistently have a favorable model to follow. Seating can be rotated from time to time so that the teacher may be near different voices and thus give more effective vocal assistance.

Many classrooms, however, do not lend themselves to flexibility of this sort and teachers must use the prevailing arrangement of desks in the room. Some teachers prefer that the children remain in their regular seats during the music period. By doing so they avoid the confusion of changing seats and also establish the idea that singing is a part of regular life in the classroom and can take place at any time.

Whatever arrangement is used, the teacher must know how each child sings and must give individuals consistent help and encouragement. To achieve this goal, one practice has been to assign "music seats" on the basis of singing voices. The best singers are seated in the back rows of the room so that their voices come forward to the poor singers seated in the front rows. By being close to the teacher, the poor singers receive more help.

This plan of seating has been useful to many teachers and still is recommended by some supervisors. Its strength lies in its provision for a definite method of dealing with problem voices. Because the teacher must classify voices in order to assign seats, he becomes aware of the level of vocal development in each child. Teacher awareness is the first step in the development of good singing voices. Teachers who do not arrange this formal seating very often neglect to evaluate individual voices.

On the other hand, this seating has weaknesses that may be more or less pronounced, depending on the teacher's use of the plan. Children as well as adults are sensitive about their singing voices. When a teacher assigns seats in the front row to poor singers and seats in the rear to good singers, there may be grave psychological reactions that prevent a child from finding whatever singing voice he might develop in a more optimistic environment.

In most situations it is preferable that the ordinary classroom seating be retained for music, but the teacher should be free to move about the room among the children as they sing. In this way he will be aware of each child's vocal development, and will be able to give individual assistance and encouragement when necessary. The teacher should carry a pitch pipe and have facility in its use so that he does not have to go to the piano each time another song is begun.

It is important also that the poor singers not be grouped together. If it is impossible within the regular seating plan to have the poor singers scattered among better singers, it is advisable to make a few seat exchanges whenever any appreciable amount of singing is undertaken.

In the primary classroom, it is neither appropriate nor necessary that formal voice testing be done. The teacher can make a much better evaluation of voices by listening as he moves about the classroom while the children sing. He can also determine abilities as individuals or small groups sing their favorite songs for other children. By the time the teacher is acquainted with the child as a personality he should also be acquainted with his voice. In the fifth and especially the sixth grades, where some part singing is done and where the tonal range of the songs may be greater, some grouping of higher and lower voices will be necessary. General listening and observation by the teacher and some application of the voice-testing procedure suggested later in this chapter for special choral groups will provide a basis for grouping.

## Quality and Values in Song Material

One of the striking observations a visitor may make in a kindergarten or first grade classroom is of the genuine, direct response that the effective teacher receives from the children. The boys and girls are carried away by the simplest story or discussion about things they have experienced. Likewise, children seem charmed by many songs. But is the appeal actually in the song itself, or is it in the setting the teacher creates for it? There is no doubt that many poor songs will "go over" temporarily with children, merely as a result of external motivation. For this reason, there is diverse opinion among teachers as to what is an appealing song for children of a certain age. The most valid criterion for judging a song's worth to children is whether or not they sing it for themselves in situations not motivated and directed by the teacher.

Children use their singing voices in three important situations:
1. They sing in groups when engaged in some physical activity. Improvisation may go into this singing, and a mere fragment of a song may be repeated over and over in a chanting manner. Songs with simple melodies and strong rhythms best serve this need.
2. They sing to themselves as they go about their own private activities or lie in bed for a nap. This singing is more crooning; it has a broader range in melody and may include parts of the wistful quiet songs the child knows.
3. They share songs with parents and the family when these songs are strongly appealing to them and to the family group.

Generally speaking, a teacher might expect that a song he likes will have appeal for the children—that is, providing he has not selected the song with some special motive in mind, such as to exemplify good manners, safety, or a trip to the zoo! Songs composed especially for didactic purposes often lack grace, are soon outgrown, and have little meaning outside the specific situation in which they were originally used.

*The Value of Folk Songs.* Beatrice Landeck is convinced that folk songs should be the basic song material for young children:

After much experience with children and music, I came to rely almost entirely on folk songs. I've found in them colorful language, vivid imagery, humor, and warmth. They never seem to be outgrown. You hear them sung by adults with as much enthusiasm as by children.

One reason American folk songs have such an appeal for children is that every child senses their vitality. Folk songs reflect every emotion from joyousness to despair. They may bounce up and down on the nonsense level or tread a stately pace.[8]

The songs selected for use in the classroom should represent many moods and feelings to provide each child with music appealing to him, and to enable the group to express a wide range of emotion through singing. Folk songs offer variety as well as genuine reflection of human feeling. A simple, reflective text counting the stars can be completely engrossing for a child.

Several parts of "Bye'm Bye" lend themselves to repetitive crooning (see page 135).

What a comforting feeling for a child to know that "All Night, All Day" (TiM III–158) someone is watching over him. Such a song as "I Wish I Were a Little Bird" (SGro–19) might enable the child to express some inner feelings to "be" a carefree bird or a fish who would "swim 'way down in the sea." "There's a Little Wheel A-Turnin' " (Bir II–20) can give expression to an inner happiness. This type of song will serve the child in his private thinking and crooning even more significantly than in group singing at school.

In other songs the topic is of such small significance that any words, or no words at all, would do. In a song such as "Jimmy Crack Corn" (Bir II–14, ABC I–70) the infectious rhythm carries the song along. "Rig-a-Jig-Jig" (see page 110) is found in many collections of children's songs. It gallops and dances along in such a delightful fashion that every child, young or old, loves to sing it. An analysis of its melodic content reveals that much of this song consists of the intervals found to be natural to the singing of children, i.e., a minor third and the upper neighboring tone. It is not surprising that children sing it so readily.

"Down in the Valley" (see page 165) is a favorite folk song of sentiment among intermediate grade children as well as their elders. With the ability to play only two chords on the guitar or ukulele an individual can accompany his own singing.

A good song need not necessarily have much of a melody: "Old House" (see page 66) is chiefly a chant built almost entirely on three tones of the minor tonic chord. The rhythm of the melody seems to be determined by the inherent rhythm of the words. For this reason, although when seen in notation the rhythm may look complicated, it is not difficult to sing. For a heavy work song this simple tune with its strong rhythm is very appropriate.

*Songs Composed for Children.* A good song need not be a folk melody. "Walk on Tippy Toe" is a song that seems to have been composed as an expression of the wonderment and sensitive feeling children have for nature's rebirth after a cold winter. Notice the quiet rhythm of this song; it flows with a smooth, regular movement. From a moderately high beginning the melody moves stepwise (with occasional thirds) to a moderately low ending. These characteristics of rhythm and melody, in addition to the fact that it is in a minor mode, make this an especially lovely song.

## WALK ON TIPPY TOE

*Lightly*                                             *Words and music by Philip Alshin*

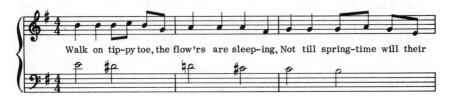

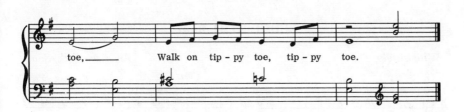

Walk on tip-py toe, the flow'rs are sleep-ing, Not till spring-time will their
buds be peep - ing, Walk on tip - py toe, tip - py
toe,_____ Walk on tip - py toe, tip - py toe.

From GROWING WITH MUSIC, *Book Two,* by H. R. Wilson *et al.* © 1966 by Prentice-Hall, Inc., Englewood Cliffs, N.J. Reprinted by permission.

The melody of this song lies within the prescribed range for children's voices; the song text reflects human feelings and is compatible with the quiet rhythm and simple melody. This is a lovely song that will surely evoke a mood in singers, thus providing the personal enrichment, described in Chapter One, which is an important value of music.

Although a lovely song, related to a subject of interest to children, may be an inspiring addition to the repertoire, the teacher should resist the temptation to use a poor song just because the text is appropriate to the topic at hand. Many teachers have composed, or have written down songs composed by their pupils, as a creative outgrowth of a unit of study. These are admirable creative products in the atmosphere in which they were inspired and took form. It is desirable that teachers compose music or inspire and guide their pupils in composition.

Unfortunately, when the majority of these songs are removed from the situation that inspired them, they lose their initial value as creative achievements and do not measure up as lasting song material. It is not necessary that all the songs used be folk songs, but the fact that a song has existed long enough to become a "folk song" indicates that it has vitality beyond its original use.

**SONGS AND
SINGING VOICES**

Basic school music books have been published for many years, and with changes in the teaching emphasis, the selection of songs has changed. The prospective classroom teacher should become well acquainted with the series of books used in the school system in which he expects to teach. For those who do not know what books will be available to them, it is recommended that a general use be made of several series listed in Appendix B.

## Song Subjects and Types

Believing that children enjoy songs related to their own daily interests in the home, with the family, or among school friends and neighbors, editors of many of the basic music books have organized song material around these topics. If the song itself is good, the fact that the subject is of immediate concern to the children will make it even more welcome.

*Songs of Personal Interest.* The child from five to seven is the center of his own universe; his interests and concerns do not range far. He will be delighted with such a simple, repetitious song as "Hush, Little Baby."

### HUSH, LITTLE BABY

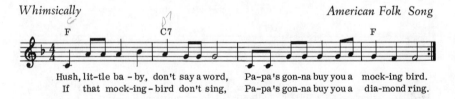

*Whimsically*                                                            *American Folk Song*

Hush, lit-tle ba - by, don't say a word,    Pa-pa's gon-na buy you a    mock-ing bird.
If    that mock-ing - bird don't sing,    Pa-pa's gon-na buy you a    dia-mond ring.

If there is a new baby at home, as there is with so many children of this age, it is "my baby." Thus the French lullaby "Fais Dodo" (GwM II–52, MMYO K–21), and other similar songs represent a topic close to the kindergarten or first grade child and will appeal to the baby's entire family.

Storybook characters have sung themselves into the hearts of young children for many generations. Mother Goose characters such as "Humpty Dumpty," "Little Jack Horner," and "Three Little Kittens" will find a place in the repertoire. Other characters from folklore like "John the Rabbit" (AFlk–100, MMYO K–150) soon become friends when children sing about them.

*Songs of Activity.* A song may be so strongly rhythmic that, regardless of the text, it will suggest skipping, running, galloping, or marching. Singing games, folk dances, and other songs evoking vigorous movement were discussed in Chapter Three. In addition, children sing about what they are doing or are going to do. "What Shall We Do?" (GwM K–76) and other chanting songs lend themselves to improvisation on endless activities during the school play periods or with friends at home.

## WHAT SHALL WE DO?

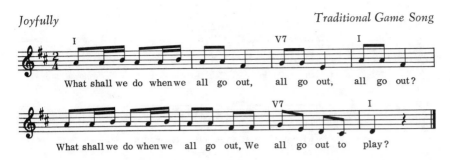

*Joyfully*                                   *Traditional Game Song*

*Patriotic and Holiday Songs.* As the class becomes more proficient in singing, the repertoire will expand in several directions; art songs as well as folk songs should be included. Among the important songs heard in the community are the patriotic songs, Christmas carols, and songs of thanksgiving. Many of these have become traditional in the United States, and children can sing them along with their families. However, some of them lack the simplicity of folk songs; they are wide in range and more difficult to sing. When it seems appropriate, the younger children may experience such songs by hearing others sing them, by hearing recordings, or by singing only the refrain.

Young children do not need many patriotic songs. "America" and "God Bless America" are two of the easiest and will enable the children to join in at any community gathering. In the third grade "America, the Beautiful" is an important song to be learned. Fourth graders can begin to learn "The Star-Spangled Banner." Although this song is the national anthem of the United States the learning of it is delayed until the fourth grade because it is generally a difficult song to sing and has an exceptionally wide range. In the fifth grade other patriotic songs are learned as a part of the study of United States history.

Christmas brings a wealth of traditional songs, and some questions about how many of these have a place in the public school. Teachers in different communities find different answers. If a song is a thing of beauty and a joy to sing, it may be used regardless of its cultural or religious heritage. However, many of the carols are too difficult musically for young children and too deeply religious in text for school use.

A number of secular carols are suitable for children in any school. The jolly Swedish carol "Now It's Christmas Time" and old English carols such as "Christmas Is Coming" and "We Wish You a Merry Christmas" are delightful and easy.

SONGS AND
SINGING VOICES

**193**

## WE WISH YOU A MERRY CHRISTMAS

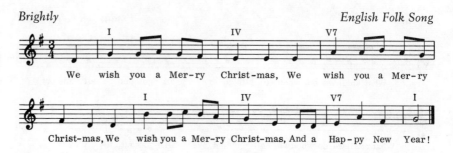

*Brightly*                                    *English Folk Song*

We wish you a Mer–ry Christ–mas, We wish you a Mer–ry
Christ–mas, We wish you a Mer–ry Christ–mas, And a Hap–py New Year!

"O Come, Little Children," "The Friendly Beasts," and "O Christmas Tree" are appropriate carols for children. Two spirituals, "Mary Had a Baby, Yes, Lord" and "A Band of Angels," make unusual additions to the Christmas repertoire. Current holiday songs with the childlike simplicity of "Frosty the Snowman" and "Rudolph the Rednosed Reindeer" are appropriate for school use.

Carols and customs from Sweden, Mexico, and many other countries can broaden the appreciation of Christmas as well as give a basis for an acquaintance with people in other lands. Older children will enjoy songs such as the Spanish carol, "Fum, Fum, Fum" (DMT VI–185, MMYO VI–91). Almost any size play, pageant, or tableau can be developed around the topic "Christmas in Other Lands."

In addition to the Christmas celebration, a teacher might consider the Jewish December Festival of Lights, as children are led to share an appreciation of traditional songs of holidays that receive less public attention. "Hanukkah" (ExM II–76, DMT I–79), "O Hanukkah" (Bir IV–128, DMT IV–151), and others are available in the basic song books. *A Treasury of Jewish Folklore*[9] by Ausubel is an aid to the teacher in his search for interesting material about the Jewish faith and customs.

Thanksgiving may be highlighted by appropriate songs. "A Thankful Song" (Bir I–91) and the following old English round, found under different titles in the basic music books, seem especially appropriate.

## SONG OF THANKS

*With dignity*                                    *Old English Round*

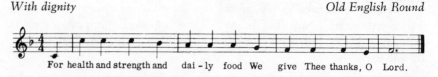

For health and strength and dai–ly food We give Thee thanks, O Lord.

By kind permission of J. Curwen & Sons Ltd., 24 Berners Street, London, W.1.

From the third grade upward children may learn "Come, Ye Thankful People, Come," the chorale "Now Thank We All Our God," "For the Beauty of the Earth," and other traditional harvest songs that are a part of the

American heritage. There are a number of "turkey" and "pumpkin" songs, but few of them have genuine musical worth.

Easter is a holy day, rather than a holiday, and as such is even harder to deal with in the public schools, where all faiths are represented, than is Christmas. Songs that treat of Easter as a time of waking earth and flowers are usually quite acceptable.

Schools associated with a religious organization, of course, have the opportunity of utilizing much fine religious music in the singing repertoire for children. However, even in these schools, the teacher should take care to see that the music is appropriate for children, both in the text and in the simplicity of the melody.

*Art Songs.*   Songs that have been composed so artistically that the music conveys the meaning and feeling equally with the text are considered art songs. Many of the songs by Schubert, Brahms, Grieg, and other composers are too difficult for children to sing, although they may be heard on recordings or performed by soloists or choral groups. Since it is important that boys and girls become acquainted with the more famous art songs as well as a wide variety of voice types (see the outline of concepts under timbre in Chapter Two), a number of good recordings of such songs should be available in the school record library.

Among the art songs that primary children can learn to sing are Brahms' "Lullaby," Mozart's "Cradle Song," Barnby's "Sweet and Low," Humperdinck's "Little Man in the Woods," and other songs from the children's opera *Hänsel and Gretel.*

Boys and girls in the intermediate grades can sing a wider variety of art songs. Such songs as "Passing By" by Purcell, "Thou Lovely Tree" by Handel, "Beautiful Dreamer" by Foster, "The Linden Tree" and others by Schubert will be found in the basic series music books.

A number of composers of the romantic style in music wrote groups of short pieces in different moods, but related to a single topic. From such a song cycle comes Schubert's "Whither?" ("Wohin?"), which is a lovely flowing melody accompanied by a gentle, rapid piano part suggesting a babbling brook. The excerpt shown on the next page gives one an idea of Schubert's famous style of song writing.

A few chorale melodies and excerpts from oratorios can be learned by intermediate grade singers: "How Brightly Shines the Morning Star" by Bach, "Now Thank We All Our God" by Crüger, and "Oh, Rest in the Lord" by Mendelssohn. In addition to such excellent works by earlier composers a number of recognized contemporary composers have written songs especially for children. Some of these songs are found in the series music books and they should be used widely so that children may experience varied song literature, especially that by composers of their own day. Many distinguished composers have written songs for children; among the contemporary composers are Benjamin Britten, "Old Abram Brown" (MMYO IV–31), and Zoltán Kodály, "Riding with the Cavalry" (ExM IV–42).

**195**

# WHITHER?

### "Wohin?" from the song cycle "Die schöne müelerin"

*Moderato*

*Franz Schubert*

I — heard a brook - let rush - ing from — out the rock - y — spring, Far — down the val - ley rush — ing, so — fresh and won - drois — clear. I know — not what im - pells — me to go where 'ere it — leads, But I — must — fol - low

af ter with my walk - ing stick__ in__ hand, But__

I must fol - low__ af - ter, with my walk - ing stick__ in__

hand.

This is an excerpt of the first five phrases from a longer song. Transposed from the key of G; translated from the German.

*"Community" Singing.* Because it was felt that the schools had an obligation to help boys and girls become acquainted with the music used in the community, teachers in the elementary grades have included patriotic, community, and camp songs in the singing repertoire for many years. Such old favorites as "Swanee River," "Down by the Old Mill Stream," "Sailing," "Old Black Joe," and others were considered basic community repertoire. In looking through the school music books today one fails to find these old favorites. Does the omission indicate that taste in "community" songs has changed or that community singing as it once was known is no longer an important activity among our people?

Perhaps both factors are involved. People sing together in smaller groups at home and on picnics, more often than in community gatherings. The repertoire has changed, although the standard patriotic and holiday songs are still sung. In some communities the music of a particular national group is more important than songs that might be considered typical of the American heritage. Many of Stephen Foster's songs, once considered basic repertoire, are encountered chiefly in the study of the musical heritage of our country. Most people are acquainted with them but few know the words so well that they can be sung in their entirety. When young people sing around the campfire they are more likely to sing current popular songs and interesting folk songs of other countries, such as "The Happy Wanderer" (TiM III–94), "Zum Gali Gali" (DMT IV–52), and "Kum Ba Yah" (MoM IV–123), than

"Camptown Races," "Down by the Old Mill Stream," and "Tenting Tonight," which were the "popular" songs of an earlier day.

In each community teachers should determine what essential heritage songs will serve this basic need for children and adults in that region. Such songs should be included in the repertoire used in the schools.

*Songs from Other Cultures.* Most of the songs heard in the United States have their roots in the musical tradition of Western Europe. They are chiefly major or minor in tonality, and they are harmonically oriented. With worldwide communication today people and music of other cultures are a part of the world of every child. Although the musical traditions differ, peoples all over the world have similar concerns and activities. Their songs can be shared by children here because the music is appealing and helps children identify with people in other lands.

Recent basic music books include original texts for some folk songs. When the words can be presented correctly these should be used in the original language for interest and for the cultural enrichment that it brings to the singing program. In elementary schools where foreign languages are taught, folk songs are an important part of the project.

At the intermediate level, songs related to the social studies become very important. Consideration will be given such a correlation of material in Chapter Nine when some recommendations are made for the organization of units of study based on such topics.

## BROADER SINGING EXPERIENCES

Opportunities to sing in larger and more varied groups outside the classroom should be provided for pupils from the third grade upward. The all-school assembly "sing" is an activity to which pupils in small schools look forward. In larger schools grade-level "sings" and a special chorus are enriching activities.

Younger children find the smaller social group of the classroom compatible with their needs; they are not able to sing all of the songs suitable for older voices. For these reasons assembly singing should be a more frequent activity in the intermediate grades.

### The Singing Assembly

In schools where an assembly hall is available, pupils from all classes can come together biweekly or monthly to sing songs they have learned in their classrooms. Some schools are built with soundproof, folding walls between adjacent classrooms. The walls can be opened so that two or three groups may simultaneously see and hear a demonstration or a film. Such an arrangement provides opportunities for the sharing of musical experiences by larger groups. The thrill of many voices singing together gives this activity its major appeal. When a school houses a large number of classes on one grade level it may be advisable to have grade-level "sings" utilizing songs closely related to classwork at a given level.

Teachers and student leaders may get together each month to decide what new songs will be used in the following assembly. In selecting such songs these criteria are valid:

1. Musical appeal is highly important; do the pupils really like to sing this song?
2. Songs that are simple in melody and rhythm are best for large-group singing.
3. Unison as well as easy two-part songs, including rounds, "partner songs" (two that fit together harmonically), and songs with easy descants, can be used.

The school principal and music consultant will need to see that music is available to all classes and that all have a satisfactory means of learning it.

Assembly singing is traditionally accompanied by the piano. If the group is very large, a single piano may not give enough support for the entire group. Some songs, especially those sung in harmony, are best sung unaccompanied. Carefully planned assembly singing can serve as an extension and enrichment of the basic music program in the classroom. Although such large-group singing has strong appeal as an occasional activity, it loses much of its impact when scheduled too often. Administrators and teachers delude themselves if they believe this kind of experience alone can provide adequate music education for children at any age.

## Special Choirs

Special choral groups, led by a trained director, should be available for intermediate grade pupils who have a particular interest in singing. Such singing enriches their musical experience and also prepares them for choral work in the high school, church, and community.

The music consultant or a skilled teacher may organize such a group. Membership should be open to all fifth and sixth grade students on the basis of interest and, to some extent, singing ability. Whatever selection seems necessary should be done with due consideration for the needs as well as talents of individuals who are interested. Fourth grade students might be included, although some prestige is achieved by limiting membership to the older children. Sixty voices will provide a good-sounding group capable of singing three parts when a large number of children need to be accommodated. Smaller groups of thirty or forty selected singers will also provide a good ensemble.

A choral group should meet two or three times weekly to make satisfying progress. It should not be a substitute for classroom music. Rehearsal within the school day is the most desirable arrangement. However, it may be necessary to practice before school or at noon. After-school rehearsals are not recommended because boys and girls are too tired for satisfactory accomplishment. A compromise may be made by extending the 30- or 40-minute rehearsal into a school session for 15 minutes in the morning, before or after lunch.

Membership should be selective as well as elective. The voices selected should be clear and flexible with a reasonably wide range. Voices can be auditioned individually or in groups of two or three. Since children sing more easily and naturally a song they know well, choose a song such as "America, the Beautiful" to be sung in two different keys that reveal the range of the voices.

## AMERICA, THE BEAUTIFUL

Samuel A. Ward
Text by Katharine Lee Bates

*Majestically*

The range in the key of B♭ is

In the key of E♭ the song begins like this:

O    beau – ti – ful    for    spa – cious skies

The range is then

Those children who sing easily in the higher key should be considered for the high part in three-part singing. Those with a more limited range should sing the middle part, and those capable of singing A below middle C with an easy, free tone can be assigned to the low part. (In the key of G the lowest note in "America, the Beautiful" is A.)

In the United States elementary school choirs traditionally sing many of their songs in two or three parts. Part-singing can be beautiful when the boys and girls are sufficiently experienced to listen to the total effect and to stay in tune. It is most effective when unaccompanied. In some schools, however, emphasis has been placed on part-singing to the exclusion of unison singing. A select group of children's voices singing in unison a lovely art song such as "Children's Prayer" from *Hänsel and Gretel,* a suitable sacred song such as "Oh Lord, Most Holy" ("Panis Angelicus"), or an excerpt from Bach's aria, "My Heart Ever Faithful" (see page 202) is a musical treat for any audience and provides a genuine thrill for the performers as well.

SONGS AND
SINGING VOICES

# MY HEART EVER FAITHFUL
## (Aria from Cantata No. 68)

*Presto*

J. S. Bach

My heart___ ev-er faith-ful, Sing prais-es, re-joice___

prais-es, re-joice; re-joice,___ sing prais-es, Your

Je-sus is here; my heart___ ev-er faith-ful, sing prais-es re-joice;___ re-

joice,___ sing prais-es___ your___ Je-sus is here!

This is an excerpt from a longer aria (measures 1–15 and 51–52). Transposed from the key of F; translated from the German.

The accompaniment in this song is important because it will acquaint the children with the pervading style of baroque music, a strong steady rhythm and a firm bass line supporting the rather florid upper voice. The slight melismatic character of the vocal line suggests the joy expressed in the words.

"Papageno's Magic Bell Song" from Mozart's opera *The Magic Flute* is well suited to children's voices, and it is a good example of the simple clear harmony and balanced form of music in the classic style. The light texture of the accompaniment and the subject of the text add to its appropriateness for children's voices. The key in which the song is shown here is suitable for most average singing voices, but the song may be done in the key of F or the key of G if the upper voices can sing higher without strain. The children would have no trouble learning the simple German text for this song.

### PAPAGENO'S MAGIC BELL SONG
#### (from Finale to Act I, The Magic Flute)

ring-eth so glo-ri-ous, it__ ring-eth so fair! La-la-
klin-get so herr-lich, das__ klin-get so schön! La-la-

**SONGS AND
SINGING VOICES**

**203**

Transposed from the key of G. Play small notes in refrain second time only.

CHAPTER
SIX

"Shadow March" by Alec Rowley is representative of contemporary songs written especially for children's voices. The accompaniment is colorful and adds to the descriptive qualities of the music. The children should be made aware of the descending augmented chords that accompany "the crooked shadows," as well as other interesting features that label this as music of the twentieth century.

## SHADOW MARCH

Alec Rowley
Words by R. L. Stevenson

*Mysteriously*

All round the house is the jet-black night; It stares thro' the win-dow pane; It crawls in the cor-ners, hid-ing from the light, And it moves with the mov-ing flame. Now

**205**

SONGS AND
SINGING VOICES

**207**

Numerous publishers of choral music have works for children's voices. (See Appendix B for names and addresses of such firms.) Most fifth and sixth grade series music books contain some part songs that may be used by such choral groups, but it is advisable to extend the repertoire beyond that used in the classroom music program. Ethel Kinley lists songs in several arrangements for unchanged voices in the Appendix of her book, *Fundamentals for Singers*.[10] A great variety of unaccompanied two- and three-part songs would be appropriate. These could include "Bicinia" and "Tricinia" by the sixteenth century composer Praetorius as well as those by the twentieth century Hungarian composer Kodály.

In the repertoire that he selects let the director strive for a balance of experiences for these young singers and avoid the error of asking them to sing consistently difficult arrangements in which they fail to realize the full musical appeal of the song. An audience is a challenge if performances are well spaced and do not become the chief purpose of the choir's existence. Certainly such a choir should sing frequently for groups of children within the school. Some teachers think only in terms of public performance and fail to see the real values of the choir:

1. To provide an extended singing experience for talented and interested pupils.
2. To acquaint all children, singers as well as listeners, with a more artistic and varied repertoire of songs than is ordinarily sung in the classroom.
3. To develop musicianship and skill in reading notation through contact with a greater variety of music.

### Mass Choruses

It is important to give all children in the intermediate grades an opportunity to sing occasionally in a performing group. In a massed choir all children in specified classes can be brought together to rehearse and polish selected compositions. If the songs are studied and memorized in the individual classrooms, the large-group rehearsals can be limited to three or less. One such project a year, planned for simplicity, can be very beneficial. If multiple parts are to be sung, each class should present a balanced group. The real ends of music education are not served when different parts are learned in different rooms and combined only in the mass group. Children who are accustomed to hearing the harmony in their classrooms will understand the composition from a musical point of view and will be more sensitive singers in the large organization.

The repertoire for such a mass chorus should be more limited in range and general complexity than that used by a choir of select voices. Descant and partner songs are effective; there are good descant arrangements of "America, the Beautiful" and "The Battle Hymn of the Republic" which could be used with orchestral accompaniment for a finale if this is desirable. Many unison songs and easy part-songs from the basic series music books are appropriate for such a chorus. Variety in style and mood as well as carefully planned sequence in the choice of musical compositions is essential to an artistic program.

The teacher who would direct rehearsals and the performance of a group of several hundred children should plan and chart his strategy well in advance. Children and assisting teachers should know exactly when and how to enter the hall, where to sit, when and where to stand, and other details. Only under such well-planned direction can the essential values of such an undertaking be realized.

In this chapter we have shown the full scope of the vocal program in the elementary school, beginning with the individualized singing of the kindergartner and advancing to the select choral group in the intermediate grades. The teacher who participates in this work must look even deeper into singing in the classroom to find out how children build skills and concepts that enable them to participate musically on ever more advanced levels. Detailed studies of classroom procedures are given in Chapter Seven.

## ACTIVITIES FOR COLLEGE CLASSES

A. Questions for Review
1. Describe the variation of tone quality and range in young children's voices.
2. Outline the various techniques through which the singing voices of kindergarten and primary children can be improved.
3. Describe the characteristics and range found among singing voices of children in the intermediate grades.
4. Outline the techniques that are recommended for remedial work with problem voices of intermediate grade children.
5. Describe the various opportunities for singing that should be provided children throughout the elementary school. Why are different opportunities needed for different groups?
6. What different kinds of songs should be provided for children of various ages and in different singing situations?
B. Written Assignments
1. Select two basic music books that are used at the grade level of your teaching interest. From these books choose two or three good songs related to several important singing interests (holidays, seasons, activities, correlated study topics, etc.) of children in that grade. Organize the song titles under topical headings in such a manner that other titles can be added later. For each song include the source and page, and brief teaching notes showing (a) musical activities that are suitable, (b) the most important musical concepts children might develop from their experiences with that song, and (c) tone calls that might be used for the improvement of voices.
2. Among "popular" songs not found in the music series books select one or two that you recommend as appropriate for study by children in the grade level of your choice. Submit the music and brief teaching notes for each song as outlined above. If you do not find songs you consider appropriate state why those you viewed were unsuitable.

C. Classroom Project

Sing for the college class any favorite easy folk song; accompany yourself on the Autoharp, the piano, or any other instrument that is appropriate. After you have sung the song once or twice invite the class to sing along with you.

---

## CHAPTER NOTES

1. Satis N. Coleman, *Creative Music for Children* (New York: G. P. Putnam's Sons, 1922), pp. 100–105. Reprinted by permission.
2. Beatrice Landeck, *Children and Music* (New York: William Sloane Associates, Inc., 1952), pp. 30–39.
3. Gladys E. Moorhead and Donald Pond, *Music of Young Children* (four volumes and two twelve-inch records) (Santa Barbara, Calif.: The Pillsbury Foundation, 1941–1951).
4. George E. Reynolds, *Environmental Sources of Musical Awakening in Pre-School Children* (Ed. D. Dissertation, University of Illinois, 1960), Microfilm Order No. 60-3983.
5. John S. Shelton, *The Influence of Home Musical Environment upon Musical Response of First-Grade Children* (Ed. D. Dissertation, George Peabody College for Teachers, 1965), Microfilm Order No. 66-4419.
6. Emma Dickson Sheehy, *Children Discover Music and Dance* (New York: Holt, Rinehart & Winston, Inc., 1959), pp. 68–71.
7. Ruth Crawford Seeger, *American Folk Songs for Children* (New York: Doubleday and Company, Inc., 1948).
8. Beatrice Landeck, *Children and Music* (New York: William Sloane Associates, Inc., 1952), pp. 52 and 55. Copyright 1952 by Beatrice Landeck. Reprinted by permission.
9. Nathan Ausubel, *A Treasury of Jewish Folklore* (New York: Crown Publishers, 1948).
10. Ethel A. Kinley, *Fundamentals for Singers* (Toronto: Clarke, Irwin and Co., Ltd., 1953).

### Other References

Carl Fischer, Inc.: *Songs for Pre-Teentime* and other publications for unchanged voices.

Gary, Charles L., editor, *The Study of Music in the Elementary School* (Washington, D.C.: Music Educators National Conference, 1967). Pp; 162–163.

Ginn and Company: *Partner Songs, More Partner Songs,* and other publications for unchanged voices.

Harewood, Maria Donata (Stein) Lascelles, Countess of (editor) and Ronald Duncan, *Classical Songs for Children* (New York: C. N. Potter, 1964).

Jacques, Reginald, *Voice-Training in Schools* (London: Oxford University Press, 1945).

*Juilliard Repertory Project for Kindergarten through Grade Six,* Roger Sessions, Director, developed through a grant from the United States Office of Education. Publication pending.

Lloyd, A. L., *Folk Songs of the Americas* (London: Novell & Co. Ltd., 1965).

Summy-Birchard Publishing Company, *Vive la Musique!,* French folk songs for unchanged voices, and other choral collections.

Timmerman, Maurine, *Let's Teach Music* (Evanston, Ill.: Summy-Birchard Publishing Company, 1958). Pp. 113–114, "Suggested Supplementary Song Sources."

Mathews, Paul Wentworth, *You Can Teach Music* (New York: E. P. Dutton and Co., Inc., 1953). Chapter 3, "The Common Sense Way to Singing."

Mills Music, Inc.: *The Festival Song Book, Mills First Chorus Album,* and other publications for unchanged voices.

Mursell, James L., *Music and the Classroom Teacher* (Morristown, N.J.: Silver Burdett Company, 1951). Chapter 6, "Singing."

Neil A. Kjos Music Co.: *Our First Songs to Sing with Descants, From Descants to Trios,* and other publications for unchanged voices.

Nordholm, Harriet, *Singing in the Elementary School* (Englewood Cliffs, N.J.: Prentice-Hall, Inc., 1966).

Oxford University Press: *Children's Songs of Denmark, Children's Songs of Italy,* and other publications for unchanged voices.

Shawnee Press, Inc.: *Little Folk Songs, One for the Melody,* and other publications for unchanged voices.

Sheehy, *op. cit.* Chapter 4, "Singing."

Staton, J. Frederic, *Sweet Singing in the Choir* (Toronto: Clarke, Irwin and Co., Ltd. 1942).

SONGS AND
SINGING VOICES

# 7

# Management of the Singing Situation

Singing is a very important activity in the elementary school classroom. It is often combined with the use of movement and the playing of instruments as described in previous chapters, but singing demands certain unique management skills on the part of the teacher and these need special study. In this chapter the singing voice as a valuable teaching tool will be considered along with practical skills such as tuning up to sing a song and using accompaniments of several kinds.

Extensive analysis will be given various ways in which songs are taught, first as aural experiences for young children and later through the use of books. More advanced situations wherein older children learn to sing harmony parts and groups of boys and girls compose their own songs are also areas of concern for the teacher.

## PREPARATION AND NEEDED SKILLS

Much can be done to prepare a teacher to carry out a useful program of singing in the elementary classroom. A teacher who feels inadequate for this task may lack understanding of vocal production and experience in singing more than he lacks a basic ability to sing. Everyone can explore the possibilities of his singing voice and will benefit from the understandings he gains from such study even though, for a few, it may be too late or the time may be too short to make much progress with vocal training.

Learning to tune up to sing a song and studying the principles of good singing and song accompaniment will be useful to the teacher whether he uses the techniques himself or directs children in acquiring these skills.

### The Teacher's Voice

The most desirable singing example that can be provided children is a teacher who sings and who shares a love of singing with his pupils. With training, many more classroom teachers could experience the satisfaction of helping children learn to sing. The teacher needs the flexible, natural voice of the good folk singer rather than the highly developed voice of the concert artist or operatic star. Simplicity in expressing through song the sentiments appropriate and appealing to children is the basic requirement.

Most teachers develop good enunciation and projection of ideas when they tell stories to children, but often they forget that this *same* technique must be employed in singing to children. Flexible, active use of the lips and tongue, as well as vitality in facial expression, will go a long way in putting a song over.

One of the teacher's initial problems is to become aware of the range of the child voice and to relate this to his own vocal range. Many beginning teachers believe that, because the child voice is high, they cannot provide a suitable example. Very often these teachers have no clear conception of the range of the average adult voice, nor do they realize that with use and some directed practice the range of the voice can be extended.

*Vocal Development.* Disuse of the singing voice, lack of understanding of the normal range, and unfamiliarity with the production of tones in the head register are the beginning teacher's chief problems. The following paragraphs give some practical suggestions for vocal development.

Support of the singing tone by effective use of the diaphragm is an important consideration in vocal production. To discover the action of the diaphragm (1) sit erect or stand and place the hands, thumbs pointing backward and fingers forward, at the lower edge of the rib cage; (2) inhale and exhale deep breaths, keeping the shoulders and upper chest quiet but expanding the lower ribs and the muscular area below; (3) pant like a dog on a hot day to put the diaphragm into observable action. When an infant sleeps on its back this normal action of the diaphragm is readily observed.

Singing tones can be produced without the optimum use of the diaphragm, but good breath support is essential for the production of tones with maximum resonance, accurate intonation, and freedom, especially in the upper register.

The proper focus of the tone and the utilization of nasal resonance contribute toward a good singing voice. Try to focus the tone forward, just behind the upper front teeth so that a slight vibration is felt in the upper teeth and the lips as the following exercise is sung:

mee may mah moh moo, mee may mah moh moo, *etc.*

When the desired sensation is achieved, try to maintain it during the singing of several different pitches:

mee may mah moh moo, mee may mah moh moo, *etc.*

Finally sing a song with a short range that can be accommodated in the middle register of the voice, about as follows:

"Go Tell Aunt Rhodie" is such a song:

## GO TELL AUNT RHODIE

Sadly                                                      *American Folk Song*

Go    tell Aunt    Rho - die,    Go    tell Aunt    Rho  -  die,

Go    tell Aunt    Rho - die, our    old gray goose is        dead.

One should maintain the necessary breath support and forward focus of the tone in experiments with the quality of the lower register. In this case the tone is amplified by added resonance in the mouth and chest. Sing "Go Tell Aunt Rhodie" in the key of A to hear the quality of the low register (sometimes called the "chest voice").

Go    tell Aunt    Rho - die,    Go    tell Aunt    Rho  -  die, *etc.*

Many people sing entirely in the middle and lower registers and believe they cannot sing above C or D:

Individuals do differ in the ease with which they sing in different registers but most young people can learn to use a few tones in the upper register (sometimes called the "head voice") if they are shown the essentials of its production. Several approaches can be taken:

1. Using adequate breath support and a forward focus of the tone, begin in the middle register and make a siren sound upward on the vowel "oo." Try this several times and finally sustain the highest tone that is achieved:

oo - - oo    oh - - oh

When the desired tone is obtained, broaden the vowel to "oh."

2. Using the syllable "mee," leap an octave and come down the tonic triad:

mee  mee  mee  mee    mee,    mee  mee  mee mee    mee, *etc.*

Sing this exercise in successive lower and higher keys; try it with different vowel sounds such as "may" and "moh."

3. Slide up to and sustain a pitch in the upper register, then sing a familiar song at that level, first using the vowel "mee" and then using the words:

mee  mee mee  mee  mee,  mee  mee mee  mee mee mee, *etc.*
Go  tell Aunt  Rho - die,  Go  tell Aunt  Rho  -  die, *etc.*

Blow the tone lightly as though blowing a bubble; strength and added resonance can be developed later. In the first few experiments of this kind the vocal mechanism will tire very readily because the production of high tones requires greater contraction of the vocal cords. Like other muscles of the body the vocal cords should be gradually trained in activities that are out of the ordinary for the individual.

4. Try to maintain the same sense of breath support and tonal placement while singing broader vowels. Learn to sing with the mouth open (the width of two fingers between the front teeth is a common rule) for better tone production.

Most unused adult voices will produce D with reasonable comfort.

Compare this with the average untrained child's range, C to D and possibly E:

There is no disparity. True, children should learn to sing higher when they have the vocal capacity, but in classroom singing the range given will permit the development of a large repertoire of songs.

*Use of the Male Voice.* Children can learn songs from hearing the male voice, which sounds an octave lower. However, because the range of the child voice lies within the range of the female voice, the woman teacher is at an advantage in providing a singing example. Some men teachers have developed the falsetto voice so that they can employ it comfortably in the actual child voice range. But the falsetto has a quality of tension about it that sets an unnatural example for children. The use of this voice is actually unnecessary if a few precautions are taken when the normal male voice is used.

In the early stages of singing for children, the man should present a few songs in the middle register, D up to B—the easiest range for children when they sing an octave higher.

If he uses a higher tenor voice, children may attempt to imitate his actual pitch on the higher tones of a song, and then find the lower notes in the song below their range. "Go Tell Aunt Rhodie," shown here in the key of F, would be appropriate, or if necessary it could be sung a third lower, in the key of D (see page 216), and still lie within the child voice range.

After the man has had experience teaching songs in a limited middle range he may select those with a wider range. The following techniques will assure correct placement in the child voice:
1. Play the melody on the piano or bells in the child voice octave as the teacher sings in his octave.
2. Train the children to take the tonic note from the pitch pipe (which sounds in their octave) and to sing to the first note of the song.
3. Employ the voice of an accurate child singer as a sample for others learning a song.
4. Play the melody on the violin, flute, clarinet, recorder, or other instrument in the soprano register. (When the teacher cannot sing as he plays, he will have to be sure the children have previously heard the song enough to know how the words fit the melody.)

Similar difficulties may arise in the use of a recorded male voice, although many of the better singers have eliminated this problem by careful choice of range. In some cases the teacher will find it necessary to help establish the child voice at the proper octave-above level through using the pitch pipe or piano so that the children will be correctly oriented at the beginning of the song, or, if the teacher is a woman, singing the first note or phrase in the proper octave.

Every prospective elementary teacher should have as much singing experience as possible. Some individual coaching is valuable, but the chief need is to sing in a group where good diction, musical phrasing, and accurate intonation are emphasized. The teacher should be able to sing the scale and the tonic chord in tune, for his example will be copied by many children.

The teacher who does not sing well in tune may ask another teacher to teach new songs to the class, or he may find melodic support in an instrument. In addition, he should study recorded materials and learn techniques for using them. Every teacher who has a sincere desire to do so will find some means by which singing can be made a vital part of the classroom activities.

## Tuning Up to Sing a Song

When a piano or other chording instrument is used to accompany singing, the player always gives the tonic chord or plays a fragment of the melody to establish the tonality of the song. In classrooms that have no piano, a pitch pipe has been the traditional means of establishing the starting tone. However, if the children are to sing with the Autoharp or bells, the pitch should be taken from the instrument rather than from the pitch pipe. When a record is used, the tonality is set by the recorded introduction, and no other tuning is necessary.

To assure a suitable singing range, songs should be sung in a predetermined key. Teachers who guess at the first tone of a song not only get the singers off to a false start, but put an obstacle in their path. Some children have excellent tonal memories which, if correctly developed, might lead to the possession of a fine sense of pitch. When a song is sung every day at a somewhat different pitch level, any development in this direction is thwarted. Furthermore, a child with a good pitch sense is bound to be confused because, for him, the song sounds different each time it is sung in a different key.

Any teacher who can learn to sing the tonic chord in tune may successfully use the pitch pipe. It is advisable to buy a chromatic, twelve-tone pitch pipe so that any key note may be sounded. Pitch pipes with tones between middle C and third-space C are more convenient to use than those with tones from F up to high F on the treble staff because the lower tones are more easily matched by the untrained voice.

*Tuning Up from a Key Note.* To sing a song in a major key, the following tuning procedure is recommended when only one tone is sounded on the pitch pipe, piano, or other instrument.

1. Find the key note of the song from its key signature. (See Appendix A–IV for key signature explanation.)
2. Sound the key note on the pitch pipe, sing "do" (1) on that tone, and then sing up or down the tonic chord to the tone on which the song begins, usually "do," "mi," or "so" (1, 3, or 5). (See Appendix A–IV for explanation of sol-fa syllables.) Notice that "so" is an accepted shortening of the traditional "sol."
3. Sing the first word of the song on the correct pitch.

As an example, to tune up for "Three Little Kittens" the key note G is sounded on the pitch pipe and then the following pattern is sung.

do    so    Oh, three lit - tle    kit - tens they    lost    their mit - tens *etc.*

Often inexperienced teachers sing the syllable pattern correctly but fail to start the first word of the song on the correct pitch; hence rule 3 is important for beginners.

**219**

This tuning up process should be accurate and quick. The teacher should train himself to remember pitches so that he is able to maintain the pitch level of a song without undue repetition of the tuning up process.

Prospective teachers often ask: "Wouldn't it be a shorter process to sound the tone on which the song begins?" If the song is very familiar and the melody comes immediately to mind, it is possible that no problem will arise, unless a song previously used has left a different key in the memory of the singers. Most songs are key-centered, and the tuning up process not only gives the singer the first tone of the song, but it also accustoms his ear to the key in which he will sing. Notice that in "Three Little Kittens" the tuning up pattern, "do" (1)—"so" (5), is reversed in the first two notes of the song. After hearing this portion of the tonic chord, the ear is prepared not only for the first tone but for the second and succeeding tones in the example, all of which lie in the tonic chord.

During the first grade the children should learn to sing "do" (1) to match a tone sounded on the pitch pipe or other melody instrument, and then, under the teacher's direction, sing the tune-up for a particular song. Pupils in the third and fourth grades should take an active part in tuning up with the teacher's assistance.

In the fifth and sixth grades pupils can learn to tune up independently. Such training gives them a need for knowing key signatures and understanding the significance of the key note. A metal or plastic pitch pipe may be *briefly* immersed in a cool sterilizing solution between use by different individuals. Often pupils rotate the responsibility for tuning up, one child being in charge for a two-week period. When a new song is learned it therefore becomes the responsibility of the pupils to understand the tuning up procedure rather than leaving such operations exclusively in the domain of the teacher.

The teacher may provide pupils with a key-signature chart such as is shown in Appendix A–IV, or the pupils can learn to find the key note by looking at the key signature. The following rules apply: In the key signature the last sharp to the right is scale step 7 (ti). The last flat to the right is scale step 4 (fa). The key note is 1 (do) or 8 (do).

*The Minor Mode.* It is important that children sing songs in the minor as well as in the major mode. (See Appendix A–IV for examples of minor scales.) Since it has a different organization of tones, a minor scale has a different sound. The teacher should note that both the minor and the major can convey a variety of moods: whimsical, merry, mysterious, sad. The combined elements of rhythm, shape of the melody, and the mode of the scale determine the mood of the song. "Simple Simon" is an example of a lively song in the minor mode.

## SIMPLE SIMON

J. W. Elliott
from Mother Goose

In this, as in songs in the major, tone calls (see brackets above song) can be used to bring characteristic melodic fragments to the attention of the children. The system of sol-fa syllables used to label tones in the minor is the same as that used for songs in a major key, with the exception that the tonal center in minor is "la-do-mi" rather than "do-mi-so."

The first step in tuning up is to determine the position of "do," assuming the song to be in a major key:

"do"

In "Simple Simon," "do" remains on the second line regardless of the mode determined. If it is in the major mode, the key will be G and the tonic chord that establishes this key in the ear will be G-B-D (do-mi-so). If it is in the minor mode, the ear should be oriented to the minor tonic chord, E-G-B (la-do-mi), of E minor by hearing:

do   ti   la   do   mi

The singing should stop on the tone of the chord on which the song begins (in this case, mi). If one needs to know the name of the key, he must remember that "la" is the tonic tone in a minor song and, therefore, this particular example is in the key of E minor.

But is it in minor? Any one or all three of these clues will help determine the mode:

1. The song ends on "la" ("Simple Simon" does). This is a reliable clue, because a major song will not end on "la." A song in the minor, however, may end on "do" or "mi."
2. The "core of tonality" in the song as a whole is "la-do-mi" (the minor tonic chord). The tones of the song center around this minor chord more than they do around the major tonic chord, "do-mi-so." (Notice how the melody of "Simple Simon" is woven around these notes.)

3. "So," and sometimes "fa," may be raised by a sharp or a natural sign. The tones are then called "si" (see) and "fi" (fee). This tonal alteration indicates the harmonic or melodic form of the minor mode (see Appendix A–IV for analysis) and is a very good clue on which to base a decision about mode. "Simple Simon" is in the natural minor mode, and so these alterations do not occur.

When one is in doubt about the mode of a song, he should tune up using whichever tonic chord will best prepare him to sing the first phrase. After fifth and sixth grade pupils have had considerable experience with minor songs, they can learn to tune up independently. It is well that they learn to sing and hear the difference between major and minor chords. A good direct example is given when they are instructed to sing the following after sounding the major key tone as determined by the key signature.

*Transposing a Song.* Should a teacher change the key of a song to make it more singable for himself or for the children? Certainly, if he has sufficient understanding of the child voice to make a sound judgment and if he knows how to transpose. The comfortable range for the child voice lies between middle C and D or E in the octave above (see page 177), but other factors should be considered.

1. Some children may be able to sing tones higher or lower than those indicated, but in a classroom situation the vocal development of the majority should determine the range.

2. The character and topic of the song determine, to some extent, the range of the song. A song about the sky, clouds, or birds might have a higher general range than one concerned with machinery, an elephant, or vigorous activity.

3. The pitch level of sustained or repeated tones needs more consideration than does the pitch of occasional higher or lower tones. A song with a brief high E or F may be much easier to sing than one in which D, the highest tone, is sustained or repeated several times. On the other hand, middle C or B♭, when encountered briefly, may be acceptable, but a song that sustains or repeats these pitches several times should be transposed upward if the upper limit permits.

Raising or lowering a song a half step or a whole step is generally enough to remove range problems. The practice of beginning a song in an undetermined lower key, without reference to a pitch pipe or piano, invariably leads to careless teaching and poor singing. The development of a concept of pitch is fully as important as the development of other musical concepts in the elementary grades. Much progress in this direction can be made through the use of proper tuning procedures.

Although considerable skill and training are needed to transpose a melody on an instrument, there is no great problem when the voice alone is used. This well-known singing game will serve as an example:

### THE FARMER IN THE DELL

*Lively*                                                                 *Traditional*

1. Determine the key in which the song is written (G) and the scale step on which the song begins (so).
2. Judge whether transposition is really necessary; note the lowest and the highest tones in the song (D–E). Might they both be moved upward or downward and still remain within acceptable limits? If so, will one half step or a whole step higher or lower better meet the singing requirements of the class? This is an activity song which may become screeching in quality if sung too high. The song may be moved down a whole step and the lowest tone will still remain within the child range.
3. Having decided what transposition is necessary, the teacher sounds a new key tone on the pitch pipe, as much higher or lower than the original key note as was judged necessary. This tone substitutes to the ear for the home tone, "do." All the notes in the song retain their original numbers or syllable names. G was the original key and F, a whole step lower, is the new key note, "do" (1). The first tone of the song remains "so" (5).

so  do

The teacher may pitch a new song lower or higher if the change seems justifiable. He should then listen to discover whether the range is suitable for the group. If so, the song should thereafter be sung in that key.

Intermediate grade pupils can gain understanding about voice range and keys by discussing and experimenting to determine the key most appropriate to their voices. The poorest singer in the group may turn out to have the best understanding of the tuning up process and of the necessity for transposition.

### Teaching Musical Notation

When one learns to play a musical instrument he needs to learn the names of the notes on the staff and how to manipulate the instrument to produce a given tone. If the instrumentalist's music-making is not limited to reading notation but also includes improvising or "playing by ear" he will also need to develop the ability to hear the relationship of tones to a key center. For the singer this problem of relating tones to one another and to a key center is present whenever he sings without an instrument to sound the tones for him. Thus in singing it has become a practice to use scale numbers or the sol-fa syllable system to establish the relationship of tones within a scale. Either of these ways of teaching skill in reading music vocally can be successful if used consistently in an organized manner. Tuned instruments (Song Bells, resonator bars, glockenspiels, etc. as described in Chapter Five) are also valuable aids in teaching reading skills and developing concepts about melody.

The development of skill in reading notation should start with the development of concepts about the characteristics of melody such as its high and low tones, movement by large steps and small steps, etc., many of which are outlined in Chapter Two. Young children usually do not know what is meant by "high" or "low" in music. Research[1] has shown that children up to the fourth grade relate "high" and "low" to volume ("turn it up" or "turn it down") rather than to pitch. For this reason much attention must be given to these concepts and to related skills in the kindergarten and primary grades before general use of standard notation is undertaken.

*Early Observations of Melody.* Kindergarten and first grade children need to be helped to notice some of the important characteristics of melody found in the songs they sing. Many songs have obvious high and low tones. In "Bye'm Bye" attention can be drawn to high and low tones (see brackets in song, page 135).

To associate these tones with high and low the teacher may use his hand to show high and low in space as the song is sung; the children may indicate high and low with their hands and sing these tones as a tonal pattern:

"high,    low"

The old French folk tune used for the song "Halloween Night" moves down the scale gradually in the first two phrases; it moves directly down the scale in the last phrase. The children can move their hands down step by step to show this melodic movement. If the song is sung in the key of C a child may play the key of C bells along with the descending voices. In the second grade, when the children are accustomed to handling music books, they may see how the notes move down the staff, one step at a time.

In addition to hand levels the teacher may give a visual representation on the chalkboard with blank notation. The first phrase of "Halloween Night" is represented in blank notation below the song.

## HALLOWEEN NIGHT

*Gaily*                                          *French Folk Tune*

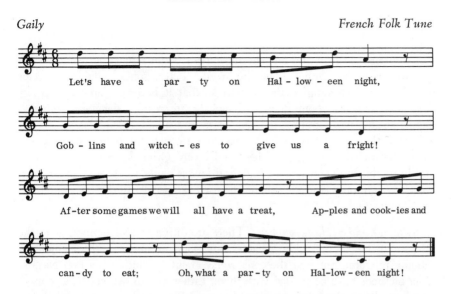

Let's have a par - ty on Hal - low - een night,

Gob - lins and witch - es to give us a fright!

Af - ter some games we will all have a treat, Ap - ples and cook - ies and

can - dy to eat; Oh, what a par - ty on Hal - low - een night!

From Discovering Music Together, *Book Three* by Charles Leonhard, Beatrice Perham Krone, Irving Wolfe, and Margaret Fullerton. © 1967 by Follett Publishing Company, Chicago, Illinois.

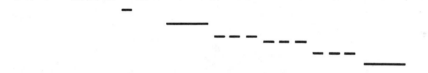

Other songs such as "My Little Ducklings" (Bir II–80, DMT I–35a) show the scale ascending. "Three Dukes" has an upward line on the tonic chord, another common melodic movement that second grade children can begin to recognize. Blank notation can be used to show the relative relationships of these tones (see page 226).

## THREE DUKES

*Briskly*                                        *American Singing Game*

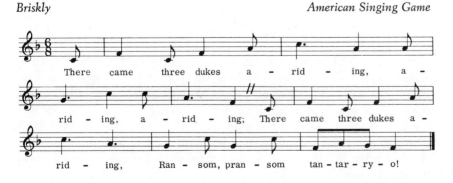

There came three dukes a - rid - ing, a -

rid - ing, a - rid - ing; There came three dukes a -

rid - ing, Ran - som, pran - som tan - tar - ry - o!

Children may hear the melodic movement better when they sing a short pattern with "la" rather than the words. Later, sol-fa syllables or scale numbers may be sung to the pattern so that it becomes more specifically defined. Concepts about details of melody are readily developed when a flannel board with staff-related tone bars is available (see Chapter Five). Children then can see the notation on the staff, play the tone bars, sing, and show the melodic movement with hand levels. Other keyboard instruments aid in establishing concepts of high and low as well as large and small intervals between tones, and they should be used extensively in the ways described in Chapter Five.

*Syllables and Scale Numbers.* There are differences of opinion as to the use and value of the sol-fa syllables and scale numbers in the elementary singing program. Some of the controversy about syllables has arisen because poor methods have been used with them. Either system, when properly used, can help define the relationships of tones within a scale. Scale numbers are favored by teachers who make extensive use of keyboard instruments. The sol-fa syllables are favored by those who have a predominantly vocal approach. Some teachers successfully combine the two, showing the relationship of the syllables and numbers in the major scale with a diagram such as that shown here.

|   |     |     |
|---|-----|-----|
|   | mi' | 3'  |
|   | re' | 2'  |
| 8 | do' | 1'  |
| 7 | ti  |     |
| 6 | la  |     |
| 5 | so  |     |
| 4 | fa  |     |
| 3 | mi  |     |
| 2 | re  |     |
| 1 | do  | 8,  |
|   | ti, | 7,  |
|   | la, | 6,  |
|   | so, | 5,  |

From the third grade such a chart made of tagboard can be helpful as pupils assist in determining syllable or number names for specific melodic fragments. Many songs move both above and below the "home tone," and so fragments of both higher and lower octaves should be shown, but not in a single column, because the completeness of the octave must be evident. A short line at the top or the bottom of a syllable number indicates its location above or below the other tones in the pattern when there is a question about the octave intended.

When used with singing, the syllables have certain advantages over numbers:

1. They are easier to sing and more euphonious since they use the basic vowel sounds.
2. Once learned, the syllable combinations are more easily remembered in their *sound* relationship to the scale tones.
3. Chromatically altered tones may be sung easily by changing the vowel sound in the syllable (see Appendix A–IV).

Earlier in this chapter one method of using syllables in the minor mode was shown. Generally speaking, this syllable system, using the "relative" tonic relationship of minor and major, is preferred in the elementary school and is used in the basic series music books. However, its effective use is limited to songs in the natural minor mode.

Scale numbers, when applied to the minor mode, are a point of differing opinion among music educators. Some basic series music books maintain the tonic note ("home tone") in any key or mode, as "one" (1) of the scale. When the syllable system described above is used, the tonic note, "la," is called "one" (1) in the minor scale. This scale-number system is essential in the study of chords and harmonic relationships. However, other basic series music books maintain the "relative" tonic relationship of minor and major in assigning scale numbers as well as syllables. That system, in which the minor tonic note is labeled "la" and also is called "six" (6) in scale numbers, is not recommended.

*Beginning Use of Syllables.* To affix the labels to the scale tones, children should sing and hear tonal patterns with syllables.

"Tone calls," used for the development of voices, become, in the second and third grades, "tonal patterns" that are identified by means of the syllables. Each tone call suggested in Chapter Six, page 179, is a common tonal pattern found in many songs. The two examples from "Are You Sleeping?" are the patterns of do-so -do and mi-fa-so. The "Rig-a-Jig-Jig" tone call is do-ti-la-ti-do. Pupils should sing the patterns rhythmically, first with the original words and then with the syllables.

In some second and third grade books the syllables are printed over the music at important points in the song. These syllables may identify short tonal patterns, as described above, or outline entire phrases that show important melodic construction. The teacher can use the printed syllables to help children analyze the melody in a simple way, or the children can sing the syllable pattern to accustom their ears to its sound.

In the nineteenth century the English music teacher, John Curwen, developed hand signs for the sol-fa syllables (see Appendix A–IV). Teachers of the *Choral Method*[2] developed by the eminent Hungarian composer, Zoltán Kodály, use Curwen's hand signs whenever syllables are sung, beginning with simple exercises and songs for very young children. The hand signs are an important part of the *Threshold to Music*[3] method which uses techniques recommended by Kodály.

Another technique, dating back to the early New England singing schools, is to memorize a syllable stanza for familiar songs. An occasional song in which *each phrase is a basic tonal pattern* (such as "Are You Sleeping?") may be sung with an added stanza in syllables; but it is not a good practice to sing every song with syllables. Other songs that may be broken into common tonal patterns are:

"The Cuckoo" (TiM III–78)        "Three Dukes" (GwM II–102)
"Jingle at the Window" (GwM II–19)    "Skip to My Lou" MoM II–152)
"Row Your Boat" (ABC III–44)       "Susy, Little Susy" (Bir III–149)

The syllables can be introduced in tonal patterns in the second grade, if the patterns were used often as tone calls throughout the first grade and early in the second grade. After the syllables have become familiar, the scale as a whole may be presented (late second or early third grade). The teacher must decide when the children can benefit from understanding the relationship of the syllables one to another, and the relationship of the many tonal patterns to the whole scale.

A few songs, such as the French folk tune on page 225, have the entire scale within the melody. The whole scale of syllables may be explained in relation to such a song. If the children do not know a suitable song, the teacher may use the syllable chart to explain the makeup of the scale. The children enjoy singing the scale, especially if one child accompanies the class playing the scale on the bells.

Singing of tonal patterns should continue, and the tones should be related to the syllable chart so that pupils see the relationship of the pattern to the entire scale. All work with tonal patterns should be done in reference to songs rather than as isolated drill. In a new song a significant pattern may be the first part of the song that the children sing; later, syllables will identify the pattern specifically. A number of techniques may be used to give the children experience with tonal patterns in many songs. Some suggestions follow.

After a familiar song has been sung, the teacher might ask: "What tonal pattern did we find in this song?" "Who can sing the pattern with the words?" "Let's sing it together." Give individuals or small groups an opportunity to sing it as a special help for voices. "Who can sing it with the syllables?" If the syllable chart has been introduced: "Who can point out the syllables as we sing the correct ones for this tonal pattern?" In later stages, if the pattern is simple, the teacher might ask: "Who can play this pattern on the bells?"

To practice aural identification of tonal patterns, the teacher may sing a known tonal pattern with "loo" instead of with the words or syllables. The children identify it by singing it with syllables. In all use of tonal patterns, the tonic note must be sounded and the tonal pattern heard in relation to it. When the work is done in connection with a familiar song that has been correctly tuned for singing it is easy to keep in mind the relationship to the tonic.

Common melodic fragments that comprise tonal patterns are the following:

1. tonic chord: do-so-do; do-mi-so; so-mi; do-do; do-do; etc.
2. scale line: do-re-mi; mi-re-do; so-la-ti-do; so-fa-mi; etc.

3. neighboring tones:   so-la-so; do-ti₁-do; do-re-do; mi-fa-mi; etc.
4. combinations:   so-la-so-mi; mi-do-ti₁-do; mi-re-mi-do; etc.
5. dominant chord:   so₁-ti₁-re; re-ti₁-so₁; etc.

The first four groupings are most common and should be very familiar to children in the fourth grade. The dominant chord patterns can be introduced and mastered as children of the fourth and fifth grades use that chord on the Autoharp. For most effective use the patterns should be limited to five tones in length.

The minor tonic chord and typical fragments from the natural minor scale should be used as tonal patterns in the primary grades. This should be done strictly on the basis of providing experience in hearing the different tone color, and no attempt at analysis should be made at this level. Children who have sung syllables in major keys will enjoy these new patterns. Good minor tonal patterns in "Simple Simon" (see page 221) are:

Go -ing  to  the  fair
la₁ - ti₁ - do - re - mi      *and*      Let me taste your ware.
mi - re - do -  ti₁ - la₁

Many Halloween songs are in the minor mode. When the minor tonic chord (la₁-do-mi-do-la ) can be found in a tonal pattern having the necessary brevity and feeling of completeness it should be used. "On Halloween" (DMT II–131) has fine tonal patterns: mi-fa-mi; la-mi-mi-la, and la₁-ti₁-do-re-mi. A number of folk songs such as "The Tailor and the Mouse" (DMT III–78) and "Ah, Poor Bird" (GwM II–10) have tonal patterns that are very good to point up minor key characteristics.

In the third grade, children can begin to identify tonal patterns visually, if identification by ear has been well established. Tonal patterns such as "so-do-so" occur in many songs. Children may "frame" the tonal pattern in the book by laying one pointer finger on each side of the pattern. The children can construct tonal patterns on a staff-lined flannel board and play them on the related tone bars.

In the early primary grades, children should not be concerned about the key in which a song is written. For most people, the syllables have the same sound relationship in any key. When the children begin to *see* the tonal patterns, it is necessary to explain that "do" changes location on the staff in different songs, and that all the other syllables move in relation to "do." The teacher can explain that the scale numbers or syllables are like a yardstick; when the one-inch mark is moved the three-inch mark moves also and stays the same distance away. The position of the key note can be marked on the flannel board or chalkboard with an x on the proper line or space.

*Intermediate Grade Use of Syllables.*   When consistently used, syllables can be an important means of helping pupils learn to hear basic melodic fragments. At the intermediate grade level, when more challenging melodic material is used, such studies should be continued. The syllable chart should include the half steps. Some chromatic alterations are found in major as well as minor songs, and these should be discussed in terms of their relationship to the unaltered tones of the scale. (See Appendix A–IV.) When a song with altered tones is first encountered, an analysis of the chromatic scale may be made. "Sleep and Rest" by Mozart contains several alterations:

# SLEEP AND REST

*Gently*                                                                  *Mozart*

Sleep, oh, my dar - ling, and rest,___ Birds are a - sleep in their nest,___
re - di - re
Gar - den and mea - dow are still,___ Bees hum no more on the rill.___
la - si - la
In through the win - dow so bright___ Shines the moon's sil - ver - y light;___
so - fi - so
Nes - tle your head on my breast;___ Sleep, oh, my dar - ling and rest;___
Oh, sleep, ___ and___ rest.

In this song the half steps (re-di, la-si, so-fi) should be rehearsed by singing the descending half steps, "do-re-di-re" or "so-la-si-la," etc., to hear and feel the closeness of the half step. Other songs containing chromatic tones are "Santa Lucia" (ABC VI–22), "Wonderful Copenhagen" (ExM VI–184), "Masters in This Hall" (GwM V–210), and "What Child Is This?" (TiM VI–65). The latter two are in the minor mode and will give students experience with the raised sixth and seventh scale steps of the minor (see Appendix A–IV for classification of minor scales).

The chromatic syllables become easier to sing if the ascending and descending chromatic scale is sung a few times whenever alterations are found in a new song. Chromatic bells and the piano keyboard help establish the *sound* of the chromatic scale. The tones may be played slowly and sung with the letter names: C, C♯, D, D♯, E, F, etc.

The sol-fa syllables were designed for use with key-centered melodies, those built around a scale with the tonic note (do) as the musical "center of gravity." When modulations (changes in key) occur within a song, the location of "do" must be shifted with the key center; this leads to considerations generally beyond the understanding of the intermediate grade student. Songs in the harmonic and melodic minor are not well adapted to the use of the syllable system wherein *la* is the tonic note.

The tones in the tonic chord do-mi-so (1-3-5) have characteristics of stability and repose. Of these, the tonic tone gives the greatest feeling of repose. When a person plays the tonic chord and sings the third or the fifth (mi or

**CHAPTER
SEVEN**

**230**

so), he will feel a tendency to move to "do." When he sings the root of the chord, "do," there is a sense of arrival. Most songs end on the key tone for this reason. Pupils who learn to use the Autoharp will have experience with the dominant seventh ($V_7$) chord. This chord, which comprises scale steps 5,-7,-2-4 (so,-ti,-re-fa), is characterized as "restless." The seventh scale step (ti) is called the "leading tone" because of its very strong tendency to move to 1 (do). An understanding of the characteristics of the scale steps that make up these chords will assist the children in singing melodies centered around the chords.

*Singing Intervals.* As pupils become more proficient music-makers and deal with more varied song literature, they will need more than this scale-centered and primary-chord-centered understanding of melodic organization. Sixth grade pupils should begin to be aware of the measured distance (the intervals) between tones of scales and chords. Then when the key center changes or eludes definition, as it often does in contemporary music, the singer still is able to find his way from one note to the next.

In the primary grades children observe intervals in general terms as steps, skips, or large jumps. Later they name them with syllables or scale numbers. Sixth grade pupils can discuss tonal relationships more specifically; they can learn to hear, recognize, and sing *particular* intervals. There is no definite order in which the intervals should be presented, but when a particular interval in a song arrests attention, it may be identified and sung in isolation a few times so that the children hear its sound and see it in notation. At other times when scales and chords are sung, the intervals may be identified as to their position in the scale or chord and their sound. Pupils can learn that the intervals in the major tonic chord are these:

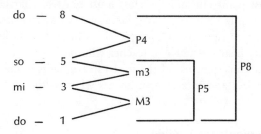

The difference in sound between a major third (M3) and a minor third (m3) is important, for the arrangement of these intervals within the chord determines whether the chord is major or minor. For effective use the sound of important intervals must be memorized. Some people remember the sound of the minor third (m3) by associating it with the first ascending interval in Brahms' "Cradle Song":

Lul - la - by    and good - night!    With__  ro - ses  be - dight __ *etc.*

**231**

The perfect fourth (P4) is the interval from "so," (5,) up to "do" (1); the first ascending interval of "Taps" helps keep this sound in mind:

Violin strings are tuned in perfect fifths (P5), and this idea of sound can strengthen the identification of the interval from "do" (1) up to "so" (5) or the descending fifth from "do" (1) down to "fa," (4,), which is more difficult to hear. Intervals are classified in Appendix A–IV.

The study of intervals should grow out of the song repertoire and should be identified in terms of the scale or chord in a particular key. Such a study is begun in the sixth grade; later, in choral classes, a broader study of intervals can be undertaken. What is suggested here is a bridge between the scale-centered approach in the lower grades and the need to read intervals in more advanced choral work.

*The Use of Scale Numbers.* Many teachers prefer the use of scale numbers to the use of sol-fa syllables. This is a very satisfactory approach as long as the children gradually and consistently are learning to recognize and to hear the tonal relationship between notes of the scale and various chords. The approach can be much the same as that described in the use of sol-fa syllables, with numbers being sung instead of the syllables.

Melody instruments should be used a great deal, and the children should be able to recognize and sing the scale steps integral to each of the principal chords, as well as the major scale and the alterations for the minor scale. The teacher must point out and the class must practice characteristic patterns as they are encountered in good song literature. Many suggestions for the use of scale numbers were made in Chapter Five under the consideration of melody and harmony instruments. The teacher who prefers the use of scale numbers should make consistent use of the tuned instruments in combination with the children's voices and in accompaniments wherein the children build chords.

## Accompaniments for Singing

Traditionally, a piano has been a part of kindergarten equipment, but it has not always been readily available to other grades. If well played, a piano accompaniment adds interest, color, and support to the singing. The teacher who does not play the piano can arrange to have a special music teacher, parent, secretary, or talented upper-grade student serve as accompanist. When a piano is not available in the classroom, one can usually be found in the auditorium or multipurpose room, which can be reserved for occasional singing periods. In many schools a small piano is mounted on large rubber casters so that it can be rolled from one classroom to another as required. Other instruments such as the Autoharp and guitar can be used as accompanying instruments for classroom singing.

*Use of the Piano.* The piano should be used as an enrichment rather than as a constant accompaniment to classroom singing. Poor use of the piano often has led to the recommendation that the piano not be used with children's singing. Picture the teacher sitting at the piano with his back to the children, accompanying every song with loud improvised chords. This situation violates at least three important principles in the teaching of singing:

1. Singing should be shared by teacher and pupils; there should be eye contact and rapport, much as there is in storytelling.
2. The teacher should know the vocal development of each pupil and should work in such a flexible manner that children often have an opportunity to sing alone or in small groups and to try their voices on tone calls. The teacher who *always* sits at the piano cannot possibly be aware of each child's vocal development, and cannot give him the personal help he needs almost daily.
3. The rhythmic chording, which is easy to play and "keeps the singing going," is musically unsuitable for many children's songs.

Some songs, such as "Go Tell Aunt Rhodie" and "Yankee Doodle," may appropriately be accompanied by broken chords on the piano. (Appendix A–V shows the use of three principal chords in the keys of C, G, and F with various rhythms.) However, the manner of playing should support rather than cover up the voices. The left hand should play near the middle of the keyboard with a light, crisp touch for lively numbers and a legato touch for smooth flowing songs. Since each song should be expressive in its own way, the accompaniment should help to establish the appropriate mood and feeling. Accompaniment books for some of the music texts show piano parts that are varied and not difficult.

With the achievement of greater independence in singing, children should be challenged to hear more in the music as they sing. For this reason, they should have more experience singing with accompaniments. Because the piano adds interesting harmonies and rhythmic effects, the teacher must use techniques that train the children to listen as they sing, so that the ensemble is heard. In some accompaniments, the composer includes musical characteristics that express the idea or mood in the song. As an example, the famous lullaby by Brahms opens with a rhythmic accompaniment that suggests the rocking of a cradle. The harmony in the first two phrases is quieting in that it centers around the tonic chord. At the beginning of the third phrase, at the words "If God will . . . ," a seventh chord and an octave leap in the melody are introduced. The rhythm changes a bit and the whole effect is more dramatic and less restful than the opening. On a very small scale this is "tone painting" by the composer.

MANAGEMENT OF
THE SINGING
SITUATION

**233**

## CRADLE SONG
### (Wiegenlied)

*With gentle motion*                                              *Johannes Brahms*

Lul-la - by and good-night, with_ ro - ses o'er-
*Gu-ten A - bend, gut Nacht, mit_ Ro - sen be-*

spread, slip_ in - to thy_ bed there_ pil - low thy
*dacht, mit Näg-lein be - steckt schlupf_ un - ter die*

head. If God will thou shalt wake when the morn-ing doth
*Deck. Mor-gen früh, wenn Gott will, wirst du wie - der ge -*

break, if God will thou shalt wake when the morn ing doth break.
*weckt, mor-gen früh, wenn Gott will, wirst du wie - der ge - weckt.*

Transposed from the key of E♭.

In some accompaniments no separate movement or musical ideas appear. The piano may move along with solid chords that hold up the melody much as pillars support a bridge. The hymnlike accompaniments for "Praise to the Lord" (MoM III–32), "Vesper Hymn" (ExM III–215), and "America, the Beautiful" (see page 200) are examples.

*The Strumming Instruments.* All over the world people enjoy singing at home and in community gatherings. To accompany this informal singing various instruments are used—guitar, banjo, ukelele, and zither, as well as piano. A parent or other person in the community who plays one of these instruments skillfully can be invited to the school to play for the children; a teacher who is able to play should do so often to accompany the singing in his classroom. When musically played, the strumming instruments make the most appropriate accompaniment for many folk songs.

Although not every song lends itself to this type of accompaniment, song books designed for school use show chord markings that enable the teacher to play the more suitable songs. Different styles of strumming should be used, depending on the type of song being accompanied. Strumming styles heard on recordings made by Josef Marais, Burl Ives, Sam Hinton, and Pete Seeger are good examples. Many good instruction books for learning to tune and to play the guitar and other strumming instruments are available in local music stores. The ukulele is considerably easier to play but it is much more limited in the songs for which it can provide a suitable accompaniment. Tuning and chord tablatures for the ukulele and the guitar are shown in Chapter Five.

The Autoharp was described in considerable detail in Chapter Five. Many teachers of primary as well as intermediate grades learn to play this instrument with facility. It lends itself to many of the interesting strumming styles used on the guitar and the banjo. The teacher who would like to enhance his Autoharp accompaniments should study and practice the procedures recommended in *The Many Ways to Play the Autoharp.*[4]

## TEACHING THE SONG

In just what setting will a teacher plan the first singing of a song? A dynamic situation may arise into which a new song fits perfectly. One day Billy told, with mixed awe and excitement, about the arrival at home of his new baby sister. Did Billy know a song to sing to his sister? No, he wasn't that well prepared for her arrival. His kindergarten teacher remedied the situation immediately by teaching Billy and the class "Hush, Little Baby" (see page 192). No "motivation" was needed; the song was "right" for a situation such as can arise in any classroom. This teacher had been working with small children for three years, and during that time she had collected a useful repertoire of songs. She said that her most successful song teaching occurred when she could meet the children's immediate needs for personal expression in song.

In any setting, one prerequisite is this: the teacher must know the song well before he presents it. If the song is taught from a record, the teacher should know the words so that he can sing along with the record when necessary. If he is using only his voice he must be able to tune up quickly and get the song under way without losing the interest and attention of the children.

In his planning, the teacher must examine the possibilities for the use of simple instruments and bodily movement, so that he will be able to guide the children in their exploration of such enrichments. Many young teachers underestimate the need for having a complete command of material and activities.

There is no single formula for presenting a new song. The variable factors are many: the song itself and its appeal, the mood and atmosphere in the class, the teacher's ability to sing a song and to project an idea. A teacher who has a lovely voice and an intimate way of singing can captivate the entire class, and may need little additional aid to make the children enthusiastic about singing. Teachers who are less gifted vocally, and cannot project a mood well, need to give considerable thought to their presentation and should use various methods of motivating the class. In the primary grades, pictures and other objects may be used to capture and hold interest as the teacher sings a song a time or two.

In presenting a song to young children the teacher should hold the interest and attention of the children in much the same manner as he does when he tells a story. He should sing with clarity so that the children can understand the words and discuss the ideas in the text. As often as possible, the melody and the words should be given together (i.e., sung rather than spoken) so that the process of learning the melody is shortened. If the teacher's enjoyment of the song is shared by the children, they will be eager to make it their own. Obviously such a situation can exist only when the teacher truly likes the music himself. The song that has sufficient appeal will not present formidable teaching problems. Even when the presentation of a song is done by means of a recording, it need not be an impersonal thing. If the teacher is near the record player the substitute voice does not displace the teacher's personal interest and enthusiasm.

## Teaching the Song with the Voice

A recording may be a very satisfactory way to present a song; some teachers who sing well use the recorded version to bring variety into the singing program. However, in the actual teaching of the song nothing is more effective than a reasonably good voice. For a simple, repetitious song one presentation may result in the spontaneous singing of it. Many such easy songs should be taught because they bring singing success to children with little experience and native ability. A longer song may require three days to a week of study to assure correct singing by the children alone. Even with longer songs the singing should be shared as soon as possible, the children singing along on the easy parts and the teacher singing the more difficult spots alone.

*Singing Selected Phrases.* The teacher may deal with the new song in a number of ways. After the children have heard the song, any pleasing phrase or tone call may be a starting point for them to sing. Often the last phrase serves this purpose, the children chiming in at the end as the teacher sings the song again. Whatever fragment the teacher selects should be rhythmic and interesting in its melody and words. It should be easy to sing. The harder phrases should be left until the class has heard the song several times.

The phrase endings of the folk ballad "The Little Pig" are suitable fragments for early singing by children:

## THE LITTLE PIG

*Moderately fast*                                                    *Texas*

There was an old wo-man and she had a lit-tle pig,___ Oink - oink -
oink, There was an old wo-man and she had a lit - tle pig,
Did-n't cost much 'cause it was-n't ver - y big,___ Oink - oink - oink.

The children will listen for the story as the teacher sings the song the first time. Then the teacher may say, "There is a part of this song that sounds as though the little pig had something to say. I wonder if you could sing it like this" (teacher sings, then children sing):

Oink, oink, oink

The children can imitate the teacher's example and show with hand levels how the tune moves. The teacher may then say, "As I sing the song all the way through, you be ready to come in with the little pig's tune at just the right time."

The next day the teacher will sing the song with its several stanzas as the children "help" on the phrase endings. When the children have heard the song several times, the teacher can say, "I think you are ready to sing the whole song now." The group then sings with the teacher helping in a soft voice.

Among the following "chime-in" songs the easiest repeated parts will be found either at the beginning or at the end of phrases.

"Hello, Ev'rybody" (MMYO K–4)          "O Christmas Tree" (ExM I–83)
"John the Rabbit" (MMYO K–150)       "Sleep, Baby, Sleep" (MoM K–96)
"Les Marionettes" (GwM K–97)          "The Train Is A-Coming" (Joy–103)

When the song has no distinctive phrase endings to serve as a beginning for singing by the children the teacher may sing the whole song and then discuss various points of interest. He may then repeat the phrases dealing with the points of interest, with the children singing the phrases in response. "Six Little Ducks" is an example.

## SIX LITTLE DUCKS

From *Sing a Tune,* © 1954 Cooperative Recreation Service, Inc., Delaware, Ohio. Used by permission.

After the first singing, the children might comment about the movements and sounds of ducks. A picture would heighten the interest, but the song itself is appealing, and the teacher's first singing of it would undoubtedly capture the interest of the children. Then, if he has sung it clearly and has conveyed the ideas in the text, he might talk about it: "What kinds of ducks were mentioned in the song?" After the children reply he sings:

"Can you sing that part?" The teacher sings the phrase again, and then the children sing it. He might continue: "There was one special duck; do you remember what he did?" The children answer, and then the teacher sings:

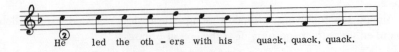

"I think you can sing that part too! Try it after I sing it now." The teacher sings and the children sing the phrase marked "2."

And so the children actually begin to learn the song as they discuss the text. The teacher may then sing the entire song and signal the group to join in on the short phrases that they know. The two antecedent phrases "3" can

**238**

be learned separately and then combined as the children sing all of the song except the transitional measures "4." These two measures should be sung by the teacher alone for a longer period of time; he can make a game of an echo effect to hold the children's interest until he is sure they have heard the song enough to sing the sequence correctly.

The technique of combining the learning of phrases with the discussion of the text is practical because it gets the singing going very soon. Talking about the words is necessary for understanding the song and helps the children remember the text, but the words should not be kept separate from the melody. The procedures used for different songs will be as varied as the songs themselves, and there will be little danger of the teacher slipping into a monotonous routine of teaching every song in the same manner.

The "phrase method" of teaching a song prevailed for many years and was well defined and organized: the teacher sang the first phrase and the children sang it back; the teacher sang the second phrase and the children echoed it—and so on through the song. The teaching example given with "Six Little Ducks" is a variation of this technique, but it is a more interesting and dynamic way to learn a song.

Although the phrase method became a routine, formalized way of teaching, it was useful because it gave the unimaginative teacher a pattern to follow. It is possible that using the varied techniques suggested above could lead to a disorganized approach to singing and could thus be confusing to the children. Flexibility and creativity are highly desirable, but the presentation must have meaning and continuity as well. Creative teaching is based on planning and imagining ahead of time just as formal, patterned teaching involves planning. With the latter, once the pattern is established a daily plan is less imperative. In creative teaching, each new song and each new class of children will suggest new, interesting approaches if the teacher will free his thinking enough to see them.

There was a time when teachers were instructed never to sing with the children. The rule was that the teacher's voice should be used chiefly as an example, and that the children would learn independence in singing if they were not assisted by the teacher. Children need to learn to sing independently, but independence is not the only concern in the early years. It is much more important that children learn to enjoy singing and steadily improve their individual abilities to sing. Singing is an activity to be shared with others. As a member of the child's school society the teacher should expect to share this enjoyment with the pupils. If a teacher sometimes sings along and sometimes listens, independence in singing will develop in a satisfactory manner.

There is another reason for the rule that teachers should not sing with their pupils: some teachers do not know how to sing softly! Their voices dominate the singing and they are not able to hear and evaluate the singing of the children. If the teacher is not able to subordinate his voice, he should not sing along at all, or he should whisper the words to give the impression of his occasional participation.

*Activity-held Interest.* Singing is only one means of making music; it should be combined with other activities to assure every child a rich musical

**MANAGEMENT OF THE SINGING SITUATION**

experience regardless of his vocal development. Rhythmic movement and the playing of simple instruments are two activities that may build interest in learning a song, and maintain interest until the song has been heard enough times to be sung in its entirety. An example is found in the finger play, "Where Is Thumbkin?" (GwM K–90) which, in the third or fourth grade, will be learned as the round, "Are You Sleeping?" The children will enjoy joining in with finger play while the teacher sings the song a few times. Soon they will spontaneously sing along with the teacher because it is such an easy song to sing.

"Three Blue Pigeons" is a simple counting song that combines finger and hand movements with the use of the glockenspiel to tell the story.

## THREE BLUE PIGEONS

*Freely*                                                                                           *American Folk Song*

(spoken by one child) One of them flew away.          (Upward glissando on Song Bells)
(spoken by all, sadly) O-o-oh!

2. Two blue pigeons sitting on the wall, etc.
   (One child) Another pigeon flew away.          (Upward glissando on Song Bells)
   (All, more sadly) O-o-o-oh!

3. One blue pigeon sitting on the wall, etc.
   (One child) And the third one flew away!          (Upward glissando on Song Bells)
   (All, still more sadly) O-o-o-o-oh!

4. No blue pigeons sitting on the wall, etc.
   (One child) One of the pigeons came back!          (Downward glissando on Song Bells)
   (All, happy) Whee-ee-ee-ee!

5. One blue pigeon sitting on the wall, etc.
   (One child) Another flew back!          (Downward glissando on Song Bells)
   (All, very happy) Whee-ee-ee-ee-ee!

6. Two blue pigeons sitting on the wall, etc.
   (One child) And the third one came back!          (Downward glissando on Song Bells)
   (All, with great happiness) Whee-ee-ee-ee-ee!

7. Three blue pigeons sitting on the wall, etc.

Other songs such as "Old House" (see page 66) and "Who's That Tapping at the Window?" (see page 103) can be learned with the creative activity as an interest-holding feature.

*The Piano as an Aid.* When teaching a new song, it is preferable to use the voice alone, not only because greater teacher-pupil rapport is possible, but because children can match tones with those of another human voice more readily than with those of an instrument. However, if the teacher feels insecure in singing unaided, he may support his voice by playing the melody line on the piano. Use of the piano is highly preferable to out-of-tune singing. The piano should be at the front of the room so that the teacher may communicate with the children as he plays. Techniques suggested for teaching a song with the voice are applicable, except that the tone is taken from the piano rather than from a pitch pipe.

On occasion the teacher may wish to make the initial presentation of a song with his voice and a piano accompaniment. This may be done if the piano is in such a position that the teacher has eye contact with the pupils and if he knows the song very well. The accompaniment should enhance the song and support but not dominate the voice.

## Using Recorded Song Materials

All companies publishing basic music books supply recordings of all or most of the songs in each book. In addition, many folk singers and artists have made fine records that appeal to children. These records are an invaluable aid to the teacher with limited singing ability, and they enrich the music program in the classroom of a competent singer as well.

*Quality and Selection of Recorded Songs.* The quality of the recordings, like that of all audio-visual aids, varies greatly, and each teacher must judge what will be suitable for his pupils. Some points to be considered are these:
1. The quality of a voice that children are expected to imitate should be pleasant and unaffected. The unnatural "operatic" type of voice should be avoided as much as the nasal twang of the "hillbilly" singer.
2. The melody should be within the vocal range of the children who will sing it. One of the chief criticisms made of earlier recordings was that the songs often were too high for the average classroom of children.
3. The interpretation should be expressive, so that the intended mood and feelings are conveyed.
4. The enunciation should be clear, so that the text is understood.
5. The accompaniment should be appropriate and musically performed.
6. The recording should be long enough that the listeners can get a good understanding of the song from one hearing. For very short songs more than one stanza might be used, or an instrumental group might repeat the song.
7. The recorded song should be accurate and should conform to that printed in the text.

The records designed to accompany basic texts and other books are listed with those books in Appendix B. A teacher who uses one of the basic series music texts should certainly use the recordings designed to accompany that book. Other records are of value to the teacher. Folkways has recorded songs from Ruth Seeger's *American Folk Songs for Children*.[5] On a record with the same title, Pete Seeger sings with a five-string banjo accompaniment. There is considerable variety among the songs and the activities they are designed to promote. Likewise, *Songs to Grow On*[6] and *More Songs to Grow On*[7] are recorded in very useful arrangements.

Charity Bailey charmed her own class with her songs before her recordings were made by Folkways. In *Music Time* she accompanies herself on the guitar, talks, sings, and invites the children to sing with her. Frank Luther has recorded for Decca Records many song-stories that are appealing to primary children. Tom Glazer, in his recordings for *Young People's Records,* has a pleasant baritone voice in a middle range so that the children have no difficulty singing with the record. He suggests many activities in connection with songs that are related to some central theme. *Young People's Records* and the *Children's Record Guild* have issued records that are especially good for individual children to use at home and in nursery school or kindergarten groups.

*Techniques in Using Records.* Teachers who do not sing well have found that recorded songs enable children to enjoy a great variety of song literature. Techniques for teaching a song with the aid of a record are as varied as those the teacher employs when using his own voice as a model. The chief problem is that difficult parts of the song cannot be isolated and rehearsed as they can be when the teacher sings and has the children sing phrases that need special attention.

In the kindergarten, which is less formal, the chief aid to the learning of a song from a recording is the repeated hearings that children demand. Easy songs present no problems if they are heard several times. In many children's records the artists invite the children to participate in various ways, and so there is little problem for the teacher.

When teaching from other records, the teacher may need to motivate listening by planning appropriate activities so that the children will hear the whole song several times before they attempt to sing it:

1. They may listen two or three times in the process of finding out what the song is about.
2. They may hear it several times as they participate with bodily movement or simple instruments.

Children and teacher should listen for phrases or tone calls where they may briefly join in the singing and then listen again as the artist sings the more difficult parts. This same technique is suggested when the teacher uses his own voice. Early singing is important, for children like to "get into the act" and should do so before their enthusiasm wanes.

Another technique is "whispering" the words as the voice on the record sings. This method is successful after the children are able to follow the text of the song printed in the music book. The practice serves two purposes:

1. It helps to establish the tempo and rhythm in the children's singing response. Often when a group of children first sing with a record, they fall behind because they cannot hear enough to follow the tempo.
2. When the rhythm and the text have been established in their minds, the children are able to connect them with the melody, which they can hear as they whisper.

This mode of participation is not unnatural for anyone who has the words before him and is hearing a recorded song for the first or second time. However, the teacher must use it with good judgment because he wants a classroom of singing children, not silent mimics.

In general, a large group of young children should not hum with a new recorded song because such humming usually results in an indefinable sound not closely resembling the melody desired, and the humming obscures the melody. On other occasions humming is an enjoyable activity to which experience and maturity bring greater accuracy.

Other techniques may be employed in the classroom of the teacher who does not sing:

1. A few children who learn songs most quickly and accurately may sing along with the recording before the entire class joins in.
2. After the record has been heard several times and the words have been reasonably well related to the melody, the teacher might play the melody on the piano or other instrument while a small group or the entire class sings. (The instrument would not be played with the record.)

In their first attempts at singing with a record, pupils should sing lightly so that they can hear the recorded voice. The teacher must regulate the volume of the machine so that it gives enough support and yet does not sound unduly loud. On the other hand if the volume is too soft, the children, in trying to sing under the record sound, will use such a hushed tone that their singing will be restrained and unnatural.

The teacher may use a recording to teach a new song and to get the singing started, but the class should occasionally sing the song unaided by the recording to develop the ability and the understanding that they can sing independently whenever they wish. The teacher may start the singing by playing the introduction on the record and then lifting the needle, or he may tune up with the pitch pipe or the piano.

Sometimes a teacher may choose to make the first presentation of a song by means of a record, and then use his own voice to assist the children in learning specific portions of the song. This procedure lends further variety to classroom singing and gives the children an opportunity to hear different voice qualities. He may also utilize the recorded version of a song as an aid to the children who are reading selected parts of the melody from notation in the music books. Even after they have learned to sing a song independently, pupils may enjoy and benefit from a rehearing of the recorded version.

Many times the recorded accompaniment may suggest to children a good way to use their own instruments. Some rhythm instruments may be added to singing with the record, and later the song may be sung and accompanied by the children themselves. These ideas may carry over to songs that are not available on recordings, and thus the entire singing program is enriched.

## The Use of Music Books

Most school districts supply a music book for each child from the second grade up. This is a basic requirement for adequate music teaching. The teacher should have single copies of several song books in addition to the basic text, for it is not possible to find in one book the variety of song literature a class should experience in a school term. For those classrooms where books are used effectively, a set of supplementary books gives the children a wider choice in songs.

Books to aid the song-learning process generally are not used until the second grade. (Earlier uses of music primers and books are discussed later in this chapter.) Some second grade teachers delay the general use of song books until midyear if many of the children do not read words well. Also, when children have not yet learned to find page numbers efficiently, the pace of the lesson is slower. However, books hold great interest for the children and will aid the music program once their use is established.

One problem that may arise is that of reading consecutive stanzas in a song if more than one stanza is written under the music line. (In some texts the second stanza is printed in verse form at the bottom of the page.) The first song of this kind encountered should be one in which two or more stanzas have previously been learned without books. Then when the printed song is before them, the children will be able to follow the unaccustomed order of the lines of the text more easily.

Some teachers solve the problem by cutting page-width markers of construction paper, which the children hold under the words they are singing and move down the page from line to line on each stanza. The teacher can see by the position of the markers which children do not understand the order of the lines. This device can be used for a few weeks, with both familiar and new songs, until the children have established the practice of reading the first line under the music score all the way through the song, and then returning to the top for the second stanza.

Teaching the melody of a new song with books in the hands of the children does not differ markedly from the techniques described earlier. However, the teacher is less concerned with other motivation, because pictures and readable words provide much of the interest. Just how a song is presented depends upon the reading level of the children and the vocabulary in the song.

The teacher may sing the song or play the recorded song and then discuss the topic and the interesting aspects of the music before the books are opened. The children depend on their ears to tell them about the song. The development of aural perception is basic at all levels of participation in music. Visual perception supports and defines in another way the sounds that the ear hears. When the books are opened, the children see the visual representation of what was heard, and the teacher gradually leads them to understand the accepted notation for specific musical effects.

At other times the books are opened to the new song; the children may notice the pictures, poems, or other items of interest on the page. They may read the text and perhaps talk about it before they hear the music. This approach can be used when the vocabulary is within the reading limits of the children. Specific musical characteristics for which the notation is familiar may be recognized, discussed, and sounded as a preliminary exploration of the way the music goes.

*Music Primers.*   Although books to aid the song-learning process generally are not used until the second grade, publishers have recognized and responded to child interest in color and pictures related to the songs they sing. The result has been a number of very attractive music books (primers) for first graders. In these small colorful song books the words and melody are included to provide a visual experience for young children. The books may be used to interest the children in learning a new song, or they may serve as an enrichment after the song has been learned.

Children cherish a colorful song book in much the same way that they do their favorite picture-story books. When they know the songs, they delight in following the tune and the words, either individually at the library table or as a group. In some of the books, the songs are arranged in story sequence so that interest is held for several pages. From this visual experience children may develop general concepts about music notation: (1) the left-to-right flow of melody on the page, (2) the rise and fall of a melody line, and (3) rhythmic notation in which groups of notes represent a steady movement:

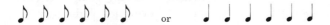

and groups of notes represent an uneven, skipping or galloping kind of rhythm:

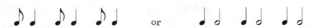

However, there should be no attempt to promote music reading per se with these primers. It is vitally important that young children learn to sing and to use singing as an expressive force in their lives before any attempt is made to interpret notation. The experience is equivalent to that of learning a language: the child learns to use the words effectively before he is required to interpret the printed symbols that represent them on the page.

*Music Books in Primary Grades.*   The same use of books carries over into the early second grade. Pupils learn some new songs taken from the music book, which will be used later, and they reestablish singing voices by reviewing many easy, familiar songs. However, there comes a time during the year when the teacher feels that books can be helpful in the learning of new songs and that the pupils will benefit by guidance in observing more in the music score.

As an example of this visual approach to a new song: a second grade teacher, in introducing "Dundee, Dundee" (see page 134), might ask the children to look at the song to see what it is about. Some of the words would be above their reading level and so he would need to discuss these and clarify the ideas in the text. Next he could ask the pupils whether they can tell anything about the way the music sounds by looking at the notes: "Is the rhythm even or uneven—does it seem to move evenly and steadily or does it have a skipping movement? . . . Yes, it is a skipping rhythm. Who can clap a skipping rhythm?" After the rhythm is established, all of the children may clap it and chant the first line of the text in that rhythm.

The teacher may then ask, "Does the rhythm skip all the way through?" The children will see that on the words "Dundee, Dundee" it does not skip. The teacher may play this pattern on the Song Bells or piano and then ask the children to sing it. One child may then play the bell part as others sing it and the teacher, alone, sings to the end of the phrase. The teacher would then sing the song from the beginning with the children chiming in on the part they now know.

Children in the third grade might be able to go further with their initial visual observations and independent interpretation. If they are experienced in playing easy piano and bell parts, one child might find the notes for "Dundee, Dundee" unaided by the teacher. With guidance, the children might recognize the basic scale movement beginning in the fifth measure which then could be sounded out on the bells or sung with sol-fa syllables or scale numbers.

At no time should this process become laborious. The teacher should give enough aid to keep the observations and singing going, but he should also lead the children to feel that musical discoveries of this sort are enjoyable challenges.

Songs in many basic music books are arranged on the page so that the phrases conform to the length of the lines. This arrangement helps children to see the construction of the song as a whole, its repeated phrases, contrasting movement, and various melodic or rhythmic motives. It is essential that boys and girls be aware of the general structure of any song they would learn either through the visual approach (reading) or learning by ear.

At this point a short discussion of music reading may be helpful. Music teachers in general are concerned that children should "learn music," which implies the development of both concepts and skills in music. There are, however, two points of view regarding the importance of reading music.

(1) The development of skill in reading music in the elementary grades requires a systematic sequential development using carefully graded materials from the first grade through the sixth grade. Song material must be selected or arranged to conform to the music reading level of each grade. Some music series books are developed on this plan, and some school music programs are organized to facilitate sequential grade-to-grade development in reading.

(2) On the other hand, many music specialists believe that broader musical experiences can be had and more musical concepts can be developed when material is selected for its basic musical appeal and its appropriateness for children of a particular age. Music series books designed by authors whose chief concern is the quality of the musical experience usually do not have enough carefully graded material to facilitate the sequential development of skill in music reading. The proponents of this approach believe that the richer, more varied musical experience and the maintenance of greater

interest in music compensate for the smaller gain in absolute reading skill. They maintain that the individual who has developed many valid concepts about music, who knows in general how to decipher a phrase of music through the use of sol-fa syllables or a musical instrument, and who is enthusiastic about music will be able to improve his reading ability any time he finds it necessary to do so.

With either system, both the aural and the visual approaches to new songs should be used with second and third grade children. Teachers' books for the basic music series give detailed suggestions for learning songs and developing music reading skills at this level. Much depends upon the particular music series adopted for use in the school.

*Intermediate Grade Use of Music Books.* Children in the intermediate grades learn songs very quickly when they have guidance and the desire to learn. At this level the teacher must not think in terms of teaching "by rote" or "by note," for the only time a song is taught by rote is when it is learned entirely by ear. Children who can read a song text and who have had considerable association with music notation should not be subjected to such song-learning conditions unless it is absolutely essential that they learn a song for which no copies are available. Every song learned with the aid of the printed page offers some opportunity to expand understanding of notation and to apply the skills developed earlier.

In Chapters Four and Five many suggestions were made about the growth of musical concepts through the use of rhythm, melody, and harmony instruments. It is expected that through these experiences, as they are promoted along with singing, pupils will learn a great deal about music and its notation. Pupils should continually be given greater opportunities to interpret notation for themselves.

Intermediate grade pupils can use either scale numbers or sol-fa syllables to analyze the melodic content of new songs. Before trying to sing a new song these children should survey it for familiar patterns. The whole song need not be sung with scale numbers or syllables if the proper *hearing* of typical patterns has been developed. When pupils recognize a group of notes as a scale line, beginning and ending at certain levels, they should be able to tune up in the proper key and hear its sound in the inner ear. However, if, when looking over a new song, the pupils come upon unfamiliar fragments, scale numbers or syllables can help them analyze and sing the troublesome spots.

As they undertake a new song, pupils should consider its rhythmic characteristics, establish the meter, and tap out rhythm patterns that may present a problem. They should consider the general contour of its melody and the repeated or contrasting phrases that determine the form before they begin singing. Experienced readers may then be ready to sing the song. Problems may arise, but they can be solved by isolation of difficult phrases.

Less experienced singers may need more assistance; they may hear the song sung by the teacher before they do any analysis. After they have a general idea of the song such students are in a better position to analyze it and to try to sing it. Some songs built around the primary chords (I, IV, $V_7$) will be read much more easily if the Autoharp is used as a harmonic background.

Inexperienced singers might use some of the melody instruments to help them work out a new song.

However the song is studied, the pupils should have a feeling of satisfaction and accomplishment. Unrhythmic, note-by-note spelling out of a melody is not a *musical* experience. On the other hand, rote teaching without any attempt to develop understanding about the music can hardly be considered "education." A varied approach to new songs is recommended, with the application of effective techniques in solving melodic and rhythmic problems and the gradual accumulation of skills.

*Independence in Learning Songs.* Children learn songs by hearing them sung by their teacher, the music specialist, or a member of the class; they hear songs played on the piano, the bells, or another instrument; they hear recordings. If they have books as they listen, intermediate grade pupils should watch the notation, observing the relationship of what is heard to what is seen, so that they are able to sing successfully at the earliest possible moment, and so that their understanding of the notation will make them better prepared to meet the next new song. The will, interest, and purpose the children have determine how rapidly they develop musical independence.

In one school where the classrooms were self-contained, the music consultant assisted once a week for one-half hour in rooms where the teacher was not a competent musician. One fifth grade class, whose teacher did no singing, was so well organized and motivated that every minute of the consultant's time was used to greatest advantage. The children were eager to learn and prided themselves upon being able to sing a song accurately the week after it was introduced. Rarely were errors made, for the consultant pointed out pitfalls at the first lesson and suggested ways in which the song could be rehearsed to avoid them. The pupils' effective use of these suggestions was based on their growing understanding of musical notation.

Two children served as song leaders who tuned the class with the pitch pipe and rehearsed the songs. At the lesson with the consultant on the week following the introduction of a song the student leaders directed the singing of the song in the manner they had developed during the week. The consultant then made suggestions for phrasing, or assisted the group in establishing a harmonizing part. Often more than one song could be introduced in one lesson because the interest and esprit de corps were high.

The songs were selected jointly by the teacher, the class, and the consultant. When songs were needed for a particular unit study, the class compiled a list of those available, and with the help of the consultant selected the most interesting and musical. Sometimes the consultant suggested songs she thought the class should learn and, because of their enthusiasm for her and for music, the children learned these as readily as any others.

When recordings were used, the pupils managed the song learning process independently. Generally one child operated the record player while another directed the singing. They understood the necessity of listening before singing, of following words and music in the book, of singing alternate phrases or the easy refrain first, and of whispering the words or singing softly in order to keep up with the recorded version. The goal was to learn to sing independently of the record and to learn to use whatever accompanying instruments seemed appropriate.

Although the teacher did not participate musically, he was an important figure in the success of this music program. He was an effective teacher who insisted upon orderly procedure and the thoughtful analysis of problems. The music consultant provided specific musical guidance when necessary and assisted in evaluating the combined efforts. Without such guidance and evaluation the pupils would have made serious errors in music; they would soon have come to the end of their resources and music-making would have stagnated.

Musical do-it-yourself programs can be excellent when organization, direction, and rapport are established by the classroom teacher, and expert assistance is given by a respected music teacher, who provides guidance from the point of view of the musical needs of the children rather than the demands of an imposed program.

## LEARNING TO SING HARMONY PARTS

Traditionally two-part singing has been done in the fifth grade and three-part singing in the sixth grade. We recommend that harmony singing be developed in these grades but that it be done in a manner compatible with the music-making skills of the children. Considerable improvisatory harmony singing should be done, much of it in conjunction with simple harmony instruments. In the self-contained classroom the program can be interesting and vital, but in most cases it does not lead to the impressive three-part unaccompanied singing that has been traditional under the direction of a special teacher. If freedom in two-part singing and some experience in simple three-part harmony can be achieved in the general classroom, a substantial basis is laid for choral singing in special groups under expert leadership.

### The Use of Rounds

Early experiences in singing harmony are provided by rounds, which can be used in many different ways, depending on the maturity and musical experience of the singers. After the melody has been learned in unison, it may be sung in two equal parts. Later, when skill in hearing and singing two parts is well developed, rounds may be sung in three or four parts. The musical value of the experience lies in the singer's ability to hear the total effect. A group should not try to sing in more parts than the members are able to hear as a whole while they sing.

In this book "Are You Sleeping?" (page 133) is an easy round that can be sung as a unison song in the first or second grade. Third graders can sing it as a two-part round. "Bells" (page 149) is another good round that fourth graders might first try in two parts.

"Spring Gladness" will serve as an example of experiences in harmony singing that may be undertaken with fifth or sixth graders.

## SPRING GLADNESS
### (Es tönen die Lieder)

*Joyfully*

*German Round*
*I.W., from the German*

New songs ring with glad-ness, For spring ends all sad-ness,

Once more hear the mer-ry pip - ing Of shep-herds up-on the hill,

La la la la la la la la la La la la la la la la la!

From DISCOVERING MUSIC TOGETHER, *Book Five*, by Charles Leonhard, Beatrice Perham Krone, Irving Wolfe, and Margaret Fullerton. © 1967 by Follett Publishing Company, Chicago, Illinois.

Since this is such a fine melody, the pupils should sing and enjoy it in unison first. Notice that in spite of the chord figurations in the first two lines, the backbone of the melody in those lines is a scale pattern upward F, G, A, and downward C, B♭, A. The song may be harmonized by the tonic and dominant chords, and voices with a limited lower range may sing the chord roots in this pattern:

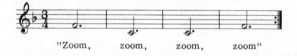

"Zoom, zoom, zoom, zoom"

Such a part should be sung rhythmically and with good resonance and sustaining quality, imitating a bass viol.

The round may be sung in three parts with this added accompaniment figure if the students can comfortably sustain that many parts. Bells or flute may play the second phrase of the melody repeatedly as a counterpart if the voices are able to regulate their volume so that a good balance is assured. Thus a four- or five-part composition can be developed from a simple round if the teacher and pupils have sufficient inventiveness and harmonizing skill.

### The Descant

A simple melody written above and harmonizing with another melody is known as a descant. One principle of its construction is that it moves *against* the basic melody; hence, when the melody moves slowly the descant may move faster and when the melody moves rapidly the descant may be in sustained tones. Also, as the melody moves upward the descant may be sustained or move downward. The arrangement of "Streets of Laredo" (see page 161) shows an excellent example of a descant.

The value of the descant in the intermediate grades is that it provides pleasing harmonic experience, but gives the less familiar part to the higher voices, which frequently sing with more independence at this age. Since it lies in a higher range and is easily heard, the descant often is sung by only three or four voices. It should accompany and not dominate the melody. Bells, Song Flutes, and other melody instruments may play the descant with or without voices. A solo instrumental counterpart is called an obbligato. Varied descants and obbligatos are suggested in the basic music texts.

Early experience in singing harmony may come in songs with simple two-part endings. The children may first hear the teacher sing the harmony part as they sing the melody. When they thoroughly understand and hear the harmony in relation to their own part, a few of the children should join the teacher on the harmony part. Later, they can sing the part without the teacher. "All through the Night" has an easy two-part ending on three phrases.

## ALL THROUGH THE NIGHT

David Owen
Old Welsh

*Quietly*

Sleep, my child, and peace at-tend thee, All through the night;

Guard-ian an-gels God will send thee, All through the night.

Soft the drow-sy hours are creep-ing, Hill and vale in slum-ber steep-ing,

I my lov-ing vi-gil keep-ing, All through the night.

MANAGEMENT OF
THE SINGING
SITUATION

### Partner Songs

Two different songs that have the same underlying harmony can be sung simultaneously as "partner songs" if desired. A simple example of this can be observed when "Paw-Paw Patch" (see page 75) and the refrain of "Skip to My Lou" are sung simultaneously in the same key.

## SKIP TO MY LOU

*Gaily*                                                                    *Singing Game*

Lost my part-ner, what will I do,    Lost my part-ner, what will I do,
Skip,— skip,—    skip  to my Lou,    Skip,— skip,—    skip  to my Lou,

Lost my part-ner,   what will I   do?   Skip  to my Lou, my    dar - ling.
Skip,— skip,—     skip  to my Lou,    Skip  to my Lou, my    dar - ling.

A great many other examples will be found in *Partner Songs* and *More Partner Songs.*[8] When the children know the individual songs well it is fairly easy to combine them as an interesting experience in two-part singing at about fourth grade level. The children should learn to sing their own part and at the same time be aware of the harmony that the two parts create.

### Singing in Thirds and Sixths

Singing thirds below the melody line is another early experience in harmony (see "In Bahía," page 79). Sometimes a harmony part may be sung a third higher or a sixth lower for a pleasing effect; because the harmony parallels the melody it is not difficult to sing. In "Tum Balalaika" (GwM V–40) we find the harmony part chiefly in thirds below the melody, but with a few measures moving in parallel sixths (see page 253).

Boys and girls should be given some experience in harmonizing "by ear" in thirds and sixths above or below a melody. When sung in the key of G, "Go Tell Aunt Rhodie" (see page 216) can have a parallel harmonizing part added a sixth below the melody throughout the song. "Skip to My Lou" may be harmonized with a part a third above the melody, except on the last note in measures two and six, when both voices should sound in unison. The pupils can be shown that D, which is a third above B, would not lie in the tonic chord, the underlying harmony at this point. The first eight measures of Brahms' "Cradle Song" (see page 234) can be harmonized a third below the melody.

## TUM BALALAIKA

*Moderato*                                                    *Yiddish Folk Song*

Maid - en, maid - en, tell___ me true, What can grow with - out___ the dew? What___ can burn for years___ and years? What___ can cry and shed___ no tears? Tum - ba - la, tum - ba - la, tum - ba - la - lai - ka, Tum - ba - la, tum - ba - la, tum - ba - la - lai - ka, Tum - ba - la - lai - ka, tum - ba - la - lai - ka, Tum - ba - la - lai - ka, Tum - ba - la - lai - ka.

From GROWING WITH MUSIC, *Book Five,* by H. R. Wilson *et al.* © 1966 by Prentice-Hall, Inc., Englewood Cliffs, N.J. Reprinted by permission.

The most important aspect of harmony singing is hearing the effect of the voices sounding simultaneously. Whether it be "Three Blind Mice" sung in two parts by second graders or a choral work of three parts sung by sixth graders, the children must be helped to hear the total harmonic effect. To accomplish this the teacher might occasionally (1) hold chords at cadences or other convenient points within the song and direct the children's attention to the harmony produced and (2) sing a phrase in parallel thirds slowly so the movement of the harmony will be heard.

Rounds sung chiefly as competition do not result in musical experiences. Singing in harmony is essentially a cooperative enterprise wherein the voices adjust to one another in an effort to make the purest harmony. Children have to be taught harmony, that is, how each interval and chord should sound. Only the teacher who has a good musical ear and has had experience singing harmony himself will be able to guide fifth and sixth grade singers in the study of part singing of which they are generally capable.

MANAGEMENT OF
THE SINGING
SITUATION

**253**

## Root Tones, Chords, and Chants

Fifth and sixth grade pupils, partly through the medium of the Autoharp, become acquainted with elementary principles of harmonization and expand their explorations to include simple chants to accompany songs. Singing the root tones is an easily understandable procedure. A song such as "Down in the Valley" (see page 165) may be harmonized by the tonic and dominant chords. The singers follow the chord changes as they sing the chord roots: "do" (I) or "so" (V₇). A different effect is achieved when "so" is held throughout the song. Harmony is possible because "so" is common to both chords (see discussion of chord accompaniments, page 164).

If more parts are desired, a solo voice or a small group may sing the melody while the class divides into three parts to sound the entire triad on a neutral or sol-fa syllable. This movement of voice parts may be used with "Down in the Valley" and other two-chord songs:

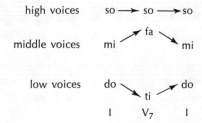

high voices     so → so → so

middle voices     mi   fa   mi

low voices     do   ti   do

    I     V₇     I

Songs harmonized with three chords—I, IV, V₇—could have added vocal harmony in the form of root tones sung on "do—fa—so—do" or chording using the progression:

high voices     so   la   so → so

middle voices     mi   fa → fa   mi

low voices     do → do   ti   do

    I     IV   V₇     I

at the appropriate points of change. "Du, Du Liegst Mir im Herzen" (see page 78) is easily harmonized in this manner.

Descants above or chants below a given melody can be created by selecting tones from the supporting chord structure. The descant suggested for the refrain of "Came A-Riding" (TiM VI–171, see page 163) is a good example of this type.

Passing tones or short scale patterns moving between chord tones also are used in creating descants and chants. The Krones, in *Music Participation in the Elementary School*,[9] have shown how to create such harmony parts. *Our First Songs to Sing with Descants*[10] and other books in the same series give good examples.

Since the guidance of intermediate pupils in singing harmony is difficult for many classroom teachers, the resource of a music consultant or a helping teacher is generally indispensable at this level of instruction. In the past the singing of harmony was done chiefly on the basis of formal parts printed in the song books. Teachers were not urged to analyze the harmonic structure with the children in order to see the relationship of the parts. The Autoharp has helped to provide a simple approach to harmony, and its use should be combined with other basic experiences in singing harmony.

After pupils in the intermediate grades have had experience playing chord accompaniments on the Autoharp and the bells, it is but one step further to show them the relationship of simple harmonizing parts to the basic chord structure. An understanding of principles of harmonization leads to better singing and opens the road for experimentation and improvisation.

## GROUP CREATIVITY IN SONGS

Creating "our own" anything gives children a sense of identification and possession. When young children create a song in the classroom, the teacher may write the music with the words on a chart so all may see it. A child may draw an illustration to be mounted at the top of the chart. Older children can write out the song themselves and by doing so can learn more about music notation. Such a project may have particular importance to an individual; it may bring music closer to him and help him to identify it as something special in his life. He may begin to explore music as a personal interest when he discovers that he and his friends can create their own melodies.

In Chapter Five methods were outlined in the use of the flannel board with adjustable, staff-related tone bars for improvisation and melody writing. This practical instrumental approach is highly recommended. The following will suggest to the teacher ways in which he can broaden the approach to creative activities in music so that more varied song texts and freer melodies can be developed through the initial use of the singing voice.

### Learning Music through Creating Music

As children create melodies for selected verses, they become more keenly aware of line and form in the melody of a composition. They begin to note, with purposeful interest, how melodies in the songs they sing rise and fall; how most songs have one high point; how melodies in a two- or three-tone range tend to be uninteresting. They may look with renewed interest at the repetition and contrast in sections of the songs they sing and think of ways to improve the form of the song they are creating.

When children write additional stanzas for an existing melody, they are made aware of the rhythm of the words and the necessary relationship between word syllables and the rhythm patterns in the melody. They should be led to hear the accents of important words and to discover that these accents correspond to the metric scheme of the music. Many other details become meaningful to pupils as they create verses and melodies. Younger children notice fewer details; the creative act itself is the most important part of the experience. The teacher must assist the children with certain technical considerations they are not yet ready to comprehend fully.

Song writing must grow out of activities that establish a readiness to create. Children who feel at home with singing find music a natural means of expression. When a topic is of concern and interest to them, children may feel the urge to express it in some new way, associating words and melody. Any classroom teacher can establish conditions favorable to the creation of melodies. He is in a better position to do so than is the special teacher who sees the children infrequently and is not acquainted with their intimate interests. However, unless the classroom teacher is skilled in identifying melodic patterns, he may need the help of a music specialist to notate the melody. The teacher may record the melody on tape as it is sung by the children. Later a musician can notate it correctly. Or the teacher may make a simple notation so that he or the children can remember the melody and sing it to a person able to write it.

Sometimes a classroom teacher may develop the idea of creating a song up to the point where the children are ready to sing their melodic ideas. Then the music specialist, if he is well known to the children so that they feel free to create in his presence, may come to the classroom to help develop the song.

### Creating Words for a Melody

Children sometimes want to add another stanza to a song they know. This relatively simple first step in creativity is important because it lends dignity and importance to an activity children carry on spontaneously in their play. The project in the classroom, however, should not be done in a way that makes this simple creative impulse a self-conscious one. The teacher should work with the natural aptitudes and habits in creativity that already exist.

Among the folk and activity songs, we find a natural setting for the creating of added stanzas. "What Shall We Do When We All Go Out?" (see page 193) and "Toodala" are two of the many songs Ruth Seeger points out as natural improvising songs in *American Folk Songs for Children*. Since the texts of these two songs are repetitive, it is not difficult to find a few words to express another idea appropriate to each song. In addition, the melody of "What Shall We Do When We All Go Out?" has the simple qualities of the universal children's chant described on page 177. This is the kind of melody the children themselves might spontaneously create on the playground, and so it is quite easy for them to find other appropriate words for it.

## TOODALA

*Easily*
*Texas*

Might-y pret-ty mo – tion too – da –la,  too – da –la,  too – da –la,

Might–y pret–ty – tion, too – da – la,  too – da–la – la  la – dy.

From *American Folk Songs for Children*. Doubleday & Co., New York, 1948. Copyright by the Texas Folklore Society, 1941. Used by permission.

"The Green Dress" (see page 54) and other songs invite the child to make up new words to please his fancy or match his activity. More thought is required to add a stanza to other songs. "Trip a Trop a Tronjes" is a lively, rhythmic melody in a foot-riding song.

## TRIP A TROP A TRONJES

*Brightly*
*Early American*

Take  a  trip  to Tron – jes,  Up  and down and  o – ver,  The

pigs  are  in  the  bean  patch, The  cows  are  in  the  clo – ver,  The

*ten.* *ten.*

ducks  are  in  the  wa – ter place, The  calf  is  in  the  long  grass

So  big  my  ba – by  is  Pop– pe–jay  vas.

From *Americans and Their Songs* (Harper & Row, publishers). Reprinted by permission of the author, Frank Luther.

Instead of "Take a Trip to Tronjes" second grade children might wish to take a trip "to the country," "to the playground," or "to Disneyland."

If Disneyland is the subject, they might sing the first phrase and find that these words can be used:

Take  a  trip  to  Dis – ney – land  *etc.*

**MANAGEMENT OF THE SINGING SITUATION**

**257**

After this beginning, facts and fancy about Disneyland would be put into words that fit the rhythmic pattern of the melody. Questions to individuals would bring out ideas that the teacher might list on the chalkboard:

"When did you go to Disneyland?"    "On our vacation"
                                    "For the holiday"
                                    "For a little trip"
                                    "In the summertime"

"What did you do there?"            "We rode on the river boat"
                                    "We had a ride on the mule's pack"
                                    "We saw Frontierland and real In-
                                    dians"

"When you went away from Disneyland what did you think about it? Did you really like it?" "I had lots of fun." "I want to go back again next year." Answers will furnish ample material for a new stanza.

The next step is to adapt the words to the melody. Ask the children to sing the new words for the first phrase and then to continue with "loo" on the second phrase as they try to find words to fit the melody. Slight rhythmic changes are often unavoidable, but not a serious deviation from the original as long as the metric beat and general rhythmic swing are maintained. Sometimes several syllables will need to be sung on one beat. Compare the following alterations:

Take a trip to Dis - ney-land   for the hol - i - day.

On ___ our va - ca - tion.

It is not necessary that the verses created by young children form a rhyming scheme. This is a refinement that can be learned later.

The chief things a teacher should do are these:

1. Be sure that the children know the melody well.
2. Keep ideas flowing so that when a phrase does not fit the music another may easily be found.
3. Have the children *sing* their ideas, either as a group or individually, to hear whether they can be adjusted to the musical phrase.
4. When an idea is especially good, suggest small word changes that will help it conform to the rhythmic scheme.

Notice that the important words in a song occur on the accent beat and that articles and sometimes prepositions are on the upbeat as in "The pigs are in . . ."

"The pigs are in---"

The words adapted should be in the mood and spirit of the melody. Decide whether the melody is lively and rollicking (as in "Trip a Trop a Tronjes") or contemplative (as in "Sleep and Rest," page 230) and more appropriate for descriptive word pictures.

## Creating a Melody

Children take unusual pride and interest in a melody they create for a poem. It may be a poem written in response to some topic of interest, or one enjoyed in choral reading or some other setting. Activities preliminary to the creation of such a melody in the classroom are those that the children use in vocal play. Simple song-chants are natural and easy for children. As Satis Coleman has suggested (Chapter Six), musical conversations on one or two tones help free the singing voice. The teacher may ask questions in a singing voice to which the children may reply:

When pupils are able to respond freely in this simple way, they will be more successful in singing melodies for verses they may choose to set to music.

Instrumental melody making, suggested in Chapter Five, is a good background for more extensive creation of songs. However, when the teacher works with the children as a group, catching, developing, and recording the melodies they sing, the melodies may be longer and much more varied than those created with a limited number of tones on an instrument.

For the first such creative experience, it is best to select a poem with considerable rhythmic movement. The first stanza of "A Swing Song"[11] by William Allingham would be a good choice:

> Swing, swing,
> Sing, sing,
> Here! my throne and I am a king!
> Swing, swing,
> Sing, sing,
> Farewell, earth, for I'm on the wing!

The teacher may write the poem on the chalkboard, with some space between the lines for notation. The children are asked to read the lines aloud several times until they find its natural rhythmic swing. The teacher may observe which words are accented and underline these. Since the accented word will fall on the accent in the music, a measure bar may be drawn before each:

> | Swing, swing, | Sing, sing,
> | Here! my throne and | I am a king!

Notice that this verse swings in two beats to the measure. Third grade classes who have worked with the metric beat and accent, as suggested in Chapter Four, may understand the placement of measure bars. They can help to identify the accents as they chant the lines.

Once the natural rhythmic swing of the verse is determined and the pupils are well acquainted with the words, the development of a melody can begin. Discuss the poem with the children. What kind of melody is required? Do the words suggest the movement of the melodic line at different points? Since it is "A Swing Song," the smooth movement of the swing should be present. Further, there should be definite high and low points in the melody. Because the last line ends with "I'm on the wing!" probably the melody should rise rather than fall at the end.

Ask the children to chant "Swing, swing, Sing, sing," to themselves as they try to find a melody for it. One child may sing softly a snatch of melody that might be a good beginning. Ask this child to sing his melody louder. Assume this to be the melody:

Immediately the teacher and/or the class should sing what was heard in order to capture it in memory. Repeat it once or twice. Does it seem like a good beginning? If so, the teacher or pupils must find suitable notation so that it is not forgotten. Perhaps blank notation, scale numbers, or syllables will help:

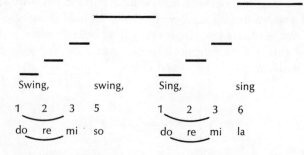

Syllables or numbers can be used if the teacher or pupils are able to tell which tone has the position of "do" or "1" in relation to the other tones. The ability to identify tonal patterns by ear is valuable. A piano or bells may be used to pick out the melody, but often, in the search for the tones sung, other tones are played that interfere with the original melody.

Once the melody for the first phrase is captured on paper or tape recorder or is secure in the memory, the next phrase must be related to it. Ask all of the children to sing the first phrase aloud and then to continue chanting or singing the next. There may be considerable sound but when someone raises his hand, the teacher should ask him to sing his melody. The teacher and/or the class immediately sings the melody as close to the original as possible. Then they go back and sing both first and second phrases consecutively. If it sounds convincing, this added phrase is put down in notation or recorded on tape. If it is not appealing to the group, other children may sing melodies for the line until something suitable is found.

It is important in this work to sing the preceding phrase as a lead into the creation of a new phrase. In this way, the two will be related to each other. If each phrase were created separately, the result might be quite disconnected.

Some teachers establish a key by playing a tonic chord and having the children sing the chord before they begin to create their melody. These teachers impose limitations on the young composers by assuming that the major is the scale suitable for a composition. Perhaps a child will hear a minor scale fragment for the first melody:

Swing, ___ swing,    Sing, ___ sing

He may not know that he is singing in the minor. His chief concern is that he has a melody that appeals to him! The major scale, although it may be more common in our civilization, has no claim to being "better" than other scales. If a child sings an unusual melody and the class finds it satisfactory, it certainly should be used. It is sometimes interesting to play an arbitrary chord progression over which a melody is improvised but, for the greatest freedom in creating a melody, no key or chord should be imposed.

The meter signature is not of concern to young children, but it may be a problem for the teacher or older pupils. It was found that "A Swing Song" moves in two beats to a measure. Common metric schemes in two beats per measure occur in ²⁄₄ and ⁶⁄₈ meter. The following difference exists:

"A Swing Song" fits the metric scheme for ⁶⁄₈. This is especially evident when three separate syllables demand three divisions of the beat:

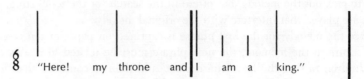

$\frac{6}{8}$    "Here!    my   throne   and | I   am   a   king."

Usually verses that are smooth and flowing in two beats will best fit into $\frac{6}{8}$ meter. More square-cut rhymes will be in $\frac{2}{4}$.

If a verse has a longer line, uninterrupted by accents, it will be better notated in $\frac{4}{4}$ meter. The first stanza of "The Idle Shepherd Boys" by William Wordsworth is an example:

> $\frac{4}{4}$   The |valley rings with mirth and joy;
>      A - |mong the hills the echoes play
>      A |never, never ending song,
>      To |welcome in the May.

If read in $\frac{2}{4}$ meter, the effect is jarring and broken by unnecessary accents:

> $\frac{2}{4}$   The |valley rings with | mirth and joy;
>      A - |mong the hill the | echoes play, *etc.*

After pupils have had some experience in such melody writing, they will find that a melody that is too closely tied to the metric scheme of the poem may be pedantic and unimaginative. The subject of the poem may suggest the meter. A lyrical imaginative text might suggest a more free-flowing, florid melody. "The Idle Shepherd Boys" might be set in a waltz rhythm with a greater variety of note lengths and some slurred passages. Children who croon to themselves might produce such a melody, while those who use music in relation to rhythm activities will create songs with a more chant-like character.

Setting a poem to music in a regular meter requires the development of a sense of the Western European musical heritage. Much folk music of other styles is asymmetrical and irregular in its meter. Rhythms in five or seven beats as well as changing meters are found in such music. Children's free singing of a text can lead to an irregular metrical setting. The teacher may find such a melody difficult to write down, but an original song of this type that is appealing and simple enough to be remembered and sung again is as valid a representation of children's creativity as are songs that conform to more traditional rhythmic settings.

When a melody has been established for the entire stanza, the children should sing it several times. If they are not pleased with all parts of it, changes can be made. A good song always gives a sense of completeness at the end, unless there is some special reason for an unfinished effect. If the new song does not sound complete, the pupils should make some adjustments in the ending. If the tonal range of the new song is too high or too low it may be transposed. Children who have had this type of creative experience will notice with greater interest characteristics of melody in the songs they sing.

In this creative activity, the chief problems are:

1. To capture the melodic ideas of the children. Sometimes the melody is sung with uncertainty. The teacher and pupils must listen carefully to sing and notate it as it was given.
2. To develop an integrated melody, not a composite of unrelated melodic ideas from several sources.
3. To use melodic ideas of the children, not unduly influenced by the teacher's notion of what the melody should be like.
4. To record the song so that it may be sung correctly later.

Composing a melody can be very important to some individuals and a fine experience for the group of children as a whole. Here the pupils are able to use all of their understanding of the elements of music and its notation. Although it may take several music periods to complete one song, it is well worth the time spent. More than one opportunity of this kind should be arranged during the year.

---

## ACTIVITIES FOR COLLEGE CLASSES

A. Questions for Review
  1. Outline the training recommended for the development of a good quality singing voice.
  2. Describe the steps involved in tuning up to sing a song in a major key; in a minor key.
  3. Describe the various techniques a teacher can use to build children's skill in interpreting notation for melody.
  4. Describe the techniques that can be used to teach songs in the primary grades.
  5. Describe ways in which children in the intermediate grades learn songs.
  6. Discuss the different approaches to singing harmony.
  7. Outline the essential steps in assisting a group to create a melody for a selected poem.
B. Written Assignments
  1. The appropriate key and the starting tone should be shown for each song title selected under written assignment No. 1, Chapter Six.
  2. Find two songs which, if transposed, would be in a better singing range for primary voices. For each song name the new key, the new range, and the syllable of the first note of the song.
  3. See that at least four songs in the collection assembled under written assignment No. 1, Chapter Six are in the minor mode.
  4. Hear the recordings of songs from two different basic music series books at one grade level. Using the seven points listed under "Using Recorded Song Materials," compare and evaluate them.
  5. Among the teaching notes for songs collected be sure you have included suggestions leading to the development of an appropriate level of skill in harmony singing in grades three and above (consider all procedures).
C. Classroom Projects
  1. Tune up with the pitch pipe and get the class successfully started singing a familiar song.

2. Select an easy but unfamiliar song that can be learned without the use of books in one or two hearings. Sing it to the class so that the words and the spirit of the song are conveyed.
3. Select and teach one song from a basic music book. Have the class use books as an aid in learning the song, and use procedures suitable for the grade level selected. If absolutely necessary, use the piano to support your voice.
4. Select a song that is well recorded. Teach the song, using the recording in combination with teaching techniques effective for the grade level selected.
5. In a small group, prepare and sing one song using some form of two-part or three-part harmony.

## CHAPTER NOTES

1. Frances M. Andrews and Ned C. Deihl, *Development of a Technique for Identifying Elementary School Children's Musical Concepts,* Cooperative Research Project No. 5-0233 (University Park, Pa.: Pennsylvania State University, September 1967).
2. Zoltán Kodály, *Choral Method,* edited by Percy M. Young and published in the United States by Boosey and Hawkes, Inc. For information on this method see Elisabeth Szönyi, "Zoltán Kodály's Pedagogic Activities," *International Music Educator,* March 1966, p. 418; and Arpad Darazs, "The Kodály Method for Choral Training," *Bulletin No. 8, Council for Research in Music Education,* Fall 1966.
3. Mary Helen Richards, *Threshold to Music* (Palo Alto, Calif.: Fearon Publishers, Inc., 1964).
4. Meg Peterson, *The Many Ways to Play the Autoharp,* Volumes I and II (Union, N.J.: Oscar Schmidt-International, Inc., 1966).
5. Ruth Crawford Seeger, *American Folk Songs for Children* (New York: Doubleday & Company, Inc., 1948).
6. Beatrice Landeck, *Songs to Grow On* (New York: Edward B. Marks Music Corporation, Music Publishers, William Sloane Associates, Inc., Publishers, 1950).
7. Beatrice Landeck, *More Songs to Grow On* (New York: Edward B. Marks Music Corporation, Music Publishers, William Sloane Associates, Inc., Publishers, 1954).
8. Frederick Beckman, *Partner Songs* and *More Partner Songs* (Boston: Ginn and Company, 1958 and 1962).
9. Beatrice and Max Krone, *Music Participation in the Elementary School* (Park Ridge, Ill.: Neil A. Kjos Music Co., 1952).
10. Beatrice and Max Krone, *Our First Songs to Sing with Descants* (Park Ridge, Ill.: Neil A. Kjos Music Co., 1941).
11. William Allingham, "A Swing Song," in *The Moon Is Shining Bright as Day* by Ogden Nash (Philadelphia: J. B. Lippincott Company, 1953).

## Other References

Christy, Van A., *Foundations in Singing* (Dubuque, Iowa: Wm. C. Brown Co., 1965).

Fox, Lillian Mohr, and Thomas L. Hopkins, *Creative School Music* (Morristown, N.J.: Silver Burdett Company, 1936). Chapter 4, "Creating Songs," Chapter 5, "Developing Original Poetry," and Chapter 6, "Developing Original Melody."

Mathews, Paul Wentworth, *You Can Teach Music* (New York: E. P. Dutton and Co., Inc., 1953). Chapter 4, "Let the Singing Begin."

Mursell, James L., *Music and the Classroom Teacher* (Morristown, N.J.: Silver Burdett Company, 1951). Chapter 8, "Creative Activities," and Chapter 9, "Musicianship."

————, *Music Education Principles and Programs* (Morristown, N.J.: Silver Burdett Company, 1956). Chapters 5 and 6, "Music Reading and Musical Growth," and Chapter 12, "Creation."

Myers, Louise Kifer, *Teaching Children Music in the Elementary School*, Third Edition (Englewood Cliffs, N.J.: Prentice-Hall, Inc., 1961). Chapter 5, "Creating Music."

Nye, Robert Evans, and Bjornar Bergethon, *Basic Music, An Activities Approach to Functional Musicianship*, Third Edition (Englewood Cliffs, N.J.: Prentice-Hall, Inc., 1968). Chapter 11, "Composing Songs."

Nye, Robert Evans, and Vernice Trousdale Nye, *Music in the Elementary School*, Second Edition (Englewood Cliffs, N.J.: Prentice-Hall, Inc., 1964). Chapter 6, "Learning to Sing," Chapter 7, "Learning to Sing Part Songs."

Perham, Beatrice, *Music in the New School* (Park Ridge, Ill.: Neil A. Kjos Music Co., 1941). Chapter 5, "Creative Learning."

Snyder, Alice M., *Creating Music with Children* (New York: Mills Music, Inc., 1957). Chapter 4, "Singing."

See Appendix B for listing of song books and records in the basic music series.

MANAGEMENT OF
THE SINGING
SITUATION

# 8

# Experiences in
# Listening to Music

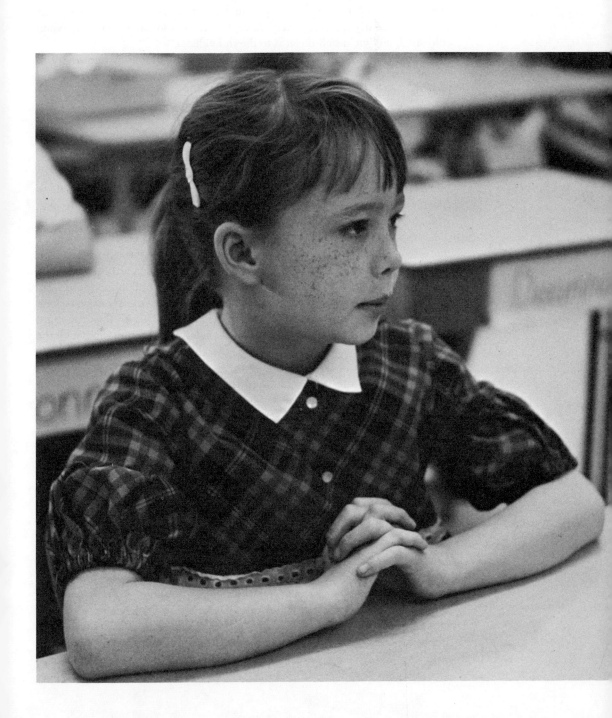

Sculpture, a visual art, is enjoyed as one sees it and perhaps feels it with his hands. Painting, likewise, is a visual art in color and design. But music must be heard. A person responds to it in proportion to his sensitivity to its tone colors, rhythm, form, melody, and harmony. Listening to music is an experience nearly everyone may have but it is also an art which, when cultivated, will yield rich rewards to the individual.

What does the individual cultivate? First, he can develop his sensitivity to the mood and ideas in the music and his freedom to respond intuitively and imaginatively to what he hears. Second, he can listen to the music of composers of different times and places and increase his capacity to hear and understand their use of the elements of music: the interplay of varied rhythms, the instrumentation, the development of a motive or a melody line and its harmonic basis, and the relationship of themes and sections. Understanding comes through guided listening and experience with music. It is the intellectual response to music. Both the intellectual and the emotional responses are important and interactive, but the emotional is more basic and, with children, should be developed in advance of the intellectual response.

Because listening to music should create a response, be it emotional or intellectual, the teacher may wish to provide avenues through which this response may manifest itself. Some children express themselves most naturally by talking, some by moving, others by the generation of sound and rhythm, and still others by painting. It is helpful but not always necessary for children to define and interpret their feelings in these ways. The important thing is that in some way, through one of the many opportunities in which the teacher makes music available to them, the children begin to listen and to respond with their imaginations.

In addition to the studies outlined in this chapter, children should have other contacts with music, experiences of a more random nature which nevertheless have value. Each teacher has his own favorite reference books and recordings, and he can adapt the appropriate material for use in his classroom. A teacher with a special musical interest can enrich the experiences of his pupils in his own unique way by sharing this interest with them.

If a teacher is to judge competently what might be of benefit to children, he must understand the limits of their ability to hear and comprehend music. Generally speaking, the child before puberty understands that which is simple, direct, and objective. The music, literature, and art to which he will respond must have these characteristics. A teacher who uses these criteria in his selection of music will reject for use with children certain otherwise excellent pieces of music. Melodies which are well defined and expressive are good as long as they are not sophisticated or sensuous in a manner not understandable to children. Rhythm has a natural appeal, but preadolescent children do not understand rhythms that are too complicated. Teachers need not be concerned about jazz before the seventh or eighth grade, for only those students who have a good understanding of simple rhythms and those who have had experiences in rhythmic and melodic improvisations will be ready to benefit musically from a study of jazz and other such improvisatory forms. Jazz and contemporary dance music are not taboo in the classroom, but they must be considered incidental rather than integral to the program in music education at this level.

The hearing of harmony, as more than a mere pleasant sound, begins to develop only in the intermediate grades. Certain subtle harmonies are not noticed by children at all, and some of the lush harmony and rich orchestrations of the romantic period overpower them. Although it is difficult to classify all the various composers according to style, the listing in Chapter Two should be useful to the elementary teacher. In each approach to listening described in this chapter, reference will be made to music of more than one style. By planning and checking the classification of composers a teacher can arrange for his pupils to hear music of the several styles during the course of a school year.

In this chapter reference is made to materials that are generally available in teacher-training institutions and may serve as examples to be explored by future teachers. Appendix B–II contains a code for the identification of important groups of recorded examples designed especially for elementary schools. Other recordings are referred to by company name or abbreviation and number. Sources of information on music and composers referred to in this chapter are listed in the chapter notes.

---

## THE FOUNDATIONS FOR LISTENING

√ Children listen to music in many ways and learn to accept it as a part of their environment. The great concern of music educators is the quality of music children hear. In answer to the basic question, "What is the value of music?" we must reaffirm the belief that the music which best serves the individual is that which is expressive of the wide range of human feeling and experience. Young children have their own levels of emotional response, and music to satisfy their needs must be supplied in various ways.

### Music as a Background

Music, like lights and color, can do much to enrich the environment. It has been a tradition of better hotels and restaurants to provide a more enjoyable atmosphere for dining through the use of pleasant music. Likewise, in business houses and factories music is used to provide a more favorable environment. Children are much more impressionable and responsive than adults. Well-selected music can help them relax during rest periods. When they are listless and tired, music in a happy mood, played as they go about their quieter activities, can help them feel cheerful and more alive.

Background music is valuable not only because it supplies a suitable atmosphere for different occasions, but because it provides another opportunity for children to hear music. Most people experience pleasure upon hearing a favorite melody. The adult rarely stops to think where he made the acquaintance of the many musical compositions he knows. We have an impressive heritage of music, but it is useful only to those to whom it is familiar. Many children do not hear a fine variety of music at home; it is the responsibility of the teacher to make it a part of classroom experience.

There are two general uses for background music in the classroom; the type of music varies with the situation. Music for resting should be melodious and soothing. It should not be rhythmically lively and should have no loud climaxes or contrasting sections. Lullabies were written for this purpose.

| | |
|---|---|
| "Berceuse," Fauré (A in M II–1) | "Cradle Song" and "Little Sandman," |
| "Berceuse," Stravinsky (A in M I–1) | Brahms |
| "Cradle Song," Schubert | "Traumeri," Schumann (BOL #63) |

Other melodies such as "Minuet" by Paderewski, "Minuet in G" by Beethoven, and "Melody in F" by Rubinstein are "classics" that everyone should know. Excerpts from longer compositions may be used if they are soothing and not interrupted with loud climaxes:

"Air" from *Suite No. 3 in D,* Bach
"Clair de Lune," Debussy (BOL #52)
"Liebestraum," Liszt
"Londonderry Air," arranged by Grainger (BOL #60)
"Nocturne" from *A Midsummer Night's Dream,* Mendelssohn
"On Hearing the First Cuckoo in Spring," Delius
"Sarabande" from *Suite for Strings,* Corelli (BOL #63)
"The Swan" from *The Carnival of the Animals,* Saint-Saëns (BOL #51, A in M III–2)
Third Movement (Adagio Cantabile) of *Quartet in D* ("The Lark"), Haydn

Some slower-moving compositions have qualities of suspense or intense passion, which make them unrestful. The popular love song should not be used because the sentiment is not suitable for young children. There is "good" music of every type: if the music of a love song is "good," it must convey the sentiment of the text. If it succeeds, it will probably be inappropriate for children.

Music used as a background should be loud enough to be heard by everyone and to obscure room noises, but not loud enough to excite the listeners. When children particularly like a musical selection, they will want to hear it often. They should know its title so that they can ask the teacher to play it. Records should not be played so often that they become tiresome.

As a background to classroom activities, music should be a change rather than a constant accompaniment. Five or ten minutes of lively music can accompany routine seat work or craft projects. Carefully timed, well-selected music can counteract fatigue and eliminate a general undercurrent of noise. Each teacher should determine what is the best "work music" for his pupils; and in doing so he can acquaint them with worthy music that will enrich their lives for many years. Some of the Strauss, Schubert, and Brahms waltzes, classical dance suites, and serenades such as "Romanze" from Mozart's *Eine kleine Nachtmusik* (A in M IV–1) are suitable. The following are readily available in educational albums:

"Badinerie," Bach (A in M III–1)
"Intermezzo," Kabalevsky (BOL #53)
"Minuet," Mozart (BOL #53)
"Petite Ballerina," Shostakovich (A in M II–1)

"Snow Is Dancing," Debussy (A in M III–1)
"Tambourin," Grétry (A in M II–1)
"Waltz of the Doll," Delibes (A in M I–1)
"Waltz No. 1," Gounod (A in M III–1)

## The Interrelationship of Musical Activities

In the highest type of analytical listening, the ability to follow a melody line within the texture of the musical composition is of basic importance. Thus, as the child learns to listen to and sing a melody, first in short fragments and later in longer phrases, he is developing his ability to follow and remember the melody line. When he tries to make his own singing express the meaning of the words of a song, he begins to understand that a melody itself can convey feeling. Later he notices specific characteristics of melodic phrases—temporary points of repose and contrasting moments of pushing forward. He then has a clue to the subtleties of phrasing that make each artist's performance unique.

The principle of balancing repeated phrases or sections with contrasting material is basic in musical design. The teacher helps the child understand such musical organization by directing attention, in songs and in music used for movement, to phrases that are the same and those that contrast.

Understanding the rhythm is as important to perceptive listening as following the melody. The listener who fully comprehends Grieg's "In the Hall of the Mountain King" recognizes the accelerando in the repetitious rhythmic motive as the outstanding feature of this music: one short four-measure theme is played eighteen times at a faster and faster tempo, with changing instrumentation and harmonies. Ravel's "Bolero" and Stravinsky's "Rite of Spring" are characterized by an insatiable rhythm that the listener should not only feel, but comprehend as the important element in these compositions.

Movement is an almost universal response to rhythm. Some listeners at concerts move their heads or fingers in time to very rhythmic music. Other listeners feel a physical response without actually moving. In the classroom, movement to music helps pupils become more aware of rhythm; they must listen to it in order to follow the music and interpret it effectively.

Following the experience of responding to "Gigue" from *Suite for Strings* by Corelli (BOL #63) through expressive movement (Chapter Three, page 80), intermediate grade children might enter into a listening lesson and make the following analysis of that music:

The music is in a lively $\frac{12}{8}$ meter with upbeats as a characteristic of most of the motives. The melodies, which are rather long, consist of short motives unified in rising or falling sequences (see brackets in the following thematic excerpt).

etc.

The music is in broad two-part form, which after several hearings reveals an AABA structure with a marked retard after the second A section, and an extended retard at the end of the composition. Within each A section there are three phrases seven or eight measures in length. The B section is only eight measures long and has the function of providing a brief contrast that leads directly to the main theme. It is interesting to hear how Corelli has taken short motives and welded them into long flowing lines that gain tension as they rise in repeated sequences and then spiral downward in extended movement toward a point of rest. This tendency to spin out long overlapping phrases is a characteristic of the baroque style in music.

The melody is predominantly in the upper part (violins), but the bass part (cellos) is also strong and has occasional melodic interest while the two inner parts fill in the harmonies with slower moving lines. This predominance of interest in the two outer voices is another characteristic of baroque music.

**CHAPTER EIGHT**

If, in addition to such analytical musical studies, children can experience through dancing the beauty of this music they will have a most worthwhile aesthetic experience. If movement is not a natural expressive medium, color and design may be used. Finger painting in delicate colors, upward arcs and downward spirals would express the mood and feeling as well.

No lines can be drawn between the classroom music activities. A lesson in "listening" or in "rhythmic activities" may motivate pupils to express with movement what they hear. Later, when they have had considerable experience in moving to music, pupils may be quite satisfied with responding through feeling, without much physical motion. The teacher must keep in mind the fact that experiences gained in the program of rhythmic activities provide a significant basis for listening.

**272**

## Materials and Equipment

Several media are useful for bringing music into the classroom. In many areas, radio and television programs are planned for use on a particular grade level. Many of these are valuable, but they do not always provide the flexible type of music program that is recommended. Some school districts provide special concerts for children. Such events are significant, but they usually are too infrequent to constitute a continuing, comprehensive program in listening.

A few teachers are able to play the piano or another instrument with artistry and can provide some of the music in the classroom. Valuable as these skills are, they do not meet the listening needs as completely as does a good quality record player and well-selected records. If a full, rich musical program is to be carried on, each classroom should have its own three-speed record player, ready for use at any time. Good recordings are likewise essential. A well-planned school record library has multiple copies of basic records that many teachers use regularly, as well as a wide variety of other records.

However, a new teacher does not always walk into his classroom and find this equipment waiting for him. Although parents and school administrators want music for children, many of them are not yet convinced of the need for a record player in every room. The limitations of a shared phonograph can be overcome only in part by careful planning. The school budget should allow for necessary equipment. If this is not the case, an interested group such as the PTA or a music club can assist in raising funds. This is a good way for these people to show their interest in music for children.

The condition of the records and the record player is important, for the value of the musical experience is determined in considerable degree by the quality in the sound heard. When children have heard high-fidelity sound through radio, in the motion picture theater, and through home record equipment, they cannot be expected to listen with interest to antiquated recordings that are scratched and worn from numerous playings. For maximum service from records, teachers should protect them from heat, dust, and scratches, which are their chief destroyers; keep them stored vertically in folders; use a good needle of the proper size; handle the tone arm carefully; touch records only on the edges or center label; and, if dust accumulates, remove it with a clean, damp sponge.

For classroom use it is essential to have a record player that can operate at three or four speeds. Some recordings of songs from the basic music texts and a few older, still useful records are available only at 78 RPM; the majority of standard "classics" must be played at 33⅓ RPM; many children's records are available on 45 RPM; transcription discs (16 RPM) are sometimes used for literature and longer programs.

Schools should avoid purchases of cheaply made record players because they are so often in need of repair. Those with very small speakers and poor amplifying equipment have inferior tone quality. Because selected portions of recordings are played in shorter periods of time, an automatic record changer is neither necessary nor advised for school use.

Another useful piece of equipment is the phonograph to which headsets are attached for individual listening in literature as well as in music. With this equipment, children who are especially interested in music have an opportunity to select private listening fare from a collection of recorded stories or music, without distracting the remainder of the class. This is another means of meeting individual needs and enriching the school program.

## DESCRIPTIVE ELEMENTS IN PROGRAM MUSIC

Music is often categorized as either "program music" or "absolute" music. In program music the composer has established a descriptive title or program notes concerning his intent in the music. The categories are not mutually exclusive. Program music may have a well-defined form, and absolute music may have strong descriptive implications. Short descriptive compositions are excellent studies for both primary and intermediate grades. Many of these are portions of larger musical works that later may be studied in their entirety.

### Short Stories in Music

Some compositions are based on traditional stories. A classic example among pieces for children is MacDowell's "Of a Tailor and a Bear," based on one of Grimms' fairy tales. The story can be found in TiM II–100 to 102. The children may discuss the story briefly and then listen to the recorded music. After the first hearing the children should be ready to dramatize or tell how the music suggests a part of the story. If they do not include important details in their comments, the teacher may ask: "How did you know when the bear was taken away?" "How did the tailor feel at the very beginning of the music?" "You didn't notice?—Let's play a little of the music again to find out." After the discussion, the children can listen to the record again for more of the story details. On another day one of the children can tell the story as he remembers it; the record can then be played while the pupils listen for items that were not mentioned. Again, the music and its relationship to the story can be discussed, and, if desired, all or parts of it may be dramatized or used as motivation for art work.

The brief composition "Sleepy Time" from *Memories of Childhood* by Pinto (BOL #68) is based on a short poem. The obvious programmatic details include:

A cuckoo clock sounding six times as the composition begins
A cradle-rocking movement and melody
A break in the music suggesting something disturbing, perhaps the owl in the tree
Frightened "mama" cries of the dollies
A return of the comforting lullaby

This composition is so short that it is best not to describe it, for there is then no opportunity for the listeners to use their own imaginations. Before playing the record the teacher may say, "What do you do to make the baby sleep?" "Yes, we very often rock him. Listen and show me where you hear rocking music in this piece. You will hear some other things too, and since you have such good imaginations we will play the music first and then you can tell what you heard."

After hearing the music the children should be encouraged to discuss what they noticed. Then the recording may be played again once or twice so that everyone can hear and evaluate the interpretations given by individuals. There are no "right" interpretations for any of the different parts of the music, but there are those that would be less appropriate. Several playings of these compositions are necessary if the children are to notice and include the musical details in their interpretations.

"Danse Macabre" by Saint-Saëns (BOL #59) is a longer descriptive composition. There are a few specific program notes on the music, but the major portion of the interpretation is left to the listener's imagination. This is the dance of "Death" and all his ghostly followers in the graveyard on Halloween night. The harp strikes twelve tones indicating the arrival of the magic hour of midnight, and then "Death" tunes his fiddle in preparation for the revelry that goes on until the cock crows, announcing the arrival of dawn. Throughout the composition the spirits dance, sometimes in a frenzy of movement and sometimes sadly; the wind blows and the skeleton bones rattle. Many of the impressions conveyed by this music could be shown in art or expressive movement. A translation of the poem by Henri Cazalis, on which the musical composition was based, may be found in Baldwin's *A Listener's Anthology of Music,* Volume II.[1] The musical themes and the imaginative interpretation given in the book may provide a helpful background for the teacher. A composition on a similar idea, "Night on Bald Mountain" by Moussorgsky (BOL #81), will be enjoyed by students in the fifth and sixth grades.

## Longer Tales in Music

Among the longer works is Prokofiev's *Peter and the Wolf,* which has narration incorporated with the music. Musical themes and pictures of the instruments are shown in TiM III–62 to 64. The important thing to notice here is that both the music and the narration tell the story: Peter is a happy boy, and so the stringed instruments play a happy melody to represent him in the musical story; when the duck and the bird have an argument one hears the argument in the music between the oboe and the flute, which take the parts of these characters. In Chapter Three this and the following composition were cited as appropriate for interpretation through expressive movement.

*The Nutcracker Suite* by Tchaikovsky (BOL #58) may first be heard in relation to the story. With younger children at the first hearing, the music can be played as a background for the story told in *The Music Box Book*[2] by Skolsky. The "Miniature Overture" can describe the children's party, and the "March" can suggest the midnight magic when the toy soldiers parade around the Christmas tree and the great battle ensues between the mice and Prince

Nutcracker's army of toys. The remaining sections are a part of the entertainment provided Marie during her dream-visit to the land of the "Sugar-Plum Fairy." Musical themes and synopses of the story are available (TiM III–34 to 42, ExM II–80 to 81, DMT III–165 to 167).

The teacher must practice in advance, reading the story aloud, making vocabulary adjustments necessary for his own effective narration, and timing the recording to see how long he should wait during each break in the story. The objective is to direct the children's attention to the music as much as possible so that it may suggest the mood and events. The total program will take about 45 minutes. With younger children it is advisable to present it in two lessons. A stop after "Arabian Dance" makes a good break; at the second session the children can assist in a review of the first part of the story in preparation for hearing the remainder. After the pupils have heard the music integrated with the story, they should be able, at later hearings, to listen to sections of the music alone and remember the story that goes with it. Any complete orchestral recording of Tchaikovsky's *Nutcracker Suite* may be used. It is preferable that children *first* learn to know the music in the form in which Tchaikovsky wrote it rather than in a modern "pops" version, entertaining though it may be.

Other descriptive compositions based on stories and legends are these:

Coates, *Cinderella* (BOL #57)
Grieg, *Peer Gynt Suite* No. 1, (BOL #59) (see also DMT IV–122)
Dukas, *Sorcerer's Apprentice* (BOL #59)
Ravel, *Mother Goose Suite* (BOL #57, A in M IV–2 and V–1)

## Character and Animal Sketches

Musical literature abounds in sketches that are impressions of characters or animals and their activities. Among the musical pictures that delight children are "Golliwog's Cakewalk" from the *Children's Corner Suite* by Debussy (BOL #63); "Fairies and Giants" from *The Wand of Youth Suite* by Elgar (A in M III–1); and "The Little White Donkey" (A in M II–1) from *Histories No. 2* by Ibert.

Classroom topics, special days, pictures, and songs may suggest musical sketches that pupils would enjoy hearing: "Clown" from MacDowell's *Marionettes* and Donaldson's circus suite, *Under the Big Top* (BOL #51). Selected "portraits" from Saint-Saëns' *Carnival of the Animals* (BOL #51) are useful to the primary teacher: "The Royal March of the Lion," "Hens and Cocks," "The Elephant," and "The Swan," which was suggested also as music for quiet resting. Some compositions by contemporary composers will be meaningful to children: Copland's "Scherzo Humoristique: The Cat and the Mouse," Bartók's "Diary of a Fly" (A in M I–2), and "Bear Dance" from *Hungarian Sketches* (A in M III–2), and Thomson's "The Alligator and the 'Coon" from *Acadian Songs and Dances* (A in M III–2). These sketches can be used in the classroom in many ways and at different times if the teacher has a flexible program.

When one goes to an art gallery and sees a picture, he looks at it from various angles. He makes himself receptive to the feeling the artist was trying to convey and perhaps agrees that the painter did successfully give the subject life and feeling on the canvas. A similar thing takes place when one hears a musical sketch at a concert; he listens, and if he is in a receptive frame of mind the characterization in the music has meaning for him. This type of an experience can come to children if a receptive frame of mind can be established.

Sometimes a teacher may give the pupils a descriptive background before playing a particular number. The atmosphere created is much like that of storytelling. Baldwin's books, *Music for Young Listeners*,[3] which were designed for intermediate grade readers, are also an excellent source of ideas for the primary teacher. *The Green Book* contains notes about the composer Edward MacDowell and his love for the tales of Uncle Remus. Br'er Rabbit, Br'er Fox, and the Tar Baby are related characters. Musical themes are given to help the children hear MacDowell's characterization in "Of Br'er Rabbit." Having separate musical themes played on the piano helps pupils identify musical ideas within the fabric of the total composition. This technique is used more often with older children, who also benefit from seeing the musical themes written out on a chart or on a projected transparency.

Some parts of the music heard for storytelling or as musical portraits may later be interpreted in color and design with finger paint, colored chalk on wet paper, or watercolors. Individual pupils may hear a piece of music and then draw pictures of their impressions of it. Sometimes the teacher may use art expression to motivate the class for listening to music. When this is done, the art supplies should be prepared ahead of time and each child should have them ready for use when the music is played.

Before they begin to paint, the group may wish to discuss briefly what they hear, and the title of the music may be used as a guide for the picture content. "Little White Donkey" by Ibert (A in M II–1) is a sketch in which the music suggests the spirit of the donkey and his unpredictable inclination to trot along or shy, balk, and sit back on his haunches. The music should be played several times so that the children may reflect its spirit as much as possible in their pictures.

Another whimsical musical portrait is "The Little Train of Caipira" by Villa-Lobos. It was written as the "Toccata" in *Bachianas Brasileiras No. 2* (A in M III–1). Listening to the music one can see and feel this little back-country train as it starts out from the station, runs merrily across the countryside, stops to take on produce, and finally arrives at its destination. In the resultant art expression, the spirit and whimsical characterization of the train are more important than the form which it takes in the picture.

More experienced listeners should give progressively more consideration to the means by which the composer creates specific effects. Toward this end the teacher might ask: "What events do you hear in the journey of the little train?" "Do you find a melody that might characterize the train itself?" "Can you sing part of it?" "How does the music show that it is a little train rather than a big one?" In reply to all of these questions pupils should consider the composer's means of creating the effect heard—the instruments used for specific effects and the use of rhythm to assist in portraying the feeling.

**277**

## Music Conveying Ideas and Mood

Composers do not limit themselves to picture painting. Some of the most delightful musical sketches are those in which the composer tries to convey an idea or a mood to the listener. Debussy wrote an impression of "Snow Is Dancing" in his *Children's Corner Suite* (A in M III–1). Robert Schumann's *Scenes from Childhood* includes "Strange Lands and People," "Curious Story," "Catch Me If You Can!" and "The Pleading Child." Children will enjoy these quiet sketches if the teacher can present them in the right setting. Baldwin's notes in *The Green Book*[3] are helpful.

Mendelssohn composed many short reflective pieces. "Spring Song," more than suggesting a picture, tells how the composer felt on a lovely spring day. Compositions of this type may be used as background for resting or they may engage the attention of the pupils for a short time. Some of the children may have a word or two to say about the feeling the music arouses in them. A good vocabulary of descriptive adjectives is very helpful when children begin discussing what they hear in music. Descriptive words on the chalkboard help children in their discussions and at the same time build vocabulary. Description is useful, but the teacher should remember that music can convey feelings and impressions that go beyond words. If words could speak as well, there would be no need for music.

In the study of music children should be guided in discovering how the various elements of music are combined to create a certain mood. Even in the primary grades children can observe that the speed (tempo) at which a piece is taken, the mode (major or minor) in which the melody is set, and the choice of instruments and the techniques used in playing them help create a certain mood.

Some composers who use landscape titles are really mood painters. Grieg's "Morning" from *Peer Gynt Suite No. 1* (BOL #59) reflects his strong feeling for the forested mountains and the fjords of his native Norway. *The Grand Canyon Suite* by Grofé (BOL #61) follows his day at the Grand Canyon from "Morning" to "Sunset." Some sections, such as "On the Trail" and "Cloudburst," are very impressionistic of scenes and events; other sections are more reflective of feelings. Intermediate grade children find these descriptive compositions easy to understand.

There are many sources for information on program music. The BOWMAR ORCHESTRAL LIBRARY (BOL) and the RCA Victor Series, ADVENTURES IN MUSIC (A in M), are designed especially for teachers. The albums in each of these series are listed in Appendix B–II. Much material is included in Baldwin's books, *Music for Young Listeners*, for which the musical compositions are recorded in the MUSICAL SOUND BOOKS.[4] Notes from concert programs and record jackets are good sources. The teacher who is continually expanding his own musical horizons can add books on music appreciation to his personal library. Bernstein's *An Introduction to Music*,[5] Stringham's *Listening to Music Creatively*,[6] and Copland's *What to Listen for in Music*[7] are good choices. There is interesting material in several paperbound books now available. As the teacher's musical experience is broadened, he will enjoy sharing some of his reading and listening with his class.

# COLOR, DESIGN, AND FORM IN MUSIC

Children should learn that a musical composition is an expression of musical ideas within a design. They should also have experience in directing their attention to musical line, design, and color without the necessity of projecting specific meaning into it.

## Experiences with Art and Music

The association of color and design in visual arts with these characteristics in music is meaningful to children and gives them a new and challenging reason for listening to music.

Just as in the visual arts we have colors that are "cool," "warm," "restful," or "active," so in music the composer has a whole palette of tone color with which to work. The various orchestral instruments have distinctive tone colors and, although these in themselves do not produce a mood or a scene, they are contributing factors. Rhythm and the flow of melody in music easily find their parallels in the rhythm and dynamics of line and design in art.

Simple contrasts help pupils discover how music's tone color, rhythm, and melodic movement can be interpreted in terms of color and design. As an introduction to this idea two short, contrasting musical compositions may be used. There should be no contrasting sections *within* the two numbers. "Träumerei" by Schumann and "March" from *The Love for Three Oranges* by Prokofiev (BOL #54) are good contrasts.

The teacher should tell the class the plan of action and then play both numbers consecutively so that the contrast is quite evident. The titles should not be given, for children are more free in their interpretations when they work from the impressions they receive directly from the music. After the initial hearing, each composition should be played several times as the children make their color design for it.

Pupils who have had considerable art work and much experience interpreting music through bodily movement might be asked to make, without preliminary discussion, designs on two papers, one to represent each musical composition. Some children may need guidance, which could be given by asking them to interpret the music first through bodily movement. Discussion may follow: "How would the graceful movements be shown on paper?" Color qualities can be brought in—cool colors, warm colors, and feelings associated with each.

Many times adults as well as children, in their initial experience relating design to music, immediately respond to the rhythm by making the crayon, brush, or fingers move in time to the music. This is a natural reaction because people are accustomed to keeping time to the music, but it does not lead to the most expressive design. The essential process is to hear the music, notice the characteristics of the melody and rhythm, and recreate the design as line and color on the paper. The procedure cannot be explained directly to young children; they must discover it through experience and by evaluating the work of others as expressions of the music heard.

When the two designs are finished, the children can hold them up in pairs to see the difference in design and color. "Can everyone tell which design represents each piece of music? What tells us?" The comparison of *color* in the two designs should be an important item. "Träumerei" is restful and graceful in rhythm and melody. Repose may suggest pastel colors and light application of the medium. When crayons are used, the flat side of a broken piece produces a broad, restful line. In contrast, "March" is very active, and has dissonant tonal combinations. Red and orange may be considered active colors; intense application of blues and greens gives more feeling of activity than do light strokes of the same colors. Combinations of certain colors promote a greater feeling of activity.

The arrangement of *lines* may provide the contrast between pictures. "Träumerei" has a smooth, flowing melody line; the phrases rise in two levels and then fall back in smooth spiraling movements. Curved lines may express this type of melodic movement. On the other hand, "March" is erratic and angular; visual design related to it may have sharp corners bumping into other lines.

How the *space* in a design is used may suggest the relationship of the elements in the music. If the music sounds "busy," the busyness might be conveyed by small intricate shapes, as in "Flight of the Bumble-Bee" by Rimsky-Korsakov (BOL #52). A piece of music that is not broken up by an interplay of parts may be interpreted on paper with no clear-cut divisions of the space.

Often teachers are satisfied with one successful "experiment" with color and design in music. This is unfortunate for it is not until the third or fourth experience that the children feel at ease making designs to music; it is only then that they begin to interpret sensitively what they hear.

The following are suggested as contrasting numbers which may be used. Pastel and smooth-flowing rhythms:

| | |
|---|---|
| "Minuet," Boccherini | "On Wings of Song," Mendelssohn |
| "Barcarolle," Offenbach (A in M III–1) | "To a Wild Rose," MacDowell |

Lively color contrast and angular design:

| | |
|---|---|
| "Chinese Dance" from *The Nutcracker Suite*, Tchaikovsky (BOL #58) | "Polka" from *The Golden Age*, Shostakovich |
| "Dagger Dance" from *Natoma*, Herbert (A in M III–1) | "Fire" from *Gayne Ballet Suite No. 2*, Khachaturian |

For further discussion of design as used in music and art, see Chapters Eleven and Twelve of *Preparation for Art* by June King McFee.[8]

## Discovering Principles of Design and Form

The basic principles of form employed in musical composition can be observed in connection with short instrumental works as well as with song literature. Contrast that is evident in *two-part* (binary) form can be seen in the stanza and refrain of a song. *Three-part* (ternary) form employs the principles of contrast and balance. Such forms are basic to musical composition in general. Many of the short sketches mentioned in the previous section are based on the simple three-part form. "March of the Dwarfs" by Grieg (BOL #52) and "Andalucia" from *Spanish Suite* by Lecuona (A in M IV–1) are other examples. Children of the intermediate grades can understand even more of the composer's art of design in music.

When the principle of repetition after contrast is extended (ABACADA etc.), a rondo is the result. Haydn's "Gypsy Rondo" (BOL #64) has five broad sections and a coda in the design of ABACA Coda. Each main section has two or three long phrases with interrelated themes, but the principal theme in the A section is always clearly identifiable. The three main themes are as follows:

A Section

B Section

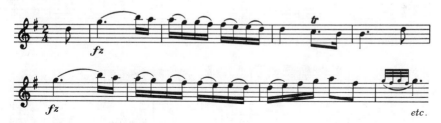

C Section

"Grand Walkaround" from *Cakewalk Ballet Suite* by Gottschalk (A in M V–1) is in modified rondo form: Introduction, ABABACA Coda. Well-known rondos by Mozart are "Romanze" from *Eine kleine Nachtmusik* (A in M IV–1) and "Alla Turca" from *Sonata in A Major.*

Another musical form in which children can easily hear thematic changes in sections is the Minuet and Trio commonly found as the third movement of

**281**

classical symphonies by composers such as Mozart and Haydn. The form is found in other compositions as well; "Menuetto" from *Divertimento No. 17 in D* (A in M V–2) by Mozart is an excellent example.

Variation on a single musical idea is an old technique in musical composition; composers of the baroque era used it extensively. Of the many types of variation, the ornamental treatment of a melody is an easy one for children to understand. Johann Sebastian Bach often used a hymn tune, known as a chorale, around which he composed an elaborate composition. "Jesu, Joy of Man's Desiring" (ExM VI–74) is a chorale that the children may sing, both before and after they hear the florid accompaniment Bach gave it (A in M V–1).

In the classic era, Mozart arranged many sets of variations on well-known musical themes. One such theme, which boys and girls know as "Twinkle, Twinkle Little Star," he arranged into a set of twelve variations. This work (Köchel No. 265, in C major) may be found in collections of his piano works and on records (Angel 35069). The original title was *Twelve Variations on "Ah vous dirais-je, Maman."* When children know a theme as well as they do this one, they have no problem hearing and understanding the techniques in variation the composer used. Of the twelve variations, the fifth, eighth, ninth, and tenth are the most simple and show clearly four different treatments of the theme. The first eight measures of the theme in the simple statement as Mozart presented it are shown here:

Variation V is a change in rhythm:

Variation VIII is set in a minor mode; it employs passing tones filling in the melodic line, and has imitation in the lower line. The series of suspensions (tying the last beat in one measure to the first beat in the next, where the harmony changes, so that a dissonance occurs) beginning in measure two create rhythmic syncopation that heightens the tension of the melodic line:

Variation IX is again in major, similar to Variation VIII in the use of suspension and imitation, but without the embellishment of passing tones:

Variation X employs a rhythmic embellishment and an important addition of chromatic passing tones that give the melody line new strength. It is preferable that the pupils hear and analyze the variations by ear first. Later the teacher may put the notation on the chalkboard.

Dohnányi used the same theme in "Variations on a Nursery Tune" for orchestra and piano, Opus 25. If the art of variation is interesting to sixth grade pupils, they may hear a portion of this work. Pupils can compare this more recent composer's treatment of the theme with that of Mozart. Excerpts of the Dohnányi musical variations and some discussion of them are given in Baldwin II.[1] Recordings are available (Cap. SP-8373).

Another set of variations that may be used after the theme has been made familiar is the fourth movement of Schubert's *Quintet in A Major* ("The Trout") for piano and strings. The first three variations and the last maintain the original theme with clarity. "The Trout" song can be found in several of the basic music series: the theme and teaching suggestions for the theme and variations movement are given in *Teachers Guide to Music in the Elementary School*,[9] pages 114 to 116. The guide also contains themes and teaching suggestions for the American dance tune "Pop! Goes the Weasel," set in the form of a theme with variations by Cailliet (A in M IV–1), and "The American Salute" by Morton Gould (A in M V–1), an arrangement of the old song "When Johnny Comes Marching Home."

Haydn wrote the second movement of his *Surprise Symphony* (BOL #62)

**283**

as a theme with four variations. This is a well-known work; the theme, which is thirty-two measures long, is often used in elementary classes because it has the loud "surprise" chords. However, the variations are considerably more involved than those in the compositions suggested above.

Composers use their thematic material in varied ways in other types of composition. They employ rhythmic changes, the use of different instruments, fragments and different combinations of the original melodies as well as extensions and embellishments of these melodies.

A group of children, captured by the idea of analysis, discovered the design in Brahms' "Hungarian Dance No. 5" (BOL #55). They observed characteristic uses of instruments, repetition, contrast, embellishment, and extension in the handling of the themes. Brahms used four themes, two in each section of a broad sectional pattern: ABA (minor, major, minor).

Having discovered the broad outline of the form, the children noticed that Theme 1 is composed of one musical idea that is embellished and extended in its repetition. The teacher helped the pupils understand the composer's varied treatment of a musical theme by suggesting the analogy of making two *different* dresses from one basic pattern. Lace and bows might be "embellishment," sashes and ruffles might be "extension," and a change of color might be the use of different instruments, etc. The second theme in Section A has three phrases based on one musical motive, played in sequence, retarded, and supplied with a fast ending.

Section B is interesting in that the rapidly moving phrases of Theme 3 are followed by the curious accordion-like effects of Theme 4. Since the composition is based on folk dance themes, such effects, suggesting the traditional use of violin and accordion by the Hungarian folk dance musicians, are quite understandable. This concert piece vividly portrays the spirit of these people and is an artist's interpretation of the folk music that inspired it.

## Larger Musical Forms

A larger musical form with which older children should become acquainted is the suite. They will readily understand that a suite is a group of related items, whether it be a suite of furniture, rooms, or musical compositions. There are three prominent types of suite in music. The oldest is the *classic dance suite,* a group of contrasting dances. In their earlier listening, pupils have heard some of these singly, especially the gavotte, gigue, and minuet. When such suites are heard as a unit, the contrast among the dances adds interest. Suggested for study in intermediate grades are these:

The Little Nothings, Mozart (The Green Book³)
Suite No. 3 in D Major, Bach (The Blue Book³)

Suite for Strings, Corelli (BOL #63, Music to Remember¹⁰)

Some of the suites for solo instruments are also appropriate if the teacher is well acquainted with the music and can select three or four shorter contrasting movements. The use of bodily movement is an important aid in realizing the distinct rhythmic differences in these dances.

The *ballet suite* is a later form in which the music of a ballet has been rearranged for concert performance. If *The Nutcracker Suite* has not been studied in its entirety earlier, fourth grade pupils will find it very rewarding listening, for it is a story as well as a suite of contrasting dances. Themes from *Petroushka* by Stravinsky are shown in Bir V–152 to 155. Single compositions from ballet music that may be used at this level are "Waltz" from *The Sleeping Beauty* by Tchaikovsky (A in M IV–1), "Swanhilde's Waltz" (A in M II–2) from *Coppélia* by Delibes, "Sabre Dance" and "Dance of the Rose Maidens" (A in M I–2) from *Gayne Ballet Suite* by Khachaturian and many others suggested in the various basic series music books.

*Orchestral suites* of a programmatic nature also are introduced in the intermediate grades. Descriptive notes are available in the record albums, in the basic series music books as well as in other sources. These notes should be used to give the class an understanding of the composer's intention. Suites often studied are these:

*Mother Goose Suite,* Ravel (*The Green Book*[3], BOL #57)

*Children's Corner Suite,* Debussy (*The Crimson Book*,[3] A in M III–1)

*Peer Gynt Suite,* Grieg (Baldwin II,[1] BOL #59)

*Grand Canyon Suite,* Grofé (Baldwin II,[1] BOL #61)

*Carnival of the Animals,* Saint-Saëns (*The Green Book*,[3] BOL #51, TiM III–84)

*Pictures at an Exhibition,* Moussorgsky-Ravel (Baldwin II[1])

Other suites of special interest may be included. Classes that study American music may like to hear Aaron Copland's suite, *Billy the Kid* (A in M VI–1), in which the composer uses frontier melodies. *Suite Symphonique* by Ibert is delightful in its descriptive qualities. The six short movements express musically six aspects of Parisian life.

The *tone poem* is a larger descriptive work of a narrative or a contemplative type that has the unity of a single composition. Intermediate grade pupils enjoy tone poems that are sufficiently vivid and not too long. Descriptive notes and musical themes help the children hear the sequence of events and are of assistance in studying the way the composer has used his musical materials. The previous listening experience of the children will determine how much verbal description and explanation must be given in order that they may find the music understandable. Active listening demands that minds be engaged by the music. The following numbers are listed in a general order of difficulty. Sources for information about each are also given.

"Danse Macabre," Saint-Saëns (Baldwin II,[1] BOL #59)

"Invitation to the Dance," Weber (*Music to Remember*[10])

"Sorcerer's Apprentice," Dukas (Baldwin II[1]; BOL #59)

"Night on Bald Mountain," Moussorgsky (Baldwin II[1]; BOL #82)

"The Moldau," Smetana (Baldwin II[1]; BOL #60)

"On the Steppes of Central Asia," Borodin (A in M VI–I)

Such longer compositions usually make up a unit of study in themselves. Two or three lessons should be devoted to each suite or tone poem so that the music can be heard several times; the composer's more obvious techniques in the use of rhythm, melody, harmony, form, and instruments should be studied. In any of this experience with descriptive music the teacher may encourage boys and girls to express the musical pictures and designs in art work or in creative writing. Occasionally the entire class may undertake such a project, but more often the individual should be encouraged to pursue these activities in his free time. If a record player with headsets is available the pupils may play the music whenever they want fresh inspiration for their creative work.

An introduction to opera is possible in the intermediate grades. The songs and recorded music from *Hänsel and Gretel* by Humperdinck can be combined with a study of the story. A synopsis of the play with the important songs can be found in ExM III–124 to 129. Excerpts from recordings should be used but it is not advisable to present the complete recorded version unless the children have had a chance to see the opera on the stage. When the story of the opera and its chief musical themes are known to the class, a study of the Prelude to the opera may be undertaken (BOL #58, A in M V–2).

The BIRCHARD OPERA SERIES[11] is an excellent collection of simple dramatizations of opera stories with arrangements of the most famous musical selections. Many of the operas studied in the intermediate and upper grades are included in the series. OPERA STORIES FOR YOUNG PEOPLE[12] is a series of stories of operas that can be coordinated with school performances.

*Amahl and the Night Visitors* is a short opera by the contemporary composer Menotti. Both a book[13] giving the story and recordings are available and the opera itself usually is presented on television during the Christmas season. Songs, musical themes, and a brief libretto for Mozart's fanciful opera, *The Magic Flute,* are shown in Bir IV–50 to 59.

The music of *Carmen* by Bizet is captivating and often is combined with the story in a listening unit for sixth grade. Portions of arias may be used, but at this age children tend to prefer orchestral versions unless the teacher is able to develop in them an appreciation for the operatic voice. The opera singer spends years developing his voice to its greatest capacity. Since he is a dramatic actor as well, and sings from a stage in a large auditorium, he must be able to express and project to his audience all shades of feeling in his singing. On the other hand, the folk singer performs to a small audience; his is a more intimate type of singing, much closer to that natural to young people.

Children who have an opportunity to hear and see an operatic singer on stage will more readily understand his dramatic production; they will have an appreciation for operatic singing as an expressive art that has a place in the world of music. If such direct experience is not possible, the teacher will need to develop an appreciation for the voice in other ways and he must be selective in his choice of recordings.

Other opera overtures and excerpts often used are these:

*William Tell* Overture by Rossini (*The Blue Book,*[3] A in M III–I)
"Overture" and "Dance of the Comedians" from *The Bartered Bride* by Smetana (Baldwin II,[1] A in M VI–2)
"Ride of the Valkyries" and "Magic Fire Music" from *Die Walküre* by Wagner (*The Blue Book,*[3] BOL #62)

"Prelude" to Act III of *Lohengrin* by Wagner (A in M VI–I)

Musical events in the community and particular interests of the class or the teacher may provide the incentive for other studies in opera at the intermediate level.

### Contemporary Music as a Resource for Creativity

Musical composition of the twentieth century has moved away from traditions of the classic and romantic periods into new forms. Composers use widely varied sources for musical sound (other than the traditional orchestral instruments) and they use different scales as bases for their music. Rhythm is characterized by changing meters, polyrhythmic writing, and unusual use of syncopation and accent. Interesting harmonies are derived from the use of seconds and fourths rather than chords built on thirds.

Children are very receptive to contemporary music and some studies in simple musical composition by children have been successfully related to this music. *Experiments in Musical Creativity* sponsored by the Contemporary Music Project[14] outlines approaches taken in three different studies wherein children explored original sound sources and combined interesting sounds and rhythms into simple musical forms. The original approaches to musical composition taken by contemporary composers suggest many easy ways for children to begin creating music. The creative activity as well as the development of understanding and acquaintance with contemporary music were important factors in these projects.

The *Manhattanville Music Curriculum Program*[15] is a four-year study designed to help children discover concepts of music through their own creative exploration. Extensive use is made of available musical literature in various styles as a source of information on certain problems in composition. Several cycles, levels of learning, and levels of action have been defined and are applicable to various age levels.

Teachers will find that continuing work with contemporary music can lead children to explore their own creative music-making potential more readily than music of other more traditional styles. Contemporary music has had little previous attention in the music curriculum of the elementary school but the two publications cited above suggest ways in which it can have direct application in the lives of children. Many compositions by composers of our times have been included in the record series designed for elementary schools.

## COMPOSERS, INSTRUMENTS, AND CONCERTS

Other important purposes of the listening program are (1) an acquaintance with the sounds and the characteristic uses of the various orchestral instruments, (2) some opportunity to hear them played in actual concerts, and (3) some familiarity with the music of famous composers in the several periods of musical style and music of other cultures. Resources for the teacher will enable him to select information and music for the compilation of a unit that he can present in a convincing manner. Each basic music series for the intermediate grades contains special information on two or three selected composers. Pictures of the composers are often given, and songs and recorded compositions are usually suggested. Materials for the study of music in other cultures are listed in Chapter Nine, pages 303–304.

### Resources on Composers

All of the basic series music books contain biographical notes and musical themes and songs by various famous composers. The teacher can use his graded music book as his primary resource and find supplementary material in some of the following: *Music for Young Listeners* by Baldwin contains biographical material and selected compositions with teaching notes. Opal Wheeler and associates have written children's books on the composers and their music. Among these are *Joseph Haydn, The Merry Little Peasant,*[16] *Franz Schubert and His Merry Friends,* and *Stephen Foster and His Little Dog Tray.*

The recordings in the VOX Music Master Series combine the story and the music of the most famous composers under titles such as "Johann Sebastian Bach, His Story and His Music." *Young Keyboard*[17] is a magazine published monthly for study by intermediate grade boys and girls. The publication includes recordings and other teaching aids and often features the music of one composer as the topic for the month.

Any study of a composer should be combined with a study of his music. Biographical facts are not as important as are human incidents that make the composer a real person to the children. Many people have the erroneous impression that the music of the "masters" is predominantly serious and pompous. Actually, Bach, Mozart, Haydn, and other composers wrote much of their music for the people and events in everyday life. That which is suitable for children is delightful in its gaiety and humor, delicacy, or wholehearted aggressive spirit. To listeners who are receptive, the best revealer of the composer is the music he has written.

### Knowing Orchestral Instruments

Children have a great interest in musical instruments. An acquaintance with those in the orchestra is a natural extension of the exploration of sound in simple instruments. Such an acquaintance should not be technical, and in the primary grades it need include only the more common instruments.

Very helpful material for elementary studies in the science of sound and instruments of the orchestra is given in many of the basic series music books. With these and the following resources it is possible to give children a general knowledge of all the instruments of the orchestra by the end of the sixth grade.

An important way for primary children to learn to know the instruments is through hearing them in the background music for resting and quiet activities. Violin, cello, and piano solos can be used in these ways and, as they are played, the teacher may show the picture of the instrument. In this way the sound of the instrument becomes familiar. Flute, trumpet, and clarinet might occasionally be heard in solo. Until the boys and girls have become well acquainted with the individual sounds of the instruments, it is not possible for them to identify one particular instrument in a group.

Many very effective recorded stories about the instruments are available for children. The first or second grade teacher will find "Tubby the Tuba" (Columbia, Cl-671), "Pee Wee the Piccolo," and "Rusty in Orchestraville" an excellent means of making these instruments and their sounds known to the class. In the third grade more information may be given the children; "The Wonderful Violin" (YPR-311) and "The King's Trumpet" (CRG-5040) are good choices. These recordings are quite informative and yet they keep the study on the story level appropriate in these grades.

In addition to hearing the recorded stories and voices of the instruments, it is important that children have an opportunity to see the instruments first hand. Older children in the school may bring violins, clarinets, or trumpets into the classroom and show the primary children the essentials of the instruments. Demonstrations help not only the children who see the instrument close at hand but also the older child who explains his instrument. *Young Audiences, Inc.*[18] is a national organization designed to provide live concerts of fine music for children in schools. The performers are professional musicians who also have the ability to communicate verbally with children. Approved groups (numbering from three to five members) are available in many parts of the country. Studies of musical instruments, elements of music (rhythm, melody, harmony, etc.), and forms of music are often topics around which the compositions heard on the programs are organized.

Children in the intermediate grades should make a systematic study of the four "families" of instruments in a symphony orchestra. An outline such as this may be followed:

| The Strings | The Woodwinds | The Brass Winds | Percussion |
|---|---|---|---|
| violin | piccolo | trumpet | snare drum |
| viola | flute | French horn | bass drum |
| cello | clarinet | trombone | tympani |
| bass viol | oboe | tuba | cymbals and gong |
| | English horn | | assorted small |
| | bassoon | | rhythm instruments |
| | | | xylophone, orchestra |
| | | | bells, celeste |

**EXPERIENCES IN LISTENING TO MUSIC**

These books, records, and pictures are valuable in organizing such a study:

Books:

*Tune Up*[19] contains excellent photographs and brief descriptions.

*Picture Book of Musical Instruments*[20] contains pen sketches of the instruments with historical résumé on each.

*The Wonderful World of Music*[21] tells of the development of instruments in an interesting, beautifully illustrated historical study for young readers.

MUSICAL BOOKS FOR YOUNG PEOPLE[22] is a series of small books about instruments and other musical subjects for intermediate and upper grade pupils.

Recordings:

*Pan the Piper* by Kleinsinger-Wing (Columbia, Cl-671). This is a fanciful narration of the beginnings of the instruments with musical examples.
*The Wonderful Violin* (YPR-311)
*The King's Trumpet* (CRG-5040)
*Licorice Stick, Story of the Clarinet* (YPR-420)
*Piano to the Harpsichord* (YPR-411)
Those above contain musical examples and verbal explanations of essential points.

*Instruments of the Orchestra* (Columbia, Victor, Decca). Single instruments play excerpts from symphonic literature.
*Meet the Instruments*[23] (Bowmar Records with filmstrips)

Motion pictures:

*Music for Young People* Series[24]—"Introducing the Woodwinds," "Percussion, the Pulse of Music," and others
*We Make Music*[25]—"The Bassoon," "The Violin," and others

Pictures of the instruments:

*Meet the Instruments*[23] (Bowmar Records, full-color charts)

As a result of their studies of the instruments, children can be led to feel that learning to play an instrument is a privilege and a challenge. They should understand that, of the many kinds of instruments, some are easier to learn to play than others. The ideal, most expressive "instrument" is the human voice. The musical prestige of all the other instruments is determined by how expressively and sensitively they may be played. The stringed instruments are given great prestige, for when well played they come nearest to the qualities heard in the human voice. The player "makes" the tone with his bow and his fingers and therefore has control over the finest shading of nuances in the melody. The more "automatic" an instrument is, i.e., the less *directly* its tone production is controlled by the player, the less expressive and artistic the instrument can be. For this reason accordions and electric organs have less stature as musical instruments.

## Classroom Concerts

Pupils should have opportunities to hear excellent musicians in person. When young children are close to the performer, they can see and hear him and his instrument to good advantage. Small concerts, in the classrooms or in a slightly larger room where three or four classes may gather together, are best at the primary level. *Young Audiences, Inc.,* or competent local artists may provide concerts similar to the following:

A principal and music supervisor, determined that their primary children should have music under the most favorable circumstances, planned an annual series of three concerts. These took place in the kindergarten room because it happened to be the largest space with good acoustics. In order that the intimacy of the concert might be maintained, only three or four classes at one time attended a performance.

To enable the children to center their attention on one or two instruments, only soloists and small ensembles performed. Each concert was thirty minutes long, for it was considered important that the experience be a short, successful one, which would leave the children eager to hear the next. The artists were chosen for musicianship and personality appeal. They were members of the community who were actively engaged in music, although not professional in the field, and occasional outstanding high school or college musicians. In every case the performers were delighted with their young audiences, who listened with much receptivity and enthusiasm.

All of the numbers performed were short and there was ample contrast in the program. One concert featured a pianist and a cellist. The pianist performed Mozart's lively rondo "Alla Turca" from the *Sonata in A Major* and followed this with the tranquil "Träumerei" of Schumann. In these two compositions the children were easily able to discern the contrasting rhythmic and tonal possibilities of the piano. Ibert's "Little White Donkey" is colorful "picture" music and, as the third piano solo, was especially appealing to the children.

To see the artist performing was a very important part of these concerts. The cellist discussed the important parts, of her instrument and gave the children samples of the different techniques that would be used. Her numbers, too, were varied—"The Swan" by Saint-Saëns and then an arrangement of "Londonderry Air" in which the melody was played in both low and high registers. Contrast and a more lively technique came in the "Waltz" from *Music for Children*, Opus 65, by Prokofiev.

Before the concert careful orientation in each classroom had prepared the children to meet their artist friends and to understand something about the instruments they were to play. Because many of the children had never before been to a concert, the teachers gave careful attention to a discussion of "concert manners." The children learned that one never talks during the playing of a number; they were interested in how and why they should applaud to show their appreciation. It was found that the children liked the formality surrounding the concert. After returning to their classrooms, the children discussed the music, and the teachers answered questions.

Children's concerts such as this do not just "happen." They are the result of purposeful planning. In every community there is talent that may be used for the benefit of children in the primary school. We need more teachers who will promote the experience of live music for children as a recognized part of a vital music education program.

## Concerts for Older Children

Pupils in the intermediate grades should have opportunities to attend concerts either of a type designed especially for young listeners or of the community concert variety. While concerts at the primary level should be intimate and informal, boys and girls from the fourth grade upward should be given some large-concert experience.

A small city school district, located 200 miles from a metropolitan center, arranged a series of three annual concerts for all of the pupils above the second grade. The plan began modestly with support from a PTA concert committee and the music supervisor. Over a period of four years the children heard a fine boys' choir, a professional string-woodwind orchestra, and several soloists. They attended musical plays and performances by an established ballet company. Many of the children had no other contact with talented musicians, dancers, and actors.

The project was unusual in that *all* pupils and their teachers attended. Programs were designed on the artistic rather than on the showmanship level; much care was taken in the selection of music, and all concerts were less than one hour in length. In addition, the music supervisor planned and, in some cases, presented material for preconcert orientation. Teachers, administrators, music personnel, and parents were enthusiastic; all agreed that quality in the performances and careful planning were the essential features in the series.

Many cities have their own symphony orchestras and opera companies, and often special school concerts are arranged. Key personnel in making concert attendance a successful activity are the school principal and the classroom teacher. If these people do not actively support the project, more often than not many of the children are not enthusiastic. If the concert is an all-school activity, the indifferent teacher may bring a group of children who do not know how to be members of a concert audience.

A teacher's enthusiasm for a community concert series may interest pupils so much that the parents buy tickets for them. Pictures of performing artists, newspaper clippings, and programs brought by children can be arranged on the tack board in the music center. Thus, important local musical events are brought to the attention of the class. Student reports after attendance at a concert may promote interest in future concerts.

Important musical events on radio and television should be given the same type of attention. Leonard Bernstein's televised Young People's Concerts have gained widespread interest and should be brought to the attention of the children. Some fifth and sixth grade pupils will be ready to read Bernstein's book by the same title.[26] The teacher who reads the announcements of such programs can discuss and evaluate them ahead of time with the class. A student music committee may be set up to keep the class informed on programs of particular interest during each week. Occasionally a teacher can plan preliminary classroom music activities that will increase the value of the out-of-school listening experience.

Many homes have fine collections of recorded music. As musical forms, such as marches, dances, opera, are considered in the classroom, pupils may explore their families' collections for similar or contrasting compositions. Likewise, a student who is studying an instrument with a private teacher may know a comparable march or dance which he could play for his fellow students. Much can be gained from class analysis of the musical elements in the composition played by the student. Individuals would be led to see that their "pieces" are not just collections of notes, but that those notes make rhythm patterns and melodies; the melodies are supported by harmonies and are set in certain patterns of phrases and sections, just as are the compositions heard on recordings or in concerts.

Generally speaking, one of the daily music lessons in each week should be centered on listening. It will be necessary to plan well in advance to arrange concerts by performers for children in the various grades, but two or three such events each year are highly recommended. The teacher who loves music but has had little opportunity to develop his own performance skills may find that his enthusiasm and resources in this area will enable him to foster children's musical growth and appreciation through activities related to music listening in a very significant way.

## ACTIVITIES FOR COLLEGE CLASSES

A. Questions for Review

✓ 1. What kinds of general experience with music provide the foundation for listening as a distinct musical activity in itself?

2. Discuss the various kinds of program music, and outline the teaching techniques that are recommended to make this valid material for musical study.

✓ 3. Describe the several techniques a teacher can use to focus attention on tone color, design, and form in music.

4. What resources are available for the study of individual composers and music of a particular style?

✓5. Make an outline of the four groups of instruments in the orchestra. Describe the several techniques players of each group can use to vary tone production and thus change musical expression as needed for different compositions.

6. Describe the kinds of concert opportunities that should be made available to children at different grade levels.

B. Written Assignments

1. List and briefly describe four compositions you believe would be suitable background music for resting or quiet activities in the grade level of your choice.

2. Select two short character sketches in music and find poems, stories, or pictures that seem especially appropriate for use with each.

✓3. Select a short musical composition that is descriptive. Listen to it a number of times and write an imaginative story based on what you hear in the music.

4. Select one short descriptive composition that you find appealing. State first the general descriptive implications which you hear in the music. Study carefully the rhythm, melody, harmony, form, dynamics, and instrumentation of the composition, and insofar as possible state how the use of each contributes toward the descriptive effect.

5. Select one suite, one tone poem, or some music from opera that will be appropriate for the intermediate grade of your choice. Become familiar with the music and prepare teaching notes that would enable you to present the music effectively if you were asked to do so next week.

6. In the basic music book from which you may teach, find material designed to assist in a study of one composer. Outline the information given; list other suitable material available to you.

C. Classroom Projects

1. Play for the college class your choice of a descriptive composition under written assignment No. 3. Through skillful questioning and rehearing

**EXPERIENCES IN LISTENING TO MUSIC**

**293**

of the composition as necessary, draw from the students satisfactory answers to these questions:

a. What descriptive effects are heard in the music?

b. How does the composer use the musical elements to achieve these effects?

Use bodily movement or other forms of creative response that may be suitable in this study.

2. Select two short contrasting compositions that may be expressed in color and design. After hearing the music, create your impression of each, using finger paint, watercolor, or crayon.

---

## CHAPTER NOTES

1. Lillian Baldwin, *A Listener's Anthology of Music,* Volumes I and II (Morristown, N.J.: Silver Burdett Company, 1948).

2. Syd Skolsky, *The Music Box Book* (New York: E. P. Dutton and Co., Inc., 1946).

3. Lillian Baldwin, *Music for Young Listeners: The Green Book, The Crimson Book, The Blue Book* (Morristown, N.J.: Silver Burdett Company, 1951).

4. MUSICAL SOUND BOOKS (recordings) (Scarsdale, New York: Sound Book Press Society, Inc.).

5. Martin Bernstein, *An Introduction to Music* (Englewood Cliffs, N.J.: Prentice-Hall, Inc., 1951).

6. Edwin John Stringham, *Listening to Music Creatively,* Second Edition (Englewood Cliffs, N.J.: Prentice-Hall, Inc., 1959).

7. Aaron Copland, *What to Listen for in Music,* Revised Edition (New York: McGraw-Hill Book Co., Inc., 1957).

8. June King McFee, *Preparation for Art* (Belmont, Calif.: Wadsworth Publishing Company, Inc., 1961).

9. Marion Jordalen *et al., Teachers Guide to Music in the Elementary School* (Sacramento: California State Department of Education, 1963).

10. Lillian Baldwin, *Music to Remember* (New York: Silver Burdett Company, 1951).

11. Harriet Nordholm, BIRCHARD OPERA SERIES, *Hansel and Gretel, The Magic Flute, Carmen,* and others (Evanston, Ill.: Summy-Birchard Company, 1951).

12. OPERA STORIES FOR YOUNG PEOPLE, *The Magic Flute* by Stephen Spender, *The Bartered Bride* by Johanna Johnston, and others (New York: G. P. Putnam's Sons, 1966).

13. Gian-Carlo Menotti, *Amahl and the Night Visitors,* narrative adaption by Frances Frost (New York: Whittlesey House, McGraw-Hill Book Co., Inc.).

14. Contemporary Music Project, *Experiments in Musical Creativity* (CMP₈) (Washington, D.C.: Music Educators National Conference, 1966).

15. Ronald Thomas, *Manhattanville Music Curriculum Program,* supported by the Arts and Humanities Division of the United States Office of Education, Contract No. 6-1999. Scheduled for completion in 1969.

16. Opal Wheeler and Sybil Deucher, *Joseph Haydn, The Merry Little Peasant* and other biographies (New York: E. P. Dutton and Co., Inc., 1936).

17. *Young Keyboard,* from KEYBOARD PUBLICATIONS, 1346 Chapel St., New Haven, Conn. 06511.
18. *Young Audiences, Inc.* 115 East 92nd Street, New York, N.Y. 10028, or 21 Columbus Avenue, San Francisco, Calif. 94111.
19. Harriet Huntington, *Tune Up* (New York: Doubleday & Company, Inc., 1942).
20. Marion Lacey, *Picture Book of Musical Instruments* (New York: Lothrop, Lee and Shepard Co., Inc., 1951).
21. Benjamin Britten and Imogen Holst, *The Wonderful World of Music* (New York: Garden City Books, 1958).
22. Robert W. Surplus, Editor, MUSICAL BOOKS FOR YOUNG PEOPLE (Minneapolis: Lerner Publication Co., 1963).
23. *Meet the Instruments* and other Bowmar productions, available from Bowmar Educational Records.
24. MUSIC FOR YOUNG PEOPLE SERIES (films), distributed by NET Film Service.
25. *We Make Music* film series, Film Associates, Los Angeles, California.
26. Leonard Bernstein, *Leonard Bernstein's Young People's Concerts for Reading and Listening* (New York: Simon and Schuster, 1962).

## Other References

Hartshorn, William C., "The Role of Listening," Chapter XI from *Basic Concepts in Music Education,* edited by Nelson B. Henry. The Fifty-seventh Yearbook of the National Society for the Study of Education (Chicago: University of Chicago Press, 1958).

McMillan, Eileen, *Guiding Children's Growth through Music* (Boston: Ginn and Company, 1959). Chapter 5, "Listening Adventures for Children and Teachers," and Appendix B, "Supplementary Materials for Listening."

Myers, Louise Kifer, *Teaching Children Music in the Elementary School,* Third Edition (Englewood Cliffs, N.J.: Prentice-Hall, Inc., 1961). Chapter 6, "Listening."

Sheehy, Emma Dickson, *Children Discover Music and Dance* (New York: Holt, Rinehart & Winston, Inc., 1959). Chapter 9, "Phonograph Records, Radio, Television," and Chapter 10, "Concerts."

Snyder, Alice M., *Creating Music with Children* (New York: Mills Music, Inc., 1957). Chapter 6, "Listening to Music."

Timmerman, Maurine, *Let's Teach Music* (Evanston, Ill.: Summy-Birchard Publishing Co., 1959). Chapter 5, "Let's Listen," with listings of recordings, films, and books, pp. 142–148.

Taylor, Katherine Scott, "An Autochthonous Approach to Music Appreciation," *Music Educators Journal,* February–March 1949.

Zimmerman, George H., "Art and Music Mix Well," *Music Educators Journal,* June–July 1956.

See Appendix B–III for record companies and other firms supplying catalogs of current recordings.

**EXPERIENCES IN LISTENING TO MUSIC**

# 9

# Implementation of the
# Music Education Program

We have traveled a long road in delineating the kind of education in music that should be provided for elementary school children. The challenges of the first chapter return in these final pages: a music program cannot be extracted from a textbook, but must be created by the inner promptings of teachers charged with the responsibility for it. Teachers are resourceful individuals, capable of meeting the challenges and assuming the responsibilities given them. Although the complete program outlined here cannot be awarded, like a diploma for faithful study, it can be recreated by each teacher according to the needs of his pupils, his own talents, and the reservoir of skill available in others.

At this time it should be possible for the prospective teacher to come to some conclusions about the value of music for his pupils and the broad objectives for the music program he would like to carry out. During the study of this final chapter the student should formulate statements on these two points to provide a foundation for the final shaping up of his early plans for teaching music.

Teachers need to plan ahead to make studies in music yield the greatest benefits for their pupils. Such planning should be so broad that it can include general arrangements encompassing the full year as well as detailed analysis of daily teaching procedures. Some sample plans for music lessons as well as other organizational suggestions are included in this chapter to help the new teacher get his work successfully under way.

A realistic approach to teaching music requires that the individual evaluate his own skills in music and teaching to determine in what areas he may need assistance. Music specialists often need the help of experienced classroom teachers in refining their teaching skills and in learning how to cope with individual differences and other problems. On the other hand, the general teacher usually needs the help of a person more thoroughly trained in music. It is quite probable that studies and experiences in the class for which this book was designed will reveal to the student some of his strengths as well as his limitations in music and will enable him to plan a music program in which he will be able to compensate for handicaps he recognizes.

Every teacher needs some approaches to the evaluation of skills and concepts that are developed by his pupils. This is necessary not only because most school administrators and parents expect a report of growth on the part of the children, but because evaluative procedures help the teacher know in what areas his work is most effective and where he needs to challenge himself to seek more adequate techniques and materials. In this chapter suggestions are given to help the teacher in evaluation of both the musical achievement of the children and the music program itself.

Frequent references have been made to relationships between music, the social studies, and other areas of the curriculum. We know that experience with the music of other peoples can bring an individual into dynamic association with the spirit and feelings of those peoples. This is the reason teachers find music such an important part of social studies. Daniel Prescott says: "If we teach art subjects in such a way as to induce feelings, surely our children will understand the stream of history, will sense the on-goingness of civilization as they never can through mere verbal symbols describing those times. . . . Indeed, the aesthetic arts should render the same service of interpretation and crystallization to the point of feeling within our own culture."[1] In this chapter some consideration will be given to the interrelationship of music with the areas of science and the social studies.

## MUSIC AND OTHER AREAS OF THE CURRICULUM

In the school curriculum music can be meaningfully related to science, physical education and dance, visual and language arts, as well as the social studies. The classroom teacher is a key person in the implementation of such an interrelationship of subjects, but the music teacher must know what materials to recommend for the particular class concerned.

Considerable attention was given the relationship of music to physical education and dance in Chapter Three of this book. Several suggestions were made in Chapter Eight for the use of art activities and story telling in connection with listening to music. Children's poems, nursery rhymes, and jumprope chants were suggested as material for creative melody writing in Chapters Five and Seven.

All of these activities can be expanded if the teacher and children have the interest and resources to do so. Since the basic music series and other curriculum publications offer additional approaches and materials that can be used, no further attention will be given these areas in this book. However, science and the social studies have important relationships to music that will be considered briefly in this chapter.

### Music and Science

A study of the scientific principles of tone production and resonance can be part of elementary projects in science at different grade levels. The children can investigate the different ways tone is produced; they should consider the source of tone (the vibrating object) and the amplifier of the tone (the resonating body). After children learn these principles and relate them to the several kinds of musical instruments, they can begin to understand why an instrument produces a tone with particular characteristics of loudness and timbre.

Music has been associated with mathematics and astronomy since the days of Aristotle, but not because of its rhythmic aspect—that two quarter notes equal a half note, and so on. Although the notes are named as fractions, quarter, half, eighth, etc., rhythm is too flexible to be arithmetic; we work with duple, triple, and quadruple beats and divisions of the beat, but from the point of view of flowing muscular response rather than as arithmetical concepts. Rather, music is associated with mathematics through the relationships of tones to each other. The octave is the basis for the division of tones into musical scales. When children of the intermediate grades learn intervals (the octave, fifth, fourth, third, etc.), they begin to work with the harmonic series in music, the real basis of a relationship between music and mathematics. Some simple science exhibits show how a vibrating string is divided into partials. At this level, however, we usually do not try to show how the ancients arrived at the harmonic series.

The student should decide to what extent a study of sound can be incorporated in the science projects recommended for the grade he expects to teach. What relationships can be drawn between the scientific studies and musical tone? Some basic music series have units on the science of sound (see TiM IV–162, Bir VI–142). Several library books for children will be useful in the classroom: Kettelkamp, *The Magic of Sound,*[2] *Singing Strings* and others; Berger and Clark, *Science and Music: From Tom-Tom to Hi-Fi;*[3] Pine and Levine, *Sounds All Around.*[4]

## Social Studies: Resources and Organization

At every grade level there are opportunities to use music within the framework of the social studies to help children expand their cultural horizons and increase their understanding of themselves and other people. The social studies program in the primary grades is determined by the interest areas of children of these ages. In the kindergarten and first grade areas of concern center on the home, the family, and the school. It is important that the teacher draw on the musical heritage of races and nationalities other than just his own in his attempt to bridge the gap between home and school in our multi-cultural society.

Second and third grade social studies center in part around the community and its resources: the city with its services and activities; the farm and the various people, animals, and work associated with it. Many third grade classes study American Indians. Authentic Indian songs tend to be modal in quality (that is, their melodies are based on scales having arrangements of intervals different from the familiar major or minor), and so a different musical sound is experienced when they are used in the classroom. It is much better that children have an opportunity to sing authentic songs of these peoples, when simple, appropriate examples can be found, than that they merely sing songs which are composed *about* the Indians. The latter may lack musical quality, and they do not project the imagery and feeling of the ethnic groups. Almost every third grade book in the various series contains groups of songs which may be used in a general study of Indians.

It is not necessary to limit the singing of ethnic songs to those times when a social studies unit is in progress. Peoples all over the world have similar activities and their songs can be shared by children here merely because they are appealing. "Lullaby" (TiM III–29) and "We-Um" are both lullabies with the characteristic quality of Indian melodies.

## WE-UM

*Quietly*                                                   *Cherokee Indian Lullaby*

We-um, we - um, we-um, we - um, We-um, we - um, we - um, we-

um, we - um, We - um, we - um, we - um, we - um.

"We-Um," from *Grammar School Songs* by Charles Farnsworth, Charles Scribner's Sons.

Songs and dance music of other peoples will enrich both the singing and the listening repertoire. Recent basic music books include original texts for some folk songs. When the words can be presented correctly these should be used in the original language for interest and for the cultural enrichment that the language brings to the music program.

In the social studies of the intermediate grades, students are concerned with the people of their own community and with those as far distant as Asia and Europe. Historically such studies may go back beyond the Mayflower to the earliest cultures from which contemporary society sprang. When music is related to such topics, teachers and pupils should study it from both the historical and the geographical points of view. When the pupils see how various aspects of music have developed and are related down through history, they will more surely understand the close relationship of peoples. In most areas city, county, and state curriculum planners have determined the topics to be used in each grade. Once the study is limited to a region or a particular period in history the teacher may determine the values that musical resources might have within the total study. In some units the use of related music may be very worthwhile, and for a time the greater part of the musical activities of the class may be centered around the study.

The classified indexes of the basic music books list appropriate songs for a variety of subjects. Some of the recent books and listings from recording firms suggest specific recordings. No one source contains all the most desirable music, and therefore it is advisable that a teacher provide himself with specialized supplementary books. The music consultant should be of service in gathering or recommending such materials.

The study of music related to the social studies topic need not be limited to folk music. Composers identified with a country make important contributions to the culture; pupils should hear representative instrumental and vocal music of these composers. As far as possible the pupils should understand the ways in which the composer's nationality, his time in history, and the events of his life influenced his music. Such an understanding depends on the background and maturity of the pupils and the extent to which they can understand such basic social considerations.

*Regional Studies.* Fourth grade social studies often are related to the country, section, or state in which the children live, or to type-regions of the world such as the hot, dry countries or the cold countries.

Material relative to local areas is compiled in state or county courses of study and generally is not available in national publications. Often there is a shortage of good usable musical material that is authentic rather than "arranged" and adapted. Local libraries, historical societies, and museums may be sources of information having some bearing on music of the locality. Available material will center around (1) a tribe of native Indians, if any, (2) immigrants (early or more recent) who brought their folk music with them, and (3) particular historical events of local interest commemorated in song.

Some of the type-regions studied offer good opportunities for a consideration of related music. *Literature and Music as Resources for Social Studies*[5] contains information and musical examples from most of the countries of the world. The other references listed at the end of this chapter suggest sources of information and music. Some curriculum bulletins list all of the music available on each topic, but many such listings are unselective and often include a large number of songs of little authenticity and musical value. Such lists are useful as resources, but the teacher must judge each song or musical reference by its genuine worth in the topic concerned.

In addition to musical criteria, a teacher might evaluate songs in terms of the following:

1. Is this a song actually sung by the people being studied, or has it merely been composed about them?
2. If it is sung by the people themselves, of what significance·is it? Does it reveal them as a particular type of people, of a particular occupation? Is it genuinely expressive of human feeling and experience? Is it a good representative of its type?
3. If the song has been composed *about* the life and circumstances of a particular people, is it a good song in itself? Does its musical and poetic quality make a genuine contribution to the study of the topic at hand?

Recorded music typical of the countries or regions studied is of importance. Some valuable recordings of this nature are cited in Chapter Four, page 107. Fourth grade children are not interested in extensive listening of this sort, but short examples designed to give them the flavor of native music can be valuable and impressive. Someone must select the music to be heard by the class as a whole; in some cases a small committee of children can assist in determining what will be of greatest interest to the entire group.

When ethnic music is heard it should be studied with respect to its rhythmic elements, melody, harmony or lack of it, and instrumentation. Older pupils are able to deal with these questions much more extensively than younger pupils.

*Music in the United States.* In many schools fifth grade children study the American scene from the landing of the Pilgrims to the present day and from the East Coast to the West. The music applicable to this study is varied and should constitute a large part of the musical experiences during the year.

Several fifth grade music books center around music of the United States, and therefore it is not difficult to obtain appropriate literature.

There are several points to be noted with regard to the use of American folk music. Genuine folk music is an expression of a people; it expresses their concerns, moods, love, and relationship to their work, family, and the world. The music has lasting value as a part of American life insofar as it is truly expressive of these things.

Such music has an important place in education and should be studied in such a way that these expressive factors are brought to the attention of the students. Certainly not all cowboy or riverboat songs are important. Outstanding examples of each type of song should be chosen. Some songs may be included because they have an important historical significance. Others may be included on the basis of musical considerations. The teacher should endeavor to use not only those that are the best representatives of each type but also those that give the pupils varied musical experiences in melody, mood, rhythm, and accompaniment. Because the United States is a collection of immigrants from many countries, folk music of other lands has its place in a study of American music; well-known melodies of other countries complement the study of folk music in this country.

A number of important resource books are available for use by the teacher and the pupils. *Literature and Music as Resources for Social Studies*[5] devotes fourteen chapters to literature and music in various times and areas of this country. For teaching purposes the study should be divided into smaller units such as "Music of the Colonial Period" and "Music of the Western Frontier." Kinscella's *History Sings*[6] gives representative incidents and stories designed to bring readers into a close relationship with the people throughout the history of America.

In Part Two, Materials, of *Teaching Music*,[7] Raymond Elliott has listed available school music materials pertinent to studies of different nationalities, and to the development of America as it paralleled cultural developments in Europe. Here the teacher will find listings of folk music as well as music of important composers representing the various style periods in music. Elliott relates the exploration of the Western Hemisphere to the European Renaissance and the American Colonial period to the European baroque era (1600–1750) in a simple, helpful way.

Patriotic and service songs may be learned by fifth grade children. Often the occasion and purpose of a song's origin is as important as the song itself, for only in that setting are some songs fully appreciated. The children should hear recordings of fine soloists and choirs singing these numbers. The historical background of this music may be found in *History Sings*, in Lyons' *Stories of Our American Patriotic Songs*,[8] and in other sources. These books are understandable to children and may serve as references for student reports.

*Widening Horizons of People and Music.* Music books at the sixth grade level reflect a broader source of music. Some sixth grades study Canada, Mexico, or countries in Central and South America. Other classes look closely at the Philippines, Japan, Africa, or Australia. Perhaps only one or two such topics will be considered, but the related music is plentiful and interesting. Topical indexes in the basic music series suggest authentic songs; Tooze and Krone[5] give a few pertinent facts about the important characteristics of the music of any country; the Library of Congress and commercial companies such as Folkways, Columbia, and Victor have made recordings of the native music in many lands; and a number of films are available as enrichment for such a study.

Short films showing a series of musical activities by native performers are most useful. Good recent publications include those by the University of Washington Press,[9] the West German Institut für den Wissenschaftlichen Film,[10] and Film Associates.[11]

Sixth grade children can be very capable musicians; when previous training has been good, they can sing and play melodies and rhythms with little guidance from their teacher or the music specialist. These pupils may do research reading on selected topics and report on their findings. The extent of such activities, of course, depends on the resources available at a suitable reading level. Because of the relative maturity and the greater musical skills of these pupils, a study of music can have considerable significance in a social studies unit.

*Developing a Resource Unit.* When building a resource unit in which music is related to social studies and other classroom activities, the teacher should consider the following questions:

1. In the selection of the literature, which music is authentic and appropriate? Are there possibilities for student reports on the backgrounds of this music? If so, what readings are available? Where?
2. Are recordings of authentic native music available? Which would be most appropriate for use with this class? Are there reliable sources of information about this music?
3. How are the character, customs, and life of the people reflected in the music? If they were a primitive tribe, were they generally peaceful or warlike, agrarian or hunters? Are religious and social customs revealed? If they were immigrants and settlers, what were their life purposes and outlook, social and religious customs, occupations, and everyday concerns with living?
4. What are the important distinctive melodic, rhythmic, and harmonic characteristics of this music? How much of this information should be brought to the attention of the pupils?
5. What use of musical instruments was made in the period or region? Did instruments vary with the music and the occasion? Are similar instruments available, or can they be made by the students?
6. What possibilities exist for the use of bodily movement and for the playing of instruments in authentic or nearly authentic ways with this music?

Teachers and pupils often arrange a culminating program around the activities of the study. Pupils sing, perform typical dances, and dramatize events related to the topic. Parents or other classes may be invited to the classroom. If these programs are closely related to the everyday studies and activities, they are quite justifiable educational enterprises, a sharing of what has been learned in a particular study rather than a "program" in the formal sense. Drama, art, poetry, music, and dance may be combined to provide a colorful and interesting presentation.

Social studies topics vary in their musical importance. Occasionally a topic may have rich musical potential, and for a time little other music is studied. Other topics may offer little of genuine musical value or interest, and the attention may be focused in other directions. Certainly the teacher should explore the possibilities for musical enrichment with whatever units are used.

## EVALUATION AND PLANNING

Evaluation and planning are reciprocal parts of the teacher's work. The growth and achievements of children shine forth in their musical activities and responses of various kinds, and the teacher must continually evaluate this progress in order to make valid plans for the next stage of the music studies.

### Evaluation for Various Purposes

In the elementary school, evaluation of progress made in music is not so much a grading of the pupil as it is a grading of the program itself and the implementation of that program through effective teaching. Because of its varied, natural appeal children respond with enthusiasm to music when it is brought to them in vital, meaningful ways.

Evaluation is a constant function of the teacher for he bases the content and procedures of his lessons on his awareness of the level of skills and understanding held by the children. In his first musical contact with the group he should be able to discern the general level of response in the activities undertaken. He then plans succeeding lessons for reinforcement or for the introduction of new activities and material leading to a gradual development of new skills and concepts.

Singing, playing instruments, responding to music through bodily movement, verbalization, and art media, as well as creative work in music are ways in which children reveal growing knowledge and skills in this subject. The teacher must realize that response in any single activity cannot be taken as a measure of a child's total musical achievement. There may be a child who, due to lack of early vocal experiences, does not yet sing well, but other activities and responses may suggest that he is growing in musical concepts and other skills in quite a satisfactory manner.

The teacher who has worked with the activities chapters in this book in conjunction with the content of Chapter Two will have an adequate basis for his evaluation whether he gives a test designed to measure the child's achievement in each area or whether he is familiar enough with each individual in the class to note progress as demonstrated in classroom musical activities. In an evaluation based on the outline of concepts and skills related to rhythm what general skill in response to rhythm might a teacher see at a given grade level? When might a child discriminate and respond at will to the metric beat, the melody rhythm, and the accent? At what point might a child clap a rhythm (1) in response to a pattern he has heard? (2) in response to a pattern he sees in notation? A study of the recommended teaching techniques and activities in this book should suggest other ways in which a child might reveal his development in rhythm.

In each area of musical concepts, growth should be evaluated in terms of the child's responses to music. His ability to respond and to make music, and his understanding of the sound and function of music, are of far greater importance than facts that may have been memorized.

Most classes are supplied with books for music study and these provide an outline of work as well as a basis for evaluation. Some of the series contain short tests or games that can aid in the evaluative procedure (see especially the pages for "Recapitulation of Learning" in each book of the Making Music Your Own Series, and pages for "Evaluation of Children's Musical Growth" in the Exploring Music Series).

There are two kinds of commercial music tests available for use with children in the fourth grade or above. Musical achievement tests are designed to measure learning in its several forms. Musical aptitude tests purport to measure natural ability for music, such skills as hearing differences in pitch and rhythm. Needless to say, it is not possible to tell exactly where natural ability ends and musical learning begins. To some extent the one enhances the other. The *Elementary Music Achievement Tests*[12] are a recently developed test battery that may have some value in a school district where there is a well-planned program of music education with continuity from year to year.

If the school administration requires formal grades in music, the teacher should consider the musical potential and evaluate in terms of individual achievement. One point of caution should be observed: it is a mistake to give the highest possible grade in music to a pupil who has a limited musical potential. The highest grade should be reserved for those who both have and use their natural ability; next highest grades may go to those who have enthusiasm and who participate in spite of lower natural endowment. When a child who is not capable of doing first quality work is given the highest grade, he and his family are given the erroneous impression that he has superior musical potential. A brief written report or a conversation with a parent is better than a number or letter grade in music for children in primary classes.

In the last analysis, evaluation of the program must be made in terms of what music is doing and can continue to do for the individual. If music is to continue to have beneficial effects throughout life, there must be continuous growth in response to it, and growth in the individual's ability to participate in it in progressively more mature ways. If the prospective teacher, as a result of the studies and musical experiences suggested in this text, can objectively evaluate his own music teaching potential he will be better prepared to assume the responsibilities assigned to him here.

## PLANNING FOR MUSICAL GROWTH

As a teacher looks ahead to his music program for the year he first needs to view the span of time and the relationship of music to the children's lives.

There are seasons and holidays to be commemorated with music, and social and personal interests to be highlighted. Then he must consider the variety of musical activities in which children can engage and which vary in their appeal and suitability for different children. A class of 25 or 30 children is a dynamic group that must gradually learn to work together and to accommodate their individual differences. Although it will not be possible for the teacher to make firm plans for his music program until he actually is acquainted with his class, there are ways in which he can organize his material and procedures ahead of time.

Planning should be done with regard to several spans of time. First the year can be blocked out into five or six periods framed by established school grading periods or holidays and vacations.

The opening period should be planned to accomplish several objectives:

1. Reestablish the variety of school musical activities, review familiar musical material, and rebuild skills that have not been used during the summer.
2. Acquaint the teacher with the various musical abilities of the children.
3. Serve as an evaluation-planning period during which the teacher can decide the pace of activities and materials to be used during the year.

The closing month of the school year can be used to summarize and review the musical learnings that have taken place during the year and to reinforce them whenever possible by new musical settings.

Study in each of the four remaining periods can be centered on musical concepts that the teacher thinks might be developed out of the materials and activities to be used. Each of these learning periods should be planned to include all of the different musical activities (singing; playing instruments; responding to music through movement, art media, and verbalization; and creating music) at a level appropriate to the class.

The next level of planning should be on a weekly basis. In this plan the teacher blocks out objectives for the week in terms of skills to be brought into focus through the use of certain musical activities. To assure variety and interest at least one new musical composition (song or recording) should be introduced each week. These pieces can vary in length and difficulty depending on the musical skill of the class. Other musical materials will include (1) well-known favorite songs of the children and (2) songs or other kinds of music that are being reviewed.

In his planning each week the teacher should study the materials to see what musical concepts might be developed and what activities or procedures would best highlight the desired learnings. All instructional materials (special records, books, charts, and instruments) that will be needed should be gathered together when the teacher makes his weekly plan. Continuity within the weekly plan can be achieved in several ways:

1. By using some of the same materials for several days, but varying the activities or focus of the study in terms of the elements of music that are considered.
2. By centering on the same activities or study of musical elements, but giving examples and experiences with different songs or recorded material.

It is recommended that music have a place in the daily schedule of every class. Ten or fifteen minutes may be long enough for a special music period in kindergarten and first grade if music is used frequently at other times during the day. Generally a daily twenty-minute music period should be planned for the primary grades and a twenty-five-minute period for the intermediate grades.

It has been shown in this book that the music activities are interrelated; it is useful for the teacher to plan two or three lessons a week combining singing with the use of rhythm or melody instruments, one lesson a week centered on movement, and one centered on listening. Special concerts, experiences with art media, and creativity should be featured once or twice during each of the six learning periods throughout the year.

The daily lesson plan is drawn from the broader plan for the week and generally should include three levels of musical material: one or two items that are familiar and especially enjoyed by the class, something that is being reviewed and polished, and some new item or new emphasis. Each lesson should focus on some concept or skill that is being developed within a span of two or three lessons. Following are seven sample lesson plans utilizing musical material available in this book.

## LESSON PLAN FOR KINDERGARTEN

*Orientation:* This lesson is from a unit of study undertaken during the month after Easter. The subject emphasis is the out-of-doors, birds and animals.

*Focus:* Singing supported by simple use of hand movements and instruments for enrichment. Preparation for dramatization to begin on the next day.

| OBJECTIVES | MATERIALS AND PROCEDURES |
|---|---|
| 1. To sing a familiar song and to give individual children an opportunity to sing tone calls and play sound effects on the Song Bells; appreciation of expressive use of voices (happy and sad). | 1. "Three Blue Pigeons" (see page 240). Discuss excitement and sadness in a voice: How would we say "One came back!" if we were happy about it? Prepare one child to play a glissando upward and downward as indicated in song. Sing with children as they count on fingers (1–2–3) while one child makes an upward glissando as birds fly away and a downward glissando as birds come back. |
| 2. To introduce a new song and help children chime in on an easy tone call, count up to 10, and notice rhyming words. | 2. Show a picture of a frog. Discuss picture and lead to introduction of song "Over in the Meadow" (see page 178). After singing the first stanza have children sing the tone call "Hop, said the one." |

Point out the rhyming words "sun" and "one" and ask the children to see if they can find two more rhyming words. Sing the second stanza, emphasizing the word "blue" and have the children supply the rhyming word "two."

Sing five stanzas as children count successive numbers on their fingers and chime in on the tone call.

3. To sing a familiar song related to a dramatization to be developed over several lessons.

3. Show picture of a duck. Sing with children "Six Little Ducks" (see page 238).

Have one child use guiro for sound effects on "Quack, quack, quack," as six others pantomime the ducks.

Explain that a recording has been made to accompany a whole story about a duck. Ask the children to listen for actions the duck might make during the story.

Play the first part of the *Dance a Story* record "Little Duck" (MoM K–177); explore the possibilities for dramatizing the first part of the story. Explain that this will be carried further at the next lesson.

4. Explain that the whole story could be shown in movement, and that the children will have a chance to try out more of their ideas in the next lesson.

---

## LESSON PLAN FOR FIRST GRADE

*Orientation:* This lesson is planned for early spring. The children have had considerable experience using bodily movement to express rhythm and to dramatize the mood of songs; they can use rhythm instruments fairly well in response both to the metric beat and to the melody rhythm.

*Focus:* The study of mood and the exploration of elements that contribute to the musical feeling in selected songs.

| OBJECTIVES | MATERIALS AND PROCEDURES |
|---|---|

1. Review a familiar song in a manner that will bring attention to the qualities of movement and of expressive feeling.

1. "Walk on Tippy Toe" (see page 191). Have children sing and listen for the mood of the song; discuss. Sing and have a few children express the music in bodily movement. Ask: "How does the music make us feel the mood?" (by its

steady rhythm and smooth, descending melody) Sing minor tone call: *la-do* ("toe") and notice its gentle upward movement.

2. To relate mood to a contrasting song well known to the children; to notice melodic movement and give voice training with tone call; to contrast the metric beat with the melody rhythm.

2. Sing "Rig-a-Jig-Jig" (see page 110). Discuss the mood and the characteristics that create the mood (fast tempo, galloping rhythm, and strong beat). Sing again, using rhythm sticks on metric beat and chop sticks on melody rhythm to stress the spirited quality. Sing tone call "Heigh-o, heigh-o, heigh-o" and have individuals sing back; point out the leap to a high pitch for this tone call which makes the song seem lively.

3. To introduce a new song and focus attention on listening as a source of information in music; to make the initial study of the song that of its mood and how it is achieved.

3. "The Fog Horn" (see page 311 and use record: ExM I–51, 3A2). Instruct children to listen and to discover the mood in the music and what the song is about.

Play the recording, then discuss: "Did you notice any interesting sounds in the music?" (a fog horn sound, quivering sound, monotonous accompaniment) "What feeling does the music give us?" (mysterious, lonely, eerie) "What helps the music express this feeling?" (the instruments and how they are played) Listen again and discuss further if necessary. (See teacher's notes in music book.)

Practice the tone call "Foggy" and then have children chime in when it occurs (replay recording).

4. Conclusion

4. Review the idea that different music creates different moods; the words of the song may help make the mood but the rhythm and melody also determine the mood, which may be lively and gay, quiet and gentle, or lonesome and mysterious, as these three songs are.

**310**

# THE FOG HORN

Music by W. S. Haynie
Words by Edith N. Chase

*Slowly and mysteriously*

Fog - gy, fog - gy o - ver the wa - ter,

Fog - gy, fog - gy o - ver the bay, And

through the fog the boats go slow - ly

While the fog horn tells them the way.

**IMPLEMENTATION
OF THE MUSIC
EDUCATION
PROGRAM**

# LESSON PLAN FOR SECOND GRADE

*Orientation:* This lesson is planned for use in the late fall of the year. The children will begin using music books in January. Now they are developing concepts of melodic movement by ear and by seeing simplified notation. They have used sol-fa syllables (or scale numbers) on both scalewise and tonic chord patterns.

*Focus:* The study of melody: scalewise versus chordwise, small steps versus large leaps, using sol-fa syllables (or scale numbers) and blank notation.

| OBJECTIVES | MATERIALS AND PROCEDURES |
|---|---|
| 1. To identify a type of tonal movement in the melody of a familiar song; to rehearse and identify the tonic chord pattern. | 1. "Three Dukes" (see page 225). Tap rhythm of song and ask children if they can identify it. "What kind of rhythm is it?" (uneven) "What songs do we know with that kind of rhythm?" If the children do not name the song, chord it on Autoharp and sing melody with "loo." "Now, what song is it?" "How do we know?" (the tune tells us) All sing the song. "Does the melody move by steps or by skips?" (by skips)<br><br>All sing the first line slowly, using hand levels; then teacher sing and show syllables or scale numbers on chart. All sing first phrase with syllables or scale numbers. Show melody in blank notation on a chart. Sing again using coconut shells on steady beat (1–2). |
| 2. To identify another type of tonal movement in a familiar song, and to rehearse scalewise movement. | 2. "Go Tell Aunt Rhodie" (see page 216). Ask children to sing the song and to be prepared to discuss how the melody moves (chiefly scalewise, with a few skips). Sing again as children show hand levels.<br><br>Repeat tone call at the end ("Our old gray goose is dead"). Sing syllables or scale numbers and have children sing that phrase in the same way. Do the same with the first phrase, "Go tell Aunt Rhodie." Show a chart with blank notation for this phrase and compare it with blank notation for "Three Dukes." Notice that one moves by steps and one by skips. |
| 3. To gain information by listening (aural training); to identify different kinds of tonal movement in the melody of a new song. | 3. "Here Dances Biba Butzemann" (see page 313). Give title; ask children to listen to find out who the character is and what he does |

(discussion relative to the "sandman"). Sing again and have children listen to learn the first phrase. Rehearse and have children sing it whenever it occurs. How many times did that phrase occur? (three) Is the song the same all the way through? Listen again to find out how the melody moves (some of it moves by skips and some by steps). Show two phrases of blank notation; ask which shows the first part of the song. Sing again as children sing the A phrase and pat the metric beat.

4. Conclusion

4. Review the main idea: that some melodies move by steps and some move by skips; one song may have one phrase that moves by skips and one that moves by steps.

## HERE DANCES BIBA BUTZEMANN

*Crisply*

*Folk Song from Germany*

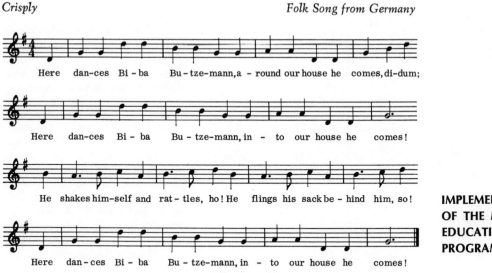

Here dan-ces Bi-ba Bu-tze-mann, a-round our house he comes, di-dum;

Here dan-ces Bi-ba Bu-tze-mann, in-to our house he comes!

He shakes him-self and rat-tles, ho! He flings his sack be-hind him, so!

Here dan-ces Bi-ba Bu-tze-mann, in-to our house he comes!

**IMPLEMENTATION OF THE MUSIC EDUCATION PROGRAM**

# LESSON PLAN FOR THIRD GRADE

*Orientation:* The class has used rhythm instruments a great deal to sound the steady beat, the rhythm of the melody, and the accent. They have learned to read rhythm patterns from charts.

*Focus:* A study of rhythm showing the difference between compound duple and simple duple meter; introducing the $\frac{2}{4}$ meter signature and seeing rhythm patterns on the page.

| OBJECTIVES | MATERIALS AND PROCEDURES |
|---|---|
| 1. To center the attention on meter, showing the relationship of beat, accent, and typical rhythm patterns within a familiar song. | 1. "Three Dukes" (see page 225). Have the class sing with the steady beat |

sounded on rhythm sticks. Help them discover that the rhythm swings in twos:

♩. ♩.
(1    2)

Sing again, with drum sounding on the "ones."

Ask the children to play the rhythm of the melody on chop sticks. What rhythm pattern is heard most?

♪| ♩    ♪ ♩    ♪| ♩
(lay   one  -  lay   two  -  lay   one)

Have a child chant and sound this pattern on coconut shells; show the pattern on a chart as the class chants and claps the rhythm.

There is one part of this song that has another rhythm pattern. Where is it? What is the pattern?

(one  lah  lay,  two)

Show notation on the chart and have children clap and chant the rhythm. Sing entire song again with three-part rhythm accompaniment.

2. To learn a new song using the same rhythm and to identify rhythm patterns in notation.

2. "Dundee, Dundee" (see page 134). Tell the children that this song has the same rhythm as the previous

song so the same accompaniment can be played. Children should listen to find out what the song is about as the teacher sings the song and the drum and sticks sound the accent and metric beat. Discuss. Help children learn the first phrase, then chime in as teacher sings the whole song.

Open books, find and frame the galloping rhythm pattern in several places. Chant and clap

one lah lay, two la lay

in this rhythm, then chant and clap

lay one - lay two - lay one.

Help children sing each two-measure phrase of the stanza. Sing the entire song with rhythm accompaniment.

3. To contrast simple duple meter (found in a well-known song) with compound duple meter. To see $\frac{2}{4}$ meter in notation.

3. "This Old Man" (see page 112). Tell the children that they have studied another kind of rhythm quite a bit. Show patterns on charts and ask children to chant

(one and two, - one and two -)

and tap the rhythm with chop sticks.

Open books, discuss meter signature and patterns seen. Establish metric beat and have children tap rhythm of the melody. Sing the song with a three-part rhythm accompaniment (steady beat, melody rhythm, and accent).

4. Conclusion

4. Review the idea that there are two kinds of rhythm that swings in twos (duple meter). Chant and clap a pattern from each song to contrast the two.

**IMPLEMENTATION OF THE MUSIC EDUCATION PROGRAM**

# LESSON PLAN FOR FOURTH GRADE

*Orientation:*    This is a lesson in late spring for children who have had some introduction to Autoharp playing and accompanying. They understand usage of the sol-fa syllables (or scale numbers), but they do not read fluently.

*Focus:*    Study of musical form.

| OBJECTIVES | MATERIALS AND PROCEDURES |
|---|---|

1. To sing a familiar song for pleasure, to develop expressive singing, and to study phrase structure.

1. "All the Pretty Little Horses" (see page 162). Sing the song expressively with Autoharp accompaniment without opening books. Ask the children to sing the song again, move their arms to show the phrase structure and be ready to tell how many phrases there are and which are alike (four phrases, AABA, with the last part of every phrase the same).

Repeat and have a child draw phrase marks on chalkboard and label (AABA). Ask children to open their books and look at the song. Help them discover that although the third phrase is different all the phrases end in the same way. Have the class sing the song again as one child plays the repeated descending line on Melody Bells.

2. To see like and unlike phrases in a new song, define the form, and learn the song with the aid of sol-fa syllables (or scale numbers) and a recording.

2. "Little Sandman" by Brahms (see page 318 and a recording such as DMT IV, Album L403). Ask children to open their books and study the song to find out what it is about and to see which phrases are alike and which are different. Discuss the subject and how the song should be sung (quietly). Have a child outline the form on the chalkboard:

A
A
B
C

Play recording as children move arms in phrasing arcs to confirm the form of the song. Ask: "Is the mood of the performance as you expected it would be for this song?" Show the notation for the first phrase on a chart; have the children discover that it moves almost entirely step-wise. Locate "do" (or scale step 1) and have them sing the song with sol-fa syllables or scale numbers.

Play the recording and have children sing the first two phrases with the performers and follow the notation in the book for the last two phrases of the song.

3. To notice antecedent–consequent phrases in a familiar song; to practice 2-chord Autoharp accompaniment and conducting in $\frac{2}{4}$ meter.

3. "Hush, Little Baby" (see page 192). Have one child press chord buttons, one strum and give tune-up note, and one conduct the song as the class sings.

Ask children to sing again and to stop at the end of each two-measure phrase. Which phrase ending sounds complete? Which does not? (end of measure 2 sounds incomplete) Ask Autoharp player what chord he is playing in each case. Demonstrate and discuss the incomplete close on phrase ending with the $V_7$ chord. As they sing the song again ask the children to notice how this song alternates between two phrases that have almost the same melody, but produce a different effect because of the harmony used. The effect is that of a question and answer.

4. Conclusion

4. Note that phrases in different songs have different relationships: AABA, AABC, and AA' as examples in the lesson today, and that the length of a phrase depends on its rhythmic, melodic, and harmonic construction, not just the number of measures involved. Each song is somewhat different from every other song.

IMPLEMENTATION
OF THE MUSIC
EDUCATION
PROGRAM

**317**

## LITTLE SANDMAN

*Slowly*                                             *Arranged by Brahms*

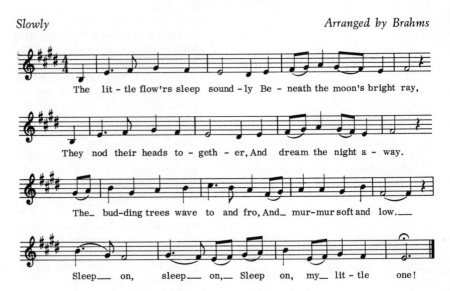

The lit - tle flow'rs sleep sound - ly Be - neath the moon's bright ray,

They nod their heads to - geth - er, And dream the night a - way.

The_ bud-ding trees wave to and fro, And_ mur-mur soft and low._

Sleep_ on, sleep_ on,_ Sleep on, my_ lit - tle one!

---

## LESSON PLAN FOR FIFTH GRADE

*Orientation:*     This lesson is planned for the middle of the year. The children play the Autoharp and have practiced conducting easy songs.

*Focus:*     Singing harmony. The class has had some experience singing rounds and easy endings in two parts.

| OBJECTIVES | MATERIALS AND PROCEDURES |
|---|---|
| 1. To sing and hear two-part harmony in a familiar round; to review the idea of harmony created by tones in parallel thirds, and to develop skill in listening to harmony while singing. | 1. "Bells" (see page 149). Sing the song first in unison, then in two parts with student conductors. Sing some phrases slowly and emphasize listening for the harmony where it moves in parallel thirds. |
| 2. To review a song previously sung in unison, and to add harmony in parallel thirds to selected parts of this song. To develop skill in listening to harmony while singing another part. | 2. "Tum Balalaika" (see page 253). Sing melody in unison with Autoharp accompaniment, one child playing and one conducting.<br><br>Children sing melody softly and listen to harmony created when teacher sings lower part on first two phrases of the refrain.<br><br>Divide class and sing parallel thirds on first two phrases of refrain; follow by singing two phrases of stanza. Repeat until the two parts are secure.<br><br>Ask the children to sing the whole song with the teacher carrying the |

3. To review a familiar song and listen for two part harmony on phrase endings.

4. Conclusion

alto part alone on the third and fourth phrases of stanza and refrain.

3. "All through the Night" (see page 251). Have one child conduct as the class sings the song with the two-part ending. Ask the children to listen to the harmony and describe the movement of the parts. Discuss the wedge movement from thirds to an ending in sixths. Set up resonator bells so two children can play the two-part ending as the class sings the song again.

4. Point out that harmony is produced when two voices sing different but compatible parts at the same time. The simplest harmony is made when two voices move in parallel thirds, but interesting harmony is made when voices move in opposing directions.

## LESSON PLAN FOR SIXTH GRADE

*Orientation:*    The class has had considerable experience listening to music; they can follow a theme and observe its recurrence as they listen.

*Focus:*    Listening for rondo form and hearing the relationship of themes and varied treatment of them.

| OBJECTIVES | MATERIALS AND PROCEDURES |
|---|---|
| 1. To hear an unfamiliar composition and to note its general characteristics. | 1. "Gypsy Rondo" (BOL #64, and see page 281). Ask the children to listen to the entire composition to discover whatever they can about it. Play record, then discuss observations (the general character, rapid pace, etc.) |
| 2. To focus on the principal theme and discover the form of the music. | 2. Show a chart of Theme A; play the theme fairly slowly on the piano and have children sing it on "loo." Repeat two or three times until it is quite familiar.<br><br>Replay composition and ask children to raise their hands whenever they hear the theme. |

IMPLEMENTATION
OF THE MUSIC
EDUCATION
PROGRAM

**319**

Discuss the fact that the theme is played more than once in several sections of the piece.

Ask children to listen to discover in how many sections this theme appears (three sections).

Replay and then discuss what happens in between (A?A?A). Are the parts between the A sections the same or different? When the children discover that there are two different parts, define the form as ABACA and identify it as a "rondo," a composition in which one main section returns after each of two or more contrasting sections.

3. To notice the combination of themes making up each section.

3. The children should notice that each of the large sections is made up of two or three different themes. This observation can be explored at a later lesson.

4. Conclusion

4. Recall other sectional forms that have been studied by the class: AB, ABA, minuet, and trio. Rondo form is a more extended kind of sectional form that was used extensively by classic composers such as Haydn, Mozart, and Beethoven.

---

The inexperienced teacher may find that these plans contain too much material for him to cover in one twenty-minute lesson. If this is the case he should omit some of the detail. In general, a lesson that uses less than three songs probably will lack the desired variety. Much will depend upon the musical ability of the children; those with less skill will need more help from the teacher in learning new material.

These plans are offered as samples centering on different musical activities and the development of various skills and concepts. The teacher will have to develop his own style of planning and presenting a lesson; much will depend upon his musical abilities, personality, and rapport with children. Films such as "Discovering Form in Music," "Discovering Melody and Harmony," "What Is Rhythm?," and others produced by Film Associates[11] that show elementary school music lessons centered on the development of concepts may be helpful to prospective teachers.

## Children with Special Needs

Many school districts provide instruction for children who for various reasons are not able to attend a regular class. There are special small classes for physically disabled children, for those who are mentally retarded, and for those who are emotionally or socially maladjusted.

Music is fully as important in the lives of these children as it is in the lives of well-adjusted, physically sound youngsters. As a matter of fact music should have more of a place in the curriculum for these children for it has recognized therapeutic value. The rhythm of music can facilitate coordinated movement and speech; certain kinds of music can quiet anxieties, release feelings into therapeutic expression, and give pleasure to those whose lives are restricted in various ways.

In spite of their limitations exceptional children have most of the basic interests and needs of other children. Much of the program in music recommended for children in general can be adapted to children with special needs. The teacher will need to consider the disabilities of the children, choose simple but attractive music, and plan those activities in which the children can be successful. *Music for Exceptional Children*[13] is a publication that has helped teachers adapt the music program to the needs of children in special classes. *The Journal of Music Therapy*,[14] *The Volta Review*,[15] and other professional publications in different fields occasionally include articles describing the use and value of music for children of various disabilities.

In this area, as in others, the teacher's personal initiative in searching out ways of bringing music into the lives of these children will be a most important factor, for the work is even more individualized than that in a regular classroom. Frequent visits by the music specialist may bring added resources and evaluation of the appropriateness of the program for the children for whom it is planned.

## Talent from Varied Sources

The discussion in this book has been based on the premise that the chief motivator of music in the education of children must be the classroom teacher. When the teacher knows what kind of music program may be developed, he can go a long way toward achieving it in spite of his own musical limitations; he may find specific music skills in others: the music consultant if he has one, the special music teacher, the classroom teacher next door, a parent, the school secretary, or an upper grade student. Of all these people, only the music consultant is likely to know as well as the teacher what kind of music program is needed in a particular classroom. Even this expert will need conferences and visits to the classroom to work with the teacher and the class before he is able to give the best advice and assistance. Administrators should provide enough music specialists to assist the general teacher with this important task.

When a special music teacher is employed to work in several classrooms on a regular schedule, he should feel that he is a member of the teaching team for each group of children. Part of his responsibility should be that of initiating musical activities that the pupils and the classroom teacher can carry on in his absence. Under such an arrangement the music program must be tailored to the needs of each class, and the two teachers must discover how their individual teaching talents can be made to complement one another.

The music consultant is an assistant, a resource person, and an advisor to teachers. If a music consultant has a realistic schedule, with no more than seventy-five teachers to assist, he can come to each school once or twice a week and go into the rooms of those teachers who need his aid. With a schedule such as this, the music consultant who knows each teacher's abilities with regard to music is able to (1) give assistance in the planning of the music program for the class, (2) suggest and provide new and varied materials to meet specific needs in that classroom, and (3) use his own musical skills to supplement the experiences that the classroom teacher is able to provide. In the pursuit of these objectives the music consultant's greatest assets are his warmth of personality and his ability to help the teacher and pupils with whom he works to feel able in their own musical activities.

If the music consultant is available but does not visit often enough to do more than assist in the planning, the teacher must find music skills in others.

In one school district the music consultant had two needs in mind when she arranged to have talented fifth and sixth grade pianists aid the primary teachers in music. The teachers knew that they needed more help than the consultant could give personally, and the consultant felt that the older students needed an outlet for their musical talent and training. These students could both sing and play the piano. Although it was necessary to plan the work so that it did not interfere with their regular studies, the whole project was a challenge to the older students and very helpful to the primary teachers.

If a consultant is not available to set up such a program, an individual teacher might seek out an older student whom he knows to be musical and eager to cooperate in such a venture. By planning ahead, the teacher can utilize the student's talent for teaching new songs and for providing accompaniments for familiar songs, rhythmic activities, and dances. In such a cooperative undertaking, it is necessary that the teacher know good music teaching techniques and that he discover how the student's talents may best be utilized to assist in effective teaching.

Many teachers find that another teacher is willing to assist in specific ways. If the two work together in planning, and if the classroom teacher himself carries on as much of the program as he is able, the specific help given can be of great value. Occasionally a parent who has special skill may be invited to come into the classroom on a more or less regular basis. He may assist in special ways, such as providing instrumental accompaniments, singing, or helping to notate original songs. The teacher does not abdicate his responsibility for the program, but plans together with the musician to use this special skill in the most advantageous ways.

In some schools, elementary teachers practice a daily exchange program wherein one teaches music while the other teaches another subject such as physical education. This exchange may provide more skilled music teaching

for both classes, but it tends to isolate the classroom teacher from the musical activities and interests of his pupils. He may develop a disinterest in these activities and do little to include music in significant ways at any other time of day. In all of the situations in which the skill of another person is used, the teacher must maintain an active interest in music for his class. He must assist in planning the program and do as much as he can to increase his own music teaching skills. Under such arrangements a great number of elementary teachers can become capable music teachers within their own classrooms.

## A New Teacher Beginning the Year

School administrators generally are pleased to employ a teacher who is fully prepared to do all of the music teaching in his classroom, and there are a few beginning teachers who are qualified to reply unequivocally that they can do this. Many others may answer in the affirmative, but they should also inquire whether there is a music specialist who can give them advice and assistance in some areas.

When a candidate has significant limitations in this field, it is advisable that he state these when he accepts the position. If his general letters of recommendation are good, this will not disqualify him, but it may have some bearing upon his placement in the district and will enable the administration to provide assistance for him.

When his assignment is assured, the teacher should find out what music books are in use, what access he will have to a good record player, what records are available, and so forth. He will then make adjustments in his music teaching plans in preparation for this specific assignment. As he establishes himself in the classroom he can arrange different centers of activity and interest. Among these, there should be a music center where he will place a few well-chosen items: an easy-to-play instrument or two, a colorful song book, pictures or posters giving promise of musical activities to come.

On his visits to the district or county school libraries the teacher should look for books that will aid the development of musical interest and knowledge. Enrichment reading books, many of which are cited in this text, can be among those that he makes available to his pupils. Supplementary song books can be evaluated and reserved for use at a specific time during the school year.

It is hoped that the teacher will have a record player and some records for use the first day of school. It may be a short day, but certainly there will be a few minutes when music can be used to refresh the spirits of both pupils and teacher. The primary teacher may have a short song-story, such as "The Shoemaker and the Elves,"[16] which he would like to play for the boys and girls. If they begin to join in singing the repetitious parts of the refrain, all well and good; if not, another day will be soon enough to suggest it. At the intermediate level an interesting recording of a good folk singer may serve as an introduction to a social studies unit; a descriptive composition such as an excerpt from Ferde Grofé's *Grand Canyon Suite* may reflect holiday travels.

During the first few days, the new teacher should use music informally, helping the children feel that music is a part of life in that schoolroom. They may experiment with and play the instruments at certain times. The teacher can show an interest in their simple discoveries and listen to the songs they hum or croon at work and play. Older children may be provided with number notations for a song or two that they know. The bells or xylophone will then immediately be a playable instrument for them. Informal groups may enjoy singing with the Autoharp.

Events will occur that will suggest a song the teacher knows and can teach; a song-story may invite the children to sing along. If kindergarten or first grade children become tired, an action song or finger play will wake them up, or a lullaby will relax them. Soon music will have a well-accepted place in the classroom, and the teacher can begin to provide a more balanced program. He may look for a musical assistant to help in specific ways. He will begin to know the musical abilities of his pupils, and, thinking in terms of the first visit of the music consultant, he can jot down his musical problems and needs.

Too often the teacher does not make it easy for the consultant to help him. Either he covers up his problems when the consultant is present, or he fails to give any prior thought to the assistance this person can give. If the consultant is scheduled to arrive on a particular day, the new teacher should make an effort to find out when he could have a conference with him, and what type of service the consultant is in the habit of giving. If he wants a sample lesson in a particular musical activity, he should let the consultant know a day ahead so that he might come prepared.

Whereas a music specialist may be quite successful teaching music with his voice and a pitch pipe as his total equipment, a less talented teacher will need something more. His pupils can benefit from the use of books, records, and instruments. The music consultant may be able to assist the new teacher in getting these or in setting up a systematic plan for their later acquisition. With these material helps, a judicious use of available music talent, and a keen sense of the value of music, classroom teachers can do much to make music a significant part of education in the elementary school.

## ACTIVITIES FOR COLLEGE CLASSES

A. Questions for Review
   1. State briefly the relationship which music has to the following areas of the school curriculum: (a) physical education, (b) art, (c) literature, (d) science, and (e) social studies.
   2. What different purposes are there for evaluation in music? What testing resources are available, and what recommendations are made for grading?
   3. Describe the various levels and types of planning that are recommended for classroom music.
B. Written Assignments
   1. Outline a plan for a month or six weeks of music study at the grade level of your choice. Indicate the musical materials you will use

throughout this time, the more important concepts to be developed, and the activities to be used with each composition. From this general plan write a detailed plan for one lesson following the outline of the plans shown in this chapter.

2. Prepare a unit of work related to social studies at the grade level of your choice. You may draw on previously developed resource units if available, but you should include only material that you have been able to evaluate and that is available in current sources. Include songs as well as recorded material if possible and cite sources for all material. Indicate the more important musical concepts to be developed and the activities to be used with each composition. From this unit write a detailed plan for one music lesson following the general outline of the plans shown in this chapter.

C. Classroom Projects

1. Using the plan developed under written assignment No. 1 or No. 2 above, teach the lesson to the college class, assuming these to be the elementary children for whom the plan was written.

2. With a small group, prepare a thirty-minute culminating program to be presented in the college class at the end of the term. Using drama, art, literature, music, and dance in simple but effective ways, develop a theme related to some aspect of social studies or other topic of interest at the grade level the group selects.

---

## CHAPTER NOTES

1. Daniel A. Prescott, *Emotion and the Educative Process* (Washington, D.C.: American Council on Education, 1938), p. 225. Reprinted by permission.

2. Larry Kettelkamp, *The Magic of Sound* (New York: William Morrow and Company, 1956); *Singing Strings* (1958); *Drums, Rattles, and Bells* (1960); *Flutes, Whistles, and Reeds* (1962).

3. Melvin Berger and Frank Clark, *Science and Music: From Tom-Tom to Hi-Fi* (New York: McGraw-Hill Book Co., Inc., 1961).

4. Tillie S. Pine and Joseph Levine, *Sounds All Around* (New York: McGraw-Hill Book Co., Inc., 1959).

5. Ruth Tooze and Beatrice Krone, *Literature and Music as Resources for Social Studies* (Englewood Cliffs, N.J.: Prentice-Hall, Inc., 1955).

6. Hazel Gertrude Kinscella, *History Sings* (Lincoln, Nebr.: University Publishing Company, 1948).

7. Raymond Elliott, *Teaching Music* (Columbus, Ohio: Charles E. Merrill Books, Inc., 1960), Part 2, "Materials," pp. 195–312.

8. John Henry Lyons, *Stories of Our American Patriotic Songs* (New York: The Vanguard Press, 1942).

9. Washington Films, Ethnic Music and Dance Series, Robert Garfias, editor (Seattle: University of Washington Press).
    "Marimba Music of Mexico," black and white, 7 minutes.
    "Classical Music of India," color, 12 minutes.
    "Music of Vietnam," color, 5 minutes.
    "Program of Songs by Lightnin' Sam Hopkins," black and white, 9 minutes.

IMPLEMENTATION OF THE MUSIC EDUCATION PROGRAM

10. Excellent short films representing the music and dance of various tribes in the Central Sudan region available from Institut für den Wissenschaftlichen Film, Western Germany.

E 1027 Djonkor (Zentralsudan, Süd-Wadai), "Preisgesang mit Harfenspiel" (two harp players and a singer), sound-color film, 6½ minutes.

E 1027 Djonkor (Zentralsudan, Süd-Wadai), "Festorchester" (individual players on flutes and drums, then ensemble), sound-color film, 11 minutes.

E 1029 Bulala (Zentralsudan, Süd-Wadai), "Fiedelspiel und Preisgesang eines Spielmanns" (male players on drum and fiddles and female singers), sound-color film, 7½ minutes.

E 1030 Haussa (Zentralsudan, Süd-Wadai), "Spielen der Schalmei libo" (free-reed flute), sound-color film, 4½ minutes.

E 1023 Dangaleat (Zentralsudan, Süd-Wadai), "Kindertänze" (children dancing), sound-color film, 9½ minutes.

11. Film Associates, Los Angeles, California.

"Discovering the Music of Japan," color, 22 minutes.

"Discovering the Music of Africa," color, 22 minutes.

"Discovering Form in Music," "Discovering Melody and Harmony," "What Is Rhythm?" and others.

12. Richard Colwell, *Elementary Music Achievement Tests* (Chicago: Follett Publishing Company, 1967).

13. Jack Coleman, Irene Shoepfle, and Virginia Templeton, *Music for Exceptional Children* (Evanston, Ill.: Summy-Birchard Company, 1964).

14. *Journal of Music Therapy* (Lawrence, Kans.: National Association for Music Therapy, Inc.).

15. *The Volta Review* (Washington, D.C.: Association for the Deaf).

16. "The Shoemaker and the Elves," a song-story sung and told by Frank Luther (Decca C.U.S. 8). Also found in *Singing on Our Way* (Ginn and Company).

## Other References

Lehman, Paul, *Tests and Measurements in Music* (Englewood Cliffs, N.J.: Prentice-Hall Inc., 1968).

Mathews, Paul Wentworth, *You Can Teach Music* (New York: E. P. Dutton and Co., Inc., 1953). Chapter 9, "Music Doesn't Walk Alone."

Myers, Louise Kifer, *Teaching Children Music in the Elementary School*, Third Edition (Englewood Cliffs, N.J.: Prentice-Hall, Inc., 1961). Chapter 12, "Music's Role in Understanding Other Peoples." Bibliography and Sources of Materials, pp. 333–344, annotated and under headings (1) "Background in Music" and (2) "Music's Role in Understanding Other Peoples."

Nye, Robert Evans, and Vernice Trousdale Nye, *Music in the Elementary School*, Second Edition (Englewood Cliffs, N.J.: Prentice-Hall, Inc., 1957). Chapter 11, "Music and Other Areas."

Perham, Beatrice, *Music in the New School* (Park Ridge, Ill.: Neil A. Kjos Music Co., 1941). Pp. 35–44, "Correlation and Integration," and Chapter 10, "Evaluation."

Pierce, Anne E., *Teaching Music in the Elementary School* (New York: Holt, Rinehart & Winston, Inc., 1959). Pp. 32–34, "Evaluation of Pupils," and Chapter 9, "Music: Servant and Master."

Timmerman, Maurine, *Let's Teach Music* (Evanston, Ill.: Summy-Birchard Company, 1958). Chapter 7, "Let's Live with Music," pp. 177–187, and suggested sources of materials, pp. 199–202.

# Appendix A

# Reference Material for Music Theory and Notation

## I. METER AND RHYTHM

*metric beat*—the underlying framework of regular pulses around which the rhythm of music is organized. The beat is usually represented by one of the following symbols:

♪ = an eighth note (numerically indicated by 8).

♩ = a quarter note (numerically indicated by 4).

♪ = a half note (numerically indicated by 2).

*tempo*—the speed of the metric beat, designated by:
(a) metronome marking indicating the number of beats per minute, e.g., MM = 72.
(b) traditional Italian terms that suggest mood and type of movement as well as pace:

| | |
|---|---|
| *grave*—slow, solemn | *moderato*—moderate |
| *largo*—very slow and broad | *allegretto*—moderately fast |
| *largamente*—slow and stately | *animato*—animated |
| *lento*—slow | *allegro*—quick, lively |
| *adagio*—leisurely | *scherzando*—playful, lively |
| *andante*—moderate and flowing | *vive*—lively, brisk |
| *andantino*—slight modification of andante, generally quicker | *vivace*—brisk, fast |
| | *presto*—very fast |

(c) words qualifying the above and suggesting more definite expression:

| | |
|---|---|
| *assai*—very | *molto*—very much |
| *cantabile*—in a singing manner | *non troppo*—not too much |
| *dolce*—sweet | *più*—more |
| *giocoso*—humorous, playful | *poco*—little |
| *grazioso*—graceful | *sempre*—always |
| *leggiero*—light, graceful | *sostenuto*—sustained |
| *maestoso*—majestic | *tranquillo*—calm, quiet |
| *meno mosso*—less movement | *très*—very, most |

(d) simple English equivalents of the Italian terms.
(e) variation within the established tempo indicated by:
 *accelerando, accel.*—increase tempo gradually
 *ritardando, rit., rallentando, rall.*, decrease tempo gradually
 *a tempo*—in the original tempo after a change

ad libitum—at will, with freedom from strict metric regularity

rubato—fluctuation or not in strict time

(f) rhythmic treatment of an individual note:

> an accent

⌢ fermata—hold or lengthen

**sf** sforzando—a heavy accent

meter—a systematic grouping of the metric beats.

measure—one unit of metric beats.

bar lines—vertical lines to frame the measure.

meter signature—figure given at the beginning of a composition to indicate the metric organization.

simple duple meter:

$\frac{2}{8}$ ♪ ♪ | ♪ ♪ |   $\frac{2}{4}$ ♩ ♩ | ♩ ♩ |
   1  2   1  2      1  2   1  2

$\frac{2}{2}$ 𝅝 𝅝 | 𝅗𝅥 𝅗𝅥 |   or ¢ which is *alle breve*
   1  2   1  2           (sometimes called "cut time")

simple triple meter:

$\frac{3}{8}$ ♪ ♪ ♪ | ♪ ♪ ♪ |
   1  2  3   1  2  3

$\frac{3}{4}$ ♩ ♩ ♩ | ♩ ♩ ♩ |
   1  2  3   1  2  3

$\frac{3}{2}$ 𝅗𝅥 𝅗𝅥 𝅗𝅥 | 𝅗𝅥 𝅗𝅥 𝅗𝅥 |
   1  2  3   1  2  3

quadruple meter:

$\frac{4}{8}$ ♪ ♪ ♪ ♪ | ♪ ♪ ♪ ♪ |
   1  2  3  4   1  2  3  4

$\frac{4}{4}$ ♩ ♩ ♩ ♩ | ♩ ♩ ♩ ♩ |   or C (sometimes called "common time")
   1  2  3  4   1  2  3  4

$\frac{4}{2}$ 𝅗𝅥 𝅗𝅥 𝅗𝅥 𝅗𝅥 | 𝅗𝅥 𝅗𝅥 𝅗𝅥 𝅗𝅥 |
   1  2  3  4   1  2  3  4

*duration*—the length of time assigned to a note or rest:

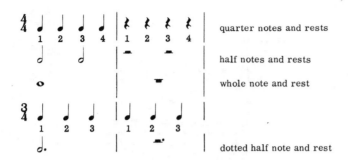

quarter notes and rests

half notes and rests

whole note and rest

dotted half note and rest

*even division* within the beat showing eighth ( ♪ ) and sixteenth ( ♪ ) notes with flags and beams, rhythm syllables:

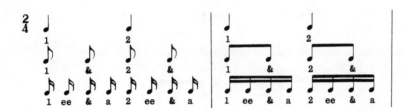

*uneven division* within the beat showing the use of the *dot* to indicate the additional time of one-half the value of the note it follows, a *tie* binding together two notes on one pitch level, and eighth and sixteenth rests:

*compound meters:*

*duple:*

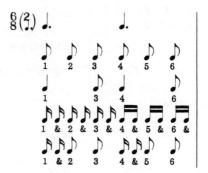

*triple:*

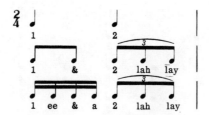

comparison of subdivided duple meter and compound duple meter:

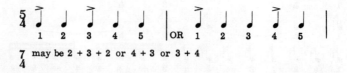

*triplet* division within one beat:

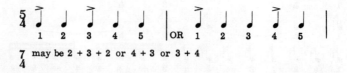

*combination meters*—groupings of two or three beats within one measure:

$\frac{7}{4}$ may be 2 + 3 + 2 or 4 + 3 or 3 + 4

*rhythm*—the flow of the tones in music in short patterns or in longer phrases toward a point of release. Rhythm is related to the underlying metric structure but is not limited to it. Whereas meter is framed by measure bars, rhythm flows across them. Rhythm patterns may cut across measures:

*anacrusis*—an upbeat leading to the accent:

$\frac{6}{8}$ ♪ | ♩ ♪♩ | ♪ ♩ 2 etc.
6 | 1 3 4 | 6 | 1

OR $\frac{2}{4}$ ♫♫ | ♫ ♪ | ♫♫ | ♫ ♪ etc.
& a | 1 & | & a | 1 &

*syncopation*—a shift of the accent from what would be its normal position in the underlying metric scheme. Achieved by:

(a) failure to begin a tone on the normal accent: $\frac{2}{4}$ ♫♪ ♫♪ | ♫♪ ♩ :||

(b) prolonging a tone on the unaccented part of the measure: $\frac{3}{4}$ ♩♩♩ | ♩♩ | ♩ ♩ | ♩ ♩♩ :||

---

## II. DYNAMICS

Signs and terms relating to strength of sound in music:

*pianissimo* (*pp*)—very soft
*piano* (*p*)—soft
*mezzo piano* (*mp*)—medium soft
*mezzo forte* (*mf*)—medium loud
*forte* (*f*)—loud
*fortissimo* (*ff*)—very loud

*crescendo, cresc.,* ——————— —an increase in loudness.

*diminuendo, dim., decrescendo, decresc.,* ——————— —a decrease in loudness.

---

## III. PITCH

The *grand staff* and a diagram of the piano keyboard:

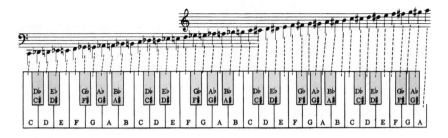

*G clef* establishes the pitch for higher voices. So named because a Gothic letter G was used to locate that tone on the *treble staff*.

*F clef* establishes the pitch for lower voices. So named because the Gothic letter F was used to locate that tone on the *bass staff*.

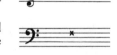

**331**

*staff degree*—a line or space on the staff, named by one of the first seven letters of the alphabet. (See grand staff, which shows names of all staff degrees on the related keyboard.)

*leger line*—a short line above or below the staff used to extend the range of tones. (See grand staff.)

*octave*—duplication of each letter name every eighth scale degree. (See grand staff.)

*half step*—the tonal distance between each consecutive key (whether black or white) on the piano keyboard.

*accidental*—a tonal alteration of the pitch indicated by a given staff degree. Its influence lasts during the measure in which it appears and is canceled by the bar line.

    *sharp* (♯)—raises the tone one half step.

    *flat* (♭)—lowers the tone one half step.

    *double sharp* (✕)—raises the tone one whole step.

    *double flat* (♭♭)—lowers the tone one whole step.

    *natural* (♮)—cancels other accidentals or the influence of a sharp or flat in the key signature.

*enharmonic tones*—a single pitch notated in different ways and called by two or more different names, depending on the key in which the composer is working.

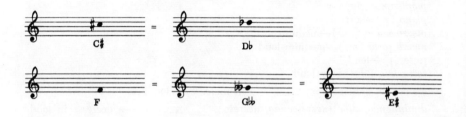

---

## IV. SCALES AND CHORDS

*major scale*—a group of seven different tones in a particular pattern of whole and half steps. Half steps occur between the third and fourth and the seventh and eighth tones of the major scale:

$$1 \quad 2 \quad \overset{\wedge}{3 \ 4} \quad 5 \quad 6 \quad \overset{\wedge}{7 \ 8}$$

*key center*—the tone on which a scale is built (also called the "tonic" note or tone).

*scale numbers*—a general means of naming the tones within a scale.

*sol-fa syllables*—Italian syllables naming the tones within a scale.

C major scale showing number, syllable, and letter names on two staves:

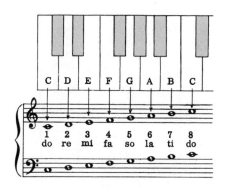

F major scale

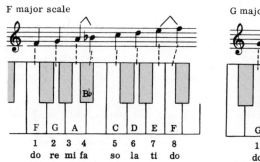

| 1 | 2 | 3 | 4 | | 5 | 6 | 7 | 8 |
|---|---|---|---|---|---|---|---|---|
| do | re | mi | fa | | so | la | ti | do |

G major scale

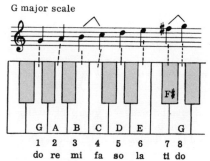

| 1 | 2 | 3 | 4 | 5 | 6 | | 7 | 8 |
|---|---|---|---|---|---|---|---|---|
| do | re | mi | fa | so | la | | ti | do |

*key signature*—sharps or flats placed on the staff immediately after the clef sign to designate the key center and to alter the pitches of the staff degrees to provide the correct arrangement of whole and half steps:

**F major**

1 2 3 4 5 6 7 8

**G major**

1 2 3 4 5 6 7 8

*common major key signatures* (in addition to those already shown):

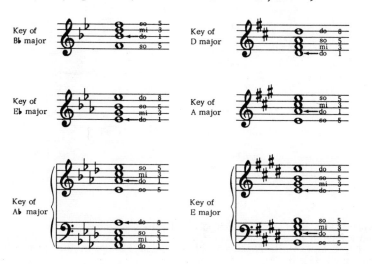

Key of Bb major

Key of Eb major

Key of Ab major

Key of D major

Key of A major

Key of E major

*circle of keys* showing the number of sharps or flats in all key signatures:

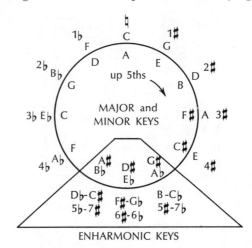

From Howard A. Murphy and Edwin J. Stringham, *Creative Harmony and Musicianship: An Introduction to the Structure of Music* (Englewood Cliffs, N.J.: Prentice-Hall, Inc., 1951). Used by permission.

*chromatic scale*—a group of twelve tones, all one half step apart. (See grand staff under Section III.)
sol-fa syllables for chromatic scale (showing ascending and descending forms):

Hand signs for tones of the major scale*

|  |  |  |  |  |  |
|---|---|---|---|---|---|
|  |  | **do'** |  |  | Do' |
|  |  | **ti** |  |  | Ti |
| (pronounced *tay*) | ♭7 te | | li ♯6 | | La |
|  |  | **la** |  |  |  |
|  | ♭6 le | | si ♯5 | | So |
|  |  | **so** |  |  |  |
|  | ♭5 se | | fi ♯4 | | Fa |
|  |  | **fa** |  |  |  |
|  |  | **mi** |  |  | Mi |
|  | ♭3 me | | ri ♯2 | | Re |
|  |  | **re** |  |  |  |
| (rah) | ♭2 ra | | di ♯1 | (*dee*) | Do |
|  |  | **do** |  |  |  |

**APPENDIX A**

* Note: These hand signs are a modern adaptation of those used by the nineteenth century English music teacher, John Curwen. See Peter W. Dykema and Hannah M. Cundiff, *School Music Handbook,* New Edition (Evanston, Ill.: Summy-Birchard Company, 1955), p. 74.

*interval*—the distance between two tones, determined by the number of staff degrees involved.

Intervals between the key tone of the major scale and each of the other tones:

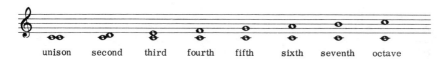

| unison | second | third | fourth | fifth | sixth | seventh | octave |

Qualifying sizes of intervals in the major scale (as above):
   *perfect* (P): unison, fourth, fifth, octave.
   *major* (M): second, third, sixth, seventh.
   *minor* (m): one half step smaller than major intervals.
   *diminished* (d): one half step smaller than minor or perfect intervals.
   *augmented* (A): one half step larger than major or perfect intervals.

Other common intervals between notes of the major scale:

   3 − 5 = m3          5 − 8 = P4
   mi  so              so  do

   6 − 8 = m3          4 − 8 = P5
   la  do              fa  do

*triad*—a chord of three tones, built in thirds.
   *root*—the tone on which the chord is built.
   *third*—the tone of the chord a third above the root.
   *fifth*—the tone of the chord a fifth above the root.

*major triad*—a chord in which the lower third is major and the upper third is minor:

*minor triad*—position of major and minor third reversed:

*diminished chord*—the triad built on the seventh step of the scale and consisting of two minor third intervals.

*triads of the major scale,* classified as to size with scale numbers, chord numbers and names:

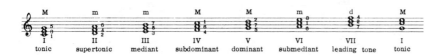

| I | II | III | IV | V | VI | VII | I |
| tonic | supertonic | mediant | subdominant | dominant | submediant | leading tone | tonic |

*dominant seventh chord*—a four-tone chord built on the fifth step of the scale:

V7

**335**

*minor scales:*

>*natural minor*—containing the same tones as the major scale but with a tonal center a minor third lower; half steps fall between second and third, and between fifth and sixth steps of the scale:

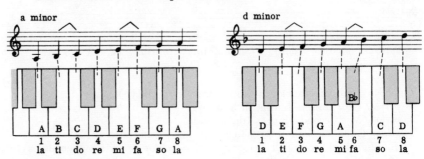

*harmonic minor*—same as the natural minor but with the seventh step of the scale raised so that the following pattern is formed:

(descent is the same)

*melodic minor*—the sixth and seventh steps of the scale are raised in ascent and unaltered in descent:

*pentatonic scale*—a scale built of five tones. The most common is that which represents the major scale with the fourth and seventh scale steps omitted:

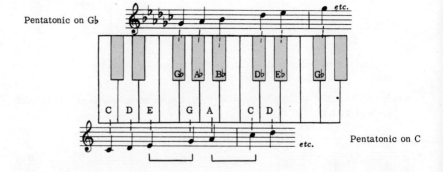

## V. ELEMENTARY PIANO ACCOMPANIMENTS

*chord inversion*—the arrangement of the tones of a chord so that one other than the root is the lowest tone. The IV and V₇ chords in the following example of chord progressions are inverted forms.

*chord progression*—the movement from one chord to another.
  *common chord progression* using inverted chords:

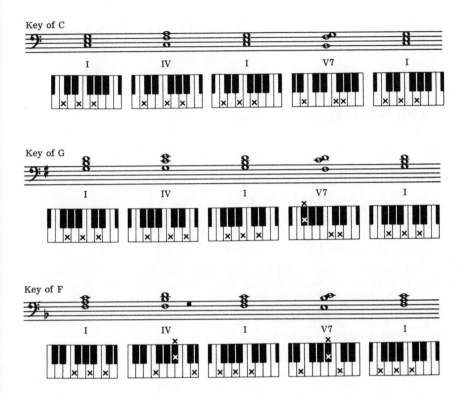

*rhythmic use of chord progressions* in accompaniments:

## I. BASIC MUSIC SERIES (with reference code)

Allyn and Bacon, Inc., 150 Tremont St., Boston, Mass. 02111. THIS IS MUSIC Series, 1967, William R. Sur *et al.*, editors.
> TiM—*This Is Music,* Kindergarten and Grades I–VI
>> Teacher's edition for each level
>> Pupils' books II–VI
>> Recordings for all books
>> Accompaniment book II–VI
>> Wall charts I–VI

American Book Company, 55 Fifth Ave., New York, N.Y. 10003. MUSIC FOR YOUNG AMERICANS Series, Second Edition, 1966, Richard C. Berg *et al.*, editors.
> ABC—*Music for Young Americans,* Kindergarten and Grades I–VI
>> Teacher's annotated edition for each level
>> Pupils' books II–VI
>> Recordings for all books

Follett Publishing Company, 1010 West Washington Blvd., Chicago, Ill. 60607. DISCOVERING MUSIC TOGETHER Series, 1966, Charles Leonhard *et al.*, editors.
> DMT—*Discovering Music Together,* Grades I–VI
>> Teacher's edition for each level
>> Pupils' books for each level
>> Recordings for all books

Ginn and Company, Statler Building, Boston, Mass. 02117. THE MAGIC OF MUSIC Series, 1966, Lorrain E. Walters *et al.*, editors.
> MoM—*The Magic of Music,* Kindergarten and Grades I–VI
>> Teacher's edition for each level
>> Pupils' books II–VI
>> Recordings for all books

OUR SINGING WORLD Series, Enlarged Edition, 1959, Lilla Belle Pitts *et al.*, editors.
> *Our Singing World,* Kindergarten and Grades I–VI
>> Teacher's book K–I
>> Pupils' books I–VI
>> Piano accompaniments II–VI
>> Guide and teaching suggestions K–III and IV–VI
>> Recordings for all books

Holt, Rinehart and Winston, Inc., 383 Madison Ave., New York, N.Y. 10017. EXPLORING MUSIC Series, 1966, Eunice Boardman and Beth Landis, editors.
> ExM—*Exploring Music,* Grades I–VI
>> Teacher's edition for each level
>> Pupils' books for each level
>> Recordings for all songs and listening lessons

Prentice-Hall, Inc., Englewood Cliffs, N.J. 07632. GROWING WITH MUSIC Series, 1966, Harry Wilson *et al.,* editors.

    **GwM**—*Growing with Music,* Grades K–VI
        Teacher's edition for each level
        Pupils' books I–VI
        Recordings for all songs

Silver Burdett Co., Park Ave. and Columbia Rd., Morristown, N.J. 07960. MAKING MUSIC YOUR OWN Series, 1965, Beatrice Landeck, Harold Youngberg, Mary T. Jaye *et al.,* editors.

    **MMYO**—*Making Music Your Own,* Kindergarten and Grades I–VI
        Teacher's edition for each level
        Pupils' books I–VI
        Recordings for all songs

    MUSIC FOR LIVING Series, 1956, James L. Mursell *et al.,* editors.
        *Music for Living,* Grades I–IV
        Teacher's edition for each level
        Pupils' books I–VI
        Recordings for all books

Summy-Birchard Publishing Company, 1834 Ridge Avenue, Evanston, Ill. 60204. THE BIRCHARD MUSIC SERIES, 1962, Karl Ernst *et al.,* editors.

    **Bir**—*Birchard Music Series,* Kindergarten and Grades I–VI
        Teacher's edition for each level
        Pupils' books II–VI
        Recordings for all books
        Wall charts for grades I–VI
        Instrumental easels to accompany books III–VI

    **Joy**—*The Joy of Music, Early Childhood,* 1967, Roberta McLaughlin and Patti Schliestett, editors.
        Teacher's book, Kindergarten
        Recordings

Code references for song books not in the basic series:

    **AFlk**—*American Folk Songs for Children,* Ruth Seeger. New York: Doubleday and Company, Inc., 1948.
    **SGro**—*Songs to Grow On,* Beatrice Landeck. New York: Edward B. Marks Music Corporation, Music Publishers, William Sloane Associates, Inc., Publishers, 1950.

## II. RECORD SERIES (with reference code)

ADVENTURES IN MUSIC, A New Record Library for Elementary Schools, RCA Victor Recording Corporation (Le = "long play," Les = "stereo"). A teacher's guide is included in the folder for each volume. (See alphabetical listing of music on following pages.)

    Grade 1, Volume 1 (Le/Les 1000) (**A in M I–1**)
    Grade 1, Volume 2 (Le/Les 1010)* (**A in M I–2**)
    Grade 2, Volume 1 (Le/Les 1001) (**A in M II–1**)
    Grade 2, Volume 2 (Le/Les 1011)* (**A in M II–2**)

* Available in late 1969.

Grade 3, Volume 1 (Le/Les 1002) (**A in M III–1**)
Grade 3, Volume 2 (Le/Les 1003) (**A in M III–2**)
Grade 4, Volume 1 (Le/Les 1004) (**A in M IV–1**)
Grade 4, Volume 2 (Le/Les 1005) (**A in M IV–2**)
Grade 5, Volume 1 (Le/Les 1006) (**A in M V–1**)
Grade 5, Volume 2 (Le/Les 1007) (**A in M V–2**)
Grade 6, Volume 1 (Le/Les 1008) (**A in M VI–1**)
Grade 6, Volume 2 (Le/Les 1009) (**A in MVI–2**)

BOWMAR ORCHESTRAL LIBRARY (**BOL**), Bowmar Educational Records. Each album is accompanied by wall charts of the themes and suggestions to the teacher. (See listing of music on following pages.)

GREYSTONE CORPORATION, Educational Activities Division, whose affiliates are:
Children's Record Guild (**CRG**)
Young People's Records (**YPR**)

MUSICAL SOUND BOOKS, created by the Sound Book Press Society, Inc. These recordings accompany books of the same titles by Lillian Baldwin (see Chapter Notes, Chapter Eight).
*Music for Young Listeners*
Green Section, MSB 78001–78018
Crimson Section, MSB 78019–78038
Blue Section, MSB 78039–78051
*Tiny Masterpieces for Young Listeners*, MSB 78301–78320

RCA Victor RECORD LIBRARY FOR ELEMENTARY SCHOOLS
*Rhythmic Activities* (album numbers: WE–71 to WE–76)
*Listening Activities* (album numbers: WE–77 to WE–82)
*Singing Activities* (album numbers: WE–83 to WE–86)
*Special Activities* (album numbers: WE–87 to WE–91)
Singing Games      Music for Rhythm Bands
Music at Christmastime      Patriotic Songs
Music of American Indians


## Adventures in Music—Musical Contents


**APPENDIX B** *Anderson:* Irish Suite—THE GIRL I LEFT BEHIND ME, Gr. 5, Vol. 2
*Arnold:* English Suite—GRAZIOSO (7th movement), Gr. 1, Vol. 2
    English Suite—ALLEGRO NON TROPPO (5th movement), Gr. 2, Vol. 2
*Bach:* Cantata No. 147—JESU, JOY OF MAN'S DESIRING, Gr. 5, Vol. 1
    LITTLE FUGUE IN G MINOR (Arr. by L. Cailliet), Gr. 6, Vol. 1
    Suite No. 2—BADINERIE, Gr. 3, Vol. 1
    Suite No. 2—RONDEAU, Gr. 2, Vol. 2
    Suite No. 2—GIGUE, Gr. 1, Vol. 1
*Bartók:* Hungarian Sketches—BEAR DANCE, Gr. 3, Vol. 2
    Hungarian Sketches—EVENING IN THE VILLAGE, Gr. 5, Vol. 2
    Mikrokosmos Suite No. 2—JACK-IN-THE-BOX, Gr. 2, Vol. 1
    Mikrokosmos—DIARY OF A FLY (Moto perpetuo, No. 142), Gr. 1, Vol. 2
*Beethoven:* Symphony No. 8—SECOND MOVEMENT, Gr. 6, Vol. 1
*Berlioz:* The Damnation of Faust—BALLET OF THE SYLPHS, Gr. 1, Vol. 1

*Bizet:* L'Arlesienne Suite No. 1—MINUETTO, Gr. 4, Vol. 2
   L'Arlesienne Suite No. 2—FARANDOLE, Gr. 6, Vol. 1
   Carmen—CHANGING OF THE GUARD, Gr. 3, Vol. 2
   Carmen Suite—DRAGOONS OF ALCALA, Gr. 2, Vol. 2
   Children's Games—THE BALL; CRADLE SONG; LEAP FROG, Gr. 1,
   Vol. 1

*Borodin:* IN THE STEPPES OF CENTRAL ASIA, Gr. 6, Vol. 1

*Brahms:* HUNGARIAN DANCE No. 1, Gr. 5, Vol. 2

*Cailliet:* POP! GOES THE WEASEL—Variations, Gr. 4, Vol. 1

*Carpenter:* Adventures in a Perambulator—THE HURDY-GURDY, Gr. 5, Vol. 2

*Chabrier:* ESPAÑA RAPSODIE, Gr. 5, Vol. 1
   MARCHE JOYEUSE, Gr. 4, Vol. 1

*Charpentier:* Impressions of Italy—ON MULEBACK, Gr. 5, Vol. 1

*Cimarosa:* Cimarosiana—NON TROPPO MOSSO (3rd movement), Gr. 2,
   Vol. 2

*Coates:* London Suite—KNIGHTSBRIDGE MARCH, Gr. 5, Vol. 2

*Copland:* Billy the Kid Ballet Suite—STREET IN A FRONTIER TOWN, Gr.
   6, Vol. 1
   The Red Pony Suite—CIRCUS MUSIC, Gr. 3, Vol. 1
   The Red Pony Suite—DREAM MARCH, Gr. 2, Vol. 2
   Rodeo—HOE-DOWN, Gr. 5, Vol. 2

*Corelli-Pinelli:* Suite for Strings—SARABANDE, Gr. 6, Vol. 2

*Debussy:* Children's Corner Suite—THE SNOW IS DANCING, Gr. 3, Vol. 1
   La Mer—PLAY OF THE WAVES, Gr. 6, Vol. 2

*Delibes:* Coppélia—WALTZ OF THE DOLL, Gr. 1, Vol. 1
   Coppélia—SWANHILDE'S WALTZ, Gr. 2, Vol. 2
   The King Is Amused—LESQUERCARDE, Gr. 1, Vol. 2

*Dvořák:* SLAVONIC DANCE No. 7, Gr. 4, Vol. 2

*Elgar:* Wand of Youth Suite No. 1—FAIRIES AND GIANTS, Gr. 3, Vol. 1
   Wand of Youth Suite No. 2—FOUNTAIN DANCE, Gr. 2, Vol. 1
   Wand of Youth Suite—SUN DANCE, Gr. 2, Vol. 2

*Falla:* La Vida Breve—SPANISH DANCE No. 1, Gr. 6, Vol. 1

*Fauré:* Dolly—BERCEUSE, Gr. 2, Vol. 1

*German:* Henry VIII Suite—MORRIS DANCE, Gr. 1, Vol. 2

*Ginastera:* Estancia—WHEAT DANCE, Gr. 4, Vol. 1

*Glière:* The Red Poppy—RUSSIAN SAILORS' DANCE, Gr. 6, Vol. 2

*Gluck:* Armide Ballet Suite—MUSETTE, Gr. 2, Vol. 2
   Iphigenie in Aulis—AIR GAI, Gr. 1, Vol. 1

*Gottschalk-Kay:* Cakewalk Ballet Suite—GRAND WALKAROUND, Gr. 5,
   Vol. 1

*Gould:* AMERICAN SALUTE, Gr. 5, Vol. 1

*Gounod:* Faust Ballet Suite—WALTZ No. 1, Gr. 3, Vol. 1

*Grainger:* LONDONDERRY AIR, Gr. 4, Vol. 2

*Grétry:* Céphale et Procris—GIGUE (Arr. by Mottl), Gr. 1, Vol. 1
   Céphale et Procris—TAMBOURIN (Arr. by Mottl), Gr. 2, Vol. 1

*Grieg:* Lyric Suite—NORWEGIAN RUSTIC MARCH, Gr. 4, Vol. 1
   Peer Gynt Suite—ANITRA'S DANCE, Gr. 1, Vol. 2
   Peer Gynt Suite—IN THE HALL OF THE MOUNTAIN KING, Gr. 3,
   Vol. 2

*Griffes:* THE WHITE PEACOCK, Gr. 6, Vol. 1

*Grofé:* Death Valley Suite—DESERT WATER HOLE, Gr. 4, Vol. 1

**341**

*Guarnieri:* BRAZILIAN DANCE, Gr. 6, Vol. 2

*Handel:* Royal Fireworks Music—BOURRÉE, MENUETTO No. 2, Gr. 3, Vol. 2
Water Music—HORNPIPE, Gr. 2, Vol. 1

*Hanson:* For the First Time—BELLS, Gr. 1, Vol. 2
Merry Mount Suite—CHILDREN'S DANCE, Gr. 3, Vol. 1

*Herbert:* Babes in Toyland—MARCH OF THE TOYS, Gr. 2, Vol. 1
Natoma—DAGGER DANCE, Gr. 3, Vol. 1

*Holst:* The Perfect Fool—SPIRITS OF THE EARTH, Gr. 6, Vol. 2

*Howe:* SAND, Gr. 2, Vol. 2

*Humperdinck:* Hansel and Gretel—PRELUDE, Gr. 5, Vol. 2

*Ibert:* Divertissement—PARADE, Gr. 1, Vol. 1
Histories No. 2—THE LITTLE WHITE DONKEY, Gr. 2, Vol. 1

*Kabalevsky:* The Comedians—MARCH AND COMEDIANS' GALOP, Gr. 3, Vol. 1
The Comedians—PANTOMIME, Gr. 1, Vol. 1
The Comedians—WALTZ, Gr. 1, Vol. 2

*Khachaturian:* Gayne—DANCE OF THE ROSE MAIDENS, Gr. 1, Vol. 2
Masquerade Suite—WALTZ, Gr. 4, Vol. 2

*Kodály:* Háry János Suite—ENTRANCE OF THE EMPEROR AND HIS COURT, Gr. 4, Vol. 2
Háry János Suite—VIENNESE MUSICAL CLOCK, Gr. 2, Vol. 1

*Lecuona:* Suite Andalucia—ANDALUCIA, Gr. 4, Vol. 1

*Liadov:* Eight Russian Folk Songs—BERCEUSE, Gr. 1, Vol. 2

*Lully:* Ballet Suite—MARCH, Gr. 3, Vol. 2

*McBride:* PUMPKIN EATER'S LITTLE FUGUE, Gr. 2, Vol. 2
Punch and the Judy—PONY EXPRESS, Gr. 1, Vol. 2

*McDonald:* Children's Symphony—ALLEGRO, Gr. 3, Vol. 2
Children's Symphony (3rd Movement)—FARMER IN THE DELL, JINGLE BELLS, Gr. 2, Vol. 1

*MacDowell:* Second (Indian) Suite—IN WARTIME, Gr. 5, Vol. 1

*Massenet:* Le Cid—ARAGONAISE, Gr. 1, Vol. 1

*Menotti:* Amahl and the Night Visitors—MARCH OF THE KINGS, Gr. 1, Vol. 2
Amahl and the Night Visitors—SHEPHERD'S DANCE, Gr. 4, Vol. 2

*Meyerbeer:* Les Patineurs—WALTZ, Gr. 2, Vol. 1

*Milhaud:* Saudades do Brazil—COPACABANA, Gr. 4, Vol. 2
Saudades do Brazil—LARANJEIRAS, Gr. 2, Vol. 1
Suite Provençale—MODERE (3rd movement), Gr. 1, Vol. 2

*Moore:* Farm Journal—HARVEST SONG, Gr. 1, Vol. 2

*Moussorgsky:* Pictures at an Exhibition (Orchestrated by Ravel)—BALLET OF THE UNHATCHED CHICKS, Gr. 1, Vol. 1; BYDLO, Gr. 2, Vol. 1; PROMENADE No. 1, Gr. 1, Vol. 2

*Mozart:* Divertimento No. 17—MENUETTO No. 1, Gr. 5, Vol. 2
Eine kleine Nachtmusik—ROMANZE, Gr. 4, Vol. 1
The Little Nothings—PANTOMIME, Gr. 1, Vol. 2

*Offenbach:* The Tales of Hoffman—BARCAROLLE, Gr. 3, Vol. 1

*Pierné:* Cydalise—ENTRANCE OF LITTLE FAUNS, Gr. 2, Vol. 2

*Prokofiev:* Children's Suite—WALTZ ON THE ICE, Gr. 3, Vol. 2
Summer Day Suite—MARCH, Gr. 1, Vol. 1
Lieutenant Kije—TROIKA, Gr. 2, Vol. 2
Winter Holiday—DEPARTURE, Gr. 2, Vol. 1

*Ravel*: Mother Goose Suite—THE CONVERSATIONS OF BEAUTY AND THE BEAST, Gr. 5, Vol. 1
Mother Goose Suite—LAIDERONNETTE, EMPRESS OF THE PAGODAS, Gr. 4, Vol. 2

*Respighi*: Brazilian Impressions—DANZA, Gr. 5, Vol. 2
Pines of Rome—PINES OF THE VILLA BORGHESE, Gr. 4, Vol. 1
The Birds—PRELUDE, Gr. 2, Vol. 2

*Rimsky-Korsakov*: Le Coq d'Or Suite—BRIDAL PROCESSION, Gr. 4, Vol. 1
Snow Maiden—DANCE OF THE BUFFOONS, Gr. 2, Vol. 2

*Rossini*: William Tell Overture—FINALE, Gr. 3, Vol. 1

*Rossini-Britten*: Matinees Musicales—WALTZ, Gr. 1, Vol. 2
Soirées Musicales—BOLERO, Gr. 2, Vol. 2
Soirées Musicales—MARCH, Gr. 1, Vol. 1

*Rossini-Respighi*: The Fantastic Toyshop—CAN-CAN, Gr. 2, Vol. 1
The Fantastic Toyshop—TARANTELLA, Gr. 3, Vol. 2

*Saint-Saëns*: Carnival of the Animals—THE ELEPHANT, Gr. 1, Vol. 2
Carnival of the Animals—THE SWAN, Gr. 3, Vol. 2

*Scarlatti-Tommasini*: The Good-Humored Ladies—NON PRESTO IN TEMPO DI BALLO, Gr. 4, Vol. 2

*Schubert*: Symphony No. 5—FIRST MOVEMENT, Gr. 6, Vol. 1

*Schuller*: Seven Studies on Themes of Paul Klee—TWITTERING MACHINE, Gr. 2, Vol. 2

*Schumann*: Scenes from Childhood—TRÄUMEREI, Gr. 4, Vol. 2

*Shostakovich*: Ballet Suite No. 1—PETITE BALLERINA, Gr. 2, Vol. 1
Ballet Suite No. 1—PIZZICATO POLKA, Gr. 1, Vol. 1

*Sibelius*: Karelia Suite—ALLA MARCIA, Gr. 5, Vol. 1

*Smetana*: The Bartered Bride—DANCE OF THE COMEDIANS, Gr. 6, Vol. 2

*Sousa*: SEMPER FIDELIS, Gr. 3, Vol. 2
STARS AND STRIPES FOREVER, Gr. 4, Vol. 2

*Strauss, R.*: Der Rosenkavalier—SUITE, Gr. 6, Vol. 1

*Stravinsky*: The Firebird Suite—BERCEUSE, Gr. 1, Vol. 1
The Firebird Suite—INFERNAL DANCE OF KING KASTCHEI, Gr. 5, Vol. 2
Petrouchka—RUSSIAN DANCE, Gr. 1, Vol. 2

*Taylor*: Through the Looking Glass—GARDEN OF LIVE FLOWERS, Gr. 3, Vol. 2

*Tchaikovsky*: Nutcracker Suite—DANCE OF THE SUGAR PLUM FAIRY, Gr. 1, Vol. 2
Nutcracker Suite—DANCE OF THE REED FLUTES, Gr. 1, Vol. 2
The Sleeping Beauty—PUSS-IN-BOOTS, THE WHITE CAT, Gr. 3, Vol. 1
The Sleeping Beauty—WALTZ, Gr. 4, Vol. 1
Swan Lake—DANCE OF THE LITTLE SWANS, Gr. 1, Vol. 1
Symphony No. 4—FOURTH MOVEMENT, Gr. 6, Vol. 2

*Thomson*: Acadian Songs and Dances—THE ALLIGATOR AND THE 'COON, Gr. 3, Vol. 2
Acadian Songs and Dances—WALKING SONG, Gr. 1, Vol. 1

*Vaughan Williams*: FANTASIA ON "GREENSLEEVES," Gr. 6, Vol. 2
The Wasps—MARCH PAST OF THE KITCHEN UTENSILS, Gr. 3, Vol. 1

*Villa-Lobos*: Bachianas Brasileiras No. 2—THE LITTLE TRAIN OF CAIPIRA, Gr. 3, Vol. 1

*Wagner*: Lohengrin—PRELUDE TO ACT III, Gr. 6, Vol. 1

*Walton:* Façade Suite—VALSE, Gr. 6, Vol. 2

*Webern:* Five Movements for String Orchestra—SEHR LANGSAM (4th movement), Gr. 2, Vol. 2

## Bowmar Orchestral Library—Musical Contents

**BOL #51 ANIMALS AND CIRCUS**
*Saint-Saëns,* CARNIVAL OF THE ANIMALS: Introduction, Royal March of the Lion, Hens and Cocks, Fleet Footed Animals, Turtles, The Elephant, Kangaroos, Aquarium, Long Eared Personages, Cuckoo in the Deep Woods, Aviary, Pianists, Fossils, The Swan, Finale
*Stravinsky,* CIRCUS POLKA
*Donaldson,* UNDER THE BIG TOP: Marching Band, Acrobats, Juggler, Merry-Go-Round, Elephants, Clowns, Camels, Tightrope Walker, Pony Trot, Marching Band

**BOL #52 NATURE AND MAKE-BELIEVE**
*Grieg,* MARCH OF THE DWARFS
*Donaldson,* ONCE UPON A TIME SUITE: Chicken Little, Three Billy Goats Gruff, Little Train, Hare and the Tortoise
*Tchaikovsky,* THE LARK SONG (Scenes of Youth)
*Grieg,* LITTLE BIRD (Vöglein)
*Liadov,* DANCE OF THE MOSQUITO
*Rimsky-Korsakov,* FLIGHT OF THE BUMBLE BEE
*Donaldson,* SEASON FANTASIES: Magic Piper, The Poet and His Lyre, The Anxious Leaf, The Snowmaiden
*Torjussen,* TO THE RISING SUN (Fjord and Mountain, Norwegian Suite #2)
*Debussy,* CLAIRE DE LUNE

**BOL # 53 PICTURES AND PATTERNS**
*Rossini-Respighi,* PIZZICATO (Fantastic Toyshop)
*Bizet,* MARCH—TRUMPET AND DRUM (Jeux d'Enfants), IMPROMPTU—THE TOP (Jeux d'Enfants)
*Lecocq,* POLKA, GAVOTTE (Mlle. Angot Suite)
*Kabalevsky,* INTERMEZZO (The Comedians)
*Schumann-Glazounov,* GERMAN WALTZ—PAGANINI (Carnaval)
*Donaldson,* BALLET PETIT
*Mozart,* MINUET
*Handel,* A GROUND
*Schumann-Glazounov,* CHOPIN (Carnaval)
*Liadov,* VILLAGE DANCE
*Debussy,* EN BATEAU (In a Boat)
*Donaldson,* HARBOR VIGNETTES: Fog and Storm, Song of the Bell Buoy, Sailing

**BOL #54 MARCHES**
*Pierné,* ENTRANCE OF THE LITTLE FAUNS
*Prokofiev,* MARCH
*Elgar,* POMP AND CIRCUMSTANCE #1
*Berlioz,* HUNGARIAN MARCH (Rakoczy)
*Alford,* COL. BOGEY MARCH
*Pierné,* MARCH OF THE LITTLE LEAD SOLDIERS
*Prokofiev,* MARCH (The Love for Three Oranges)
*Ippolitov-Ivanov,* CORTEGE OF THE SARDAR (Caucasian Sketches)
*Schubert,* MARCHE MILITAIRE
*Sousa,* STARS AND STRIPES FOREVER
*Rodgers,* THE MARCH OF THE SIAMESE CHILDREN (The King and I)

**BOL #55** DANCES, PART I
*Wolf-Ferrari,* DANCE OF THE CAMMORISTI
*Guarnieri,* DANCA BRASILEIRA
*Kabalevsky,* GAVOTTE
*Dvořák,* SLAVONIC DANCE #1
*Copland,* HOE-DOWN (Rodeo)
*Walton,* FAÇADE SUITE: Polka, Country Dance, Popular Song
*Brahms,* HUNGARIAN DANCE #5
*Waldteufel,* SKATER'S WALTZES
*Khatchaturian,* MAZURKA, GALOP (Masquerade Suite)

**BOL #56** DANCES, PART II
*Vaughan Williams,* FOLK DANCES FROM SOMERSET (English Folk Song
  Suite)
*Benjamin,* JAMAICAN RUMBA
*Corelli,* BADINERIE
*Smetana,* DANCE OF THE COMEDIANS
*Lecocq,* CAN-CAN, GRAND WALTZ (Mlle. Angot Suite)
*Strauss,* TRITSCH-TRATSCH POLKA
*Rossini-Respighi,* TARANTELLA (Fantastic Toyshop), WALTZ (Fantastic
  Toyshop)
*Waldteufel,* ESPAÑA WALTZES
*Guion,* ARKANSAS TRAVELER
*Khatchaturian,* RUSSIAN DANCE (Gayne Suite #2)

**BOL #57** FAIRY TALES IN MUSIC
*Coates,* CINDERELLA
*Mendelssohn,* SCHERZO (Midsummer Night's Dream)
*Ravel,* MOTHER GOOSE SUITE: Pavane of the Sleeping Beauty, Hop o' My
  Thumb, Laideronette, Empress of the Pagodas, Beauty and the Beast, The Fairy
  Garden

**BOL #58** STORIES IN BALLET AND OPERA
*Menotti,* SUITE FROM AMAHL AND THE NIGHT VISITORS: Introduc-
  tion, March of the Three Kings, Dance of the Shepherds
*Humperdinck,* HÄNSEL AND GRETEL OVERTURE
*Tchaikovsky,* NUTCRACKER SUITE: Overture Miniature, March, Dance of
  the Sugar-Plum Fairy, Trepak, Arabian Dance, Chinese Dance, Dance of the
  Toy Flutes, Waltz of the Flowers

**BOL #59** LEGENDS IN MUSIC
*Saint-Saëns,* DANSE MACABRE
*Grieg,* PEER GYNT SUITE #1: Morning, Ase's Death, Anitra's Dance, In the
  Hall of the Mountain King
*Dukas,* SORCERER'S APPRENTICE
*Saint-Saëns,* PHAETON

**BOL #60** UNDER MANY FLAGS
*Smetana,* THE MOLDAU
*Torjussen,* LAPLAND IDYLL, FOLK SONG (Fjord and Mountain, Nor-
  wegian Suite #2)
*Grainger,* LONDONDERRY AIR
*Sibelius,* FINLANDIA
*Coates,* LONDON SUITE: Covent Garden, Westminster, Knightsbridge March

**BOL #61** AMERICAN SCENES
*Grofé,* GRAND CANYON SUITE: Sunrise, Painted Desert, On the Trail,
  Sunset, Cloudburst; MISSISSIPPI SUITE: Father of Waters, Huckleberry
  Finn, Old Creole Days, Mardi Gras

**BOL #62** MASTERS IN MUSIC
*Bach,* JESU, JOY OF MAN'S DESIRING

**345**

*Handel,* BOURRÉE FROM FIREWORKS MUSIC
*Haydn,* VARIATIONS ("Surprise" Symphony)
*Mozart,* MINUET (Symphony #40)
*Beethoven,* SCHERZO (Seventh Symphony)
*Grieg,* WEDDING DAY AT TROLDHAUGEN
*Schubert,* MINUET (Symphony #5)
*Wagner,* RIDE OF THE VALKYRIES
*Verdi,* TRIUMPHAL MARCH (Aida)
*Brahms,* HUNGARIAN DANCE #6
*Mahler,* SECOND MOVEMENT, SYMPHONY #1

**BOL #63** CONCERT MATINEE
*Debussy,* CHILDREN'S CORNER SUITE
*Corelli-Pinelli,* SUITE FOR STRING ORCHESTRA: Sarabande, Gigue, Badinerie
*Haydn,* MINUET ("Surprise" Symphony)
*Verdi,* ANVIL CHORUS
*Grieg,* NORWEGIAN DANCE IN A (#2)
*Schumann,* TRÄUMEREI

**BOL # 64** MINIATURES IN MUSIC
*Zador,* CHILDREN'S SYMPHONY
*Schubert,* THE BEE
*Haydn,* GYPSY RONDO
*Schumann,* WILD HORSEMEN, HAPPY FARMER
*Couperin,* LITTLE WINDMILLS
*Leo,* ARIETTA
*Liadov,* MUSIC BOX
*Gounod,* FUNERAL MARCH OF THE MARIONETTES
*Elwell,* DANCE OF THE MERRY DWARFS (Happy Hypocrite)
*Villa-Lobos,* LITTLE TRAIN OF CAIPIRA

**BOL #65** MUSIC, USA
*Copland,* SHAKER TUNE (Appalachian Spring)
*Thomson,* CATTLE & BLUES (Plow That Broke the Plains), FUGUE AND CHORALE ON YANKEE DOODLE (Tuesday in November)
*McBride,* PUMPKIN-EATER'S LITTLE FUGUE
*Gould,* AMERICAN SALUTE
*Cailliet,* POP GOES THE WEASEL
*Ives,* LAST MOVEMENT, SYMPHONY #2

**BOL #66** ORIENTAL SCENES
*Koyama,* WOODCUTTER'S SONG
*Donaldson,* THE EMPEROR'S NIGHTINGALE
*Folk tune,* SAKURA

**APPENDIX B**

**BOL #67** FANTASY IN MUSIC
*Coates,* THREE BEARS
*Prokofiev,* CINDERELLA: Sewing Scene, Cinderella's Gavotte, Midnight Waltz, Fairy Godmother
*Donaldson,* MOON LEGEND
*Tchaikovsky,* SLEEPING BEAUTY WALTZ

**BOL #68** CLASSROOM CONCERT
*Tchaikovsky,* ALBUM FOR THE YOUNG
*Stravinsky,* DEVIL DANCE
*Bartók,* THREE COMPOSITIONS
*Pinto,* MEMORIES OF CHILDHOOD

**BOL #69** MUSIC OF THE DANCE: STRAVINSKY
FIREBIRD SUITE: Koschai's Enchanted Garden, Dance of the Firebird, Dance of the Princesses, Infernal Dance of Koschai, Magic Sleep of the Princess Tzarevna, Finale: Escape of Koschai's Captives

**346**

SACRIFICIAL DANCE (The Rite of Spring)
VILLAGE FESTIVAL (The Fairy's Kiss)
PALACE OF THE CHINESE EMPEROR (The Nightingale)
TANGO, WALTZ AND RAGTIME (The Soldier's Tale)

**BOL #70** MUSIC OF THE SEA AND SKY
*Debussy,* CLOUDS, FESTIVALS
*Holst,* MERCURY (The Planets)
*Wagner,* OVERTURE (The Flying Dutchman)
*Thomson,* SEA PIECE WITH BIRDS
*Debussy,* DIALOGUE OF THE WIND AND THE SEA (The Sea)

**BOL #71** SYMPHONIC MOVEMENTS, NO. 1
*Tchaikovsky,* THIRD MOVEMENT, SYMPHONY #4
*Beethoven,* SECOND MOVEMENT, SYMPHONY #8
*Mozart,* FIRST MOVEMENT, SYMPHONY #40
*Schumann,* SECOND MOVEMENT, SYMPHONY #4
*Brahms,* THIRD MOVEMENT, SYMPHONY #3
*Saint-Saëns,* FOURTH MOVEMENT, SYMPHONY #3

**BOL #72** SYMPHONIC MOVEMENTS, No. 2
*Dvořák,* FIRST MOVEMENT, SYMPHONY #9 (From the New World)
*Beethoven,* FIRST MOVEMENT, SYMPHONY #5
*Britten,* FIRST MOVEMENT, Boisterous Bourrée (A Simple Symphony)
*Hanson,* SECOND MOVEMENT, SYMPHONY #2 (Romantic)
*Sibelius,* FIRST MOVEMENT, SYMPHONY #2

**BOL #73** SYMPHONIC STYLES
*Haydn,* SYMPHONY #99 (Imperial)
*Prokofiev,* CLASSICAL SYMPHONY

**BOL #74** TWENTIETH CENTURY AMERICA
*Copland,* EL SALON MEXICO
*Bernstein,* DANZON (Fancy Free), SYMPHONIC DANCES (excerpts) (West Side Story)
*Gershwin,* AN AMERICAN IN PARIS

**BOL #75** U.S. HISTORY IN MUSIC
*Copland,* A LINCOLN PORTRAIT
*Schuman,* CHESTER (New England Triptych)
*Ives,* PUTNAM'S CAMP (Three Places in New England)
*Harris,* INTERLUDE (Folk Song Symphony)
*Phillips,* MIDNIGHT RIDE OF PAUL REVERE (Selections from McGuffey's Readers)

**BOL #76** OVERTURES
*Strauss,* OVERTURE (The Bat)
*Brahms,* ACADEMIC FESTIVAL OVERTURE
*Mozart,* OVERTURE (The Marriage of Figaro)
*Berlioz,* ROMAN CARNIVAL OVERTURE
*Rossini,* OVERTURE (William Tell)

**BOL #77** SCHEHERAZADE BY RIMSKY-KORSAKOV

**BOL #78** MUSICAL KALEIDOSCOPE
*Borodin,* ON THE STEPPES OF CENTRAL ASIA
*Ippolitov-Ivanov,* IN THE VILLAGE (Caucasian Sketches)
*Borodin,* EXCERPTS, POLOVTSIAN DANCES (Prince Igor)
*Glière,* RUSSIAN SAILORS' DANCE (The Red Poppy)
*Bizet,* CARILLON, MINUET (L'Arlesienne Suite No. 1), FARANDOLE (L'Arlesienne Suite No. 2), PRELUDE TO ACT I (Carmen)
*Berlioz,* MARCH TO THE SCAFFOLD (Symphony Fantastique)

**BOL #79** MUSIC OF THE DRAMA: WAGNER
LOHENGRIN: Overture to Act I, Prelude to Act 3

THE TWILIGHT OF THE GODS: Siegfried's Rhine Journey
THE MASTERSINGERS OF NUREMBERG: Prelude, Dance of the Apprentices and Entrance of the Mastersingers
TRISTAN AND ISOLDE: Love Death

**BOL #80** PETROUCHKA BY STRAVINSKY (Complete ballet score with narration)

**BOL #81** ROGUES IN MUSIC
*Strauss,* TILL EULENSPIEGEL
*Prokofieff,* LIEUTENANT KIJE SUITE: Birth of Kije, Troika
*Kodály,* HÁRY JANOS SUITE: Viennese Musical Clock, Battle and Defeat of Napoleon, Intermezzo, Entrance of the Emperor

**BOL #82** MUSICAL PICTURES: MOUSSORGSKY, PICTURES AT AN EXHIBITION, NIGHT ON BALD MOUNTAIN

**BOL #83** ENSEMBLES, LARGE AND SMALL
*Britten,* YOUNG PERSON'S GUIDE TO THE ORCHESTRA
*Gabrieli,* CANZONA IN C MAJOR FOR BRASS ENSEMBLE AND ORGAN
*Bach,* CHORALE: AWAKE, THOU WINTRY EARTH
*Schubert,* FOURTH MOVEMENT, "TROUT" QUINTET
*Kraft,* THEME AND VARIATIONS FOR PERCUSSION QUARTET
*Mozart,* THEME AND VARIATIONS (Serenade for Wind Instruments) (K361)

**BOL #84** CONCERTOS
*Grieg,* FIRST MOVEMENT, PIANO CONCERTO
*Brahms,* FOURTH MOVEMENT, PIANO CONCERTO #2
*Mendelssohn,* THIRD MOVEMENT, VIOLIN CONCERTO
*Castelnuovo-Tedesco,* SECOND MOVEMENT, GUITAR CONCERTO
*Vivaldi,* THIRD MOVEMENT, CONCERTO IN C FOR TWO TRUMPETS

**BOL #85** MUSICAL IMPRESSIONS: RESPIGHI, PINES OF ROME, FOUNTAINS OF ROME, THE BIRDS (Prelude)

**BOL #86** FASHIONS IN MUSIC
*Tchaikovsky,* ROMEO AND JULIET (Fantasy-Overture)
*Bach,* LITTLE FUGUE IN G MINOR
*Ravel,* SUITE NO. 2 (Daphnis and Chloe)
*Mozart,* ROMANZE (A Little Night Music)
*Schoenberg,* PERIPETIA (Five Pieces for Orchestra)

---

## III. RECORD COMPANIES AND SOURCES OF CATALOGS FOR EDUCATIONAL USE

APPENDIX B

*Bowmar Records,* Inc., 622 Rodier Drive, Glendale, Calif. 91201.

*Capitol Records,* Educational Dept., Capitol Tower, 1750 North Vine St., Hollywood, Calif. 90028. Capitol and Angel Records Educational Catalog.

*Columbia Records, Inc.,* Educational Dept., 799 Seventh Ave., New York, N.Y. 10019.

*Decca Records,* a division of MCA Inc., 445 Park Avenue, New York, N.Y. 10007.

*Educational Records Sales,* 157 Chambers St., New York, N.Y. 10007.

*Folkways/Scholastic Records,* 50 West 44th St., New York, N.Y. 10036.

*The Franson Corporation,* Institutional Trade Division, 100 Sixth Ave., New York, N.Y. 10013. Distributors of *Children's Record Guild* and *Young People's Records.*

**348**

*Keyboard Jr. Publications, Inc.,* 1346 Chapel St., New Haven, Conn. 06511.

*Motivation Records,* a division of Argosy Music Corporation, Mamaroneck, N.Y. 10543.

*RCA Victor Record Division,* Educational Dept., 155 East 24th St., New York, N.Y. 10010.

*Rhythm-Time Records,* P.O. Box 1106, Santa Barbara, Calif. 93102.

*Sound Book Press Society, Inc.,* 36 Garth Road, Scarsdale, N.Y. 10583.

*Vox Productions, Inc.,* 211 East 43rd St., New York, N.Y. 10017.

---

## IV. FILMS, LISTINGS FOR EDUCATIONAL USE

*Brandon Films, Inc.,* 221 West 57th St., New York, N.Y. 10019. Catalog available with listing of about 25 music films.

*Contemporary Films,* a division of McGraw-Hill, Inc., 330 West 42nd St., New York, N.Y. 10036; 828 Custer St., Evanston, Ill. 60202; and 1211 Polk St., San Francisco, Calif. 94109

*Coronet Films,* 65 E. South Water St., Chicago, Ill. 60601. Catalog available, listing about 25 music films.

*Educom, Ltd.,* Box 388, Mt. Kisco, N.Y. 10549. Transparencies for overhead projector featuring songs and teaching units for opera.

*Encyclopaedia Britannica, Inc.,* 425 N. Michigan Ave., Chicago, Ill. 60611.

*Film Associates,* 11559 Santa Monica Blvd., Los Angeles, Calif. 90025. Short teaching films in color: "New Discovering Music" Film Series, "We Make Music" Film Series and others.

*Hoffberg Productions, Inc.,* 321 West 44th St., New York, N.Y. 10036. Annotated listing of films for rental or sale includes a group of short films for study in music appreciation.

*Institut für den Wissenschaftlichen Film,* Gottingen, den Busenstrasse 10, Gottingen, Western Germany.

*The Jam Handy Organization,* 2821 E. Grand Blvd., Detroit, Mich. 48211. Film strips with recordings.

*Johnson-Hunt Productions,* Films for Modern Learning, 16 Spear St., San Francisco, Calif. 94105.

*Library of Congress,* Washington, D.C. 20540. Catalog to Motion Pictures and Film Strips.

*Music Educators National Conference,* 1201 16th St., N.W., Washington D.C., 20036. Donald Shetler, *Film Guide for Music Educators* 1968. Also *Music Education Materials,* a selected, annotated bibliography, edited by Thomas C. Collins. See "Instructional Resources," pp. 145–160.

*NET Film Service,* Audio-Visual Service, Indiana University, Bloomington, Ind.

*S.L. Film Productions,* 5126 Hartwick St., Los Angeles, Calif. 90041

*Teaching Film Custodians, Inc.,* 25 West 43rd St., New York, N.Y. 10036. Annotated listing of "Motion Pictures for Music Classes" available on request.

*Washington Films,* University of Washington Press, Seattle, Washington 98105.

*H. W. Wilson Company,* 950 University Ave., New York, N.Y. 10052: "The Educational Film Guide," Eleventh Edition, with annual supplements. Generally available in libraries.

---

## V. COMPANIES SUPPLYING CLASSROOM INSTRUMENTS AND OTHER EQUIPMENT

*Children's Music Center,* 5373 West Pico Blvd., Los Angeles, Calif. 90019.

*Educational Music Bureau, Inc.,* 434 South Wabash Ave., Chicago, Ill. 60605.

*Fender Musical Instruments,* a division of Columbia Broadcasting System, Inc., 1402 East Chestnut, Santa Ana, Calif. 92701. Electronic Piano Classroom System.

*Gamble Hinged Music Co., Inc.,* 312 So. Wabash Ave., Chicago, Ill. 60604. Classroom instruments, library materials, teaching aids. Catalog available.

*Hargail Music Press,* 157 West 57th St., New York, N.Y. 10019. Specialists in recorders, and music for recorders and other instruments.

*M. Hohner, Inc.,* Andrews Rd., Hicksville, Long Island, N.Y. 11802. Representative for Sonor musical instruments for schools.

*Jensen Mfg. Division,* The Muter Co., 6601 So. Laramie St., Chicago, Ill. 60638. Manufacturer of recorders.

*Kitching Educational,* a division of Ludwig Drum Co., 1728 N. Damen Ave., Chicago, Ill. 60647. Mallet-played instruments and rhythm instruments.

*Wm. Kratt Co.,* 988 Johnson Place, Union, N.J. 07083. Chromatic pitch pipes, harmonicas.

*Lyons,* 688 Industrial Drive, Elmhurst, Ill. 60126. Classroom instruments of all kinds, educational recordings, other materials and equipment. Catalog available.

*Magnamusic-Baton, Inc.,* 6394 Delmar Blvd., St. Louis, Mo. 63130. Distributor of Studio 49, Munich, Germany, Orff instruments and related materials. Catalog available.

*National Autoharp Sales Company,* P.O. Box 1120, University Station, Des Moines, Iowa 50311.

*Oscar Schmidt-International, Inc.,* Garden State Road, Union, N.J. 07083.

*Peripole Inc.,* 51–17 Rockaway Beach Blvd., Far Rockaway, Long Island, N.Y. 11691. Rhythm, melody, harmony instruments, and other materials. Catalog available.

*Rhythm-Band, Inc.,* P.O. Box 126, Fort Worth, Texas 76101. Distributors of all kinds of classroom instruments, materials, and equipment. Catalog available.

*Scientific Music Industries, Inc.,* 1255 S. Wabash Ave., Chicago, Ill. 60605. Manufacturers of Tone Educator Bells and Swiss Melodé Bells.

*Targ and Dinner Inc.,* 2451 No. Sacramento Ave., Chicago, Ill. 60647. Distributors of American-Prep Tone Bells.

*Viking Company,* 113 So. Edgemont St., Los Angeles, Calif. 90004. Distributors of Tone Educator Bells and Swiss Melodé Bells.

*Walberg and Auge,* Musical Instruments, Route 20 at Millbury St., Auburn, Mass. 01501. Manufacturers of percussion instruments.

*Willis Music Co.,* 440 Main Street, Cincinnati, Ohio 45202. Educational music, records, teaching aids. Catalog available.

*The Wurlitzer Company,* Music and Education Department, DeKalb, Ill. 60115. Pianos, electronic pianos, and other equipment.

## VI. PUBLISHERS OF CHORAL MUSIC FOR CHILDREN'S VOICES

*Associated Music Publishers, Inc.,* a subsidiary of G. Schirmer, Inc., 609 Fifth Ave., New York, N.Y. 10017. *Choral Music Catalog* lists music for children's chorus.

*Carl Fischer, Inc.,* 56–62 Cooper Square, New York, N.Y. 10003. Octavo editions and collections for unchanged voices.

*Concordia Publishing House,* 3558 So. Jefferson Ave., St. Louis, Mo. 63118. Octavo editions, Christmas and sacred music.

*Marks Music Corporation,* 136 West 52nd St., New York, N.Y. 10019. Folk song collections, choral collections, operettas, music for recorders and other melody instruments. Classified descriptive list available.

*Mills Music, Inc.,* 1790 Broadway, New York, N.Y. 10019. General Catalog lists a variety of music for elementary schools including Foreign Language Music Study Books with records, musical plays, and operettas.

*Neil A. Kjos Music Co.,* 525 Busse St., Park Ridge, Ill. 60068. Collections include descants and other arrangements by Beatrice and Max Krone.

*Oxford University Press,* Music Department, 44 Conduit Street, London, W.1. Octavo editions of folk and composed music as well as song collections and musical plays.

*Theodore Presser Company,* Presser Place, Bryn Mawr, Pa. 19010.

*G. Schirmer, Inc.,* 609 Fifth Ave., New York, N.Y. 10017.

*Shawnee Press, Inc.,* Delaware Water Gap, Pa. 18327. Choral collections and other song books for children.

# Glossary*

*a cappella*—choral singing without instrumental accompaniment.

*Alberti bass*—continuous broken chord accompaniment in the left hand on a keyboard instrument.

*alto*—the lowest female voice, or instruments and written parts sounding in the upper middle range of tones.

*arco*—playing a stringed instrument with the bow.

*aria*—an extended solo melody for voice with instrumental accompaniment, usually from an opera, oratorio, or cantata.

*art song*—a composed song in which the poetry, melody, and accompaniment are balanced and mutually contribute to the total expressive effect.

*authentic cadence*—the strongest harmonic effect of arrival at the close of a musical phrase; a dominant chord in root position moving to a tonic chord in root position. Qualified as *perfect* or *full* when the melody comes to rest on the tonic note, and *imperfect* when the melody ends on the third or fifth of the tonic chord.

*ballad*—a simple, narrative song of several stanzas with a refrain.

*band*—a group of instrumental players, chiefly wind and percussion instruments.

*baroque*—the style of art, architecture, and music following the Renaissance; generally in a grand style, highly decorated, and colorful. Applicable to much music composed between 1600 and 1750.

*bass*—the lowest male voice, or instruments and written parts sounding in the lowest range of tones.

*basso profondo*—a deep bass voice, powerful and solemn.

*binary form*—a basic musical form of two sections, the second being the logical completion of the first.

*blues*—a characteristic of some jazz, derived from a type of early American Negro song, wherein certain degrees of the scale are used both flatted and natural, resulting in "blue notes" or chords.

*bourdon*—a low tone of long duration as in the drone bass of the bagpipe.

*bourrée*—a seventeenth century French dance in quick duple meter beginning with an upbeat; used as a movement in instrumental suites.

*cadence*—a pause or point of rest in melody and harmony; it is momentary or final, depending upon its position at the end of a phrase, period, or musical work as a whole.

*canon*—meaning "according to law," the musical application of which is the exact imitation of one voice by another at the same or at a different pitch level, with each voice starting at a different time.

*chorale*—a hymn tune characteristic of the German Protestant church.

*chorale prelude*—an organ composition based on a chorale melody and designed as a prelude to the congregation's singing of the chorale.

*classic*—in a general sense, music of established value; specifically, music of the Viennese Classic Period (Haydn, Mozart, Beethoven).

* See also related items under *Meter and Rhythm, Dynamics, Pitch, Scales and Chords* in Appendix A.

*coda*—a concluding section designed to bring a musical composition to a satisfactory close.

*coloratura soprano*—a female voice of great agility and high range.

*concerto*—a large composition, generally in three movements, for one or more solo players and orchestra.

*consonance*— a relative term, in opposition to dissonance, applied to a combination of tones representing stability and repose.

*contralto*—see alto.

*counterpoint*—a horizontal weaving together of melodies to form a musical texture (see polyphonic).

*courante*—an early French or Italian style of dance in quick triple meter, found as a movement in instrumental suites.

*da capo, D.C.*—indicating a return to the beginning of a composition.

*dal segno, D.S.*—indicating a return to a sign: 𝄋

*descant*—a more florid part, originally improvised, sung above a given melody.

*diatonic*—music based on a scale of seven tones within an octave, consisting of five whole and two half steps in an arrangement found in the white keys on the piano.

*dissonance*—a relative term, in opposition to consonance, applied to a combination of tones representing instability and disturbance.

*duet*—a composition for two performers, with or without accompaniment.

*ethnic music*—music characteristic of a race, a nation, or a people.

*etude*—a study or short piece usually devoted to one special aspect of instrumental technique.

*exposition*—the opening section of a musical work setting forth the musical subjects to be developed later.

*finale*—the last movement of a large musical work, or the final section of an operatic act.

*fine*—end, close.

*fugue*—a composition employing imitation, but more free than a canon. "Fugue" means "flight"; two or more parts seem to chase each other, but may diverge after each entrance.

*gigue*—a movement in the early dance suite, in triple meter with some imitation.

*ground bass*—a bass part consisting of a few notes and used as a theme over which new melodies are created.

*half cadence*—a temporary close of a musical phrase, ending on the dominant chord and thus demanding continuation as from a question to an answer.

*harmony*—the vertical relationship of tones in a musical composition (chords), their succession and the relationships between them.

*harpsichord*—a keyboard instrument, forerunner of the grand piano, in which the strings are sounded by a quill or leather plectrum; a characteristic instrument for Baroque music.

*homophonic*—the texture of music in which a single melody is supported by chords in the other parts; in contrast to polyphonic texture.

*imitation*—a way of writing music in which the established theme is taken up in turn by successive voices or instruments.

*impressionism*—a style of composition, principally by Debussy and Ravel, designed to evoke a mood or atmosphere by subtle use of musical tone color and texture and unorthodox techniques in harmony. Painting has its parallel in Monet and Renoir.

*incidental music*—instrumental music designed for performance before and between acts of a play and at necessary points within the drama.

*intonation*—the accuracy with which one sings or plays in tune, with an instrument or with other voices.

*inversion*—the result of changing the relative positions of notes in a chord or voice parts in a composition.

*leading tone*—the seventh degree of the scale, which is a half step below and has a strong tendency to lead to the tonic note.

*legato*—smooth and connected; indicated by a *slur* above or below a group of notes:

*libretto*—the text, or words, of a long composition such as an opera or an oratorio.
*lied*—a German word for "song."
*lyric soprano, lyric tenor*—a light, high voice with a pleasant "singing" style.
*marcato*—notes "marked" or emphasized in performance.
*march*—music with a simple, strong, duple rhythm, in regular phrases, designed to accompany marching.
*mazurka*—a Polish dance in moderate triple meter with accents on the second and third beats.
*melismatic*—referring to a vocal melody in which many notes are often given to one syllable in the text (also "florid").
*mezzo*—medium or half. Therefore: *mezzo-piano, mp*—medium soft; *mezzo-soprano*—medium-range soprano.
*minuet*—a French dance in moderate triple meter, originating about 1650; often used as a movement in early symphonies.
*mode, modal*—an arrangement of tones in a scale, consisting of the tonal material used in a particular musical work. Major and minor scales of western European music are modes, as are pentatonic and oriental scales and the scales which are the basis of medieval church music, including Gregorian chant. The adjective *modal* usually applies to music based on the modes of medieval church music, but is not limited to church music. ·
*modern music*—that music composed between 1890 and the present; a general classification in that modern music comprises a variety of styles.
*modulation*—moving from one key to another within a composition.
*motive (motif)*—a salient, germinating feature, derived from thematic material, which is expanded and developed throughout a musical work.
*neighboring tone*—the tone a staff degree above or below a tone in a chord from which the melody comes and returns:

*obbligato*—in early music the term meant obliged, or a part not to be left out; general usage has reversed the meaning so that it now refers to an optional ornamental part, usually on a solo instrument, accompanying a given melody.
*opera*—a staged drama in which music, sung dialogue, arias, and duets with instrumental accompaniment are combined with other theatrical representations (costumes, scenery, and dancing) to produce an integrated art form.
*operetta*—a musical-dramatic work with spoken dialogue, vocal solos, ensembles, and dancing, with instrumental accompaniment; generally with a nonserious plot and in a popular style.
*opus*—a "work," usually used in reference to the chronological works of a single composer.
*oratorio*—a serious musical-dramatic work utilizing vocal recitative, arias, chorus, duets, etc., with instrumental accompaniment, but without staging or costumes.
*orchestra*—a large group of musicians playing string, woodwind, brass, and percussion instruments.
*ostinato*—a melodic or rhythmic pattern persistently repeated as an accompanying feature in a musical composition.
*passing tone*—a tone which is touched in passing stepwise from one chord tone to another:

*pavane*—a stately court dance of the Renaissance; usually in duple meter, and sometimes appearing as an introductory movement of a suite.

*period*—a unit of two or more phrases which presents a complete musical idea (analogous to a sentence in language). Within a period two phrases may provide contrast and balance wherein the first serves as the *antecedent* and the second the *consequent* phrase (in a sense, "question and answer").

*phrase*—a short musical idea with a well-defined point of arrival, but not complete in itself.

*pitch*—the property of musical sound determined by the rate of vibration of the sound waves, defined in terms of twelve semitones within an octave: A, A#, B, C, etc.

*pizzicato*—playing a stringed instrument by plucking the string with the finger instead of using the bow.

*plagal cadence*—the ending of a phrase or composition in which the subdominant chord moves to the tonic (IV–I); typified by the "amen" ending of a hymn.

*polka*—a lively Bohemian dance in duple meter, originating in the early nineteenth century.

*polonaise*—a stately Polish processional dance in triple meter; important as a stylized form of instrumental composition among the works of J. S. Bach, Chopin, and others.

*polyphonic*—the texture of music woven in horizontal melodic lines with apparent independence of each part but a compatibility of the whole.

*polyrhythmic*—the use of cross rhythm, two or more strikingly different rhythms employed in different parts at the same time.

*prelude*—an introductory movement to a suite, opera, or other work; also a short independent piece for solo or instrumental ensemble.

*program music*—music in which the aesthetic impact of tone color, melody, rhythm, and structure found in all music is specifically directed to convey an idea, mental image, or feeling of the composer. Such music is sometimes accompanied by descriptive titles or program notes by the composer.

*quartet*—a composition for four vocal or instrumental performers.

*quintet*—a composition for five vocal or instrumental performers.

*recitative*—intoned speech, used in narrative and declamatory sections of opera or oratorio, wherein melody is abandoned in favor of a few pitches on which the words are recited; provided with a very simple instrumental accompaniment.

*repeat*—a sign indicating that the passage is to be repeated:

**GLOSSARY**

*resolution*—movement from an active or dissonant note or chord to one of consonance and stability.

*rococo*—ornamental eighteenth century architecture, furniture, and music of elegance and refinement; in music, also called the "gallant style," represented by some aspects of composition by Haydn and Mozart.

*romanticism*—the characteristic of a style in literature, art, and music of the nineteenth century, representing a break with formalism and classic aims in favor of individual expression of sentiment and imagination. Characterized by music with programmatic implications, rich orchestral sonority, full and somewhat blurred outlines in harmony.

*rondo*—the form resulting from a prescribed repetition of different sections in a composition. Usually the first section is heard alternately with other sections: A B A C A D A, etc.

**355**

*round*—a canon in which the imitation is on the same pitch level and where the identical melody is sung more than once by each voice.

*scherzo*—a lively, humorous composition in triple meter, often used as the third movement in a sonata or symphony.

*semitone*—a half step, the smallest interval in the tonal system of western European music.

*sequence*—the reproduction of a pattern of tones at a higher or lower level.

*sextet*—a composition for six vocal or instrumental performers.

*solo*—a composition for one vocal or instrumental performer, with or without accompaniment.

*sonata*—a composition for one or two instruments, generally in three independent but related sections called movements. The first and often the second movements are in "sonata form," the most important organizational plan in musical composition of the eighteenth and nineteenth centuries.

*soprano*—the highest female voice, or instruments and written parts sounding in the highest range of tones.

*staccato*—a note to be played short, not connected; indicated by dots above or below the notes:

*staff*—the horizontal lines and intervening spaces on which music notation is written (see Appendix A–III).

*strophic*—the form of a song in which all stanzas of the text are sung to the same music; the opposite of "through-composed."

*suite*—a group of related compositions. (a) The *classic dance suite* is a group of contrasting dances. (b) The *ballet suite* is a concert rearrangement of music from a ballet. (c) The *programmatic suite* consists of separate compositions related to a single story or descriptive idea.

*suspension*—the effect achieved when a tone in the melody or one or more tones of a chord are held over as the harmony changes in the other parts.

*syllabic*—referring to a vocal melody in which each syllable of the text is given one note; the opposite of "melismatic."

*symphonic poem*—a one-movement, programmatic composition for orchestra (see program music).

*symphony*—a composition for full orchestra, usually in four movements; a "sonata" for orchestra.

*tenor*—the highest male voice, or instruments and written parts sounding in the lower middle range of tones.

*ternary form*—a basic musical form in three sections, each complete within itself, and the third a repeat of the first: A B A.

*tessitura*—the general range of a voice part, not taking into account occasional extremes of high or low.

**GLOSSARY**

*texture*—in music, with an analogy to fabric, the horizontal "threads" of melody and rhythm are related vertically through the resulting harmony of simultaneous sounds. Musical texture can be rich, thick, transparent, or delicate, etc., depending upon the quality and use of instrumental tone or voices, melody, rhythm (see polyphonic and homophonic).

*theme*—a distinctive melody which is a basic factor in a large musical composition such as a sonata or fugue; also "subject."

*three-part song form*—see ternary form.

*through-composed*—a song in which the music is written throughout to conform as closely as possible to the meaning and feeling of the text. Many art songs are through-composed (see strophic).

*timbre*—the distinctive tone quality of different voices and instruments.

**356**

*tonality*—the characteristic of musical composition that establishes one tone as a tonal center to which all other tones are related.

*tonic*—the key center of a scale or musical composition. The *tonic chord* is a chord built on the tonic note of a given scale (see Appendix A–IV).

*treble*—the highest part in a choral composition, or an instrument or voice performing in a high range.

*trio*—a composition for three vocal or instrumental performers.

*troubadour*—a type of aristocratic poet or poet-musician in southern France during the middle ages.

*two-part song form*—see binary form.

*unison*—the relationship of tones having the same pitch. Different voices or instruments simultaneously playing or singing the same melody do so "in unison."

*variation*—a change or elaboration of an established melody or rhythm.

# Index of Songs and Dances

# Index of Subjects

**361**

**INDEX OF
SUBJECTS**

**363**

**INDEX OF SUBJECTS**

**365**

**367**

**369**

**371**